Eirik G. Jansen

Rural Bangladesh: Competition for Scarce Resources

Eirik G. Jansen

Rural Bangladesh: Competition for Scarce Resources

Norwegian University Press

Norwegian University Press (Universitetsforlaget AS), 0608 Oslo 6
Distributed world-wide excluding Scandinavia by
Oxford University Press, Walton Street, Oxford OX2 6DP

London New York Toronto
Delhi Bombay Calcutta Madras Karachi
Kuala Lumpur Singapore Hong Kong Tokyo
Nairobi Dar es Salaam Cape Town
Melbourne Auckland

and associated companies in
Beirut Berlin Ibadan Mexico City Nicosia

Published with a grant from the Norwegian Research Council for Science and the Humanities

British Library Cataloguing in Publication Data
Jansen, Eirik G.
Rural Bangladesh: competition for scarce resources.
1. Bangladesh — Rural conditions
I. Title
307.7′2′095492 HN690.6.A8

ISBN 82-00-07617-2

Printed in Norway by
Nye Intertrykk as, Lommedalen

Contents

List of Tables

List of Appendices

Preface

There is general consensus in western industrialized countries that conditions of living have improved over the years, particularly in the field of economy. A comparison of standards of living in the 1980s with those of the 1880s and 1780s show a vast improvement. In Bangladesh, however, the complete opposite is the case. Two hundred and fifty to three hundred years ago Dhaka was a wealthy market town with half a million inhabitants and the centre of a thriving textile industry. Travelogues written by foreigners visiting Bengal describe a population comfortably off, with enough food and land for all.

Today there is hardly any country in the world where so much poverty is concentrated in so small an area and where the outlook for improvement is so bleak for such a large group of people. Of the 95 million people living in the 144,000 square kilometres of Bangladesh, 85 million live in rural areas, and of these 75 million are totally dependent on income from or paid work in agriculture. All available arable land has been worked now for many decades, but it is very unevenly distributed. Soon 10 per cent of the richest families will own more than half the land, while more than 50 per cent of the families will have nothing, thus being dependent on paid agricultural work, in fierce competition with the smallholders. Research has shown that 30–40 per cent of the population either cannot find paid work or are underemployed.

The majority of rural people in Bangladesh do not have the basic needs outlined by the international aid organizations, e.g. suitable living conditions, medical services, political rights. These things they consider luxuries which take second place to such basic needs as enough food for survival. FAO has calculated that 85 per cent of the population live below the poverty line, i.e. on a diet of less than 2122 calories per day, and 54 per cent below the extreme poverty line, i.e. on a diet of less than 1805 calories a day.

Naturally this extreme poverty is the dominating factor in the lives of the rural people in Bangladesh. This study will try to answer such questions as: How do people manage to survive under such difficult conditions? What are the relationships between people when resources are at a minimum? Why are the resources available not utilized better?

Our method of approach is one of focusing on and trying to account for the ways in which people attempt to find a solution to the problem of the fight for survival. In particular we aim at giving a detailed survey of the different assets and resources, albeit scarce, which people have, and the factors which limit, govern and direct their struggle for survival. We want to show how ecological, agricultural, technological, social, and cultural conditions limit the choice people have of satisfying their elementary needs, and to analyse to what extent the wider political and economic framework, predetermines social structures and the division of wealth. We maintain that this study, more than any previous one, documents the complicated 'opportunity situation' the people find themselves in.

A central theme of this study is how the actual lack of resources causes people to adjust their relationships to each other in a special way, thereby shaping the social patterns dominant in rural Bangladesh today. This organization of society contributes to conserving the status quo as regards the economic and political structure of rural society, and prevents mass movements of a more revolutionary kind. Another central theme throughout this study is to see by hypothesis what effect prolonging the patterns and variables we describe and analyse will have on social conditions, and which factors would maintain or change these. The conclusion we reach is depressing to put it mildly. If things continue in the same manner as now in Bangladesh, it is difficult to find historical or contemporary parallels to the extent of the catastrophe which will hit millions of people.

Acknowledgements

This study and the field work for it has been carried out intermittently over the last five or six years, during which I have received much support and inspiration from the environment at DERAP at Chr. Michelsen Institute, Bergen. DERAP (Development Economics Research and Action Programme) provides unique opportunities for research studies on Bangladesh, staffed as it is by people with years of experience in administration, reporting and research there. Few research libraries have available such a large collection of material on development economics and social science topics about the country, and it has frequent visits from research scholars in the social sciences from Bangladesh. As a social anthropologist this milieu with its broad-based approach to development economics and its integration of various research fields has influenced me much, and undoubtedly affected the choice of themes and approach in this study. From December 1976 to June 1978 and from December 1979 to March 1980 I was able to do field work in rural Bangladesh thanks to the cooperation agreement between the Bangladesh Institute of Development Studies and DERAP, Chr. Michelsen Institute.

There are many people whom I would like to thank for their help and advice during this research: Just Faaland who commented on the draft of my study and provided encouragement when I most needed it; Johan Skutle and Ole David Koht Norbye for their comments and queries on issues not sufficiently clear; Gunnar Håland, Per Tveite and Armindo Miranda for the many inspiring discussions providing thoughts and ideas. And I should like especially to thank the Bangladesh researchers at DERAP, in particular B.K. Jahangir, Barkat-E-Khuda, and Professor Mosharaff Hossain for their valuable comments on various aspects of this study. Winter 1978/79 I spent doing research at the Ethnographic Museum, University of Oslo. Throughout all my work I am deeply indebted to Professor

Fredrik Barth for his valuable guidance and intellectual inspiration, particularly as regards choice of analytical approach. Of those who helped with the field studies I should especially like to mention Nazibor Rahman, who in addition to being my assistant in several studies in rural villages, also gave me much information as to the links between social, political and economic rural life. The main source of information was the villagers of Bhaimara, with whom I lived for months at a stretch. I am very grateful to them for their hospitality, their patience, and for allowing me to have a glimpse of their everyday way of life. I should also like to thank Florence E. McCarthy and Shelley Feldman in Dhaka for their informative discussions and Egil Kåre Bakke for going through this study and offering his valuable comments. But my deepest debt in the years I have worked on this project is to Bodil Maal, for her help in collecting data in the villages and for detailed discussions of every chapter, data-processing of material and working out of tables.

In conclusion I should like to thank the administrative staff of DERAP, the library and the EDP section: Astrid Blom who has typed the manuscript and helped me actively in many ways; Kirsti Hagen Andersen of DERAP's library, and EDP consultant Grete Dahl for their willing service; and finally DERAP for providing financial support for correction of the most obvious mistakes in my English. This task has been undertaken by P. Quist-Hanssen, to whom I am also most grateful for advice on choice of phrase, interpretation, and the finer points of the language.

Bergen, September 1986
Eirik G. Jansen

Some Basic Facts About Bangladesh

Population

Around 95 million (1983) out of which 1 to 2 per cent are tribal people.

Birthrate: 45-47/1,000
Deathrate: 17-20/1,000
Rate of Growth: 2.8 per cent per annum (1965–70).

Area

144,000 square kilometres, of which 6.5 per cent are rivers.
Density: 660 inhabitants per square km, as of 1983.

Administrative divisions in Bangladesh, as of 1982

Administrative Units		*Local Councils*	*Size of population per unit*
Name	*Number*		
Division	4	—	23 million
District	19	Zilla Board	4.8 million
Sub-division	62	—	1.5 million
Thana	464	Thana Parishad (council)	200,000
Union	4,355	Union Parishad (council)	15–25,000
(Ward)	13,000		

Religion

Muslims (mainly Sunnis): 85 per cent
Hindus: 10–15 per cent
Other: 2–3 per cent

Education

Literacy: Less than 20 per cent of the population.
Enrolment in primary schools: 55–60 per cent of eligible age group.
Drop-out rates: Extremely high.

Health

Population per doctor: 11,000 (1975).
Population per hospital bed: 5,300 (1974).
Infant mortality: 130 per 1,000 live births.
Life expectancy: 42 years.

Per capita income

G.D.P. per capita (1977): U.S. $ 91.

Distribution of income

Top 20 per cent of population take 40 per cent of national income. Bottom 20 per cent of population take 7 per cent of national income.

Currency

1 Taka = 100 paisha
1 U.S. $ = Around 24.5 Taka (as of June 1983).

Units and measures

1 *crore*	=	10 million
1 *lakh*	=	100,000
1 *maund*	=	around 37 kilos
1 *seer*	=	0.9 kilos
1 *bigha*	=	0.33 acres.

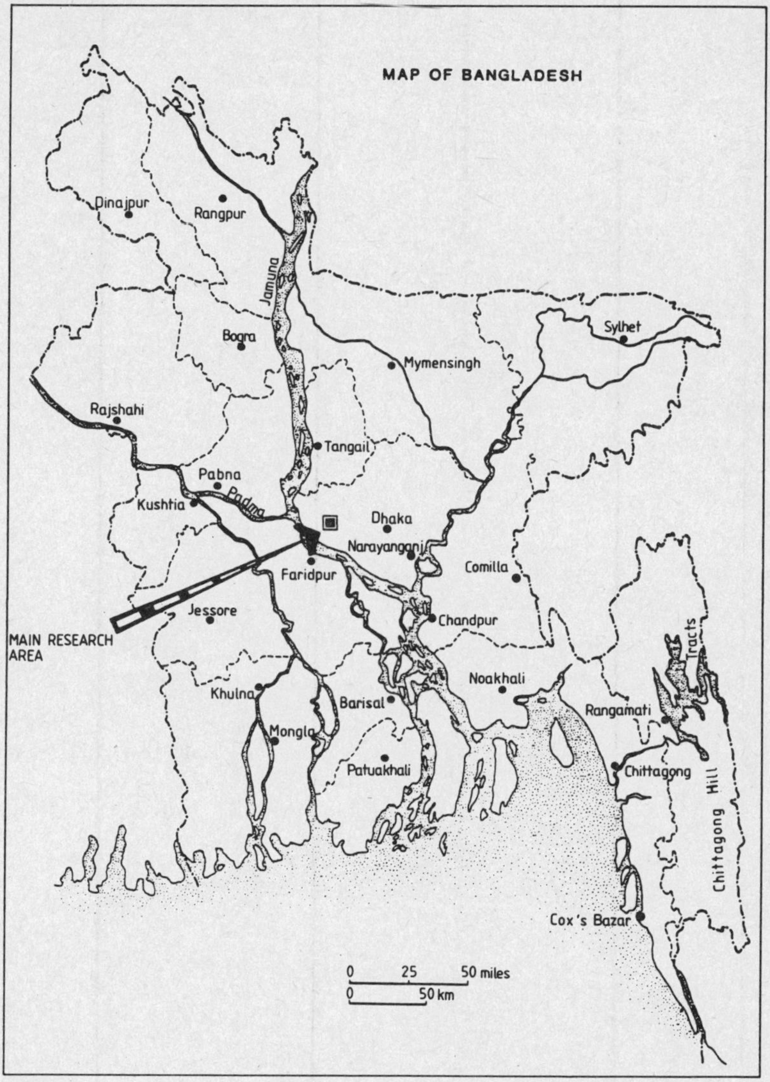

MAP OF BANGLADESH
Dinajpur
Rangpur
Jamuna
Bogra
Sylhet
Mymensingh
Rajshahi
Tangail
Pabna
Padma
Kushtia
Dhaka
Narayanganj
Faridpur
Comilla
Jessore
Chandpur
MAIN RESEARCH AREA
Noakhali
Khulna
Barisal
Rangamati
Mongla
Patuakhali
Chittagong
Chittagong Hill Tracts
Cox's Bazar
0 25 50 miles
0 50 km

1

The Problem and the Framework of the Study

Introduction

Rural Bangladesh is a land of gruelling poverty and, if the present development tendencies continue, of relentlessly deteriorating prospects. This study aims to describe and analyse, on the basis of empirical evidence from the rural villages, the processes which lead to poverty for most people and to the accumulation of property for a small group. The main thesis of the study is that the commonest way for people to maintain or improve their economic position is to secure for themselves better shares of limited resources at the expense of their fellow human beings.

In separate chapters of this study we shall describe and analyse how people in different fields, by a variety of methods, compete for scarce resources. The 'winners' in these competitive relationships normally improve their standard of living and obtain a strengthened position in society. For the 'losers', who outnumber by many times the 'winners', the result is increased impoverishment.

To be able to understand the significance of this competition one must realize how precarious and low the standard of living of these people already is. According to recent studies, 60 per cent of the rural population in Bangladesh is estimated to obtain less than 85 per cent of the calories required for a minimum subsistence.[1] What this statistical estimate implies, in practical terms, is that the majority of people in rural Bangladesh eat less than they physically need for large parts of the year or even starve. The percentage of the population living much below the minimum subsistence level is not a stable figure, however; it has been estimated that 20 years ago, only 10 per cent of the population lived in a similar situation. The outlook for the future is gloomy; all indications are that the absolute number as well as the percentage of people subsisting in extreme poverty will increase. It is against this background that the competition among people for access to sources of livelihood must be understood. Loss of livelihood has already had, and will continue to have, dramatic consequences for the majority of the population.

What are the resources and limited supply of goods for which people compete? About 75 million of the 85 million people who live in rural Bangladesh depend in one way or another on agricultural activities for their income and employment. The income from agriculture is obtained as owners of land, as employees for landowners, or as a combination of owner of land and employee. There is scarcity of both *land* and *employment,* and it is about these two sources of income that people compete.

That *land* is a limited resource seems evident when one considers the following development pattern in Bangladesh. At the beginning of this century there was, in the geographical area which today constitutes Bangladesh, one person to each acre of land. For many decades practically all the available land for agricultural purposes, 22 million acres, has been utilized. Today there are about 4 people to each acre of land, and with the existing growth of population, there could be as many as 8 people by the end of this century.[2] The productivity per unit of land has not kept up with this growth of population, and still only a very small percentage of the rural population is able to obtain an income from any source other than agriculture.

Along with the increasing scarcity of land, a change has taken place in the ownership pattern of land. Twenty years ago only a few per cent of the households owned no agricultural land; today about a third of the households are landless. According to the Land Occupancy Survey in 1977, the size distribution of agricultural land was as shown in Table 1.1:[3]

Table 1.1. Size Distribution of Agricultural Land in Bangladesh 1977.[4]

Category of peasant/worker	No of acres owned	Per cent of households	Per cent of land area
Landless	—	32.8	—
Peasants owning	0.01–2.00	44.9	25.1
,,	2.01–4.00	12.7	24.2
,,	4.01–10.00	6.9	31.3
,,	10.01–	1.8	19.3

It seems quite clear that the landless state of the poor peasant households will become an even more critical issue over the coming years. Sons of a landless person will establish their own households, and peasants with small landholdings will lose the land they own. The more land a peasant owns, the more influential he is in society and the easier it is for him to expand his landholdings further by taking over land from poor peasants.

The process of losing and gaining land goes on all over rural Bangladesh. The ratio, man-land, varies in the different regions, but there is no doubt that in almost all of the about 65,000 villages which constitute rural Bangladesh, land is very scarce, and there is an ongoing process of land being lost by some and gained by others. In this competition for land the relationships between people and the mechanisms of land being lost and gained vary from one area to the other, but the land transfer processes have important features in common all over Bangladesh.

For rural people who own no agricultural land or very little, *employment* in agricultural activities is the most important source of income. For the great majority of people who are seeking employment in the agricultural field there will be periods of the year when paid work is hard to find or simply not available. On an annual basis it has been estimated that there is 30–40 per cent underemployment and unemployment in rural Bangladesh.[5] Competition for obtaining employment is thus a regular feature of existence in the great majority of the villages. The different ways by which employment is obtained and the terms and conditions of employment contracts will vary from one area of the country to the other, but the issues related to employment will also share many common features all over rural Bangladesh.

Our material to document the competition over land and employment has been collected mostly from one particular village. We focus on the strategies people pursue in the competition for land and employment. It is useless to try to assess to what degree the material we have collected is representative, in a statistical sense, for larger areas. The circumstances which produce the competition for land and employment in the village we studied were basically the same as those operating in the other villages of the country. Statistics will not particularly illuminate the understanding we wish to obtain of people's strategies, conception and practices regarding the competition over land and employment. We therefore claim a general validity for the model of competition we shall construct.

The study area

The processes of gaining and losing land and of obtaining employment are not limited by village boundaries. When therefore we collected information on these processes, the village was not the unit of our study. We focused on the whole range of relationships in which people from the village participated, both those internal to the village and those extending to persons beyond the village boundaries. However, for the purpose of collecting quantitative information on the distribution of land and various issues related to land, the whole set of households of our particular village was our statistical universe.

Bhaimara, a village about 40 miles west of Dhaka, was the village from which we collected most of our information.[6] In 1980 we conducted a census there which showed that the total population consisted of 311 individuals who lived in 62 households. (This means that on an average there are 5 persons in each household.) The 62 households in the village altogether own 67.8 acres of land. Nine acres are homestead plots, small elevated areas where the houses are placed, and 58.8 acres are agricultural land. This means that there are 5.3 persons to one acre of agricultural land.[7] Table 1.2 shows the distribution of land in Bhaimara.

According to the villagers, in 1970 there were only 7 households that were landless. Many of the households that today own less than one acre of land will lose their land within the next 5 years. We can observe from the table that the land distribution (by chance only) corresponds very closely to the national distribution, with about a third of the households being landless, 48 per cent owning less than 2 acres, and 13 per cent owning between 2–4 acres of land.

All village studies face the problem of classifying peasants. In fact, a major theme in many studies has been discussion of the dilemmas attached to adopting different systems of classifications. Many researchers attempting to conduct a class analysis meet difficulties. What is, for instance, the class position of a family owning

Table 1.2. Ownership of Land in Bhaimara in 1980.

Group and amount of land owned[8]		No. of households	%	Amount of land owned acre	%	Size of household plot acre	%	Size of agricultural land acre	%
Landless	—	21	34	0.95	1.4	0.95	10.5	0	
Poor peasants	(0.01–0.99 acres)	22	35	13.2	19.5	3.2	35	10	17.0
Small peasants	(1–1.99 acres)	8	13	12.9	19.0	1.88	21	11	18.7
Middle peasants	(2–3.99 acres)	8	13	24.6	36.2	2.24	25	22.4	38.1
Rich peasants	(4 acres and above)	3	5	16.2	23.9	0.77	8.5	15.4	26.2
Total		62	100	67.8	100	9	100	58.8	100

2 acres of land, sharecropping one acre of land, where the father hires labourers in the peak seasons and one son works as wage labourer in the slack season and another son holds a petty-service job? In addition to finding relevant and applicable objective criteria for classes, there is the problem of whether these criteria can be used for comparison on a national level, and the problem of relating 'objective and subjective' aspects of class. In different chapters of this study we shall document how problematic the 'subjective' aspect of class (class awareness, class consciousness) is for the peasantry of Bangladesh, and how far away major collective actions based on class interests appear to be. Because of all the problems they have to face, researchers making a class analysis often end up with classifications very similar to the *economic categories* we adopted.[9]

For our purpose of understanding people's strategies, we found that a fruitful departing point was to focus on the degree of self-sufficiency people have in rice production. (Rice is without comparison the main agricultural crop; on a national basis rice is grown on 4 out of 5 acres. Nearly 85 per cent of the daily caloric intake of the rural population comes from grain, which is primarily rice.)[10] Although Bhaimara is fairly near an urban centre, the great majority of the households receive their main income from cultivating their own land and/or being employed as wage-labourers for other landowners.

The degree of self-sufficiency in rice production can be used as a measure in understanding the nature of the strategies the households pursue and the economic relationships they enter. We used our subjective judgement, based on detailed interviews with the 62 households, when we placed the households in one of the three categories; deficient in rice production, self-sufficient in rice production, surplus in rice production. Table 1.3 shows that there is no clear-cut and simple relationship between economic category of size of land owned and degree in self-sufficiency.

Only 45 of the 62 households produce rice. (This includes 4 of the 21 landless households who are sharecroppers and cultivate land owned by others.) The rice production of 31 of the 45 households (68.9 per cent) is deficient, and these have to obtain rice from outside.[12] The 17 landless households, who do not cultivate any land as owners or sharecroppers, naturally also have to obtain all the rice

Table 1.3. Self-sufficiency in Rice Production in Bhaimara in 1980.

Group[11]	No. of house-holds	No. of house-holds with rice pro-duction	Deficient in rice pro-duction	Self-sufficient in rice pro-duction	Surplus in rice pro-duction
Landless	21	4	4		
Poor	22	22	20		2
Small	8	8	4	2	2
Middle	8	8	3	2	3
Rich	3	3			3
Total	62	45	31	4	10

they consume. This means that 48 of the 62 households (77.4 per cent) in the village are not self-sufficient in the most important item of consumption. This is the main reason why households have to enter into various credit relationships, employment for others, sharecropping, sale of cash crops, mortgage and sale of land and other assets. (It should be mentioned that the self-sufficiency and surplus situation is estimated on the basis of a whole year. Some of the 14 households that are self-sufficient and have a surplus will both sell and purchase rice during the year.)

It is, of course, very difficult to give an accurate estimate of how many households are 'self-sufficient' and have a budget which on an overall basis is fairly balanced with respect to income and expenditure. Our impression, which will be substantiated in later chapters, is that about 50 of the 62 households in their present situation are in a position where their expenses are greater than their incomes, and that they are caught in a process where they gradually have to deplete and part with their fixed assets and land in order to finance their deficits. A few households have a fairly balanced budget, while about 10 of 62 households have a surplus, which varies in size, but which, indirectly or directly, is oriented towards further investment in land.

Above we have described an important aspect of the background for the emergence and development of economic, political and social relationships between people in the rural areas. Before we proceed to our analysis of these relationships, we shall in the next section briefly describe the framework of concepts and the analytical approach which we felt it necessary to adopt.

Theoretical and methodological approach to the study

Many social scientists have done research on the economic and political structure of rural Bangladesh, and quite a variety of themes and problems have been analysed. In our opinion many studies suffer from an exogenous notion as to what constitutes the important categories in which to order and present information. Our aim has been to adopt an analytical approach which is as close to the social reality of rural Bangladesh as possible. Our glimpse of social reality was naturally limited and was to a large degree determined by the field situation we found ourselves in, the contacts we made with individuals, and the specific events we experienced. No doubt, placed in a different physical and social setting of rural Bangladesh, other themes would have been taken up and our emphasis might have been different. This peculiarly subjective foundation of the analysis should be recognized, and we think it is reflected in the way we carried out our research and presented our results. We are thoroughly aware that much relevant information which might have provided relevant insight into the questions we studied, has not been 'discovered' and collected. Such information, when 'found', should be incorporated into the analysis. Therefore throughout the study we have sought to formulate our 'findings' in such a way that they can be tested and, if that be the verdict, falsified by further empirical investigation.

Below the study framework is presented and discussed in three separate sub-sections: firstly some aspects of the theoretical framework are briefly discussed; secondly, the fieldwork situation through which we collected our primary sources of information is described; finally, we list some of the topics and literature we have gone through in connection with our study. We particularly discuss our attitude to some of the literature of rural Bangladesh with a Marxist approach.

a) Theoretical frame

The analytical framework we thought best suited to capture the social reality we observed, has been developed by Fredrik Barth.[13] We shall not, at this early stage of the study be explicit and go into detail on the concepts his model and approach contain. In chapter 9 we shall review the different elements in the model, and discuss them separately. Below we shall only indicate that a central issue in Barth's approach is to account for the relationship between the acts and events individuals are engaged in and the aggregate pattern of behaviour and social systems. The concepts of *decision-making units,* the *assets and strategies* of the units, the *constraints and opportunities* for the *choices* made by the units, the *feed-back effect of aggregate patterns on the opportunity situation* of the decision-making units, underlie the analysis of our study.

The tables presented above on distribution of ownership of land may serve as a point of departure for indicating our approach. The tables present aggregate patterns of the distribution of land. The individual units are the households. The members of the households are in almost all cases related by kinship. Normally a household is built around a nuclear family. (Depending on its phase in the development cycle it can be an incomplete or an extended family.) The household members have a joint budget, being, by definition, one unit for production and consumption. It is thus these households which are the decision-making units with respect to the organization of production; whether land shall be sold or purchased; whether wage labourers shall be hired or not, etc.

It was not difficult to 'discover' that the members of the households are guided in their activities for obtaining a secure livelihood by purpose and by consciousness of choice, and that they have the ability to evaluate the consequences of their actions, and, if necessary and if possible, make new allocations if the intended goals are not achieved. Given that most households have members who live on a starvation diet, it should be easy to accept that strategies for providing a livelihood receive highest priority.

The direction of these purpose-oriented activities must be understood in relation to the context in which these activities take place. In the previous section we emphasized that the sources of income, land and employment were limited to an extent that caused fierce competition. Typically the individual households are the units operating within *dyadic* competitive relationships. We believe Barth's concept of a *transaction* is helpful to identify and give precision to the sequences of events which take place in these relationships. (See chapter 9 for an elaboration.) Both parties in these relationships (employer-employee, seller-buyer of land, landowner-tenant, etc.) try to obtain as much as possible from the other without demanding more than the other party will concede. Thus, these relationships are conducted with reference to considerations of *reciprocity*. Reciprocity, here, refers to a relationship in which each party makes an assessment of whether there is an acceptable 'balance' in 'the give and take' between the parties. It does not imply that there exists an even balance or equality between the parties. In fact, in these economic and social relationships in rural Bangladesh, one party is normally the stronger and more powerful actor, who will direct much of his efforts towards an imposition of his own conditions in the 'give and take' of the relationship and in circumscribing and controlling the scope of action of the weaker party.

Yet, as we shall see in the presentation of the material of this study, even the weaker party will have some scope for choice and manoeuvre and can to some extent resist the most onerous consequences of these relationships. The available options may not be particularly attractive to the weaker party, but the fact that they are there may cause the stronger party to come some way towards meeting the needs and preferences of the weaker party in order to ensure that a deal is actually reached.

In rural Bangladesh where the material scarcity is so extreme, there is a demand and a market for many goods and services which in other societies normally are free and available to all. It is therefore possible to start a process of transactions over a whole range of minor but vitally important items, e.g. dead branches of trees, cow dung, leaves, as well as bits and pieces of information on different topics, for instance issues of landownership. More important, however, is the fact that most landless households still own a homestead plot of land, the value of and demand for which is high. This makes homestead owners, however poor, attractive prospects for richer people who are eager to obtain this land. As we shall show, elaborate and time-consuming transactions in which a range of alternative actions come into play for the poor homestead plot owner may take place before a homestead plot changes owners.

By applying the concept of transaction in our analysis of relationships which determine income and livelihood, we do not want to suggest that all observed relationships can be best interpreted with reference to this concept. We shall see that for many purposes the household units cooperate and within the corporate unit the relationships between household units are not conducted with reference to transactional principles. Also for most of the daily activities of a routine character people will not in their relationships assess the balance of benefits and costs in a minute manner. Yet it remains a very strong impression from our field work that the actions of the members of the households observed were strikingly and nearly uniformly purpose-oriented in respect of their obtaining a livelihood and economic security. Even, at first glance apparently quite 'neutral', social games and activities in many instances were indirectly and very cleverly converted into events which strengthened the position of one actor or another in relation to economic and political issues. The reason for the concentration of almost all efforts on matters relating to economics is, of course, the precarious material condition under which people are living, which leaves little room for 'non-purposeful' activities.

The way the relationships handling scarce resources are conducted will vary. For our study of the different patterns of relationships, therefore, detailed information is needed on a variety of issues relating to how the household units are constituted, the mechanisms by which their assets are transferred, and the rules and cultural value standards regulating these transfers. We also need to understand how the wider environment and society condition the strategies adopted by the households. For this reason much of the information that will be presented in the following chapters will be material that describes the complex 'opportunity situation' of the households.

We should emphasize, at this stage, that it is not the strategies and adaptations of individual households or actors which are our object of study. We want to describe aggregate patterns of behaviour and to specify the circumstances which can explain why certain types of household adapt in particular ways, for example, why specific types of employment, mortgage and sharecropping contracts are accepted. Clearly, the aggregate patterns which are documented should not be analytically conceived just as a simple addition of individual choices; thus, for example, the level of wages in an employment contract, the terms and conditions in the prevailing sharecropping contracts, and the price of agricultural land, all have a dynamic element with feedback effects, which in turn influence the opportunity situation of the decision-making units. Throughout the study we shall be concerned with documenting these types of interconnections.

Also, at this stage, we would emphasize that much of the information we present to document the constraints on and opportunities for people's choices are more or less relevant for rural Bangladesh as a whole (agricultural technology, ecological factors, Government policies, etc.). We shall therefore in the different chapters of the study easily switch our focus from the events in the village of Bhaimara to conditions we believe pertain to the rural areas in general. Through this approach we indirectly make an assessment of the degree of representativeness of Bhaimara for the villages of Bangladesh.

b) Field-work situation and other sources of information

We used a variety of techniques to obtain information for our study, the most important being the traditional anthropological technique of field-work and living among the people studied. Most of this field-work was carried out in Bhaimara village. Intermittently over a 3-year period and covering all seasons, altogether more than six months were spent in the village. For more than a year during this 3-year period we resided in Dhaka, from where it was possible to have frequent and regular contact with people and events in the village.

Much of the social life and activities in rural Bangladesh take place behind walls, normally made of jute palings, erected around the homestead plots. The walls are set up mainly in order to keep the women in *purdah;* to 'protect' them from men who are strangers. If households are able to keep their women in *purdah* this adds to their prestige in the village. It requires a certain effort to visit 'closed' homesteads; often all ongoing activities are stopped and the women whisked into the houses before an interview can start. This means that the place in which the field worker resides to a large degree determines which activities he will observe and the ease with which he can approach persons.

More by luck than by careful planning, the principal researcher and his assistant came to live in a house which opened up to a large homestead compound where the domestic activities of 8 households took place. Most of these 8 households were agnatically related by having a common grandfather. Some of the households were 'servants', working on a regular basis for the more well-to-do households. In addition, the homestead compound was also the daily meeting place for six to seven other households, more distant relatives, who came to fetch water from an open well in the compound inside the walls. Inside the compound *purdah* was naturally not observed. The researchers were very soon defined as 'grandfathers' of the compound and were thereby put into a category which made it possible for them to move around freely. Outside the walls there was another meeting place, which was frequented by many villagers. This was the more formal place where visitors were entertained and where many men came after having prayed in the village mosque, one hundred yards away. A few yards from the visitors' place was the only hand tubewell in operation for drinking water for the village. Children and poor women of the village came to collect water here. Thus it was possible for the researchers to switch easily between the two rather different arenas and to observe and obtain contact without imposing themselves on the villagers.

Later, when contacts were established with other households in the village more easy access was obtained also to their homes. Some households even gave 'kin-terms' to the researchers in order to facilitate and welcome their coming and going to the homes. These were mainly poor households who were not so strict in their observance of *purdah;* for some of the rich households contact remained limited to their respective 'visitors' places' outside the fences where more formal entertainment was provided with tea and conversation.

Such were the circumstances under which events were observed and interviews conducted. Most people were asked informally about their *income and expenditure situation* and the options they could see for improvement in their position. Efforts were made in the interviews to collect *'life stories'* of both living and dead persons and detailed *genealogies.* Material was also collected on *plans and hopes for children.* Except for a few well-to-do families, who had ambitious marriage and educational plans for their children, most households conveyed a strong impression of how their livelihood situation had deteriorated significantly during the last couple of generations. Some households also admitted frankly that their moral standards had been influenced and changed in the face of growing material poverty. Most of these households felt that their children and grandchildren would face futures of even worse conditions than themselves.

Besides *informal interviewing* we also conducted more *structured interviews* and, for certain land plots, we made surveys of how ownership had changed during the last generations. A *quantitative survey* was conducted towards the end of the period of field-work. The survey covered information relating to land ownership, land use and credit. Visits typically lasting for a couple of hours were made to all the households in the village for completion and cross-checking of information. These occurred in the late evening when the males were at home. Most of our qualitative information we received from about 10–15 persons belonging to different economic categories. Some of the information we received from the *key informants* is presented in our different case studies. A major advantage of the approach of *participant observation* as a way of obtaining information is that the researcher is able to *transcend his own categories* of how society is ordered. Without living in the midst of a village community for a long period it would have been impossible for us to obtain an understanding of the many factors which influence people's behaviour. Most of the information we present on constraints and opportunities for people's choices is based on *primary sources* we collected ourselves, not on literature or other *secondary sources* of information.

It will become apparent throughout this study that material on certain issues has been collected also from geographical areas other than Bhaimara village. We have worked in rural districts in the Northern, Southern and Eastern parts of Bangladesh and have spent short periods in villages in these regions. Although there is scarcity and competition over land and employment everywhere, the circumstances varied. It seems obvious, for instance, that the relationships between landless tenants and landowners having as much as 100 acres or more, such as we found in the Bogra district, are different from the relationship in Bhaimara between a small-scale owner-cum-tenant operator and his perhaps equally small-scale landowner having, say, 3 acres from which a plot is share-cropped. It may be worth recording how the employment, credit and mortgage patterns observed in Bhaimara contrasted with the patterns obtained in the home village of our research assistant. His father was a peasant and a trader in Pabna district. During our visit to his house we meticulously examined how and why the patterns of employment, sharecropping and mortgage contracts, etc. differed or were similar to the patterns that we had found in Bhaimara.

Although many of the relationships we have recorded from Bhaimara can be dealt with in transactional terms within the village, there are important factors operating beyond the village, for which 'participant observation' is definitely not a particularly suitable technique for obtaining information: Such are ecological, demographic and certain cultural and religious factors, Government activities, and national and international market penetration. The impact within the village of such factors can be 'observed' and, as shown in subsequent chapters, it is possible to depict how they influence and shape the opportunity situation of the actors. However, these factors are not 'generated' at the village level, and the essence of their dynamics cannot be captured by anthropological methods.

Therefore description and analysis of the internal dynamics of these factors, which in the main are determined outside the rural areas, have been left out of our study. This is an acknowledged, yet serious limitation of our study, since we do not wish to imply that such external relationships are unimportant or irrelevant for an understanding of the dynamics of what goes on in the villages. On the contrary, the economic, social and political environment in which any particular village society finds itself in rural Bangladesh has important consequences for life in that village. We also want to demonstrate in the subsequent chapters how activities at the village level, to a varying degree, have feedback effects on the course of development of these 'external' factors themselves.

c) How available literature on rural Bangladesh influenced our study

Both before and after the fieldwork we naturally read as much as possible of the available literature about rural Bangladesh. There is little doubt that our reading about various village institutions, local judicial systems, honour systems, religious activities, the role of patrilineage and kinship relations, influenced both the direction of attention in the process of observation and what we actually recorded. Without prior knowledge of some of these institutions their significance might have been overlooked in the field or maybe differently interpreted.[14]

Many authors who describe economic and political activities in rural areas apply a Marxist framework in the analysis of their material. Much of what we learnt in the course of our study about employment, credit and land issue matters reflects and is based on insight gained from such writings. We were also, in a general way, influenced by the emphasis the Marxist literature put on the irreconcilable contradiction between rich and poor in the rural areas.

Helpful as the Marxist framework has been in some respects for our study, our analytical approach is of a very different nature. Therefore, we have been selective in picking up 'themes' generally dealt with in Marxist analysis of rural Bangladesh. Thus an important theme treated in the Marxist literature can be subsumed under the constructed macro-concepts of 'exploitation' and 'surpulus appropriation'. The empirical events and processes in which 'exploitation and surplus appropriation' are exercised in the context of rural Bangladesh are mainly in relations concerning employment, sharecropping and credit. These themes, which, in fact, constitute the main part of this study, we relate directly to the strategies pursued by the different households in their situation of scarcity of land, employment and livelihood. From this perspective the 'transactional' relationships which occur in respect of land, employment and credit could be read as an account of exploitation and surplus appropriation, and as shown in later chapters, our analysis is conducted along these lines.

Another important 'theme' on which the Marxist literature on rural Bangladesh has focused is the development of class consciousness among the rural population. It seems to be widely agreed, however, that class consciousness can but rarely be identified as a dominant factor in important events in rural Bangladesh. In our study we include an assessment of the *patron-client* relationships as a form of alliance more typically descriptive of the adaptation for households than alliances based on class interests. We shall also discuss some of the factors which hinder collective actions made on the basis of class interests.

The Marxist analysis explicitly acknowledges that the structure and dynamics of a given geographical area or village cannot be adequately understood in isolation. Our reading of the literature has provided some concrete insight about how villages are integrated, economically and politically, with the larger society both at a national and international level.

However, despite the importance and relevance of the issues on which the Marxist-oriented literature on rural Bangladesh has focused, most of it is very disappointing reading from an empirical and ethnographical point of view. Such studies as are available seem to us to be biased in their selection of empirical phenomena and to suffer from both observation and analysis being forced into the mould of a pre-established scheme: *in casu* a given mode of production. Too often the material is presented in such abstract terms and in the guise of such general concepts and theories that it is difficult to discern that one is dealing with rural Bangladesh at all. Also, when empirical phenomena, say, a table showing the sharecropping or mortgage pattern of an area are discussed, a surprisingly 'one-dimensional' interpretation is offered. Complexity is the very essence of these relationships, for example, mortgage must be understood in the ligth also of patterns of sharecropping, employment opportunities and political patronage, and this is but rarely brought into the available Marxist literature. Moreover, the varied patterns of, for example, mortgage contracts and the circumstances which produce these variations are not systematically integrated into the Marxist analysis of rural Bangladesh. Thus, the wide variation which characterizes the concrete events that come under the labels of 'exploitation' and 'surplus appropriation' seems to have escaped due attention in much of the Marxist literature. This is reflected in the relative absence of contributions from Marxist scholars towards providing and analysing detailed and comprehensive empirical data on social and economic life in rural Bangladesh.

Outline of the study

Chapter 2 will give a brief physical and ecological description of the rural area to which Bhaimara belongs. The agricultural production cycle and the available technology will be described. We shall identify the production factors which are scarce and those which are difficult to mobilize and show the consequences this has for encouraging peasants with a surplus to invest in additional land, rather than to intensify cultivation. We shall briefly indicate some of the implications which follow from this type of investment patterns. We shall also indicate some of the social and economic consequences which follow from ecological factors; how the annual floods and the inundation of the land have implications for the nature of employment contracts, which in turn affect the credit relationships.

Chapter 3 will present different aspects of the household, the 'decision-making unit'. The household's position in relation to other domestic units and the kinship structure will be discussed. The division of labour in the household will be described, as well as the process by which decisions are reached within the household. The development cycle of the different types of individual households and the reasons for the 'split-up' and 'non-viability' of households will be outlined and related to the amount of land and property owned. This chapter will also describe the inheritance rules for land property and the ways ownership of land is documented. Aspects of the system of social stratification as perceived by the villagers will be outlined, and the economic and political significance of the institution of marriage and affinal ties will be pointed out. We also outline some social groups and institutions in the rural areas and show some characteristic features of local leadership in the villages.

Chapter 4 will emphasize an important transfer mechanism of land; namely how land is mortgaged and sold. Establishment of credit relationships normally precedes mortgage and sale of land, and we describe in detail how and with whom credit relationships are entered into (kinship-member, villager, etc.). We further describe the 'budget' of expenditures and incomes of the landless, the poor, the middle and rich households. Only peasants with a 'surplus' are in a position to invest, and one of the main issues of this chapter is to show how the establishment of credit relationships becomes the initial stage for accumulation of land and capital by the rich households. We shall also discuss to what degree property of the rich households disintegrates when the children of the household divide and inherit the property. In this connection we shall explore some of the ways by which the rich households maintain their position in the next generation. Most of the information in this chapter is presented through five separate case studies.

Chapter 5 in the study discusses the practice of sharecropping, in which most of the households in the village are engaged. Sharecropping is of great economic significance to many households, and it is often combined with different types of credit and of political patronage. This chapter will show the characteristics of landowners and tenants, and outline the various terms and conditions of these relationships. In this chapter we shall also indicate how the existing land tenure system gives little incentive for increased production.

Chapter 6 focuses on employment relationships. Almost all the households of the village are involved in the labour market either as employers or employees. We discuss the points taken into consideration by employers when picking and choosing between potential wage-labourers, and give an outline of the terms and conditions of the employment contracts. We also describe the various methods practised by employers to cut the cost of wage-labour. We assess the purchasing power of wages and indicate the implications the low purchasing power of a large group has for the investment patterns of the rich.

Chapter 7 takes up a rather neglected issue in rural studies in Bangladesh: viz. the different types of disputes over ownership of land. Disputes over land and occupation of other people's land by force are in fact another mechanism for transfer of land. This chapter presents a number of case studies, each showing the different types of disputes, the evolution of the disputes, and the institutions which are called upon to settle such disputes.

Chapter 8 discusses the various ways by which the village is politically and economically integrated into a wider society with particular emphasis on various types of Government policies in rural Bangladesh, both in general and as observed in Bhaimara. We are particularly concerned with the employment effects of the Government policies. The nature of the Government itself and its special client groups, as revealed through the different Government programmes implemented, will also be discussed. This chapter will indicate how the village is integrated into a market beyond the village itself, including a brief note on how the village is integrated into a wider labour market.

Chapter 9 summarizes some main findings in the study. We also outline in detail the analytical approach underlying this study and relate the concepts and approach to the empirical material we have presented in the study. The last section of the chapter summarizes and discusses various aspects of social organization in rural Bangladesh. We shall discuss the direction of mobility in rural Bangladesh and relate this theme to the discussions on 'cyclical mobility' which have been a recurring theme of controversy in the rural studies of Bangladesh. We shall also outline some of the factors which hinder the development of class consciousness and class formation in the rural areas.

Chapter 10 will discuss some prospects for rural Bangladesh during the next decades. The analytical perspective and informal model we have presented in the preceding chapters has the advantage that it can be used to produce prognosis and predictions. On the basis of the development trends of certain variables (growth of population, employment possibilities, polarization of land holdings, Government policies etc.) we shall permit ourselves to speculate on future development trends in rural Bangladesh.

Notes

1 FAO/UNDP/Government of Bangladesh. Agricultural Mission, *Selected Policy Issues and Working Papers,* Dhaka 1979.

2 Faaland, J. and Parkinson, J.R.: *Bangladesh — The Test Case of Development.* C. Hurst Company, 1976, p. 124.

3 Jannuzi, F. Thomasson and Peach, James T.: 'Land Occupancy Survey, 1977, in: *The Agrarian Structure of Bangladesh, An Impediment to Development,* Boulder, Colorado, USA, Westview Press, 1980.

4 The land referred to in the table is agricultural land *owned* by the households, not the *operational* landholdings of the households. Agricultural land does not include homestead plots, where kitchen gardens are often situated. See Appendix 1 for a more detailed breakdown of size distribution of land owned in rural Bangladesh.

5 Faaland, J. and Parkinson, J.R., *op.cit.,* pp. 81–88.

6 *Bhaimara* is a fictitious name chosen to protect the identity of the villagers.

7 Not all the land owned by the villagers of Bhaimara is located within the village boundaries. A small part of the 58.8 acres of agricultural land is distributed in other villages of the region. On the other hand, some people not belonging to Bhaimara own agricultural land within the boundaries of the village.

8 The term peasant is descriptive and only used to classify the landowners with reference to how much land their households claim ownership rights to. The separate categories of peasant households cannot be regarded as *classes* in any sense. Our groups in Table 1.2. differ from those presented in Table 1.1. for rural Bangladesh as a whole in the amount of land owned by each group, since our categorization was adopted to suit the particular circumstances of Bhaimara village, where no peasant owns more than 5½ acres.

There were several methodological problems involved in delineating the different households of the village and dilemmas connected with which households should be included in the village. See Appendix 2 for more detailed discussion on this issue.

9 For a general discussion of the difficulties in classifying peasants see Willem van Schendel: *Peasant Mobility — The Odds of Life in Rural Bangladesh,* Van Gorcum Assen, The Netherlands, 1981, pp. 37–39. For a detailed specific discussion, based on fieldwork in one particular village, see Arens and Van Beurden; *Jhagrapur — Poor Peasants and Women in a Village in Bangladesh,* Third World Publications, 1977 (Chapters 9 and 10). For other endeavours to classify peasants see P. Bertocci 1970, G.D. Wood 1976, B.K. Jahangir 1979. S. Adnan utilized the rigorous 'E-criterion' on 'labour exploitation ratio', developed by U. Patnaik 1976 in a guide to meaningful differentiation of peasant classes. He too ends up with neat landownership strata, see *Differentiation and Class Structure in Village Char Samraj* (mimeo), Village Study Groups, Dhaka, 1977, editor S. Adnan.

10 *Area Handbook for Bangladesh,* Foreign Area Studies, The American University, Washington D.C., 1975, p. 124.

11 See Table 1.2 for amount of land peasants own in the different categories.

12 The reasons for the fact that some 'poor' and 'small' category households are self-sufficient and have a surplus in rice production are that they have a high ratio of productive members in relation to unproductive members, and that they share-crop land in addition to cultivating their own land.

13 Fredrik Barth's major analytical work is presented in *Selected Essays of Fredrik Barth,* Volume 1 & 2, Routledge & Kegan Paul, London, Boston, and Henly, 1981.

14 Probably there exist more than 25 village studies carried out by social scientists in rural Bangladesh. We have been aware of the following monographs and related articles, in English: P. Bertocci (1970, 1975, 1976, 1979); R. Mukherjee (1971); S.M. Zaidi (1970); A.K.M. Aminuel Islam (1974, 1978); G.M. Wood in M.A. Huq ed. (1976, 1981); Arens and van Beurden (1977); S. Adnan (1976, 1977); S. Adnan and Z. Rahman (1978); K. Westergaard (1979, n.d.); A. Chowdhury (1978); M. Cain (1977, 1978, 1979); B.K. Jahangir (1979, 1982a, 1982b); Hartmann and Boyce (1979, 1981); H.K. Arefeen (1977, 1982); K.M.A. Aziz (1979); Who Gets What and Why (n.d.); Van Scendel (1981a, 1981b); A.L. Arn (1976, 1978); Z. Rahman (1980); K. Siddiqui (1982); A. Jenkins et al. (1980a, 1980b); K.M. Jensen (1983).

2

The Environment and Technology of Agricultural Production

Introduction

In chapter 1 we emphasized that it was the distribution as well as the scarcity of resources which caused poverty and competition for land and employment. This competition takes place within a given physical setting and environment. In this chapter we discuss different aspects of this environment and show the constraints and opportunities the environment sets for the economic strategies people can pursue. The first section gives a description of the large river system and the types of soil which exist in Bangladesh. In the next section we give a physical description of Bhaimara village, with particular reference to how the different types of land and rivers influence the settlement pattern and the land usage.

The third and main section deals with the utilization of the various production factors in agricultural activities. We discuss how the land and water resources, modern inputs, capital equipment, draft power and the human labour force resources are exploited. In this connection we also indicate how the employment pattern and the informal credit system in the rural areas are influenced to a large degree by the annual floods when work in the fields is made difficult. A main question for comment is why some of the production factors are so under-utilized and poorly mobilized. The answer largely explains why households make so little effort to invest *'intensively'* by increasing the output per unit of land. The efforts and resources of surplus households are more directed towards investing *'extensively'*, by obtaining more land at the expense of the poorer landowners. The problems of and constraints on a better utilization of the production factors thus have clear consequences for the investment pattern and thereby the competition for acquisition of more land and the level of employment opportunities which are created.

The river network and types of land

The extensive network of large and small rivers is the most significant feature of the landscape in Bangladesh. The river network moves from north to south but includes a number of streams flowing west to east and east to west. The rivers flow through the Bangladesh plain, which is the largest delta in the world, and end up in the Bay of Bengal.

The complex river system is based upon three major rivers: The Ganges, or Padma as it is known locally, the Brahamaputra (Jamuna, locally), and the Meghna. The Ganges and Brahamaputra stem from the Himalayas while the Meghna comes through the Sylhet basin within Bangladesh. The Ganges enters Bangladesh from the west at an elevation of 34 feet above sea level and the Brahamaputra enters from the north at an elevation of 50 feet. The rivers flow on to the Bay of Bengal with a drop of only five inches per mile. If the level of the Bangladesh plain had been 40 feet lower, almost all the plain would have been submerged under water. The flatness of the landscape is thus another prominent feature of the Bangladesh scenery.

The river system is formidable in many respects. The monsoon rains and Himalayan snowmelt drain from 600,000 square miles of the Indian sub-continent and are mainly funnelled through Bangladesh. The river system also drains 45,000 of the 55,000 square miles which make up Bangladesh. Thirty-two of 33 principal rivers in Bangladesh originate outside the boundaries of the country. The annual peak flood in the Padma-Meghna network discharges as much as 5 million cubic feet of water per second (cusec), placing this river network in a class with the other largest rivers in the world (the Amazon, the Congo, and the Mississippi).[1]

The average annual rainfall varies from between 50 and 60 inches in the west to 100 inches or more elsewhere in the country. Eighty per cent of the annual rains fall during the five months from May through September. The winter months from November through March only receive about 6 per cent of the total rainfall. During the monsoon, between May and September, the country is flooded every year. About two-thirds of the country's 22 million acres of cultivated area are vulnerable to floods that can destroy crops. In addition to the land that is flooded, an estimated three million acres suffer from saline intrusion from the Bay of Bengal.

The large river system, bringing nutritious silt-laden water as 'fertilizer supply' to the land, is the main physical resource of Bangladesh. The annual silt load carried down to the estuary has been estimated at 2.4 billions tons. However, the river system also represents the greatest hazard to Bangladesh. During flooding the rivers normally erode some inches off the river banks. Under extreme conditions, which nearly every year occur in one or another part of the country, the rivers can eradicate embankments and reshape the whole landscape. Whole villages can be destroyed; lives and property can be lost when rivers flood and find new courses. Along all the larger rivers *chars* occur. This is land that is built up by the silting. Sometimes the *chars* are islands in the rivers and may erode; at other times they become a permanent part of the landscape and become inhabited and cultivated.

The perennial problem for the Bangladesh peasant before each monsoon is to guess how much land will be flooded and where and when the flood will occur. There is no certain answer to these questions, which makes it difficult for the peasant to find the optimum time for planting. There is to-day no realistic possibility of controlling and regulating the larger floods and the main courses of the rivers. The flat land of Bangladesh is composed completely of mud. There are no rocks with which to build embankments, and there are no natural storage basins for the great rivers within the boundaries of Bangladesh.

The *land* is the other main physical resource of Bangladesh. The characteristics of the land in Bangladesh from the north to the south have sometimes been summed up by geographers as 'old mud, new mud and marsh'.[2] The active delta area is in the 'new mud and marsh areas' of the middle and southern part of Bangladesh. The soils of the Bangladesh plain are alluvial deposits resulting from river action, and they lack hardening properties. The soils can be roughly divided into old and new alluviums. Old alluviums, which are dark brown and loamy, containing little sand but much clay, are mainly found in the northern part of Bangladesh. Newer alluvial soils occur mainly along the large rivers where they are annually renewed. The newer soils are generally found south of the Padma river. The new alluviums are lighter in colour and contain more sand than the older soils. The annual siltations make the soils very fertile.

There is nothing the population living in Bangladesh can do to influence the amount of rainfall, the size of the silt load arriving at the borders of Bangladesh, or the types of soil which have developed. These basic ecological factors originate outside the boundaries of Bangladesh, and the population can only make smaller adjustments in the local areas to these strong natural forces.

The physical setting of Bhaimara village

Bhaimara village is situated in the middle of the Bangladesh plain in Manikganj Thana in Dhaka district. This is an area where the large river systems meet. Bhaimara lies only some miles east of the junction between the Padma and Jamuna rivers. Bhaimara is also situated a few miles from a main tarmac road, and it only takes a couple of hours to reach Dhaka by bus. Manikganj town with the Thana and subdivisional administrative headquarters is an hour and a half away on foot. Despite its fairly central location Bhaimara has a very rural appearance. It is difficult to find any material features which distinguish the village from the more distant villages located in the interior. The main roads in and around the village are mud roads, just wide enough for rickshaws to pass. When going to the village from the main tarmac road one has to walk through 4–5 other villages before coming to Bhaimara.

The settlements of houses in Bhaimara and the surrounding areas are dispersed rather than nucleated. The reason for this is the fairly high level of the annual floods. In order to keep the houses and the homes above the water level it is necessary to erect the houses on the 'highest' elevations, normally only 5–10 feet above the agricultural land. The pattern of the placement of the houses in the area therefore follows the course of the 'high lands'. The main paths in and between the villages have also been made on the elevations, so that they can be used at least during some part of the period of flood.

For many houses in the area the natural heights of the elevations are not high enough for setting up homesteads. Here people have dug up the agricultural land and added the soil to the elevations in order to reach heights which preserve their houses from flood. The place from where the soil is taken in the field often becomes many feet lower than other parts of the field, making it difficult to use the excavated place for agricultural purposes. It can, however, serve as a pond for washing water. The pond retains the water for a long period after the flood has receded.

During the period of the year when the lands of Bhaimara and the surrounding villages are flooded, to a depth varying from 3–12 feet, only the homestead plots and a few stretches of the road are visible above the water. The homestead areas look like small islands in a large lake. The only way to move from one homestead to another, if they are not on the same elevation, is to use a boat or any other floating vessel. In the area of Bhaimara most of the agricultural land is normally flooded 4 to 5 months a year. According to the people of the area, the floods have lasted one or two months less than in earlier years, because less water has been coming out of the tributaries of the Jamuna river.

The dispersed settlement makes it difficult to distinguish between the different villages. On two sides of Bhaimara, the south-eastern and south-western sides, the boundaries between it and the neighbouring villages are drawn between houses lying on the same elevation (see map of Bhaimara village on page 28). Homestead plots lying next to each other, with houses only a few yards away, belong to different villages. In north-west and north-east the boundaries towards three other villages go through the agricultural fields.

When one arrives in the village of Bhaimara, as with the other villages of the area, it is difficult to see all the houses when walking on the small paths through the village. Almost all houses are built next to or under trees. The leaves and branches of the trees provide shade which protects people, domestic animals, and houses from the strong sunlight. Around many of the homesteads jute palings have been erected so that family life can go on undisturbed on the homestead plots.

The houses in Bhaimara are made out of local material. The walls are made with jute or bamboo mats, the main frame being constructed from bamboo stems or trunks of small trees, and the roofs are normally thatched with paddy straw. Only relatively well-to-do people have a corrugated iron sheet as roof. One house in the village

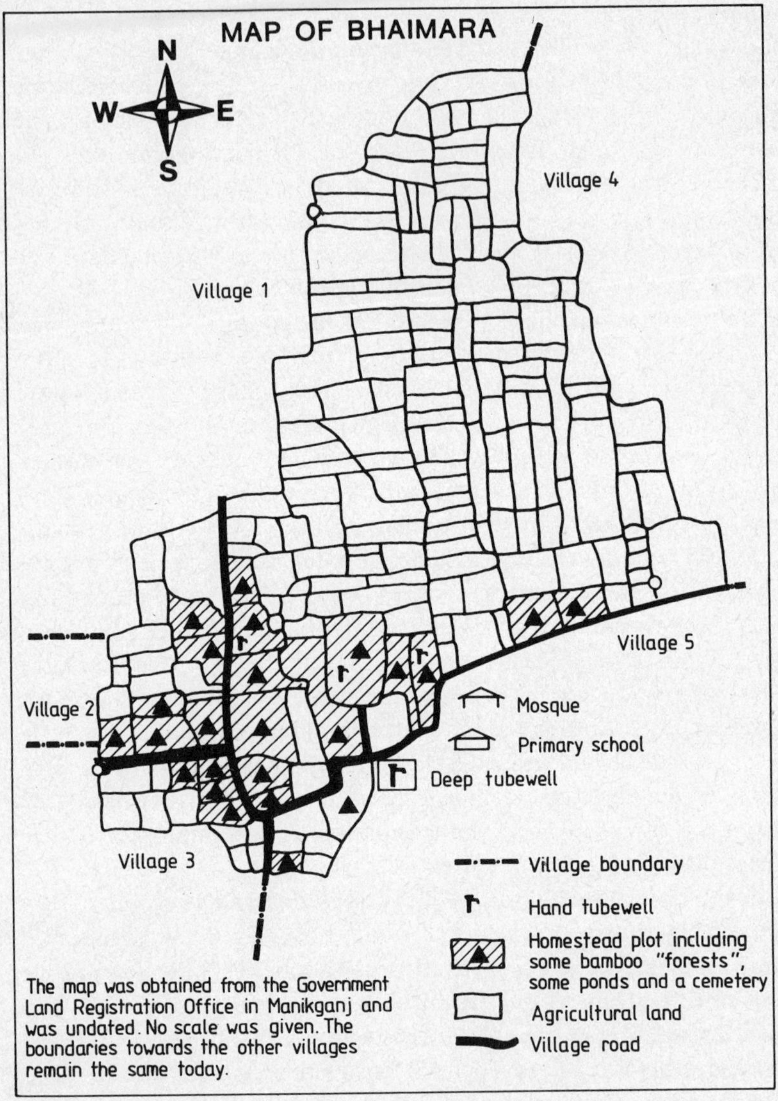

The map was obtained from the Government Land Registration Office in Manikganj and was undated. No scale was given. The boundaries towards the other villages remain the same today.

is made out of bricks. This house belong to the richest household in the village. All houses and buildings in the village, except two, belong to individual households and are used for dwellings, kitchens, and shelter for cattle. The two buildings which are not owned and used by individual households are the primary school and the mosque. Both these buildings are located on the southern border of the village, and they also serve people coming from certain sections of a couple of other villages. These houses are exclusively made out of corrugated iron sheets attached to wooden frames.

Bhaimara village has no shops, but in one of the neighbouring villages there is a bi-weekly *haat* (local market). This market is the main market place for 10–15 villages. This village also has a post office. Manikganj town is the large trade and shopping centre, having a variety of shops. All Government departments have their offices there, and Government employees reside in the town. However, the great majority of the villagers only rarely visit this town.

For an outsider the impression of Bhaimara is not one of glaring poverty. On the contrary, the village with its neat, small houses and picturesque palms and fruit-trees, small vegetable gardens and large green fields gives an impression of peace and tranquillity. But later when one comes to know how dependent the inhabitants are on agriculture for their living, how little land they own, and how little they get out of it, it becomes clear that the people are in fact very poor. Especially after one has learned how unevenly the total production is divided among the population, it becomes obvious that many people must be destitute.

Bhaimara village is small both in population and geographical extension. The average Bangladesh village has about 1200 inhabitants. Bhaimara has, as we noted in Chapter 1, only 311 inhabitants, who own only 58.8 acres of agricultural land — an average of 0.19 acre per inhabitant. The 58.8 acres are divided into 195 plots. Most of the 195 plots are placed north of the village, as seen on the map. The process of land transfer is such that people from other villages will own land within the administrative boundaries of Bhaimara, while the inhabitants of Bhaimara have some of their 195 plots in areas which belong to other villages. During the last 30 years the villagers of Bhaimara have sold many of the plots north of the village, and obtained land in the fields to the south of the village.

There is hardly any waste land in the village which could be used for agricultural purposes. The ten acres of homestead land on the elevations are already used for vegetables gardens and for fruit-trees. The few acres in front of the school and mosque are used for communal purposes: a playground for the children, a prayer field during the Eid celebration, and a pasture area for the cattle. In addition to this some tiny bamboo woods, a few ponds, and an old cemetery are situated on small elevations unsuitable for cultivation on the outskirts of the homestead plots. Thus, there is hardly any scope for expanding the agricultural area within the village boundaries. It is easy to understand that there is competition for getting as large a share as possible of the land within reach of the village. The high growth rate of the population aggrevates this situation. Bhaimara with 311 people in 1980 could, as some researchers estimate and predict for Bangladesh as a whole, almost double its population by the end of the century. This means that if the amount of land is kept constant, the villagers will have on the average about 0.10 acres each. This would be scarcity indeed, no matter how many times the production, from a technical point of view, can be increased!

Utilization of production factors in agriculture

Except for gas there are no important known natural resources in Bangladesh other than the fertile land. It has always been agriculture and related activities which have provided the livelihood for the great majority of the population in the country. The physical features of the landscape, described above, set clear limits to the organization of agricultural activities.

What aspects of agricultural production are of particular relevance for our analysis? We have already noted that the productivity of the land is very low. In fact, Japan and South Korea, which are both large rice-growing countries, produce 4 to 5 times as much rice per unit of land as Bangladesh.[3] Why does Bangladesh have such a low productivity rate and why do not the peasants apply more labour and inputs in production? These questions are complex and a variety of explanations can be put forward to answer them. First, on the basis of a technical description of how the different factors of production, land, labour and capital are utilized and combined, one might argue that the low productivity in Bangladesh is due to under-utilization and inefficient management of the production factors. Then, however, one might ask why the production factors are so poorly utilized. Here the explanation may be found, at least in part, by considering the characteristics of the distribution of ownership of land, the nature of the tenancy system, the possibilities of obtaining the necessary inputs and capital equipment, the role of the Government in rural development, the power structure in rural areas, the level of purchasing power among the landless and deficit peasants, etc.

In this chapter we focus on the more technical description of the under-utilization of the production factors. In subsequent chapters we examine why the factors of production are so under-utilized.

It is crucial for the focus of our study to understand why there is such a low productivity in agriculture. It is obvious that low productivity results in poverty and fewer employment opportunities. But the difficulties in obtaining a return on their investment per unit of land induce the 'surplus peasants' to use their surplus towards obtaining more land. The fierce competition for obtaining more land can, therefore, partly be understood against the background that for many peasants with a surplus a utilization of this surplus to increase production per unit of land is a less optimal alternative than expanding their land property. We shall, however, see that these alternative investment patterns do not necessarily exclude each other. The first option for those who have a surplus, however, is to increase their output by obtaining larger areas of land.

It thus becomes clear that the low utilization of the production factors is closely related to our focus on how well-to-do peasants have to encroach on poorer peasants' property as the safest form of investment. Below we shall describe, separately, the utilization of different production factors and show how under-utilized they are in relation to what, technically, could be an optimal utilization. We shall relate our discussion of the utilization of the production factors both to Bhaimara village and to Bangladesh as a whole.

Land

The total annual foodgrain production in Bangladesh varied during the 1970s between 10 and 14 million tons, and in the early 1980s it was ca. 13.5 million tons.[4] This means that the average production varied between 0.45 tons per acre and 0.64 tons per acre, which is a very low output by any international standard. The total production can be increased in two ways. Either the yield for each crop harvest can be increased or the number of cropping seasons per year can be increased. In the first part of this section, we shall mainly discuss the annual cropping patterns and number of agricultural seasons per year.

Annual cropping pattern

Most of the agricultural land in Bangladesh could be cropped two or three times a year if provided with irrigation as needed and with the necessary current inputs for the crops. The national average utilization of the 22 million acres of agricultural land is about 1.4 crops per year. There is a large variation in the cropping intensity and the type of crops grown in the annual cycle. These variations occur both between different regions of the country and within the individual villages. The two main 'physical' factors which explain this variation are the level of or the 'height' of the land and the fertility of the land. We have emphasized the flatness of the Bangladesh landscape, but a difference in height of only a few feet makes large differences for annual cropping patterns.

The agricultural land of Bangladesh may be classified into four categories according to the height of the land: (i) The *high* land (large parts of northern Bangladesh consisting of old alluviums belong to this category) on which even during the monsoon it is difficult to retain adequate moisture. This land only covers 8 per cent of the total cultivated area of Bangladesh.[5] (ii) *Intermediate* land, which is flooded during the monsoon but not more than to a couple of feet. This area constitutes about 45 per cent of the cultivated land and can be used for multiple cropping. (iii) *Low land,* which is flooded to between 3 and 12 feet and constitutes about 25 per cent of the area and is suitable for double cropping. (iv) *Very low land,* which is flooded to more than 12 feet and can be cultivated only when the water has receded. This type of land only represents 5 per cent of the total amount of cultivated land.

Most of the land around Bhaimara belongs to the intermediate and low level types of land. In a neighbouring village, however, there is some agricultural land which is so high that it is hardly ever inundated and ponds and canals which are so low that the land is only used for 'seedling beds'. In Figure 2.1 some graphs show typical annual croppings on the different levels of land.[6, 7]

The cropping pattern varies on the about 60 acres of land cultivated by the villagers of Bhaimara. The traditional pattern has been to cultivate *aus* or jute in the spring season, *aman* in the summer and autumn season, and winter crops (pulses) in the dry winter season. Some of the peasants broadcast *aus* and *aman* at the same time and harvest the two crops with a few months' interval, *aus* in the summer and *aman,* which takes longer to mature, in the autumn. Some of the more well-to-do peasants of Bhaimara have recently started to cultivate tobacco during the winter seasons. For tobacco cultivation, however, they need fertilizers and insecticides.

A few years ago a deep tubewell was installed in the southern part of the village (see map). This deep tubewell has technically a command area of about 50 acres and can provide water to the agricultural land of several villages. The irrigation water from the deep tubewell has changed the annual cropping pattern. During the winter season a high yielding variety of *boro* is cultivated. This is harvested in May/June, which implies that *aus* and jute cannot be grown.

It is difficult to estimate the average cropping intensity on the about 60 acres of land owned by the villagers. From the information presented above it could appear to be more than 2 crops per year, much above the national average. This is, however, not a correct figure. First, only a small part of the land is covered by winter crops. Most land lies fallow, or only fodder for the cattle is grown on the land. On some land only the *aman* crop is grown, and some peasants who have land under the command area of the new deep tubewell now only grow one *boro* crop each year, while they earlier grew broadcasted *aus* and *aman* on the land.

Haroun Er Rashid has estimated that the cropping intensity of

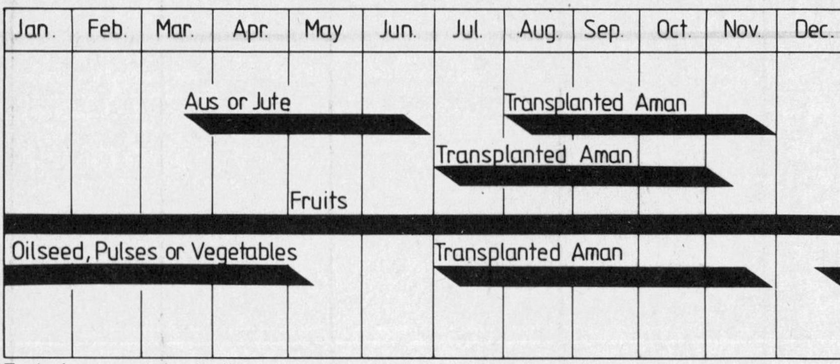

Typical present agriculture cropping pattern, High Land

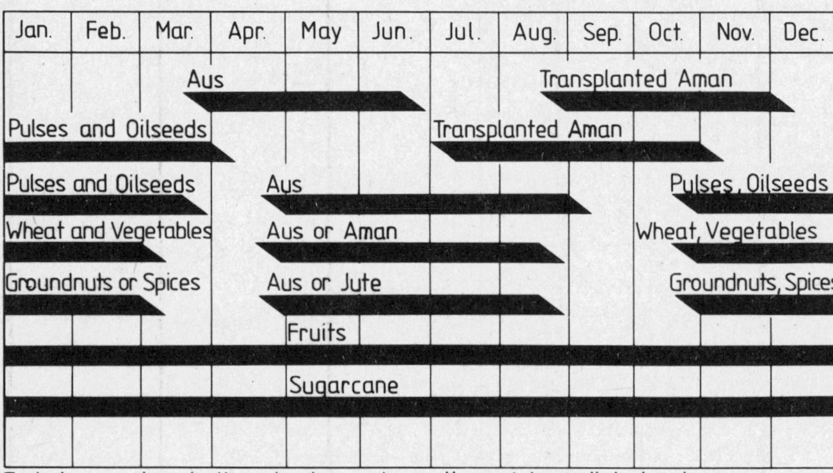

Typical present agriculture land cropping pattern, Intermediate Land

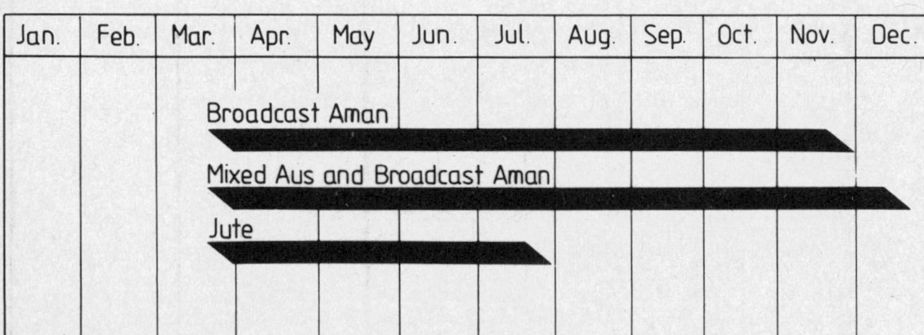

Typical present agriculture land cropping pattern, Low Land

Figure 2.1. Annual Cropping Patterns

the Jamuna-Podda floodplain area, to which Bhaimara belongs, is 170 per cent, i.e. 1.7 crops per year.[8]

In any event, two crops of rice in a year do not yield twice as much as one crop per year. According to the peasants of Bhaimara a combined broadcast of *aus* and *aman* normally does not produce much more than 1½ times a single *aman* broadcast crop.

While topography and the quality of the soil to a large degree determine the annual cropping pattern (various economic factors naturally also influence the choice of crops), the *yields* of the crops depend on other circumstances. One important factor is the climatic conditions, especially timely and adequate rainfall. The rainfall, or the expectation of it, influences the agricultural operations of ploughing, sowing, weeding and harvesting. Ploughing for the *aus-aman* broadcast crops depends on the arrival of rain from the north-west in March/April. Too much rain in April/May may damage or drown the small plants. Untimely rainfall can not only destroy one crop; it can also make it difficult for the peasants to get the right start for the next season.

The monsoon rainfall and the level of flood of the inundated land have effects beyond those of cropping patterns and yields of the crops. The rainfall and the level of the flood also make the agricultural activities highly seasonal, which has consequences for the issues on which we focus attention in this report. During the periods when the land is under water, there are no work tasks to be carried out in the fields; therefore, the households that mainly depend for their income on employment in the agricultural sector face particular difficulties during this period. The clear seasonality of income-earning opportunities, in its turn, to a large degree determines the employer-employee relationships which are established and also the nature of the credit market. This theme will be pursued in chapters 4 and 6.

Competition for land and employment is therefore both directly and indirectly related to how the forces of nature influence agricultural activities.

Fragmentation of land

Another important aspect of the usage of land is the fragmentation of the agricultural plots of the peasants. This has clear consequences for agricultural activities and for the type of technology which can be applied.

There are only a few large farms in Bangladesh. One main reason for this is the inheritance system, which divides the land of a man equally between his sons. (The inheritance system will be dealt with in the next chapter.) A peasant will often own several or many plots. When his heirs are to inherit the land, they will most often not take whole plots each. Unless the plots are very small they will divide the individual plots into smaller pieces and take one part each.

Rashid estimated that in 1970 there were 75 million plots of land in Bangladesh.[9] The table below, quoted from Rashid, shows the fragmentation of the farms (households owning agricultural land).

Table 2.1. Fragmentation of Holdings.[10]

	million	
All farms	6.14	100%
Farms not fragmented	0.62	10%
Farms with 2 or 3 fragments	1.29	21%
Farms with 4 or 5 fragments	1.08	17%
Farms with 6 or 9 fragments	1.39	23%
Farms with 10 or more fragments	1.76	29%

The 58.8 acres owned by the 41 landowning households in Bhaimara consist, as we have noted, of 195 plots. This means that the 'average' landowning household possesses 4.76 plots. Ten years ago the number of plots on the same area of land was less. In ten years from now, when the sons of some households have inherited from their fathers, the number will probably exceed 200 by a wide margin.

We found very little evidence of any process of consolidation of plots. Even a rich peasant who acquires a plot of land next to his own will often not consolidate the two plots. On the other hand, there are lower limits to the size of small plots determined by the need for reasonably efficient cultivation with the existing technology. The average size of plots in Bhaimara is (58.8 acres : 195) = 0.30 acres.

One advantage for the peasants in having their land divided into separate plots is that this fragmentation represents a certain security against unpredictable natural and climatic conditions. Often the level and soil types of the different plots belonging to one household will vary. Flood or drought can destroy the crops on one plot while the crops on another can be saved. Also, for the planning of seasonal work operations it can be advantageous for a peasant to start ploughing and planting on the low land, which is inundated first, and then move on to the plots at the intermediate level.

There are also disadvantages attached to a fragmented ownership pattern. For some peasants much time must be spent moving equipment from one plot to the other if the plots are far away from each other. Certain work operations, like ploughing, are more easily and efficiently carried out on larger plots.

Production of major crops

Table 2.2 sums up some of the issues which we have touched on so far. The table compares the average annual production in the period 1965-66 to 1969-70 with the average annual production in the period 1970-71 to 1974-75.[11]

The table shows clearly the important role of rice in agricultural production and in acreage, accounting for nearly 4/5 of all the area cultivated. It also shows that the total area cultivated declined marginally between the late 1960s and the early 1970s. Moreover, for most crops there has not been any increase in yield per acre; thus rice production remained constant while population increased by nearly 3 per cent per year.

Figures from more recent periods show that the agricultural production has increased. But for no period of any length has the agricultural production kept up with the growth of the population.

Total rice production was 13.6 million tons in 1978-79 and fell slightly the following year. For these two years about half of the production was made up of the main *aman* crop while the remainder was divided more or less equally between the *aus* and *boro* crops.[12]

Table 2.2. Acreage, Production and Yield Rates of Major Crops in Bangladesh. (Averages of 1965/66 to 1969/70 and 1970/71 to 1974/75)

	1965/66–1969/70			1970/71–1974/75		
Crops	Acreage (mill. acres)	Production (mill. acres)	Yield per acre (lbs)	Acreage (mill. acres)	Production (mill. acres)	Yield per acre (lbs)
Rice	23.9	10.7	1001.0	23.0	10.7	999
Wheat	0.2	0.07	716.8	—		
Potatoes	0.9	0.65	8153.6	—		
Sugar cane	0.4	7.5	18 tons	0.4	6.3	17 tons
Oilseeds	0.8	0.2	716.0	0.7	0.2	681
Pulses	0.6	0.2	672.0	0.8	0.2	678
Jute	2.3	1.2	1158.0	1.9	0.9	1092
Tobacco	0.1	0.03	663.0	0.1	0.04	732
Tea	0.1	0.03	656.3	0.1	0.02	512
Others	1.88			2.3		
Total area of all crops	30.7			Total 30.2 million acres		
Net cropped area including current fallow	22.4			Net cropped area 22.5 million acres		

L. Chen has estimated that the accepted minimum foodgrain consumption for Bangladesh is 15 oz (425 g) of foodgrain per head per day.[13] J.R. Tarrant states in relation to this figure:

> At no time during the last 20 years has Bangladesh produced enough foodgrain to provide her population with this amount. Despite the existence of other non-grain sources of food, Bangladesh is a food deficit country by any method of measurement and by any criteria,
>
> ...perhaps 70 million people are seriously undernourished... as they cannot afford sufficient food at current prices.[14]

In chapter 8 we shall discuss the measures the Government undertakes to bridge the gap in the food deficit situation.

Water resources

A major reason for the low agricultural production is the underutilization of the water resources. Adequate water supply is essential both for increasing the cropping intensity and for raising the output per acre for each crop. A World Bank report from 1971 has estimated that it would be possible to quadruple the rice production of the mid 1970s by the end of the century with the use of already known technology.[15]

Table 2.3. Potential Rice Production (million tons).

Year	Inputs only	Inputs plus irrigation	Inputs plus full irrigation and drainage
1983	16	26	35
1993	19	32	42
2003	22	38	51

As shown in the table, access to adequate water supplies (both surface water and groundwater) and inputs (seeds, fertilizers, pesticides, extensive services) are necessary conditions for doubling and trebling production.

Potential rice production under different circumstances is, however, at best only a tentative estimate of what is *technically* possible.

The economic costs involved for the different technical alternatives have not been considered. The cost of increasing output rises progressively with the technical measures which are added: (1) inputs only, (2) inputs + water, (3) inputs + water + drainage. Especially this last measure of drainage, which implies the establishment of large-scale water control systems, seem to be an unrealistic goal in the near future.[16] Even if the economic means were available to carry out the various measures, there would have been other constraints to tackle in order to achieve the higher output. Introduction of new technology takes place in a socio-economic environment in the rural areas which militates against reaching out to the poor and small land-owners with the new technologies. Yet, the table from the World Bank study serves to show the amount of output which could technically be achieved by the use of available technologies.

The ecological possibilities for providing irrigation water to the fields are very good. At present only some 12–15 per cent of the total cultivated area of Bangladesh is under irrigation. It has been estimated that about 16 million acres of land, 75 per cent of the total cultivable area, could be irrigated by groundwater resources, and several million additional acres could be irrigated by surface water if the necessary canals from the large rivers and their tributaries were dug.[17]

Although the potentials for better utilization of water resources are good and have been so many years, there are many reasons for the continued poor irrigation performance. According to surveys carried out in Bangladesh, most irrigation pumps are out of order only a few years after they have been installed. When the pumps do operate, they only irrigate 30–50 per cent of the area which technically they could irrigate.[18] The problems of proper utilization of installed irrigation facilities can to a large degree be ascribed to the lack of organization and skills for repair and maintenance by the peasants, as well as to the way in which the power structure of the villages operates. The uncertainties connected with irrigation, even if it is technically available, make many peasants opt for the safer, but low-yielding varieties of crops. Another reason why small peasants might decide to cultivate low-yielding varieties, even if irrigation water were available, is that they would have difficulties in obtaining the inputs needed for the high-yielding varieties.

It is clear that the more the peasant strive to increase the output per crop or for more crops per year, the more vulnerable they become to ecological, technical and economic factors which often lie beyond their control. Although the traditional varieties of *aus* and *aman* rice are low-yielding they possess certain qualities which are in their favour in the highly risky ecological environment of Bangladesh. The local low-yielding varieties are much more flood and drought tolerant than the new high-yielding varieties (HYV); they are also more resistant to insect attacks and do not need chemical fertilizers and insecticides and the same skilful supervision, as the HYV-plants. The package of inputs and the supply of water have to be carefully balanced if the crops are to yield their full potential output.

The deep tubewell installed in Bhaimara confirms many of the points made in different irrigation surveys. The pump irrigates only a small area of what is technically possible, and it has been difficult for the small peasants with land under its command area to obtain the necessary inputs for cultivating HYV's. In one particular season the pump was out of operation for one week. During this period an expensive crop was destroyed for some peasants. We return in other chapters to the role of the deep tubewell of Bhaimara for agricultural development. Here we wish to emphasize the interdependence of water and inputs when introducing the new varieties of rice. If these production factors are not co-ordinated better in their application than in the past, serious barriers to agricultural growth will continue to exist.

Modern inputs

The main nutrients for the soil in Bangladesh have always been and still are the silt-laden flood waters of the monsoon. Cow dung and oilcakes are also used as fertilizers. Cow dung has, however, an alternative use as fuel for cooking purposes. Normally, therefore cattle manure is only used on the most valuable crops, on cash crops like tobacco and in the beds of seedlings.

Chemical fertilizers were almost unknown in Bangladesh two decades ago and even to-day the consumption of such fertilizers is extremely low compared with both other rice-producing countries

(Taiwan and South Korea use 15 times more fertilizers per acre) and the recommended doses, see Table 2.4:[19]

Table 2.4. Actual and Recommended Levels of Fertilizer Use in Rice Crops, Bangladesh 1961–74 (pounds of nutrients per acre).

Period	*Aus*	*Aman*	*Boro*
Average 1961–65	2.8	1.7	9.9
" 1966–70	5.6	4.8	24.3
" 1971–74	8.2	6.2	44.1
Recommended doses*	240.0	270.0	270.0

* The figures refer to local varieties of rice. With high-yielding varieties the recommended doses would be substantially higher.

The under-utilization of fertilizers is not evenly distributed among the peasants. Chemical fertilizers are almost exclusively used by the well-to-do and rich peasants. The table shows a fast growth in the use of fertilizers for all the three crops. Although the Government in the last 15 years has subsidized fertilizers heavily in order to make them available to all, the low Government price does not apply within the villages. Since the demand is so much larger than the supply, a black market has developed and poor peasants cannot afford the high prices which are charged. Traditional varieties, grown on 85–90 per cent of the cultivated area, are also responsive to fertilizers, although not to the same extent as the HYV's. (High-yielding varieties are cultivated on 12–15 per cent of the land.)[20] There are, however, many doubts about applying expensively obtained fertilizers to low-yielding crops. In many places peasants have also found that the straw of the plant may be so weak that it bends, since it cannot carry the weight of the heavier 'crown' of the rice plant.

The modern inputs are, in most of their components, neutral as to scale. This means that the inputs can be adopted with about the same advantage to small and large farms. All studies indicate, however, as we also found in Bhaimara, that access to scarce HYV-seeds, pesticides and fertilizers is highly dependent on the economic and social position of the peasants.

Tools

The agricultural implements used by the peasants are very simple and inexpensive. The wooden plough, or ard, which is used has not changed its form during the last two thousand years.[21] Such a plough only costs 50–70 Taka. It is very light, generally only 20 to 30 pounds, makes furrows only 3½ inches deep, and does not turn the soil. According to agricultural experts this may be adequate ploughing for the rice plant, but not for some other types of crops. The depth of the furrow depends, of course, on the hardness of the soil and the strength of the draught power. Another agricultural implement in common use is a drag (*moi* — local name), which is drawn behind a pair of oxen in order to level the fields. Different types of wood sticks are used to break hard clay lumps. For harvesting short sickles are applied to cut the crops. Hand spades (a special sort of knife) can be used for weeding. The traditional equipment for post-harvesting operations is also simple and inexpensive. The basic agricultural implements are all readily available to all peasants and do not represent a constraint to agricultural growth.

Cattle

Cattle, including buffaloes, are raised primarily to serve as draught animals, but they also provide milk and meat for consumption, skins for sale, and manure for fuel and fertilizer. In 1970 there were 18.5 million cattle and buffaloes, almost one for each acre. Owing to lack of pastures and to overgrazing, the quality of the cattle is generally very poor. A large part of the cattle food is crop residue, such as rice straws and husks. The average ox only stands 3 feet 6 inches at the shoulder and weighs about 200 pounds. The draught bullocks are weak, and they only have one-tenth of the draught power of an English draught horse.[22] In an average day a yoke of bullocks can plough 0.40 acres. Since each plot of land has to be ploughed 6–8 times, a pair of bullocks can only manage to plough 5–7 acres of land per agricultural season. The cows too are in poor shape. The main purpose and function of the cow is to produce draught animals; the average yield of milk per cow is only 140 litres per year. (Cows are also used as draught animals in agriculture.)

Although most peasants have a very practical and utilitarian attitude towards cattle, ownership of a good breed of cattle also brings social status. Some of the rich peasants can afford to feed their cattle well and raise oxen which weigh many times more than the average. These animals may be valued in the market at many thousand Takas, while the undernourished poorly fed calves and cattle only cost a fraction of these sums; small calves can be bought for only 150–200 Takas.

Bullocks as draught animals are scarce, and there is strong competition for them in the peak ploughing season. The most secure basis for carrying out ploughing at the right time is for a peasant to own cattle himself. Poor people who do not own draught animals themselves may obtain a ploughing team only at less than ideal times during the ploughing season.

In Bhaimara we found that 22 of the 62 households owned cattle and 9 households borrowed cattle on a sharecropping basis, 7 from the cattle owners at Bhaimara. The 22 cattle owners owned a total of 46 cows, 28 calves, 7 oxen and 10 bullocks. It is the rich households of Bhaimara that possess most of the cattle, and it is these households that sharecrop out cattle to the poorer households. In Bhaimara there is strong competition for strong draught animals during the time of ploughing.

Overgrazing was clearly a problem. The grass in the field in front of the school was only left to grow a few millimetres before it was eaten. We often saw children in the fields picking weeds which they fed to the cattle. The most touching example of utilization of available resources we witnessed every night, when the labourer with whom we shared a homestead let the calf he had sharecropped lick the sweat and salt on his body.

Labour

We have seen that there is great scarcity both of land and of certain types of capital equipment for agricultural production, both of which hamper production. Labour is the only production factor in abundance. The labour force possesses the basic skills which are needed to increase production, except for repair and maintenance of the mechanized irrigation equipment.

It is difficult to assess the overall unemployment and under-employment situation of the country. Estimates of the rural employment situation are mainly based on micro-studies of a small number of villages and on farm management studies. These studies estimate man-days required for the different crops under various technological circumstances and given annual crop patterns. The results from these micro-studies are projected up to Bangladesh as a whole. Such estimates of labour requirements for agricultural and related activities are then compared with the available labour force of the country. According to the estimates there are 7 to 8 million man-years remaining unutilized each year. This means that one-third of the human resources are under-utilized. (There are of course many uncertainties attached to such estimates.)[23]

There is great variation in the underemployment and unemployment situation among different groups in the country during different seasons. In a later chapter we discuss which groups are hardest hit by the unemployment situation. We also emphasize that the employment prospects for the future are not bright. Already, the increase in the labour force is larger than the growth of the population, 4–4½ per cent each year. Owing to the predominance of young persons in the population, the labour force will increase by 850,000–1.1 million persons annually.[24]

At the village level unemployment is very much in evidence, particularly during the period when the land is under water and many people only sit around in their small homestead 'islands' unable to find work. During the agricultural seasons too one can observe young, strong men who are idle. Some stroll around in the villages, others sit for hours with a fishing rod hoping to catch a small fish in a tiny pond. Unemployed boys and girls and old women often spend much time in the fields picking up the left-over paddy from the harvest. None of these activities are very productive; they are usually not sufficiently remunerative even to provide a minimum amount of food for the person so engaged.

Compared to many other villages in Bangladesh, Bhaimara is atypical in that there does exist, during the dry season, a small but regular market for employment outside the village area. Adjacent to the highway, a few miles from the village, there is a brickfield factory. About 10 young men from the village are normally employed here for some months. Without this opportunity for employment the competition for labour contracts would be even greater within the village.

Unemployment creates a desperate situation for the households affected, forcing them to live in poverty and misery. The waste of human resources is especially tragic in view of the many work tasks which 'cry out' to be undertaken and which would increase production. A common feature of many of these work tasks is that a large number of persons would have to work jointly and in a coordinated way on such tasks as 'earth-digging' in order to make embankments against floods, repairing and maintaining roads, building canals for water distribution, digging ponds, etc.

But there are also other and smaller tasks which the members of individual households could carry out by themselves. Anisur Rahman has made a list of some of these small-scale tasks:[25, 26]

> Construction of dwellings, godowns, etc.; manual and semi-manual irrigation; collection of human, animal and green wastes and producing fertilizer therefrom; kitchen gardening and tree plantation; pisciculture; cultivation of more labour-intensive high-yielding variety cereals in place of traditional ones and following modern, labour-intensive cultural practices traditionally absent; manual and semi-manual transportation; rearing of silk-worms — with easy-to-grow caster leaves and producing castor oil from the seed; spinning, weaving, knitting and other cottage industries of various kinds; participation in mass literacy programmes; family planning and health extension works; extension work in so many areas; and so on. Every developing country has its own combination of numerous, literally numerous, such works that can keep the entire population engaged with relatively small complementary inputs that should not be very difficult to produce. The gain in national product, and in capital formation simultaneously, could thereby be substantial.

Why are not these activities of a large-scale or small-scale nature carried out? There are many reasons for this. For the large-scale operations of protecting land from the rivers there is no individual or institution based in the countryside which can mobilize people collectively on the scale needed. Besides, the nature of the work tasks is often such that the result would affect people differently. With individual ownership to land, it would be difficult to make a coordinated plan, taking equal care of the interests of all landowners. The Government has, however, through Rural Works and Food Work projects been able to mobilize thousands of people to participate in large-scale earth-digging projects. Nevertheless, although many projects have been carried out on a national scale, the Government effort does not amount to much in relation to total unemployment and to the work that needs to be implemented.

There are various reasons why 'small-scale projects' have not been carried out. For some people it can be lack of innovative power, lack of necessary skills, or lack of access to small inputs, which restrain them from initiating and carrying out such tasks. In many cases among the poorest people in Bhaimara we witnessed a state of apathy which reflected their condition of semi-starvation and grim poverty. In later chapters we discuss the power structure in the rural areas and show how this operates to suppress innovative efforts among poor people.

It is clear that labour could be better mobilized in the ongoing agricultural activities. The crops of a given plot could often be increased by ploughing 7 times instead of 5 times before broadcasting the seeds. The crops would also become larger by weeding three times instead of twice and by making a more thorough harvest. Sometimes there will be manpower available in the household owning the plots to make these extra efforts, but at some point a balance has to be struck between the drudgery of the work and the utility and the results of the extra labour efforts. If there is not available or willing manpower within the household, there will nearly always be wage-labourers ready to do the third round of weeding. What are the economic and social factors a household considers when deciding whether or not to employ wage-labourers for these tasks? These questions will be discussed in chapters 4, 5 and 6.

Another theme we shall take up in these chapters is the motivations and incentives the cultivators have for increased efforts in the fields. If very little of the rewards of increased labour input accrue to the labourers or the sharecroppers, but end up with the non-cultivating owners of the land, this might explain poor efforts among the cultivators.

Conclusion

In this chapter we have sought to convey an impression of the extent of under-utilization of production factors and of the difficulty of achieving a faster growth of agricultural output, as is illustrated by the meagre results of efforts made during the last two decades to provide irrigation and modern inputs. To increase production substantially it is not enough to improve the utilization and performance of one production factor; the application of modern inputs, irrigation facilities and labour has to be coordinated if output is to be augmented efficiently and significantly. It is very much the lack of coordination of the production factors rather than scarcity of such resources which causes the low level of production.

In this situation, and given the uncertainties of obtaining a satisfactory return on investment for increased output per unit of land, it is not surprising that many peasants with a surplus tend to concentrate on expanding their landholdings, which in a long-term perspective also represents a better form of security than does a correspondingly smaller landholding with a higher yield per acre. This has direct and automatic implications for deficit peasants, whose property the 'surplus' peasants seek to acquire. Throughout the study we shall, directly and indirectly discuss some of the implications which follow from this investment pattern.

Notes

1 *Bangladesh Land and Water Resources, Sector Study* (9 Volumes), World Bank, 1972, and Joseph R. Stepanek: *Bangladesh — Equitable Growth?* Pergamon Press, 1979, Chapter 8 on Water for Land's Development.

2 See *Area Handbook for Bangladesh, op.cit.*

3 See Daniel Asplund and Stefan de Vylder: *Contradictions and Distortions in a Rural Economy: The Case of Bangladesh,* SIDA, Stockholm, 1979, pp. 13–22.

4 See J.R. Tarrant: 'Food Policy Conflicts in Bangladesh', *World Development,* Vol. 10, No. 2, pp. 103–113, 1982 and *Statistical Pocket Book of Bangladesh 1981,* Bangladesh Bureau of Statistics, December 1982, p. 172.

5 Alia Ahmad: *Some Important Features of the Agrarian Economy in Bangladesh,* Working Paper No. 3, Department of Economics, University of Lund, April 1980. (The percentage distribution of land in the four categories only adds up to 83 per cent from the quoted source. Nevertheless a rough indication is given of the size of the different categories of land.)

6 Source: *Bangladesh: Rural Development in Four Thanas in Kushtia District,* International Technical Assistance Department, Ministry of Foreign Affaris, Netherland, February 1978.

7 Bangladesh has three rice crop seasons: *boro* (winter), *aus* (spring), and *aman* (summer). *Aman* is the principal crop, providing 54 per cent of the food grain, *aus* 24 per cent, and *boro* 20 per cent. *Wheat* production supplies 2 per cent of the total grain production. See J.F. Stepanek, *op.cit.,* p. 47.

8 Haroun Er Rashid: *Geography of Bangladesh,* University Press Limited, Bangladesh 1977, p. 401–402.

9 Rashid, *op.cit.,* p. 211.

10 Rashid, *op.cit.,* p. 212. Rashid has estimated the figures in a table based on the 1960 Census of Agriculture. The figures are different to-day. Since a larger proportion is nearly landless, a higher percentage of the household will probably own only one or a few plots.

11 The table is based on the Bangladesh Five-Year Plan 1973–78, p. 83, and *Statistical Pocket-book of Bangladesh, 1978* (pp. 140–145). The table is quoted from Alia Ahmad, *op.cit.,* p. 32.

12 See J.R. Tarrant, *op.cit.,* p. 105.

13 L. Chen, *An Analysis of Per Capita Food Grain Availability, Consumption and Requirements in Bangladesh: A System Approach to Food Planning,* Ford Foundation Reports, No. 24, (Dhaka 1974).

14 See J.R. Tarrant, *op.cit.,* p. 103 and p. 105.

15 Discussed in J. Faaland and J.R. Parkinson: *op.cit.,* pp. 131–134.

16 J. Faaland and J.R. Parkinson, *op.cit.,* p. 72.

17 See Biggs, S., Edwards, C., and Griffiths, J.: *Irrigation in Bangladesh,* Discussion paper 126, Institute of Development Studies, University of Sussex, 1978.

18 See Biggs, Edwards, and Griffiths, *op.cit.,* and L.M. Hannah: 'Hand Pump Irrigation in Bangladesh', *Bangladesh Development Studies,* Volume IV, No. 4, October 1976.

19 Source: Raisuddin Ahmad, *Foodgrain Production in Bangladesh: An Analysis of Growth, its Sources and related Policies.* International Food Policy Research Institute, Washington 1976. (The table quoted here is from Asplund/de Vylder, *op.cit.*, p. 19.)

20 See Joseph F. Stepanek, *op.cit.*, Chapter 6.

21 See Harun Er Rashid, *op.cit.*, p. 214.

22 See Rashid, *op.cit.*, p. 215.

23 See J. Faaland and J.R. Parkinson, *op.cit.*, pp. 84–88, and Asplund/de Vylder, *op.cit.*, pp. 19–22.

24 See J. Stepanek, *op.cit.*, pp. 41–43.

25 Anisur Rahman: *The Utilization of Labour in the Strategy for Development in the ECAFE Development Region,* paper presented for ECAFE, United Nations, mimeo, n.d.

26 Rene Dumont has made similar proposals and particularly emphasized the development potential which lies in cultivation of fish in ponds. See *A Self-reliant Rural Development Policy for the Poor Peasantry of Sonar Bangladesh* (Ford Foundation, Dhaka, May 1973) and *Problems and Prospects for Rural Development in Bangladesh* (Ford Foundation, Dhaka, November 1973).

3

Aspects of Social Organization in the Rural Areas

Introduction

The social organization and cultural factors constitute an important part of the framework within which the competition for scarce resources takes place. In this chapter our subject will be various aspects of this social and cultural setting. We start by describing different domestic units. In particular we focus on the household unit, which is the smallest decision-making unit for production and consumption purposes. We discuss how decisions are reached within a household and the division of labour between its members. We then proceed to outline the development cycle of the household and show the qualitatively different stages the household goes through. We relate the cohesiveness of the household to the stage of composition it has reached.

A main mechanism for transfer of land is inheritance. We spell out the rules of inheritance and emphasize the implications the inheritance rules have for the division and fragmentation of land properties. We show how the increasing scarcity of land forces people to adopt new practices as regards inheritance rules. In a separate section we discuss the factors people attach importance to when ranking themselves and other people in their own 'local' social stratification system. We show how the severe poverty situation most people find themselves in makes people recognize wealth (size of landholding), as a more important criterion of rank than traditional signs of status. Marriage relationships are important both for economic and political purposes. We outline the factors taken into account by parents looking for mates for their children and show that here too the economic standing of the household of the prospective marriage partner is a prime consideration. The various social institutions and groupings in the rural areas are also a context for the competition for scarce resources. We outline some of these institutions and show how the local leadership and the power structure emerge from them.

Throughout the chapter we want to depict the dilemma most people face: how to strike a balance between conforming to certain activities which are regulated by culturally defined rules and taking advantage of economic opportunities. We show in this and the next chapters that in many situations a choice has to be made between behaving properly and exploiting an economic opportunity.

The domestic units

The household unit referred to in our statistical material is in Bengali termed *chula* or *khana, chula* meaning 'hearth group' and *khana* 'eating unit'. In the following, we shall use the term household for either type.[1] The members of a household are, most often, a joint production and consumption unit. Within the household decisions are taken as to how the production factors at the disposal of the household shall be utilized and combined. The household is based on kinship-relations, and the individual households are built around one elementary family. As we shall see later, the composition of the households varies greatly. The household may consist of incomplete families, an elementary family living with other family members, or several elementary families living together in a household.

Each elementary family lives in its own house *(ghor). Ghor* literally means housing unit. The *ghor* therefore may or may not overlap and correspond with the household. Another distinct and separate domestic unit in rural Bangladesh is the *bari,* which literally means home. Normally there are several *ghors* and several households in a *bari,* but a *bari* can also consist of only one household. The 62 households in Bhaimara are part of about 25 *baris.* Each *bari* has a homestead yard in its midst, and the houses face this yard, which is the place where the domestic activities are carried out.

All the households belong to an agnatic lineage *(gusti). Gusti* is the term for a group of households or families all of whom are agnatically related with the exception of in-marrying wives and out-marrying daughters.[2] Married women often maintain a kind of dual *gusti* membership, both to the agnatic lineage into which they were born and the one they have married into.

In Bhaimara we counted 18 *gustis*. It was clear that the villagers of Bhaimara do not have a common conception of what the term *gusti* implies. There was much disagreement about which households belonged to which *gustis*. Generally poor households also wanted to be included in *gustis* with which they had relatively distant kin-relations. The rich households, on their side, attempting to keep their lineage as 'pure and good' as possible, often denied kin-relations with some poor households. There are also economic reasons why rich households disown their poor distant kin-relations. A recognized kin-relationship would imply certain obligations for the welfare of the poor relatives. Few households could trace their forefathers for more than three to four generations, and there have been many intermarriages between the *gustis*. Some villagers' conception of *gusti* was that it is a group of households which are agnatically related. Other villagers, however, maintained that a common ancestor was necessary to delineate the *gusti*. In our account of the number of *gustis*, each *gusti* can refer to a common, deceased male ancestor. It is in this strict sense we have used the term in other chapters where we present information on the type of social relationships which exist between the types of households and economic activities. Table 3.1 shows how many households belong to each of the 18 *gustis* and to which land-owning category the households of the *gustis* belong.

Table 3.1 shows that 7 of the 18 *gustis* only consist of one household. A few of these households immigrated to the village during the last two decades. Four *gustis* consist of two households only. In Bhaimara there are only 3 larger *gustis*, two having 11 households each and one 9 households. The table shows that the three large *gustis* have households which belong to different land-owning categories (some of the 18 *gustis* will also have member households that live in other villages). Most of the households of a *gusti* would live in close proximity to each other; some households would be sharing the same homestead yard.

Later we shall often refer to the *gusti* as patrilineage, and in chapters 4 and 5 we shall assess the role the *gusti* plays for important economic relationships.

Table 3.1. Households and *Gusti* membership in Bhaimara in 1980.

	The *Gustis* in the village																		
Group	1	2	3	4	5	6	7	8	9	10	11	12	13	14	15	16	17	18	Total
Landless		1	6		1			3	3	1	1	4	1						21
Poor	1	7	3				1				3	2		3		1	1		22
Small	2	1	1	1								1		1	1				8
Middle		1	1		2	1						1					1	1	8
Rich		1										1			1				3
No. of households	3	11	11	1	3	1	1	3	3	1	4	9	1	4	2	1	2	1	62

Decision-making within the household

Economic and social activities are planned and organized within the separate households. There is a division of authority and division of labour within each household. Normally the oldest male person, the father, the grandfather or the oldest brother is the recognized head of the household. This person is referred to as *malik, paramanik, prodhan* or *murrabi* (the term varies with the different regions of the country). Here we shall refer to him as the household head.

The household head is the member of the household who has the final say in both the internal and external affairs of the household. In economic activities the household head decides on the timing and nature of the different agricultural operations. He allocates work tasks to the male members of the household and decides if or when outside labourers should be employed. The household head also takes decisions on the credit, sharecropping and mortgage relationships which the household establishes. The nature of the decisions that are taken will, of course, depend on the economic position of the household.

There is much variation in the amount of authority the household head has and in the way decisions are reached and enforced. The authority the household head exercises will depend on how many other males there are in the household, their age and relationship to him. A household consisting of a father with young sons naturally reaches its decisions in a much more authoritative way than a household consisting of fairly equally aged brothers with separate families. The authority of a household head will also depend on the strength of his personality and his abilities. If he is at the same time the recognized leader of the *gusti,* he will carry more authority when settling internal matters in his own household. The amount of authority of the household head is also related to the size of landholding the household head possesses. If there are many 'heirs' in the household with much land to inherit, the authority of the household head increases. If, on the other hand, much of the land is registered in the names of other household members — the wife (from her father's property) and sons — these household members play an important role in the decisions concerning their land. The way the decisions are reached, whether by informal consultations among the household members or by directives from the household head, thus depends on the amount of authority the household head possesses.

Division of labour

There is a clear division of labour between the sexes. Female persons very rarely participate in agricultural activities in the fields. Their labour tasks in the agricultural sector are related to post-harvesting processes, carried out within the compound of the homestead. In addition, they perform a number of other activities for which they alone are responsible; i.e. cooking, taking care of children, rearing of poultry and livestock. There is also in each household one particular woman who is the recognized head for the labour tasks and matters which relate to the female members of the household. She is often termed *ginny* or *boro-bou* (first wife or wife of eldest male person). We shall refer to her as the female head of the household. The head of the household and the female head are often the oldest married couple. The female head may, however, also be a widow or the wife of the oldest son, or brother, in cases where the old mother, for various reasons, is not in a position to exercise her authority. Respectful sons and daughters-in-law will often address the widowed mother as the head of the household even if she is unable to function as the head.

The female head organizes the post-harvesting activities, and she also decides how much food and what type of food shall be served each day. The female head is responsible for always being able to assess how much food is left in the granaries of the household. She also has to keep separate the seeds which are needed for the land in the next season. Although they very rarely go to the fields, many women have names for the different plots their households possess, and they know exactly how much seed and what types of seeds shall be allocated to each plot.

When the male head of the household is absent or too old or sick to take decisions, a strong female head can in many cases run the household. She hires wage-labourers during the peak seasons and negotiates their wages and organizes the agricultural activities from the homestead. Women can also earn income which they pool in the household's common 'purse'. Sale of eggs and poultry or fruit and vegetables from the small gardens of the homestead plot can substantially augment the household's income.[3]

The female head of the household is also to a large degree responsible for the 'respectability', the *purdah* situation, of the females in the household. There is great variation as regards the extent to which *purdah* is observed in the rural areas. Girls less than 10–12 years and old widows can move around without loss of status more freely than young girls and married women. Women of poor households are in many cases forced by economic necessity to walk in the village in order to collect fuel, to fetch water, to work in other households, etc. The respectability of both their household and their *gusti* can suffer as a consequence of their 'visibility'. The female head of the household is vested with the task of controlling and giving permission for the movements of the females in the household.[4]

The development cycle of the household

One important factor which decisively influences the composition of the household is the stage the household has reached in its 'development cycle'. The ideal household situation, valued by all groups, is the large extended family in which the parents live with their married sons and grandchildren. (Girls nearly always move to their husband's home when they marry.) When the old parents die, the hope is that the brothers with their separate nuclear families will stay together, at least for some years, and that the eldest or most clever of the brothers will take over as household head. It is, however, very rare that an extended household of brothers with their separate families can live in a joint household for a long period. Quite often the end of the development cycle is reached when a son establishes his own family.

Table 3.2 shows the composition of the 62 households in Bhaimara and the sex of the household head.

Table 3.2. Sex of Head of Household and Type of Household in Relation to Landowning Group in Bhaimara in 1980.

	Head of household		Type of household				
Group and acres of land	Male	Female	Incom-plete family	Elementary family	Elementary family with addition	Extended patrilineal families	Total No. of households
Landless	17	4	8	8	3	2	21
Poor peasants 0.01–0.99	20	2	4	13	2	3	22
Small peasants 1–1.99	7	1	1	4	1	2	8
Middle peasants 2–3.99	8		1	1	1	5	8
Rich peasants 4 and above	3			2		1	3
Total	55	7	14	28	7	13	62

From the table we find that 28 of the 62 households are elementary families consisting of husband and wife and their children. Fourteen households are incomplete in the sense that they do not consist of a married couple with spouses living together. Seven of these incomplete households have female heads, implying that the woman, who is the outward 'spokesman' of the household, is divorced or widowed. Seven households consist of elementary families with additional members: a widowed parent or an unmarried or divorced brother or sister. Thirteen households contain two or more elementary families who are agnatically related. The table clearly shows that the more land a household owns the more complex is its composition.

An extended household lives in several houses around a homestead compound. When the household splits, there is normally no change in the physical placing of houses or lay-out of the homestead area. The only difference that can be observed is that small kitchen places, hearths, are set up next to the houses of the newly established households. When an extended family breaks up, it is nearly always the same factors which cause the split. The separate nuclear families have different labour force and consumption needs and conflicts occur when they produce together and consume jointly from the same 'pot'. A nuclear family which produces more than it consumes may feel that it 'subsidizes' those who consume more than they produce. Many nuclear families will feel that they would be better off on their own. On the other hand, residing in an extended household can give social and political protection. It also gives prestige in the rural areas to belong to a large household unit. Many well-to-do and rich families attach so much value to staying together that they decide to live together despite the distributional conflicts which may occur. Compared to poorer families, it is also clear that equal and just division of the products is not so vital for an elementary family within a richer household. Another reason for richer households to have a larger membership is that the old household head, who normally possesses all the land, refuses to allow the sons to break away from him. Mead Cain's study from a village in Mymensingh shows a typical pattern for sons establishing their own households; sons of 'large landowners' leave their father's home at the age of 28.5 years, sons of 'smaller owners' at the age of 26.3 years, and sons of landless peasants at 22.3 years.[5]

Table 3.3. Land Ownership Groups and Size of Household in Bhaimara in 1980.

	No. of members in household												
Group	1 mem.	2	3	4	5	6	7	8	9	10	11	12	13	Total
Landless	4	3	3	4	4	1	2							21
Poor	3	1	2	5	3	3	3		2					22
Small	1		2		1	2	1				1			8
Middle					2	1	1		1		1	1	1	8
Rich						1		1	1					3
Total	8	4	7	9	10	8	7	1	4		2	1	1	62
Total individuals	8	8	21	36	50	48	49	8	36		22	12	13	311

Table 3.3 shows that the 'middle' and 'rich' households contain the greatest number of individuals. This should be evident when we also know that the composition of the households is more complex among the 'middle' and 'rich' households.

From the table we find that the average size of a landless household is 3.6 members, for the 'poor' households 4.7 members, for the 'small' households 5.3 members, for the 'middle' households 8.5 members, and for the 'rich' households 7.8 members. With so few households in the different categories (especially the 'rich' category), it is of course very difficult to comment precisely on these numbers. The size of membership of the different household categories corresponds very well with what has been found in other household surveys, viz. that the well-to-do and rich households have more members than the poor and landless. In a national survey conducted in the late 1970s, Jannuzi and Peach found that on an average the landless households have 4.8 members, and landowners with more than 15 acres have 12.1 members. (In this latter number possible residential servants may also be included.) For the landowners with less than 15 acres of land, the number of members of the household increases with the amount of land owned.[6]

Another important factor which influences the size and composition of a household is the need for individuals to belong to, or at least cooperate with, a household unit so that the different work tasks needed for providing for a livelihood can be carried out. In a society with a rigid division of labour tasks such cooperation is necessary. It is impossible for a woman to participate in the work in the field and a man who cooks for himself is ridiculed. Therefore an unmarried brother will almost always stay in the household of his elder brother and eat the food prepared by his sister-in-law. An old widow will most often stay in the family of her youngest son. If the requirements for the different labour tasks cannot be met by family members, there are many ways to recruit other persons to the household. Barren couples may adopt sons (*palok* — child), permanent servants may be attached to the household (this occurs especially if the household is rich), children from other households in which the labour force is sufficient, either from the mother's or the father's side, may live and work in the household for certain periods. From Table 3.3 we find that 8 households only consist of one member. All these individuals (a crippled beggar, widows and widowers) live in houses attached to a larger homestead compound and cooperate with their agnatic kin living in the other households of the compound.

When a household containing the nuclear families of several brothers, including unmarried brothers, stays together, the different units know very well that their joint production and consumption is a temporary phenomenon. The brothers, married or not, are well aware that they will soon establish their own households. Even when living in a joint household, many start to prepare for this future split. This can be done by not handing over all they produce to the common 'purse'; some of the products will either be consumed directly or saved by the nuclear family or its individual members. The extent to which this can be practised depends on the sources of income the separate nuclear families have. If all sons are working together on jointly owned land, they will collectively control the size and value of the product, and it is difficult to take away any part of the joint product. If one or several of the brothers obtain their income from sources which the others cannot control, for instance when a group member migrates to a town or to another rural area, it can be difficult to assess what would be the net income after the cost of living is covered. In such situations it can be easy to put a little bit of the net gain aside. Also when working for others on their land or doing casual work alone, there are chances that not all the earned money goes to the common pot. In some cases the amount thus saved over a long period can be so large that a son can get hold of a small plot of land secretly. He will, of course, then not cultivate the land himself but most often lease it to the former owner on a sharecropping basis. He will not publicly take over the land until he is well established in a separate household.

Also women in a household can prepare for a future split of the household and put resources aside. The sources of income for women are petty trading done on the basis of products obtained from the homestead area. Women have different reasons for saving clandestinely; the old widow may feel she is not catered for well enough; the nuclear families of two brothers may be in the process of splitting; the wife may fear a divorce or becoming a widow and will seek to obtain a certain material security; the wife will give special support to one of the children, etc. If the woman is in desperate need, she can sell her most valuable item, the ornaments she received in her marriage ceremony. She will then tell her husband that she has lost them. In the case of one particular woman in our household the scars inflicted by her husband's beating after she told him that a stranger had robbed her of her ornaments at night, are still visible.

Another common way for brothers to prepare for a split is to obtain as much as possible of the land owned jointly by the households. Although there are detailed rules of how property shall be divided, there is much room for manipulation and by-passing of the rules. This saving and provision of property for one's own purposes, which the nuclear families or individuals in an extended household can do, may be insignificant or great. It is, of course, impossible to obtain accurate information on the extent to which such methods are practised. Whether it is practised or not, people in most households are very conscious of the fact that it occurs or can happen. Quarrels about the division of the product are common everywhere. The reason for this competition for resources within the household is of course the material poverty and the precarious situation in which the nuclear families and individuals find themselves. One's resources can best be increased at the expense of one's nearest family, with whom one is supposed to share products and property.

On the other hand, the processes described above as preparations for the split-up of an extended household can also be regarded as factors which slow down the split-up of the extended household. If some families or individuals of the extended household, especially those who produce more than they consume, did not have the possibility of consuming, saving and investing 'clandestinely', they would break out of the extended household at an earlier stage. The nuclear families or individuals who consume more than they produce are aware of this, and often have to accept that the net producers do not share all their earnings through the common purse.

Above we have shown how important the stage the household has reached is for the internal processes going on within the unit. We have seen how the joint production and consumption within the unit is a matter of degree, depending much on the fission processes going on among the members of the unit. There is a very different measure of cohesiveness in a household which is a simple elementary family from that in a household which consists of an extended family, including several elementary families. Poverty and competition for scarce resources are major factors causing larger households to split up early. The role poverty has for the composition of the family becomes particularly clear when one studies the poorest households, the households who do not possess any agricultural land.

Development cycle of landless households

We indicated above that an important factor which binds the different nuclear families together in an extended household is the amount of land they may expect to inherit after the death of the father. If the father has a large property to divide, he is in a much stronger position to keep the whole household together; with little or no land the sons may feel that economically they can benefit from separation, thus avoiding the burden of supporting non-productive family members. When a split has taken place and the land property has been divided, the break-up is irreversible. There is no way back to a joint household. The development cycle of the landless household often differs from that of the landowning household. There is no agricultural land either to bind the household together or to separate it.

In Bhaimara we found many examples of peculiar development cycles in the landless household. We were made aware of this when, for the purpose of our village survey, we went to the homestead areas of the landless households to collect information on household composition and membership. A few months later, when we came back to check the information, we noticed that the composition of the households had changed. Half a year later still, the composition of the household had reverted to a state similar to what we found at our first visit, and later on it would again have changed.

One particular case we observed over a period of one and a half years developed like this. An old husband and wife stayed together with their newly married son. It was the son who provided almost the entire income of the household. During the rainy season, when it was difficult to find employment, the son and his wife established a separate household. On our second visit we saw the new kitchen-place outside their house. The son explained that there was no possibility of providing food for four persons from his meagre income. He said it was painful for him to split the family and leave his old parents on their own, but explained that this was the only way to make the old parents take a more active role in providing for themselves. In fact, the old couple obtained loans from richer people with their small homestead plot as collateral. In addition, the old woman made some mats of bamboo material and the old man fished a little in a nearby pond for home consumption. The couple also may have received small gifts from more well-do-to people. On our third visit, which was during harvesting time, another son, unmarried, had returned from a labour migration trip to the northern part of Bangladesh. At this time both sons were employed with relatively high salaries and even the father could be asked to work a little. The old mother sometimes participated in the post-harvest activities in the home of a neighbour; for this work she was rewarded with the meals she ate during the day. In this situation the whole family of 5 persons, then an 'extended' household, had moved together again and contributed to and consumed from a common 'pot'. At our fourth visit to the homestead the household composition had again been altered. This was during a period when it was hard to obtain employment. Now the household was split along new lines. The married son and his wife provided food for the old father, while the old mother cooked in a separate kitchen for her unmarried son and herself. Neither of the sons could afford to cater for both of their parents.

We observed this process of splitting and reuniting in other landless households too. The initiative for these changes is not generally taken by the old head of the household. In a landless household his authority is to a large degree undermined by the fact that he has very little property to offer his children for their future. He therefore has no effective sanctions against what he considers undesirable behaviour. It will be the sons and 'net producers' who determine the composition of the household. Many old parents, widows and widowers, complained bitterly to us about how they had been abandoned by their sons.[7]

Rule of inheritance

We have seen that the development cycle of the household to a large degree depends on the way property is divided. For the great majority of households in rural Bangladesh, the most, and for many the only, valuable property is land, both agricultural land and homestead plot land. The main mechanism for the division of land and the transfer of ownership rights is through *inheritance*. The inheritance rules, among the Muslim population, are in the main based on the Islamic law of inheritance. This law decisively influences the ownership pattern of land in the rural areas, the fragmentation of the land, and the relationship between the household members who are due to inherit the land. The social structure of rural Bangladesh cannot be described or explained without an understanding of how the inheritance rules operate.

According to the Islamic law of inheritance, all sons inherit an equal amount of land.[8] A daughter inherits half the amount of a son. The basic non-corporate character of the patrilineage is due to the individual property rights and the possibilities which exist for the transfer for ownership rights between individual kin-members. The nature of the competition for scarce resources and also important features of the rural society are very much influenced by the fact that brothers are often rivals for the same plot of land.

From a legal point of view a Muslim woman is an heir to the property of her father, mother, husband, son and daughter. When her husband dies the widow should inherit one-eighth of his property, and if he dies childless, she should inherit one-fourth. The other part of the property will be passed on to the husband's closest relatives. If no son is born to a couple, daughters alone cannot inherit all the property of their parents, a part of the property goes to their father's brother's sons. The traditional Islamic law also states that if a son dies before his father, the grandsons and granddaughters do not have the right to inherit any property. In 1961 a secular law, incorporated in the Muslim Family Laws Ordinance of 1961, invalidated this traditional law. In spite of this invalidation, it is the traditional law which is known in the rural areas and most adhered to. Two landless households in Bhaimara claimed they lost the land they expected to inherit from their father, because their father died before their grandfather.

According to the inheritance rules the property of a man with a wife, three daughters and three sons, should be divided into seven parts at the time of his death. In practice this occurs very rarely. There are several systematic deviations from the inheritance rules. The most important is that the daughters, by tradition, do not exercise their claim on their father's property. By not taking over the land they are entitled to, they do their brothers the important service of keeping the land of the family in the patrilineal line. They also thereby ensure themselves a warm welcome in their brothers' households and can expect material support in times of crisis. In cases of early widowhood or divorce they have a place to return to if they so wish.

There have, however, always been certain types of exception to the rule that daughters should not claim any part of their father's property. In rich families women could take their share of land with less damage to their brothers. In Bhaimara, and also from villages in other areas, we heard that women from poor families had claimed their share of their father's property. Married women in poor households face a conflicting situation. On the one hand, they could secure a better standard of living for their children, their husband and themselves by obtaining some more land. On the other hand, they could easily destroy their relationship with their brothers' households by insisting on acquiring their share of the land. It will often be the husband of the wife who insists that she shall claim her share of the land. In Bhaimara we heard several stories of how husbands had pressed their wives to take the land from their brothers or at least claim a substantial compensation for not taking the land. A case that was brought up in the local court several times concerned a head of household who demanded a higher rate of compensation for his wife's rights to her section of the homestead plot. By exercising their claims, the women find themselves in the paradoxical situation that they are the 'losers' on two fronts: they do not have the security of an 'alternative' home with their brothers, and they thereby also become more vulnerable to, and less protected by, the behaviour of their husband's family.

It is very difficult to judge the extent of the practice of women claiming their share of their fathers' property. In our investigations we attempted to obtain systematic information on the number of women who had claimed their share. It was impossible to obtain accurate information on this topic. It is obviously considered shameful for a woman to take land out of her father's family. Claiming or not claiming the land is not, however, the only course open to a woman. A middle way is to demand, directly or indirectly, certain gifts or sums of money or credit on good terms in return for the assurance that she and her husband's family will not claim the land.

Another systematic deviation from the formal Islamic inheritance rules is that the widow will very seldom claim the one-eighth of the property to which she is entitled. When the land is divided after the death of the father in the homestead, the sons and/or leaders in the *gusti* will allocate some land for the specific purpose of feeding the widow. The widow will normally live in the household of her youngest son. If the widow has unmarried daughters staying with her, the land set aside for their purposes will be larger. In most circumstances the widow will not take an active part in the organization of the agricultural activities on 'her plot' of land. It is the son with whom she stays who will make the decisions concerning the usage of the land. If the widow belongs to a poor household, she is naturally allocated a small plot, which by itself may not produce sufficient food for her. If she belongs to a rich household, the land that is set aside for her may be much larger than she needs. In such a situation many of her sons may be eager to have the mother in their household. When the mother dies, her piece of land is divided among her sons.

We noted that all the sons ought to inherit equally. This is a principle which is probably practised to a large degree. It is however, very common for quarrels to occur when a large household breaks up and the land is divided. Some of the older sons will often feel they have contributed more to maintaining or expanding the household's property than their younger brothers. They may therefore claim compensation for their efforts by obtaining more or better land than their younger brothers. If an older brother is in a strong position, he may take advantage of this situation when the land is divided. The break-up of the households and the division of the land leads to a very critical period for the new households which are established, and at this stage the foundation is laid for the social and economic position of a new household. There are many stories, some of which we shall narrate later, of how strong individuals have manipulated their closest relatives in this period and by illegal means have taken over all or parts of their land. In our village survey we naively attempted to obtain information on whether the brothers had shared their property equally. The answers we got were contradictory. Some men claimed that the poverty and misery of their lives had been caused by older brothers who had 'snatched' away the share of land they were to inherit. Their brothers naturally denied this and came up with sound explanations as to why they had obtained more land than their younger brothers.

There are several ways in which the inheritance rules can be by-passed legally. Only under some circumstances does a man set up a testament before he dies. However, when a man wants to make certain that some favourite heirs or persons should have some of his land, he can make an official will. One way to protect an adopted son, for instance, is to allocate him land in a will and also arrange to have the land registered in his name. Also a wife or any other relative who would not formally qualify for inheriting much land could have their interests catered for by having land registered in their names. A favourite son can also obtain additional land by such a method. The heirs to a property cannot, however, be deprived totally by the ownership of land being transferred to any other person or institution as a gift. While a person has the right to sell part or all of his land, he cannot make a gift of his land property exceeding one-third of the whole.[9]

Unscrupulous sons have taken advantage of this way of obtaining land. They may have forced their father to register some of the land in their names. We were told several stories of how thumbprints of the old father were impressed on a piece of paper while he was asleep at night as a signature of the will his sons had made, unknowingly, on his behalf.

If the father and the sons have a strong desire to keep the land within the lineage, the father can also register all the land in the names of his sons and thereby prevent his daughters taking land out of the lineage when they marry.

We received a strong impression from the villagers that people were more on guard now when dividing inherited land than they were a generation or two ago. This leads to the question of how ownership of land is documented. We have already noted that ownership of land is private and that the owner, formally at least, has the right to use or dispose of the land as he/she may choose. Each plot of land is registered in the name of one person. For each plot there is a document spelling out its size and stating with which plots it shares boundaries. Not all plots of land are, however, registered in the name of the present owners. Inherited land is often registered in the name of the father or grandfather. Land that is purchased or obtained by gift needs to be registered in the name of the new owner. The registration document will then state who the former and present owners are, and the price the land was sold for. When land is registered in the name of a new owner, about 10 per cent of the value of the land has to be paid as tax to the Government Registration Office. A large household can therefore have their different plots of land registered in the names of the head of the household, his father and grandfather, the wife of the head, and in the name of sons if they have purchased land.

The registration document is the most important sign of ownership to a plot of land. A document in the name of a father or a grandfather is, however, just as valid as a document in one's own name. Ownership of land can also be documented through other official papers. Every 10–15 years the Government makes a land record in order to register the changes in the ownership of land and measure the size of new plots which have been made through division of property and sale of land. The owner of the land obtains from a Government official a paper stating the size of his plots and the owners of the neighbouring plots. A third type of document is the tax receipt showing that tax has been paid for a specific plot. Although tax on land is minimal for owners possessing less than 8.3 acres (=25 *bighas),* the tax receipt is a paper which also states the owner of the plot of land. All three papers are important when ownership is to be claimed.

In chapter 7 we shall outline in detail various types of dispute over ownership rights to land. Change of ownership of land due to disputes is an important transfer mechanism. People are very conscious of the fact that ownership rights to land are not established once and for all. There are different degrees of 'security' of land ownership. In particular circumstances the land to which a person claims ownership may need to be defended against others who claim ownership to the same plot of land or the same part of a plot. We shall see in later chapters how alliances between people are built up in order to gain support from others in such situations.

In this section we have attempted to convey an impression of how poverty influences the nature of the social relationship between people in the village. People are bitterly conscious and articulate about this. An old male member of the household we lived in put it this way: 'Poverty forces us to be ruthless. If we are not clever and cunning we have no chance of eating rice every day and we will leave our children without land.' Others told us about the gap that existed between ideal moral standards and their actual behaviour. A rich man of a neighbouring village admitted that 'if I acted like I talk and preach, my children would starve'. Another man said straight out: 'I cannot afford to practise and live according to high moral standards.' These statements reflect our observations as to the number of people who, owing to poverty and an insecure situation, had developed elaborate double moral standards. In the informal meeting place next to our homestead compound people who had been or were enemies competing for scarce resources could pat each other on the back and praise each other while they were actually contemplating robbing the man next to them of his property and even murdering him.

This section has also indicated that the competition for land and other scarce resources takes place between close relatives, since most property is transferred to people through inheritance. Many people said that it was particularly painful when enmity, suspicion and hatred developed between brothers fighting over land property. The inheritance system is therefore a crucial factor in preventing the family developing and pursuing major interests on a corporate basis. The fact that an attempt is often made to keep land belonging to a forefather within the family does not alter the competitive nature of relationships between brothers.

The inheritance system also has a major impact on the pattern of mobility in the rural areas. It is obvious that the division of the land of a household has a levelling effect on the potential social mobility of the sons of the household.

Social stratification

In our tables on the population of Bhaimara we have divided the households into landless, poor, small, middle and rich categories according to how much land each household owns. Such categories are naturally not used by the villagers themselves. This section will give a short description of the system of social stratification as it pertains to the Muslim part of the population (85 per cent of the population in Bangladesh are Muslim and all the 62 households in Bhaimara are Muslim).

There exists much literature on Muslim social stratification in Bangladesh. Almost all the village monographs cited earlier deal with the issue to some degree. Already at the turn of the century E. Gait discussed Hindu and Muslim stratification.[11] Mukherjee collected information on Muslim stratification from West Bengal and East Bengal in the 1940s.[12] The most recent effort to deal with the peculiar characteristics of Muslim stratification in Bangladesh has been made by H.K. Arefeen.[13] Arefeen states that the Hindu and Muslim caste systems have a number of similar features, such as that society is organized on an hierarchical basis, the practice of endogamy, and also hereditary occupations (p. 53, *op.cit.).* However, his main efforts are directed towards showing how Muslim caste differs from Hindu caste. The features that he finds differ include the absence of the strict purity-pollution notion in the hierarchy, the lack of ritual sanctions of the caste, the less rigid practice of commensality and endogamy, and the individual possibility of mobility among the Muslims. We have not considered it necessary to enter into the debate which discusses to what extent the Hindu caste concept is applicable to Muslim societies. Below we shall discuss various aspects of Muslim stratification in Bangladesh, both generally and as we found it expressed from our own investigations.

'Caste' in Muslim village societies in Bangladesh is of less importance than in most other areas of the sub-continent. The traditional Muslim distinction between the *ashraf* (high born) and *ajlaf* (low born, synonym in Bengal *atraf),* which is a common division of status among the followers of the Prophet, has not very much significance in Bangladesh today. This is partly because of the extensive adoption of *ashraf* titles and symbols during the nineteenth and early twentieth centuries.[14] In rural Bangladesh there is a nearly universal claim to *sheikh* status, one of the four Mohammedan 'tribes'; the other tribes are Sayed, Pathan, Mugal. Although people distinguish between real 'sheikhs' and 'sheikhs' who work the land themselves, the nature of 'sheikh' status is not a fruitful basis on which to discover the underlying principles of social stratification.

One way differences of status are expressed is through the usage by the different patrilineages of names and titles. Some titles have traditionally been regarded as high status titles. Some of these lineage titles function as patronymics.[15] The titles and names of the lineages derive their significance from different sources. If a lineage has belonged to the rich landowner aristocracy, or has had a specific position in the revenue collection system or local administration of the pre-independence government administrations, it may be given a certain title (e.g. Chowdhury, Khan, Kazi); each name refers to a certain position or task performed. A title or name can also be derived from a specific position in the religious system (mowlana, molla, imam). The prestige of the different titles will vary. *Mowlana* refers for instance to a religious leader with a better training than a *molla* or *imam.* Names to patrilineages can also be attached as a consequence of certain characteristics of a family or a specific occupation carried out by members of the family. In such cases the names do not become patronymics.

Respectable behaviour is associated with the claim to a lineage title with a high status which also often requires a certain material standard of living (e.g., refraining from physical work in agricultural activities). Poorer households belonging to a high status lineage will to a certain extent enjoy the respect claimed by the lineage if they have close relations with the leading households of the lineage and live according to expected rules. If the whole lineage becomes poor, it is difficult to continue to claim the title for a long period.

In Bhaimara the two most prestigious lineages are named Khan. One of the Khan lineages claim they have forefathers who collected revenue and worked in the colonial administration. Proudly they told us of how their great-grandfathers were carried around in comfortable chairs by four men when they inspected the estates they collected revenues from. The households belonging to this lineage own today between one and 3½ acres each. The male members of one of the households have started to cultivate their land themselves. People in the village, however, recognize the noble traditions of this patrilineage, even if for the last couple of generations it has declined in economic strength and status. The other Khan lineage has emerged during the last two generations, and to-day they owe their status to being educated and having jobs in the Government administration in Dhaka. They only adopted the Khan title 20 years ago, and many villagers are quick to point out that they did not obtain the title 'legitimately'. It is clear that people are very conscious of lineages with long-standing titles which have lasted for many generations and lineages which in the last one or two generations have acquired a title.

There are other ways of distinguishing families than by their title or lack of it. The villagers themselves make distinctions of households belonging to *ucha-bangsha* (high status lineage), *madhya-bangsha* (middle status lineage), and *nico-bangsha* (low status lineage).[16] Economic position and the status of the lineage in terms of its traditions, as well as the existence of a title, count when households are placed in these categories. There is often disagreement about where to place the lineages.

The distinction we found the inhabitants of Bhaimara applying when categorizing people was *Khandans* (high status) and *Girhastas* (low-middle status, 'common' people, cultivators). The *Girhastas* included everyone engaged in agricultural work in the fields. Only the Khan lineages were regarded as high status, as long as they did not perform physical work in agriculture. In order to retain the *Khandan* status, a family is expected to adhere to certain manners (language, eating habits, ways of entertaining guests, dress).

For lineages claiming high status, *izzat* (respectable behaviour) together with manners, is important. *Izzat* is a relative phenomenon and one can gain or maintain *izzat* more or less. Jahangir mentions that the *izzat* of a person (household head) depends on certain factors:

1. whether he can provide his family with food (khawa-pora);
2. whether he can maintain the privacy of women (purdah);
3. whether he has a separate room to entertain guests (kacharighor);
4. whether his women bathe in the ponds of others or not.[17]

In Bhaimara we also observed that *izzat* was strongly associated with these factors. In addition we also found *izzat* to be associated with moral standards. One of the richest men in the union, living in a neighbouring village, was not considered to have any *izzat* although he easily qualified for the four factors mentioned by Jahangir. Since he had used many dirty tricks in acquiring his landed property, people would say he was without honour *(izzat)*.

We searched actively for distinctions referring to people's different classes in terms of possession or lack of possession of the main means of production, viz. land. We did not find any concepts, generally applied, which expressed this distinction. Landless households can belong to high status lineages, and large landowners to low status lineages.

There may be disagreement among villagers as to where to place different patrilineages on a scale in the stratification system. There is, however, little disagreement about certain 'low-caste' Muslim groups being clearly separated and belonging to the lowest level in the Muslim stratification system. These low-cast Muslim groups are associated with certain low status occupations which many think are defiling. In this category are Muslim washermen, weavers, sweepers, barbers, butchers. Also groups who perform traditional surgery, like ritual circumcision of Muslim males, *hajjams,*[18] and eye-surgeons[19] are separated from the other parts of Muslim society and regarded as very low-status people. In Bhaimara we found that people whose forefathers had been professional fighters *(lathial),* called upon by rich men to protect their property physically, and people who daily carried the *zamindars* men in their portable chairs were regarded as low caste. The relationship between the owners and cultivators of land and the *ajlaf,* low-born, occupational groups is expressed in 'caste' terms.

However, it is possible for individual households of those born as *ajlaf* to raise their status. E. Gait gives a description of this process:[20]

> ...any Muhammudan who is well off, though he can not go from one caste to another, can gradually enter the ranks of Ashraf. The proverb 'last year I was a Jolha [a Muslim weaver, E.G.J.], this year I am a Sheikh; next year if prices rise I will be a Sayed' is well known, and it represents what often occurs though the process of promotion is not quite as rapid in reality as it is in the Proverb. A well to do man of a

functional group, say a Jolha, will discard the word Jolha, call himself Sheikh and assume a more respectable name, and he will slowly secure for himself a circle of friends from the poorer classes of the Ashraf community. He will then marry into an Ashraf family probably of doubtful status and his son will be recognized as a true Ashraf. The process is easier in towns than in the villages where people are more conservative, and in a distant place than near the house where a man's connections are well know.

The proverb quoted by Gait more than 80 years ago is still on the lips of people in the rural areas to-day. At present the proverb also refers to all individual mobility, not only to that between the 'low-born' occupational groups and the rest of the Muslim population.[21]

As we have seen, the place of a lineage in the stratification system depends both on its traditions and its present economic position. The same also applies to the separate, individual households. A combination of high traditional status and economic strength naturally qualifies for a higher position than only traditional status or only economic strength. In the situation people find themselves in with increasing poverty and an insecure future, 'priority' seems to be given to economic position rather than traditional status when, for example, finding a marriage partner. Bertocci reports one villager saying: 'Nowadays if one's economic position is good, one's lineage status is also good.'[22] An unmarried research investigator from a Government institute who often came to the village told us he felt like a prince in the village. Many rich fathers of girls of marriageable age were eager to meet him. The research investigator told us his father was a poor peasant living far away, but the fact that he had a Government job made him potentially, a very attractive son-in-law.

Marriage and relationships of affinity

We have seen that patrilineage ties dominate in the social organization of family life in rural Bangladesh. Despite the fact that it is an ideologically patrilineal system, kinship in practice, however, has many bilateral features. In this section we shall discuss different aspects of the institution of marriage and the ties that are established between the families of the spouses. In the context of this study marriage as an institution is important for both political and econnomic reasons. From a political point of view a marriage can create an alliance which can be used for mutual support between the families of the spouses. From an economic point of view the alliances can also be used for credit purposes. For the families of the spouses, a marriage is also an economic transaction which can constitute one of the major sources of income or expenditure during the whole period of the households' existence. Expenditure on marriages of children have to be weighed against major transactions in land property. Marriage is therefore of interest, since no other event better reveals whether people give priority to high status in the traditional system of social stratification or to economic position. From one point of view, the choice of a mate for one's child becomes a *test case* for the priority given to economic factors.

Marriage is universal in Bangladesh. The marriage is arranged by members of the families of the spouses, although men in some cases may have a certain influence on the choice of their wives. It is, however, not uncommon that the spouses meet for the first time at the marriage ceremony. A marriage concerns other people than the nearest families of the spouses. Before the final selection of the spouse is made, agreement among the leaders and the elder people of the lineage *(gusti)* is needed. Also prominent people of the *samaj* (village association, described later) have to endorse the marriage.

What do the families of the spouses have to consider when selecting a mate for their son or daughter? The families of the girls are naturally concerned about the well-being of their daughters who are sent away to their husbands' homes. Well-being and 'happiness' are closely connected to the economic and material level of the household of the husband; i.e. whether the girl can continue to maintain her 'invisibility' or whether she will have to work in other households, bathe in the public pond, etc. The family of the girl will also investigate the reputation of the family to which she will go; whether they are well-behaved, and whether there are few or many divorces in the family. The family of the boy will be particularly concerned that the girl is 'good-tempered', clever in household tasks, and beautiful (fair-skinned). Naturally they will also consider whether there are economic and political gains to expect in the future from the family of the girl.

There are many steps in the arrangement of a marriage, starting often with indirect indications from 'representatives' of the families. The most important and difficult stage is when the different types of payment between the parties are to be negotiated. The flow of money and goods between the families is often the object of much haggling and bargaining. Many potential marriage alliances have stranded because no agreement was reached on the sums which were to be transferred.

One or two generations ago most of the material goods went from the family of the boy to the family of the girl. This situation has changed. Miranda writes:

> Functionally and culturally, the marriage market is male-oriented and male-dominated, in line with the overall organization of society; in addition it is structurally a 'bridegroom's market' in the sense that, due to the gap between males' and females' marriageable ages and the age structure of the population, prospective brides are always in over-supply.[23]

The family of the groom pledges the traditional Islamic *mehr*. Part or all of the *mehr* today is deferred and will only be paid in case of divorce initiated from the boy's side. The *mehr* thereby provides some protection for the girl against a summary divorce, which is permitted by Islam. The family of the groom is also obliged to provide the bride with ornaments. Often the ornaments are borrowed from members of the groom's family and returned to them after they have been exhibited by the girl's family in the marriage ceremony.

The father of the bride incurs the largest expense in the marriage arrangement. The amount of 'dowry' he has to pay will naturally vary with his own economic position and the status and economic standing of the family to which he sends his daughter. A marriage between households where both parties are very poor or landless will only involve a sum of some hundred *Takas,* while middle and rich families will spend several or many thousand *Takas* to marry off their daughters properly. However, only among the rich were transfers of ownership rights to land part of the values exchanged between the families of the spouses. We were told that considerations of a practical nature were often the basis for this type of exchange in marriage alliances.

We were witness to and were informed about the marriage negotiations of a number of young girls and young men in Bhaimara.

The Khan family we mentioned above had two daughters of marriageable age. Both had obtained their secondary school certificate, and one of them was particularly 'beautiful'. The father of the girls wanted to marry both to university-educated men working in urban areas. One family he had contacted demanded 15,000 Takas for marrying their son, who was an officer in the army, to the beautiful daughter. Such a sum would imply that the father would have to sell about 0.60 acres of land of the 1.5 acres he owned in total for the marriage of this daughter alone. This alliance never materialized, since the father considered the sum asked for too high. At the time we left the village neither of the girls was married, and the father expressed a fear that unless he found husbands for his daughters soon, their attractiveness on the 'marriage market' would decrease.

Many households in the village faced the problem of postponing the marriage of a daughter owing to lack of resources to make up an adequate offer to the groom's family. One villager told us a proverb in this connection which is well known in rural Bangladesh:

> There are three reasons for a man not being able to sleep during the night: If he is poor, he may worry about how his family can escape starvation. If he is rich and has money and valuable items in his house, he will worry about their safety. If he has older, unmarried daughters, he will worry that their purity *(izzat)* may be damaged before they are married.

The father of the Khan household would have no difficulties in marrying off his daughters if he married them to men with an overall equal status to his own household. He would then also have to pay much less in dowry for his daughters. A main function of the marriage negotiations is therefore to balance any disparity of status or of the other criteria considered (education, age, appearance, etc.) with the value of the goods and money transferred between the parties.

The Islamic law imposes few restrictions on the choice of a spouse. Except for certain incestuous relations, as long as a person is Muslim he/she could be marriageable. In practice, in rural Bangladesh, there are many factors which restrict the selection of spouses. In Bhaimara we witnessed strong endogamous tendencies among the lineages. The girls of the Khan family would never marry a boy from an untitled lineage in the village or a nearby village, even if he came from a rich family. One representative of the recently emerged Khan-lineage told us that the only woman the *'girhastas'* (the ordinary cultivators) of the village could have from their lineage was a woman named Sharifa. She was divorced twice and by many considered mentally ill.

Many of the intense quarrels which had taken place in the village derived from families having married their children well below the standard that had been expected, without the approval of all the relevant parties. They had saved expenses by the marriage, but lost their status. In particular, marrying into a low-caste Muslim family, the *Ajlaf*-born, results in a loss of status quite different from marrying into other families below one's status. Yet, one of the distinctions we saw H.K. Arefeen make between Hindu and Muslim caste practice was the extent of the rigidity with which endogamy was observed. Arefeen differentiates between the Hindu, who has no alternative but to marry in his ascribed occupational caste *(prescribed* endogamy), and the Muslim, for whom the caste endogamy is *preferential,* while possibilities for marriage outside exist, although at a high cost.[24]

Place of marriage

Also other factors limit the selection of mates. Most of the villagers will marry their daughters away to other peasants. They naturally want to keep close contact with their daughters and the in-law after the marriage. Such contacts are difficult and costly to maintain if the daughter is married far away. In Bhaimara we found that most of the women who were in the village came from neighbouring villages or villages only a few miles away. Also the daughters who married out of the village seldom moved more than a few miles from the village.

Bertocci has emphasized the role the *market area* has for social and economic activities in the villages.[25] There is no *haat* (local market) in Bhaimara, but in the neighbouring village there is a market, which is held twice a week. For 5–6 villages this is the main market. In addition, this market also serves 10–15 other villages as one of their market places. Bertocci found that a large proportion of the marriages he recorded in Comilla took place within the 'market area'. Although we do not have quantitative information to document this relationship, we also received the impression that marriages to a large extent took place within an area defined by the possibility of obtaining information and following events. At the local market the fathers and brothers were able to hear news about their daughters/sisters. They would also have an opportunity to develop and cultivate the relations with their male in-laws (no women, except old widows and girls below 8–10 years of age, go to the market).

In addition to the preference for marrying daughters within an area where a certain contact can be kept, we also found in Bhaimara another marriage pattern. Quite a number of the married women in Bhaimara came from the same village two miles away and many of the daughters of Bhaimara had married into another village also lying within the domain of the market area. Many villagers stated that they liked to obtain their wives from some particular villages. This marriage pattern, exchange of women in specific geographical directions, naturally also increases the opportunities for keeping in touch with daughters and sisters and utilizing affinal relationships for economic and political support. However, sometimes the place of marriage is dictated by already existing vested interests in an area. A household may possess land miles away from their home. The marriage of a daughter to a man in the area could increase the value of the land for the girl's family.

There are no restrictions on marriages within the village. In fact, in larger villages, a major proportion of the marriages take place within the boundaries of the village. In the small village of Bhaimara, we found that about 90 per cent of the married women came from other villages. A couple of the marriages in the village were parallel-cousin marriages (the marriage of son and daughter of two brothers). This occurred among the more well-to-do peasants in order to keep the property within the lineage and to reduce the expenses of marriage. Aziz has a much wider sample than we have with which to assess the extent of cross-cousin (marriage between children of brother and sister) and parallel-cousin marriage. According to his survey of 1719 first time Muslim marriages, 62 (3.6 per cent) were parallel-cousin marriages and 84 (4.9 per cent) were cross-cousin marriages.[26]

Ghor-jamais marriages

One particular type of marriage should be mentioned: when the married man moves to the homestead of his wife and resides there permanently. This type of marriage is termed *ghor-jamais (jamais* = son-in-law). In Bhaimara we found that among the married couples there were four men who lived as *ghor-jamais*. Living in his father-in-law's or brother-in-law's homestead compound is a very undesirable position for a man. Ownership of the father-in-law's property is passed on to his wife and not to him. The children are reckoned as the members of his wife's patrilineage and not his.

There are normally some specific circumstances which produce this type of marriage. The family of the girl's side may lack male labourers to work in the fields. This was the situation in three of the four cases in Bhaimara. The older father of the household had no sons and only daughters. The last *ghor-jamais* had married a girl who had a minor physical handicap which reduced her chances of marrying on the same status level as her own family. Nearly all men who live as *ghor-jamais* come from a very poor economic background, most often from completely landless families, and they marry into families with a considerably higher status in the stratification system. A normal *ghor-jamais* is often ridiculed in the village, and his position in his father-in-law's house is insecure. If there is a divorce between him and his wife, he is sent away. If his wife dies before him, leaving no children, he is often also compelled to leave the home. There are many proverbs showing the weak position of the resident son-in-law: 'A son-in-law living in his father-in-law's house is often kicked by his wife' and 'no intelligent man will stay as a *ghor-jamais*'. We note that also *ghor-jamais* marriages, to a large extent, can be explained as an adaptation to the prevailing economic circumstances of the people involved in the marriage. Also polygamy can be studied in such a perspective.

Polygamy

Polygamy in the Bhaimara area is more rare than *ghor-jamais* marriages. Only two men in Bhaimara had two wives. One man found a second wife after his wife had become mentally ill. Another man married for the second time when his first wife had not given birth to any children after ten years of marriage. Both men could with 'good' reason have divorced their first wives but, out of pity and concern about their position as divorced women, permitted them to remain in their compounds. The social status and position of the women decreased, however. In the neighbouring villages a few more normal *'polygynous'* marriages were reported between rich old men and younger second wives, but these did not represent more than 1–2 per cent of all marriages. Aziz found that among 1681 married Muslim men in Matlab, Comilla, only 19 men (1.1 per cent) had two wives and only one man had 3 wives.[27]

Age of spouses

The typical marriage, according to the different national demographic surveys, takes place between a girl who has recently passed puberty (14–15 years) and a man who is as much as ten years older. There is some variation in the age of marriage. With increased education, girls tend to marry later. There is, however, little evidence pointing to the socio-economic background of the families resulting in very different ages for marriage either for girls or men.

Divorce and widowhood

We have already noted that 7 of the 62 households in Bhaimara are headed by females. In addition to these women, many women who have been married are living without husbands in households where a male person is the head.

The status and position of a woman without a husband is insecure. Traditionally one of the sons takes on the obligation of caring for his mother. A woman without a husband or sons is particularly exposed to becoming destitute.

There are two ways a woman can 'lose' her husband, either through divorce or by becoming a widow. At the age of 50 only about two-thirds of the women still have a husband, and among the women above 65 years, only one out of five women has a husband. Of the men, who almost always remarry after divorce or death of a wife, 9 out of 10 had a wife when they were above 65.[29] (Only three out of five Muslim widows and divorced women will remarry after their first marriage has been dissolved.)[30]

National surveys show that about one-fifth of all marriages end in a divorce.[31] The older the bride is at the time she enters into marriage and the better education she has, the greater are the chances for a stable marriage. The rate of divorce is a little higher in marriages where the husband is landless than in marriages where he cultivates his own land (24 and 20.9 per cent).[32] We do not, from Bhaimara, have any quantitative information on the divorce rate and variables to which it can be correlated. Divorce was, however, quite common, and with the pragmatic attitude many Muslims have towards marriage, as a contractual bond and not a sacramental relationship, divorce is a way of dissolving a marriage that does not work. In Bhaimara we found that separation between the spouses, when the woman left for her paternal home, would sometimes lead to divorce. Many villagers told us that it was poverty which was the direct or indirect cause of many quarrels among the spouses.

Fictive kinship terms

Above we have described two forms of kinship relationships, the *consanguinal* and the *affinal.*[33] An expression of the important role kinship plays in the rural areas is that many people in a village, particularly the older ones, are not called by their names but addressed by an appropriate fictive kin term. The care with which social intercourse among unrelated persons in a village is conducted depends much on the use of fictive kin terms. One consequence of the village being mainly a patriarchal society is that many of the terms used for addressing unrelated persons will be the same as those used for paternal relatives: *dada* and *dadi* (paternal grandfather and grandmother) or *jetha* and *jethi* (father's elder brother and his wife) and *chacha-chachi* (father's younger brother and his wife).[34] There are many terms, of closer or more distant type, to choose between. The term that is used depends on the relationship one has to the person who is addressed; whether he lives in the neighbourhood, in the village or belongs to the same village association. During the fieldwork we became very conscious of the importance of using the proper term when calling outside the homestead compound before obtaining permission to enter. By using a respectful term, broad smiles often awaited us inside the homestead compound.

The use of fictive kin terms not only facilitates interaction, it also creates certain obligations and rights. Fictive kin members will be added to the list of people who should receive preferential behaviour when favours are distributed (e.g. employment, credit, sharecropping contracts, etc.). In the absence of real relatives, many people who seek employment in urban areas will approach an employed villager or even an unrelated man from the villages their mothers came from to ask for assistance and favourable considerations. Aziz in his study notes:

> Sometimes fictive kinsmen of different villages are offered jobs by highly placed persons in public offices on the condition of marrying members of their closely related families. The job is given when the individual remains as a fictive kin, so that such employment is not categorized as favouritism. After some months of such employment the marriage takes place, giving no indication that it was prearranged.[35]

In addition to kin terms used fictitiously there are also other terms with which people are addressed. These terms are based on close friendship, religious or spiritual relationships between people. In a neighbouring village there lived a well-established *pir baba* (religious leader), of whom some villagers were the loyal followers. Almost all children in Bhaimara are encouraged by their parents to develop a friendship with a particular child of the same sex. If the parents approve of the relationship, a long-lasting *dosto* relationship (friendship) can be established. Such a relationship will imply material and political support between the parties when they grow up. In the meantime, the parents of the children can use this relationship for the same purposes.

Social groups and local leadership in the rural areas

We have indicated the important role which the larger and wealthy lineages can play in social, political and economic activities. There are, however, other groups and institutions besides the kinship-based ones, which are important for understanding the social context within which competition for scarce resources takes place. In this section we shall discuss certain activities connected with the *village* unit and the *samaj* (village association). We shall also, briefly, touch on the role the local leaders play in village affairs.

From a statistical point of view, Bhaimara *village* is our unit of study. There are very few activities for which the village is a corporate unit acting against other village units. There are also few types of activities which are particularly linked to and confined by the village boundaries. We have already noted that the patrilineal ties and especially the matrilineal ties extend beyond the village boundaries. The only particular activity we found where the village acted as a unit was the sports team of the boys in Bhaimara who competed with the teams from other villages.

A number of activities, including a certain type of movement of women, took place within the boundaries of Bhaimara village. It was, however, often not the boundaries of the village which imposed restrictions, but rather that the network and boundaries of other social groupings coincided with and ran parallel to the village boundaries.

We found, however, the village to be an important reference point in a unit of identification. The first question all strangers are met with is — which village do you come from? In a larger area the different villages will also be units which are referred to and have certain characteristics attached to them. '*A* is a tradition-oriented village; in village *B,* there are many educated people.' The size of the village naturally influences the cohesiveness the villagers may feel. People in a village with 3000 inhabitants divided into 5–10 *paras* (geographical areas) and many social groupings are less attached to their village than people in a village like Bhaimara of 300 inhabitants with one *para* and much overlapping of membership between the village and other social groups.

The *village* membership is, however, not completely without significance in economic and social matters. There exist obligations to support and show consideration and preference for a fellow villager. Close agnates, other members of the patrilineage, and *samaj* members come first on the list, however.

As all people belong to only one village, also all people belong to one particular *samaj.* A *samaj* is an institution which is vested primarily with the task of ensuring that people conform to a morally proper mode of conduct. The *samaj* has the authority to inflict punishments on people who deviate from the established norms.

In Bhaimara there is only one *samaj,* but this *samaj* also contains

6 to 7 households from two neighbouring villages who live on the boundaries of Bhaimara village. Larger villages in the area have several or many *samajes.* The composition of the *samaj* to which the households of Bhaimara belong has changed several times during the last decades. It has changed by taking up a few new households and it has expelled a few. Twice since the *Partition* (in 1947) the *samaj* has split into different factions, but after some years it has been reunited. The 'official' reason for the split both times was that members of the *samaj* had entered into marriages with partners which some *samaj* members approved and some did not.

A *samaj* has a certain organizational structure. The leaders of the *samaj* are called *matbars,* and they are the ones who will pass judgement on conflicts and misbehaviour. The *matbars* are generally old, respected people. Most often they are relatively well-off economically. They need to have knowledge and skills in mediating and settling disputes. They are also supposed to be impartial and balanced in their judgement and unwilling to take bribes from the parties. Often the *matbarship* is hereditary, and the eldest son of a *matbar,* if he possesses the necessary skill, will take over his father's position.

In Bhaimara there is only one *matbar* who is recognized by all the people in the village. His name is Umeth *matbar (matbar* is, like a title, added to his name). There are several reasons why he has achieved this position. His father was a *matbar,* and he was considered to have the skills necessary for being a *matbar.* He was also the recognized leader of a large and influential patrilineage in the village. An almost necessary condition for becoming a *matbar* is that one belongs to such a lineage. There are no clear limits on how many *matbars* a *samaj* may have. In addition to Umeth *matbar* there are also other older men who aspire to be or regard themselves as *matbars.* Their supporters address them with the *matbar* title added to their name. The more cases of conflict they are called upon to negotiate and the more influential they become, the stronger their position as *matbar* stands. An indication of their position is the general use of the *matbar* title added to their real names. Several times we were promptly interrupted when we referred to a particular villager as *matbar* in speaking to a man who we did not know was his enemy: 'He is not a *matbar* and he will never be one.'

Disputes and misbehaviour can be solved at different levels. Attempts are always made to settle quarrels between members in a household, a patrilineage, a village, within the smallest unit both, or all, disputants belong to. If the settlement of a dispute is not satisfactory to one of the parties, the disputant may call upon some of the *matbars* of the *samaj* to set up a kind of rural court before which the dispute can be heard and adjudicated. Such local courts operate in all villages and are called *shalish.* Umeth *matbar* of Bhaimara hears all the important cases in the village, while the other *matbars* are only appointed to hear some. An indication of the strong position Umeth *matbar* has is that, along with other well-known *matbars* from other villages, he is sometimes called upon to settle inter-village disputes.

The nature of the judgement passed by the *shalishes* is very often different from the verdict which a Government court might reach. The *shalishes* will often try to reach a compromise in a dispute, recognizing that the disputants and also the *matbars* of the case must, in most cases continue to live in close proximity to each other. Also in their judgement of the case the *matbars,* who normally know in detail the life stories of the disputants and their families, will consider a much wider variety of factors as relevant to the case than the Government courts will.

For religious purposes the *samaj* is also an important unit. During the Eid celebrations all the male members of the *samaj* gather in the Eid congregational field and offer their prayers. For many years the tradition in Bhaimara has been that after the communal Eid prayer, all the male members of the *samaj* are invited to a sumptuous meal in the homestead of the most influential Khan family. Some goats are normally slaughtered for this meal. Important *matbars* or members of households who are rivals of the Khan family will not attend this celebration.

We have noted that there is one mosque in the village. The mosque was established and built about 25 years ago by donations from two well-to-do households of an important lineage in Bhaimara. Although the mosque, in principle, is open for anyone to pray in, the congregation which assembles for worship every Friday and which contributes to the maintenance of the mosque, consists of 15 to 20 older men of the *samaj,* some of whom are the *matbars.*

In chapter 9 we shall discuss some of the effects Islam has on people's conception of the local stratification system and the nature of relationships between people.

This group of older men who worship together in the mosque are the backbone of the local and traditional power structure of the village. Not only do they control and dominate internal village affairs, they also have an important say in how external matters will influence village life. In a later chapter we shall discuss Government activities in the rural areas. The response of the *matbars* and the elder people of the *samaj* is decisive for the outcome of any Government programme. If the Government officials do not link up with the local power structure and 'pay tribute' to this group, the effectiveness of any project will be hampered. Also the candidates from the rural areas who campaign in public elections for regional and national offices will seek support from the *matbars* and the elders of the important patrilineages of the villages of the constituency they compete in. If a village candidate for a Union Parishad election is to be regarded as a serious candidate, he also needs the endorsement of some *matbars* in the village.

The story of Durzon Ali

Much of the information we have outlined on the various topics in this chapter was obtained when the stories and cases of particular persons were unravelled to us. One case was especially illustrative, since the case began rather dramatically only a few weeks after we came to the village. One day we heard that a house in the village had been torn down by some people. The owner, Durzon Ali, came weeping to the homestead we lived in and begged for the support of the older, respected household head. Durzon Ali's story summarizes many of the issues we have dealt with in this chapter. The story ran like this:

About 25 years ago Durzon Ali had to flee from his village as he and many others were suspected of murdering the Union Council Chairman. He hid in the house of his sister, who was married to a poor peasant in Bhaimara. When the murder case was finally solved, he did not return to his home village about 6 miles away. In Bhaimara he had taken on a job as palm-juice tapper. He was able to buy some trees and sharecrop other trees. During the peak seasons he helped his brother-in-law in the fields, and the latter let him use part of the homestead plot when Durzon Ali established his own family. (His wife came from a neighbouring village.) When Durzon Ali's brother-in-law died, Durzon Ali took over the small plot of agricultural land and the homestead plot, since the brother-in-law had no children or close relatives in the village. Durzon Ali, his family and his widowed sister thus had no relatives in Bhaimara and could not expect protection from their own patrilineage.

The son of Durzon Ali became a rickshaw driver in Manikganj and it was this son's marriage which was the cause of the expulsion of Durzon Ali both from the *samaj* and the village. The son of Durzon Ali married the daughter of a well-to-do peasant in a village two miles away from Bhaimara and went to live there as a *ghor-jamais*. The problem was, however, that the family and the lineage of the bride was considered to be low-caste and low-born. As we have noted there are strict restrictions for peasants claiming to be *sheikhs* on marrying into such a caste. The family of the bride had traditionally been *jolhaes* (Muslim weavers), and they therefore constituted an endogamous low-caste group. The father of the bride had run a successful business in the purchase and sale of chickens and had been able to invest much money in land. The bride was to inherit 1.5 acres of land from her father, and this was naturally an important consideration for the son of Durzon Ali.

Durzon Ali told the *matbars* of the village that he had no knowledge of his son's marriage (it was his son's second marriage) and that he would totally reject his son in order to be able to live in Bhaimara. The elders of Bhaimara had a different opinion on the matter. They claimed that it was Durzon Ali who had arranged the marriage with the poultry-dealer in order to obtain the land for his son, and that he only pretended to have no knowledge of the marriage because the elders of the *samaj* would never have permitted a marriage to a low-caste group.

Durzon Ali contacted the *matbars,* but it was clear to both him and the others that no *matbars* would bring up his case in the local court, since he was without family and supporters in the village. Durzon Ali and his family were forced to leave the village, and he took up residence with his son and his bride who had been allocated a homestead plot and agricultural land by the father of the bride.

The homestead plot of Durzon Ali in Bhaimara and his small agricultural plot were soon taken over by some influential people in Bhaimara, and Durzon Ali received a payment for his land at much less than the market value. We visited Durzon Ali many times in his new home, which was a few miles from Bhaimara. Durzon Ali always insisted on his innocence and complained about the lack of action over the major crimes the rich committed. He said that the reason for his expulsion was that a particular person wanted his land, and that this person had bribed the *matbars* so that they should not pursue the matter.

An objective comment on the case made by people not involved agreed with the assessment made by Durzon Ali about his own situation.

Notes

1 As we show in Appendix 2, the definition of the household is far from easy, and however one defines a household there will be dilemmas attached to how particular units shall be delimited. We found several cases in Bhaimara where the production unit did not overlap with the consumption unit. Several of the young yearly wage labourers we refer to later stayed permanently in the houses of well-to-do households, received all their meals there, but supported economically their own families living elsewhere. The same dilemma crops up when delimiting households who have absentee members on labour migration to other rural or urban areas. We put more weight on the economic links between members of the same 'budget' unit than on the joint residential and cooking-relationships when we grouped 'dubious' individuals. However, even our solution is inadequate for certain types of cases. For a further discussion on this issue see Appendix 2, and Eirik G. Jansen, B.K. Jahangir, Bodil Maal, and Nazibor Rahman: 'Dilemmas Involved in Defining and Delimiting Household Units in Rural Surveys in Bangladesh', *Journal of Social Studies,* No. 21, 1983, Dhaka, and Van Schendel, *op.cit.,* pp. 20–21.

2 There are different opinions on what the term *gusti* implies. K.M. Ashraful Aziz in his book *Kinship in Bangladesh,* International Centre for Diarrhoeal Disease Research, Bangladesh, 1979, states, p. 24, that all members of a *gusti* can trace their common origin to a single deceased male ancestor. A.K.M. Aminul Islam in *A Bangladesh Village,* Schenkman Publishing Company, USA, 1974, gives *gusti* a much looser meaning, as kinsmen, and states that for membership in a *gusti* the common ancestor may or may not be necessary (p. 67). J. Arens and J. van Beurden, *op.cit.,* p. 178, say that a *gusti* is a group of families tied together by relationships often other than kinship.

3 See Florence E. McCarthy: *The Status and Condition of Rural Women in Bangladesh,* Women's Section, Planning and Evaluation Cell, Ministry of Agriculture and Forests, Dhaka, 1978, and Shelley Feldman: 'Rural Infrastructural Development in Bangladesh and its Potential Consequences for Reproductive Behaviour', *Journal of Social Studies,* Vol. 7, 1980, Dhaka.

4 There is an extensive amount of literature on *purdah* and the economic implications which follow from the practice of *purdah:* See T.A. Abdullah: *Village Women as I saw Them,* Ford Foundation, Dhaka, 1974, J. Arens and J. van Beurden, *op.cit.* Part II, pp. 31–68, Shelley Feldman and Florence McCarthy, 'Purdah and Changing Patterns of Social Control among Rural Women in Bangladesh', *Journal of Marriage and the Family,* Vol. 45, No. 4, November 1983.

5 Mead Cain: 'The Household Life Cycle and Economic Mobility in Rural Bangladesh', *Population and Development Review,* Vol. 4, No. 3, September 1978, pp. 421–438.

6 F. Thomasson Jannuzi and James T. Peach: 'Note on Land Reform in Bangladesh: The Efficiency of Ceiling', *Journal of Peasant Studies,* Vol. 6, Number 3, April 1979.

7 From a statistical point of view this splitting and reuniting of household units naturally creates difficulties when preparing a baseline for a village household survey. Appendix 2 discusses this issue.

8 A clear and short outline of the Muslim law of inheritance is found in: Maurice Gaudefroy-Demombynes: *Muslim Institutions,* George Allen & Unwin Ltd., London, 1968, pp. 139–147.

9 See Aziz, *op.cit.,* p. 70.

10 For a good overview of Government land surveys and land records see Van Schendel, *op.cit.,* pp. 32–37.

11 E. Gait: *Census of India 1901,* Bengal Secretarial Press, Calcutta, 1902.

12 RamKrishna Mukherjee: *Six Villages of Bengal,* Popular Prakashan, Bombay, 1971.

13 H.K. Arefeen: 'Muslim Stratification Patterns in Bangladesh. An Attempt to Build a Theory', *Journal of Social Studies,* No. 16, 1982, pp. 51–74.

14 See Peter Bertocci: *Ellusive Villages: Social Structure and Community Organization in Rural East Pakistan,* Ph.D. Dissertation. East Lansing, Michigan State University, 1970, pp. 40–60.

15 See Bertocci, *op.cit.,* p. 56.

16 See B.K. Jahangir: *Differentiation, Polarization and Confrontation in Rural Bangladesh,* Centre for Social Studies, University of Dhaka, 1979, pp. 110–112.

17 B.K. Jahangir, *op.cit.,* pp. 86–87.

18 Bertocci, *op.cit.,* p. 46.

19 Anwarullah Chowdhury: *A Bangladesh Village, A Study of Social Stratification,* Centre for Social Studies, University of Dhaka, 1978, p. 94.

20 E. Gait, *op.cit.,* pp. 441–442, quoted from H.K. Arefeen, *op.cit.,* pp. 58–59.

21 See P. Bertocci, *op.cit.,* p. 56, and Anwarullah Chowdhury, *op.cit.,* pp. 78–108.

22 Bertocci, *op.cit.*

23 Armindo Miranda: 'Nuptiality in Bangladesh', *Journal of Social Studies,* No. 9, July 1980, Dhaka, p. 82.

24 Arefeen, *op.cit.,* p. 55.

25 Bertocci, *op.cit.*

26 Aziz, *op.cit.,* p. 59.

27 Aziz, *op.cit.,* p. 60.

28 Miranda, *op.cit.,* p. 77.

29 Miranda, *op.cit.,* p. 80.

30 Miranda, *op.cit.,* p. 86.

31 Bangladesh Population Census Report, National Volume (Dhaka), 1978, quoted from Miranda, *op.cit.*

32 *World Fertility Survey: Bangladesh Fertility Survey 1975,* Government of Bangladesh, Ministry of Health and Population Control, Dhaka, 1978; quoted from Miranda, *op.cit.*

33 Consanguinal relation (by descent), affinal relation (by marriage).

34 Aziz, *op.cit.,* pp. 76–77.

35 Aziz, *op.cit.,* p. 136.

4

Credit Relations and Transfer of Land

Introduction

The previous chapters have established a wide frame within which we need to understand how competition for scarce resources takes place. In chapter 3 we emphasized that inheritance was a major way of allocating land between households. It is obvious that in addition there exist other mechanisms for the transfer of land between households. Ten to twenty years after they have been established most households will own either more land or less. A household which inherited 10 acres of land may 10 years later own 15 acres. The more normal pattern is that a household which at the time it was established started with half an acre of inherited land, will 20 years later own no agricultural land at all. This process of transfer of ownership of land cannot be attributed to inheritance. What are the mechanisms of transfer of land which can explain these changes in land ownership?

The main aim of this chapter is to describe and analyse in detail the mechanisms by which poverty forces poor households into debt and the sale of their land to rich households. The great majority of the households in Bhaimara and in rural Bangladesh as a whole, are, as we have noted, deficit households in the sense that their expenditure is greater than their income. For most households this means that they have to establish credit relationships with the few 'surplus' households in order to cover the gap between expenditure and income.

The focus of this chapter will be on the various types of credit relationships between households; the conditions for the credit will be spelled out and the type of collateral which exists for the different types of loans will be discussed. We shall show in this chapter that credit relationships between households are part of the survival strategies of the poor and the investment strategies of the rich. The strategies and the nature of the credit relationships a household has, depend very much on the relationship the household has to its kin members, both to the paternal lineage *(gusti)* and to its affinal relations (in-laws). The strategies of a household will naturally also depend on the household's position in the rural stratification system outlined in chapter 3. In this chapter we shall, on the basis of quantitative evidence, assess the role the patrilineage *(gusti)* plays in credit relationships and the sale and purchase of land.

This chapter is built up around five case studies. Each case narrates in detail the story of the economic position and the strategies of a particular household in Bhaimara, with special reference to the types of credit relationships the household is involved in. The cases presented show households in different economic positions. The first case shows the credit relationships and survival strategies a landless household pursues. Case 2 describes a deficit household owning a small, but declining amount of agricultural land. The case of this particular household is presented next to case 3, which shows a household possessing a small surplus and expanding its landed property as a consequence of the credit relationships it has with the deficit household described in case 2. After these cases follows a description of the economic position and investment strategies of two rich households. Case 4 describes a household whose members live in a village nearby Bhaimara. The household possesses about 30 acres of land and is considered to be among the four richest households in the whole union.[1] Case 5 narrates the story of a household that belongs to Bhaimara and has its land possessions there. The members of the household live in Dhaka, which gives the credit relationships this household is involved in and its investment strategies a particular shape.

In order to understand the credit relationships and the strategies which are pursued, the wider social context and opportunity situation of the households are presented. This context will include the issues we discussed in chapter 3 on the phase the household has reached in its stage of development and its composition in terms of age and sex. We shall also emphasize the importance of having good connections and alliances with people who are part of the local power structure and with Government officials in the urban areas.

In conjunction with each case a discussion of the more general features of the economic strategies of households in similar economic positions is presented. We shall see that the categories we have applied, based on the amount of land held by the households, do not readily correspond to our labels of deficit and surplus households.

Below follows the story of the economic strategies pursued by a landless household.

Case 1. The economic strategies of a landless household

Mosum Ali's household is among the poorest in *Bhaimara* village. Mosum Ali's household is in debt to many different people. All the major debt relations Mosum Ali is involved in, are due to the fact that the expenses of his household are greater than its income. In order to understand the types of debts his household has it is necessary to have information about the material resources the household possesses, the income sources of the household, the expenditure of the household, the strategies to reduce expenditure, and the type of people Mosum Ali can call on to obtain credit.

Mosum Ali has lived in a separate household for the last 12 years. After the death of his father the sons established separate households. Mosum Ali inherited a 12 decimal homestead plot and a 20 decimal plot of agricultural land (1 acre = 100 decimals).

Mosum Ali's main income during the last years has been what he has earned as an agricultural wage-labourer. About 20–30 per cent of the value of his total income has come from the homestead plot. His homestead plot has a small vegetable garden and 4 grown fruit-trees. All the 12 years Mosum Ali has had a separate household he has been in deficit on his annual 'budget'. (Neither Mosum Ali nor any other person described in this study would set up a formal budget of their household's income and expenditure.) During the 12-year period he has gradually mortgaged and sold the 20 decimal agricultural plot and 6 decimals of his homestead plot. The money obtained from the gradual mortgage and sale of his agricultural land and half of his homestead plot has been an important additional source of income for him. For the last 5 years Mosum Ali has been left with only 6 decimals of homestead plot. Here we shall be concerned with exploring the debt relations he has entered into after he sold his agricultural land and half of his homestead plot.

Mosum Ali has a wife and 5 children, from 2 to 11 years old. The oldest boy is 8 years of age. The boy does not work regularly for others, but he provides some income for the family through various activities (fishing, occasionally weeding fields for others, looking after cattle, etc.). Another source of income for the household is provided by chicken and hens and a goat and a calf. The goat and the calf are borrowed from two more well-to-do families on a particular 'sharecropping' basis.

It is easy to account for the expenditure of the household of Mosum Ali and his family, as it is for almost all landless households. Purchase of rice constitutes by far the most important type of expenditure; 80–85 per cent of the money income earned by the household goes to buy this item alone or what people consider the poorer substitute for rice: wheat or sometimes potatoes. The household is self-sufficient in vegetables and fruit for some months, and sometimes money is earned on the sale of these items. The 15–20 per cent of the remaining expenses the household has consist of the purchase of salt, kerosene, chillies and occasionally some inexpensive fish. Twice a year Mosum Ali purchases the cheapest available *lungi,* costing 15–20 Taka. Mosum Ali's wife and their children never purchase new clothes — they receive old clothes as gifts from richer people. Only once has Mosum Ali given his wife a *sari;* that was at the time of their marriage. Thus during the whole year almost all the money available (from incomes and loans) is spent on rice, wheat and potatoes.

There is, however, a great variation in the income over the year. In the *aman*-harvest period which can last for a whole month in the Manikganj area (normally in December), it is possible for Mosum Ali to obtain employment every day. During this period the price of rice is also at its lowest point. In other months of the year, particularly during September-October, it may only be possible to get work for 5–10 days a month. During this period the price of rice is high, normally 30–50 per cent higher than after the *aman*-harvest. The budget for Mosum Ali's household in December, during the *aman*-harvest, is thus very different from that in September. In December the budget for Mosum Ali's household would roughly be (in 1980 prices):

Income (Taka)		*Expenditure (Taka)*	
30 days work, wage		1½ *seers* (1 seer = 0.9 kilos)	
10 Taka per day	= 300	of rice per day = 4.50	
Vegetables, fruit from		Taka per seer = 6.75 Taka	= 202.50
own garden and eggs		Chilli	7.50
sold in the market	50	Fish	15
	350	Kerosene	5
		Lungi	15
		Other items	10
			255

Surplus 95 Taka

In periods of the year when Mosum Ali is employed daily and the salaries are high and the price of rice is low, it is possible for Mosum Ali to save some money. In a full year, however, Mosum Ali is only employed as an agricultural wage-labourer for 200–220 days per year. In addition he may be employed for 20–30 days in non-agricultural activities (transport, housebuilding). His household's monthly budget for September is roughly:

Income (Taka)		*Expenditure (Taka)*	
8 days work,		1 *seer* of rice per day	
7 Taka wage per day	= 56	at 6 Taka	= 180
Sale of vegetables,		Salt, chillies	10
fruit, eggs	34	Wheat	30
	90	Other items	15
			235

Deficit 145 Taka

The September-October monthly budgets are always in clear deficit. In other months of the year, when Mosum Ali is employed for more than 20 days, his budget can be in balance or even show a little surplus. On the whole, however, Mosum Ali's household has had a yearly deficit for the last 2–3 years of 300–400 Taka each year. In order to obtain this amount of money, he takes up loans. Almost all the loans are spent on the purchase of rice. The credit Mosum Ali obtains can be regarded as the main method of bridging the gap between income and expenditure. Since the credit ultimately will have to be repaid in one way or the other, Mosum Ali tries as hard as he can to make the gap between the amount of income and the amount of expenditure as small as possible. There are two main ways of narrowing the gap: to increase the income or to decrease the expenditure. These strategies are pursued simultaneously.

An important strategy for generating income is to secure as much employment as possible and for as many members of the household as possible. With the present age and sex composition of the members of the household, it is only Mosum Ali who can count on receiving a normal cash wage. Mosum Ali puts much effort into being employed by various landowners as much as possible. Some landless people are employed less than he is during the whole year, other landless persons are employed more. In the present situation of the household it is not possible for Mosum Ali to increase cash income from wages. Income in kind can be obtained through employment of the eldest children and the wife. Their income will be the food and clothes and possibly other gifts they receive in payment for their work. Other sources of income in kind, and also in cash, are produce from the kitchen garden, collected cow dung, which is sold as fuel, and fish caught in village ponds. Much time is spent on these and similar activities.

The other course in order to make the deficit on the budget as small as possible is to reduce expenditure. This can also be done in various ways. To send his wife and children away to work for others can also be regarded as a method of reducing expenditure. As long as they work for others, Mosum Ali is saved the expenses for their meals and for the clothes and other items they may receive as a part of their salary.

Another way to cut expenses and reduce the deficit is to receive outright gifts, which Mosum Ali and his household members do not compensate for in terms of labour. At the *Eid* festival, the household of Mosum Ali receives gifts from the richer families. Also on other occasions the members of Mosum Ali's household may receive free food and clothes from *gusti* and *samaj* members and well-to-do villagers.

It is very difficult to estimate the amount and value of the gifts the members of Mosum Ali's household receive in one year, since in many cases it can be difficult to draw the line between gift and payment, especially if the members of Mosum Ali's household work for the families they receive the 'gift' from. Mosum Ali himself estimated that if these gifts are regarded as part of the payment along with the food, his household members received gifts, all in the form of food — and clothes — of a value of roughly 100 Taka per year.

Since rice and wheat alone account for almost all expenditure, one important strategy is to reduce the consumption of these basic food items. This is a strategy which Mosum Ali's household follows almost the whole year and a strategy which is physically felt by the household members. Only for short periods of the year do the members of the household eat well and sufficiently. In most periods of the year rice is consumed only once or twice a day; sometimes some of the members of the family can go without rice for several days. Starvation is thus a calculated and very common strategy to reduce expenses.

How has Mosum Ali been able to obtain loans to cover his 300–400 Taka yearly deficit? The most important debt Mosum Ali has, is one to a well-off, distant relative who lives in the village. Mosum Ali has mainly gone to this man when he needed money to purchase rice or wheat. As the loan increased the relative demanded a collateral for his loans. Mosum Ali has over the last years mortgaged 3 of the remaining 6 decimals of his homestead plot to him. He has mortgaged the plot for 150 Taka per decimal. (The first 6 decimals of the homestead plot Mosum Ali sold to his cousin. Mosum Ali still uses the 6 decimals of household plot sold to his cousin, but his cousin is free to come and pick the best vegetables and fruits from the homestead plot.)

Mosum Ali received a better offer from his distant relative in the village for the mortgage of the next 3 decimals than he did from his cousin. Therefore he went to him rather than continuing to sell land to his cousin. Mosum Ali realizes that if he takes more loans from his relative during the next years, he will have to sell the three decimals to him. The sale of the homestead plot will be the next step in order to cover his household deficit. One reason Mosum Ali went to his relative was that he thinks there is little chance that his relative will take over the homestead plot, even if the relative eventually acts as mortgagee and buys the rest of the homestead plot.

Mosum Ali had, however, a much better economic offer from his neighbour, Joinel Kazi, for the homestead plot. Joinel Kazi offered him 500 Taka per decimal for the purchase of the plot. Mosum Ali realized that Joinel Kazi is interested in expanding his own homestead area, and that he would have no guarantee for being able to continue to dwell on his plot after he had sold it to Joinel Kazi.

In many ways Mosum Ali is dependent on Joinel Kazi. He estimates that for at least 30 days a year he is employed by him. It was also Joinel Kazi who gradually gave him loans against a mortgage and bought up the 20 decimals of agricultural land Mosum Ali had inherited. At present Joinel Kazi is also an important source of credit for Mosum Ali. Mosum Ali has mortgaged two fruit trees to him on different occasions. The first tree he mortgaged after he had been ill for 10 days and not been able to work. He received 50 Taka for the tree. The agreement is that Joinel Kazi can pick all the fruit of the tree till the money is paid back. Two months after the 50 Taka was received, Joinel Kazi could already harvest fruit worth 80 Taka. Joinel Kazi will also have next year's harvest unless the money is paid back. The other tree Joinel Kazi took after Mosum Ali had gradually run into a debt of 70 Taka to him. At present Mosum Ali has a debt of 40 Taka to Joinel Kazi. He fears that next time he has to go and ask Joinel Kazi for a loan, a third tree will have to be mortgaged as a security for the loan.

Mosum Ali also has a different type of loan to cover the deficit. During the different seasons in the year Mosum Ali is employed by 10–15 landowners, most of them living in Bhaimara. Four of the landowners employ Mosum Ali for about 150–160 of the estimated 200 days he is employed in the agricultural sector. In seasons when work is scarce Mosum Ali will often approach his main employers to ask for an advance for work to be carried out in the near future. This happens when he has been without work for some days and expects to get employment within a few days. He will then ask for half of his wage in advance. Joinel Kazi is one of these 3–4 people whom Mosum Ali approaches for this type of loan. Only to one person, Shajahan, who employs Mosum Ali for 90–100 days per year, can Mosum Ali turn in the slack season and ask for loans and advance payment, even if it will be weeks or months before he can return the loan through deduction from his wage. Shajahan, however, can count on Mosum Ali to give his plots first priority in the hectic harvest season or other periods when labour is urgently needed. The loan he receives as payment in advance can be in cash or in kind; normally the wage he receives later is a little less than the going rate for the period.

Mosum Ali and his household are also engaged in another type of debt relationship. This is a debt relationship between households of equal economic status. Landless and poor families are very aware of the economic situation of other poor households. As soon as a poor household realizes that a neighbouring poor household has more money in hand than it consumes, members of that household are approached for loans. At one period when Mosum Ali had worked every day for a whole month he was asked to give a loan to a household where the main income-earning person had been unemployed. Similarly, when the news spread around that he had received the last instalment for the sale of the first half of his homestead plot, several people approached him for loans. Some of the poor people Mosum Ali gives and takes loans from are people he has established friendship relations with. These loans between friends are without interest even if they remain unpaid for years. For the sake of balance in the relationship, loans are not allowed to accumulate by one of the parties. It is seldom that one party has more than a 200 Taka debt to the other. The wife of Mosum Ali is also involved in many petty loans on an equal basis with other poor housewives. Every week she will several times borrow or receive a small amount of vegetables, chillies or rice from the neighbouring poor households. She will also in times of acute need ask for loans, in kind, from the more well-to-do families she works for.

There is another type of loan among the poor in which interest is involved. Mosum Ali is involved in such a relationship with another poor household. He took a 50 Taka loan from a household during a period when he had remained unemployed for several weeks. The interest on the loan is 10 per cent each month, which is the normal interest rate. Every month since he obtained the loan 6 months ago he has paid 5 Taka. The 5 Taka interest per month is partly covered by a similar loan of 30 Taka, which he gave another poor household when he had surplus money. It would, of course, be possible for Mosum Ali to refuse a poor household a loan when he had surplus money. The consequence of not giving a loan, when possibilities for it existed, would be that Mosum Ali would be denied loans when his own household was in need.

One result of the vast reciprocal network of debt relationship between poor households is that it is very difficult for the poor household to save much. On the other hand, when the households do not have money, they can approach other households and expect loans. In this way the reciprocal borrowing system acts as a security and guarantees that when sickness or unemployment strikes a household, loans can be expected, at least for a certain period.

It is important for Mosum Ali to show his creditors that he has many sources of credit to turn to when he has no money. If he had only one or two people willing to give him loans, and the creditors were aware of Mosum Ali's dependence on them, they could make the terms of the loans even less favourable.

Also when it comes to management of loans, it is important for a man to have a good relationship to a richer and more powerful man. Since Mosum Ali has a good relationship to Shajahan, Shajahan not only acts as a source of credit for him, where labour is Mosum Ali's security for the loan, he also acts as a *jamin* for Mosum Ali. (A *jamin* is a person who will guarantee that his client will repay the loan.) For many types of loans between creditors and debtors in different income groups, there will be a *jamin* who takes on the responsibility of ensuring that the debt will be repaid. Sometimes, when the *jamin* is a powerful person, he can even influence the terms and conditions on which the creditor issues his loan.

On several occasions Mosum Ali has called upon Shajahan to guarantee loans he has taken. For Mosum Ali, it is undoubtedly a source of strength that he can call upon Shajahan to act as a *jamin* under certain circumstances. This makes it possible for Mosum Ali to turn to more people when he needs credit, since the creditors can count on the loan being repaid. If it is not repaid, the creditors will have a bad relationship both with Mosum Ali and Shajahan.

Mosum Ali realizes that also in the years to come it is most probable that he will be in deficit on his annual budget. What are the other types of collateral besides his labour, homestead plot, trees and his *'jamin',* that he can mobilize in order to obtain loans? Mosum Ali inherited a small iron-sheet roof from his father, which he still owns. He wanted to sell the iron-sheet roof some years ago, but he was offered such a ridiculously low price for it that he decided to mortgage one of his trees to Joinel Kazi instead. At the time of marriage his wife received some inexpensive jewelry ornaments. These he pawned to a pawnbroker in Manikganj for about half of the market value of the ornaments. Holes in the nose and in his wife's ears, where the ornaments previsously were placed, are visible evidence of Mosum Ali's deteriorating situation. The brass pottery the household owned has all been sold; now the family only has clay and cheap aluminium kitchen utensils left. The next item Mosum Ali will sell will probably be his iron-sheet roof. A well-to-do man in the village who wants his cow house to be covered with iron-sheet has tried to get Mosum Ali to accept a *bayna* for the roof. (*Bayna* is advance payment, and the seller and buyer are bound to complete the transaction after *bayna* has been made.) Mosum Ali cannot accept a better economic offer from anybody else after the *bayna* is made, and the well-do-to man, who in this case has proposed to pay 40 Taka in advance (10 per cent of the sum of sale), will lose his money if he changes his mind about the purchase. Mosum Ali has not agreed to accept *bayna* yet; he hopes that the well-to-do man will not only buy his iron-sheet, but also employ him for some period during the year when it is difficult to obtain employment.

Mosum Ali has also been involved in a different type of credit relationship. Four times since he established his own household, he has left on labour migration trips. From Bhaimara and a few neighbouring villages landless or poor people, like Mosum Ali, leave for Rajshahi and Sylhet districts in groups of 20–30 people. People from labour surplus areas like Manikganj migrate for a 1–2 months period every year to these districts, which during the *aman* harvest season suffer from a shortage of labour. In order to cater for the needs of the family who are left behind, Mosum Ali and the other migrant labourers take up loans from rich peasants in the area, who are often the people who finance and organize the entire trip. Two *maunds* of paddy (1 *maund* = 37.2 kilograms) or 200 Taka is usually borrowed for the maintenance of the remaining family. The loan is repaid when Mosum Ali returns from the trip.

All the loans Mosum Ali takes are for consumption purposes. Sometimes he also has to take up loans to repay debts when there is a chance that the collateral for the debt can be taken by the creditor. For the major loans Mosum Ali has obtained he does not pay any interest. The reason for this is that all the creditors eventually expect to take possession of the collateral Mosum Ali has put up for the loan. Even if Mosum Ali can repay part of the loan, the creditors would consider this only to be a postponement before they receive the collateral. The sum of the accumulated loans will often be ridiculously low compared to the real value of the collateral before the creditor insists on taking possession of it.

Mosum Ali does not take up any loans for productive purposes. Being landless, he has no possibility of investing productively in agriculture. Mosum Ali has never ventured into trade and business; he does not possess the right skills for these occupations. Even if he attempted to enter in to these enterprises, it would be very difficult for him to raise the necessary initial capital through loans.

Besides the daily need for the basic food, there are other situations when Mosum Ali needs money and resources. Sickness is an unpredictable event which has struck his household several times seriously. Seven years ago Mosum Ali was sick for two months during the *aman*-harvest season. It was in this situation he sold the first decimals of his homestead plot — in order to obtain money to purchase food for his family. At first he received loans, but later he had to sell the land when the loans increased. Last year his youngest daughter fell sick. Both the local medical doctor and a 'witch-doctor' were consulted. Treatment and pills would cost more than 100 Taka. Mosum Ali could not afford this treatment, so his daughter remained unattended by the local doctors. The daughter was sick and very weak for a long period, but she survived. Mosum Ali knows, however, that he cannot afford to take up loans in order to cover expensive medical bills except for his oldest son, who will in a few years start to earn money, and for his wife and himself.

A different type of expense Mosum Ali will have to manage is the dowry for each of his three daughters. He hopes that the families where the two eldest daughters work will cover at least part of their dowry and help him in finding suitable bridegrooms for his daughters. The *gusti* of Mosum Ali, which has a certain prestige in the village, could also help with the expenses for his daughters' marriages. The leader of the *gusti,* an uncle of Mosum Ali, would have to approve the marriage. The *gusti* members, even if they keep a certain distance from Mosum Ali, would, in the eyes of other villagers, lose respect if the daughters of Mosum Ali were married to men who lived in even poorer economic conditions than Mosum Ali. He would have to manage some money on his own, 100–150 Taka, for each daughter. This money he would probably mobilize from his various credit sources.

From a social point of view, who are the people Mosum Ali can turn to and ask for assistance and loans? Ideally, it is the *gusti* people whom he can approach first. Since Mosum Ali has already received many gifts and has outstanding debts to many of them, he finds it hard continually to ask the *gusti* members for support to manage his daily expenses. He can expect to get some old clothes as gifts, and material support to cover wedding expenses for his daughters. Mosum Ali can also expect to get employment when his richer relatives need labourers on their fields. But generally Mosum Ali has found it easier to receive political support and physical protection from his *gusti* than economic assistance.

The next close group which should give Mosum Ali support is the *samaj.* During the Eid festival he receives small gifts from the richer *samaj* members. Normally a rich man would give priority to a member of his *samaj* when giving loans and employment. After *gusti* and *samaj* the group poor people can turn to for loans and favours is the villagers. In Bhaimara, as it is a small village, all villagers belong, as we noted in chapter 3, to the same *samaj.* There are, however, so many poor and landless people in the village and in the *samaj* that Mosum Ali has to compete with them as regards loans, employment and other favours.

Mosum Ali has found that the people he most easily can approach for loans are people to whom he is already economically linked. This would be the people he works for as an agricultural labourer, the families where his wife and daughters work, and households that he is in the process of selling something to (the iron-sheet roof, the trees, the homestead plots, etc.). He could also approach a household from which he has sharecropped a calf and a goat. An initially single-stranded economic relationship can thus be developed into a more complex one. The main debts and income of Mosum Ali, mentioned above are summarized in Table 4.1.

Table 4.1. Debts and Sources of Income of the Household of Mosum Ali.

Land property when the household was established in 1968:
— 20 decimals of agricultural land
— 12 decimals of homestead plot

Present land property (1980)
— 6 decimals of homestead plot

Other property (1980)
— small iron-sheet roof
— inexpensive kitchen utensils

Land sold in period 1968–1980
— 20 decimals of agricultural land to Joinel Kazi (neighbour and employer)
— 6 decimals of homestead plot sold to cousin

Mortgaged
— 3 decimals of the 6 decimals homestead plot to a distant relative
— 2 fruit trees to Joinel Kazi (same person as above)

Debts
— 40 Taka to Joinel Kazi
— Received advance wage from 3 employers (80 Taka in all)

Sources of income
— agricultural wage income of Mosum Ali 200–220 days per year
— wage income of Mosum Ali 20–30 days in non-agricultural activities (transport, housebuilding)
— sale of fruit and vegetables from own garden in local market
— irregular income in kind of wife and children
— small cash income from sale of cow dung, branches for fuel, fish
— gifts at *Eid* festival each year from rich families in village

— 50 Taka from a poor household (10 per cent interest per month)
— Petty loans incurred by wife in kind (food) from other poor households

— irregular gifts from *gusti* and *samaj* members (food, old clothes)
— interest on loan to poor household (3 Taka per month)

On a sharecropping basis
— 1 goat and 1 calf from a well-do-to household in the village

Some general features of the economic strategies of landless households

In the case above the major different strategies available to Mosum Ali were outlined. Several strategies for narrowing the deficit have, however, not been mentioned. Some of these strategies could be used and considered acceptable for landless households even poorer than the household of Mosum Ali. *Begging* is the most common of these strategies, and this way of earning an income is acceptable when the household has no male person who can earn a cash income. *Migration* to an urban centre is a very uncertain strategy, since the urban centres are already filled with a large number of unemployed people. *Criminal activities* and *disguised prostitution,* carried out by some members of the household, are naturally regarded as unacceptable strategies for securing an income. It is difficult to know the extent of these practises, but judging from cases brought in the local courts, in the rural areas, these are not unknown strategies.

Even among the households that have no agricultural land in Bhaimara, there are relatively large differences in the standard of living. The most important difference is expressed by the amount and quality of the food the members of the different households are able to consume. In many respects the situation of the household of Mosum Ali is similar to that of most of the landless households in Bhaimara village. These households will use many of the same strategies to increase income, reduce expenditure, and to obtain loans.

There are many factors which influence how well or poorly the landless households live and how big a deficit they have on their annual budget. One important factor influencing the standard of living is the age and sex structure of the household members. It was noted for Mosum Ali that at present he was the only person in the household who had a cash income. In five years time the age and sex distribution of his household will be different. The two oldest daughters will be married and separated from the household, and two sons will be old enough to be employed as agricultural wage-labourers along with their father. In a certain phase of Mosum Ali's household development cycle, the household could be self-sufficient and have a fairly satisfactory diet.

In Bhaimara 7 of 21 landless households are headed by women. Some of these households have a lower standard of living than Mosum Ali and his family at present, and several of the strategies Mosum Ali applies to earn an income, cut expenditure and take up loans, are not available to them.

Another factor influencing the material standard of the landless household is whether the household possesses its own homestead plot. Of the 21 landless households in Bhaimara 14 had homestead plots. The size of the plots varies from 2 to 18 decimals, with an average of 7 decimals. The 7 households without homestead plots are allowed to live on the homestead plots of their relatives. Lack of a homestead plot implies that the household does not receive an income from fruit trees and kitchen garden. It also means that the best security or collateral they could have for obtaining a loan is lacking.

The availability of loans also depends on the 'quality' of the labourers in the household. A hard-working and trustworthy man has a good chance of getting regular and frequent employment and, with that, possibilities for asking for advance payment and loans from his employer. The ability to work well is not the only important factor; if a person is a good political 'client' and clever supporter who can influence others, his chances of acquiring loans and other favours will be better. This means it is not only the material resources a landless person and his household possess that will decide the material standard of living for the household members. It also matters how cleverly the resources, both the economic resources and human skills, are managed.

Possibilities for loans will also depend on the support a household can manage to get from the *gusti*. A landless household will stand a better chance of obtaining loans if it is on good terms with its more well-to-do *gusti* members. More well-do-to *gusti* members can also act as *jamin* (guarantor) for a landless household on the credit market.

One factor which was not discussed in the case of Mosum Ali is the support a household can obtain from its affinal relatives. In chapter 3 we noted that this would depend on whether the woman had claimed land from her paternal property. Some of the best terms and conditions for loans are given by brothers who hope that their sister and her husband will not take the part of the land to which she is entitled according to the Islamic law of inheritance.

For some of the landless households, especially the households without a male person to generate cash income, loans cannot alone explain how the household members survive. From an economic point of view the members of these households ought not to be able to survive. Their members earn hardly any cash money and they have no homestead plot of land nor any valuable item which could be used as a collateral for obtaining loans. In order to survive for a longer period, food worth at least 0.50–1 Taka per day (1980 prices) is necessary for each person every day. To explain how the members of these poorest households survive, other factors than the loan-strategy must be found. These most deprived households, which today constitute about 10 per cent of the households in Bhaimara, survive owing to certain solidarity and supportive mechanisms which exist in the village. With the present strong tendency for an increasing number of households to lose their agricultural land and then gradually their homestead plots, a much larger number of households will end up having no possessions they can use as a security for taking up loans. It is doubtful whether the supportive measures to the poorest households can continue to operate effectively and reach all the poor when a larger number of households will have lost all their possessions. In chapter 10 we shall discuss this perspective in more detail.

The case of Mosum Ali illustrates several of the issues we have already stated that we would take up. This case clearly spelled out the seasonality of employment opportunities. We noted the severe consequences this had for the 'monthly budget' of Mosum Ali and thereby his need for credit. As long as Mosum Ali possesses an attractive and valuable collateral (land, iron-sheet roof) he will manage to finance his household's deficit during the seasons when the opportunities for income are scarce.[2] We also clearly saw how far from providing a sufficient diet for his family Mosum Ali is. His household shares this lack of purchasing capacity with many households that own some agricultural land. It is obvious that when and if these households obtain better incomes, or the price of rice goes down, purchase of more rice is the immediate response. We shall discuss certain aspects of the relationship between the level of purchasing power for the majority of the population and agricultural production and the investment pattern in chapters 6 and 8.

Some general features of the economic strategies of households with agricultural land but deficit budgets

It is difficult to state the exact number of households in Bhaimara with agricultural land that have a deficit on their annual budget. It is possible that a household with half an acre can have a balanced budget while a household with 2 acres can be in deficit and take up loans and mortgage land in order to cover its deficit. A fair number of the households with agricultural land will also be in the situation that one year they will have a balanced or even surplus budget and the next year, perhaps because of crop failures, sickness, low prices for the agricultural products or extraordinary expenditures such as a marriage, they may be in deficit. A rough estimate of the number of households with agricultural land which, over a longer period, 5–10 years, could be considered to be in a deficit situation, would indicate that 30 of the households are in such a position. This means that, including all the landless households, about 50 of the 62 households in Bhaimara are persistently in deficit and have to take up loans in order to survive. Many of the loans these households take up are not repaid, and gradually the capital and resources of the household are depleted.

Ten to twenty years ago many of the 21 landless households were in a similar situation to this category of households with agricultural land but with a deficit on their annual budget. The households that are landless today lost their land when they had to sell in order to cover a deficit on the annual budget, and also as a consequence of the division of land when the former household they belonged to split into several new households.

There are many factors which determine whether households with agricultural land have a deficit or a balanced budget: the size of agricultural land owned, the consumption pattern, the effectiveness of the saving strategies, how many productive versus non-productive members the household has, whether the household obtains extra land through sharecropping, the capacity to work of the different household members, and the overall management ability of the household members.

For this category of households too, loans represent only one of many strategies to narrow the gap between expenditure and income. Many of the strategies and types of loans are similar to those of the landless households. The most important types of loans these households are involved in, however, are loans for which *agricultural land* provides the collateral. In this section it is particularly this type of loan which will be discussed.

When loans accumulate, a plot of land is mortgaged. This means that the creditor obtains usufruct rights to the plot and retains these rights until the debt is repaid. The creditor who has obtained usufruct rights to the land can decide whether he wants to cultivate the land himself or lease the land out on a sharecropping basis.

The about 30 households with agricultural land that are at the same time in deficit are in the situation that they take up loans which already have involved, or in the future will involve, them in the mortgage and sale of their agricultural land. Many of the households in this group have sold or mortgaged land to members of their own *gusti*. Inheritance of agricultural land naturally takes place within the *gusti*. But also when it comes to money-lending, mortgage and sale of land, the *gusti* is an important institution within which land transactions occur.

The following two case studies, cases 2 and 3, describe the development of the debt relationships between two brothers. Such relationships are typical in Bhaimara, and are most probably a very common process between brothers and kin members throughout the villages in Bangladesh. One of the brothers in this case has a deficit on his annual budget which is covered by loans from his more well-to-do brother, a peasant who has a surplus. (The poor brother is here named Joinuddin (case 2) and the more well-to-do brother Eynuddin (case 3).)

Case 2. The economic strategies of a household owning agricultural land but with a budget deficit

The father of Joinuddin and Eynuddin died when they were young, but they stayed in a joint household with their mother till 1965. Then, shortly after their mother died, the two brothers established separate households. At that time Joinuddin had 3 children, one boy 2 years old and two daughters 4 and 6 years old. His brother Eynuddin, who was 6 years older than Joinuddin, had two sons, 14 and 16 years old and one daughter, 8 years old. The two brothers each inherited about half an acre of agricultural land, and they split the homestead plot which was 0.40 acre in size. Their sister married many years ago, and she lives in a village outside the union. She has not claimed any of the land and property she is entitled to. When the two brothers lived in a joint household, they cultivated their own land and 4 plots of land totalling 1.25 acres which they held on a sharecropping basis obtained from different persons. With one of these persons their father had sharecropped the same half an acre plot of land for a long period. The other plots the two brothers sharecropped had been acquired recently from various villagers. It was very much due to Eynuddin's efforts that the recent sharecropping contracts had been obtained. By all the villagers Eynuddin is thought of as being the more hardworking and clever of the two brothers. The reason for the split of the joint household was that Eynuddin realized that economically he would be much better off on his own than living in a joint household with his younger brother. Eynuddin managed to get all the land the brothers had sharecropped jointly for himself. Everyone who had sharecropped land to the two brothers when they lived together realized that it was Eynuddin with whom it would be most beneficial to have a good relationship in the future.

The split and the establishment of two households was the beginning of the long and gradual decline of Joinuddin. While his brother immediately after the split cultivated 1.75 acres land (0.50 acres his own and 1.25 acres sharecropped in), Joinuddin was left with only 0.50 acres. Eynuddin was also in possession of a pair of cows for ploughing while Joinuddin only owned a cow and a calf.

The crop from the half acre of land only provided Joinuddin's household with rice for 3–4 months per year. Joinuddin could not get any assistance from his other household members in the work in the field in the peak seasons of the year. What other opportunities did Joinuddin have to earn an income in order to provide his household with food in the remaining months of the year? The most logical alternative would be to ask for employment from peasants who needed wage-labourers. This was not, however, an easy alternative for Joinuddin. Neither his grandfather, father nor he himself had ever worked as a wage-labourer, *kamla,* and Joinuddin had doubts and reservations about being classified as a *kamla* and entering the labour market of the village along with people like Mosum Ali and other landless persons. It would not, however, lower his prestige so much if he worked for his brother. Eynuddin had two grown sons, of whom one was available for work with his father (the other son went to school). It was only in the peak seasons that Eynuddin needed labourers. The first year after the separation of the two households, Joinuddin was in the course of each year employed for about 30 days by his brother. When he did not work on his own or his brother's land, he remained unemployed.

Joinuddin very soon developed a large deficit on his annual budgets. His annual budget, in the years after the split of the joint household, showed a deficit of 1000–1200 Taka per year. Compared to Mosum Ali's yearly deficit of 300–400 Taka, Joinuddin's deficit may seem large for a household possessing half an acre of land. The large deficit accumulated by Joinuddin's household compared to Mosum Ali's household can partly be attributed to the different social and economic backgrounds of the two households. When Joinuddin lived in a joint household with Eynuddin, the consumption profile of the household was very different from that of a landless household. While rice and wheat may account for 80–90 per cent of the expenditure of a landless household, only a third of the expenditure of the joint household of Joinuddin and Eynuddin was accounted for by these items. About a third was spent on other foodstuffs: fish, meat, chillies, vegetables, etc. The last third of the expenditure went to cover various items — schoolbooks for the children, medical expenses, clothes, housing materials, gifts to beggars and the poor people, etc.

It is difficult to cut down on the material standard of living. After Joinuddin established his own household, he managed to reduce the expenditure for food a little bit by eating less fish and substituting wheat for rice for some of the meals, but clothes, medical expenses, gifts to beggars, he still paid. The other reason for the big difference in the deficit of Mosum Ali and Joinuddin is that many methods of earning an income, in cash or kind, and ways of reducing expenditure which were available to Mosum Ali, would be beneath the consideration of Joinuddin. It would be below the dignity of Joinuddin and his *gusti* to let his wife work in other households or send his children to work as permanent servants for richer people or to receive clothes and other gifts from richer people. He would never let any of his household members collect cow dung in order to sell it as fuel. The starvation strategy of not eating rice, or only very little of it for a short period, was unknown to Joinuddin, his wife and children. This strategy had the advantage, though, that it was not visible and public, and therefore could be pursued without loss of prestige.

When Joinuddin and Eynuddin lived in a joint household, they had had a fairly balanced budget over the years. A rough expression of this was that the household had not mortgaged any land in or out. The household had in certain periods taken up loans, normally cash loans or paddy before the *aman* harvest, when their stocks of paddy were depleted. The loans with interest were paid back after the *aman* harvest, and none of the loans accumulated to the extent that land had to be mortgaged. When Joinuddin established his own household, he did not have an established source of credit to turn to. However, he would have had no difficulty in finding persons willing to supply him with as much credit as he needed. All surplus and well-do-to peasants in the area realized that by giving loans to Joinuddin, they would eventually have a good chance of obtaining his half acre of land. Joinuddin knew, however, that it would be a loss of prestige both to himself and his *gusti* if the loans he took resulted in the land he, his father and forefathers, had cultivated, being taken over by someone outside the *gusti.* Joinuddin thus turned to Eynuddin for loans to cover this daily expenses. He started to approach Eynuddin for loans soon after they separated in 1965.

In the first two years after separation from Joinuddin, Eynuddin himself had a very hard time balancing his own budget. In addition to his own household's expenditure, he lent out money and paddy to Joinuddin to a total value of 800–900 Taka every year. Eynuddin cut down on his expenditure and even in some periods had a diet that was as inexpensive as that of Joinuddin's household. Eynuddin realized that the only way to keep Joinuddin's land within the *gusti* was by covering Joinuddin's deficit through giving him loans. He also knew, of course, that living on a low budget at this time in order to finance his brother's loan would enable him to obtain more land in the future.

Joinuddin also took loans from a few villagers. These loans he intended to pay back. When the loan from one of these persons on one occasion had gradually increased to 300 Taka, the person demanded either the money back or an adequate compensation for the loan. Joinuddin turned to Eynuddin and asked for a sum of 500 Taka to cover the various loans. Eynuddin promised he would help him, but said that Joinuddin's own debt to him had now become so large that he wanted to take a plot of 0.25 acres of land as mortgage for the loan. Joinuddin had very soon understood that he would not be able to pay back his debt to his brother, and he had expected that at some stage his brother would demand a piece of his land on a mortgage basis in order to have a collateral for his loan. The mortgage contract Eynuddin made with his brother involved that until the 2500 Taka were repaid by Joinuddin, Eynuddin had the right to cultivate Joinuddin's land. He could cultivate the land by himself or he could sharecrop it out to anyone he chose. Both the brothers realized, however, that there were very small chances that the loan would ever be paid back. Joinuddin knew, however, that if he improved his position, it would be easier to pay up the mortgage to his brother than to a person outside the *gusti.* Joinuddin could probably have received an economically more beneficial mortgage contract from some well-to-do people in the village, but by mortgaging to his brother he had kept the land within the *gusti.* Eynuddin let his brother continue to cultivate the 0.25 plot on a sharecropping basis. Thus not only was the prestige of the *gusti* preserved, but Joinuddin also continued to cultivate his own land, and very few of the villagers knew about the mortgage and Joinuddin's straitened circumstances. No written contract or deed was made, nor were any witnesses called when Eynuddin took the land mortgage. Only the two brothers and a few *gusti* members knew about the transaction. Economically it would have been advantageous for Eynuddin to cultivate the plot himself, since he had less land than he and his sons could cultivate. Eynuddin did Joinuddin a favour by giving him a sharecropping contract. On the other hand, this was also a way for Eynuddin to ensure that Joinuddin would continue to come and ask him for loans and eventually mortgage and sell more land to him. If Joinuddin mortgaged or sold land to other people, Eynuddin would definitely refuse to let his brother continue to sharecrop the land he had mortgaged.

Above we saw that Eynuddin had to manage to raise the 500 Taka so that Joinuddin could clear his debts to the other villagers. It was a problem for Eynuddin to obtain this sum. Normally the loans to Joinuddin had been extended in small amounts, 20 Taka one week, 15 Taxa next week, or 1 *maund* of paddy in one month. Eynuddin raised the 500 Taka by selling one of his two cows. He was promised by a friend of his, whom he often exchanged favours with, that he could borrow one of the friend's cows when he needed it for ploughing.

A comment should be made here on the relationship between the two brothers. Neither of the two brothers consider that the one 'exploits' the other. Eynuddin does not think in the terms of how he, as fast as possible and with as little expense as possible, can impoverish his brother and take over his land. Eynuddin would not use dirty 'tricks' to snatch away the land from his brother even if he could do so successfully. On the contrary, Eynuddin favours and gives priority to his brother on many occasions. When Eynuddin, for example, needs 3 man-days of labour in his fields for weeding, he would rather employ Joinuddin for three days, than hire 3 men for one day, if the work operation is of such a nature that it can be carried out over a longer period. Joinuddin would also receive gifts from his brother, clothes for the children and his wife, meat and chicken occasionally, and support to cover medical expenses, without these gifts being added to the total debt bill. Eynuddin realizes, of course, that by having a 'good' relationship with his brother which shows general concern and support, Joinuddin gains confidence in him and regards him as a 'protector'. Because he expects Eynuddin to give him both economic support and political protection in the future, he chooses his brother as the main source for credit and thereby the man who eventually will take over his land.

Joinuddin interprets his own deteriorating position as being his 'fate' in life. He does not feel cheated or exploited by his brother, since he is the first to be employed when his brother needs wage-labourers and since he receives a good wage. He definitely would have felt exploited if Eynuddin had lent him too little for the mortgage of the land. His reaction to being exploited by his brother would be to turn to other people in the village. He would have no difficulty in getting a higher rate from these persons than from his brother. They would even be in a position to raise 2500 Taka quickly so that Joinuddin could return the loan to his brother and in this way free his land from the mortgage should he change his mind about the relationship to his brother.

However, since there is a good relationship, conducted on a basis of reciprocity, it is unlikely that such a transaction would take place. The relationship between the two brothers is of a complicated and contradictory nature, though. The person Joinuddin depends upon for general support is also the person who gradually buys up his land. Many poor peasants have found that the general support given in such a creditor-debtor relationship only lasts as long as the richer person has something to gain from the weaker part. The 'turn-down' and denial of support to a client who has nothing to offer happens more often, however, if the client is not a close relative or a *gusti* member.

Although Joinuddin had, by the mortgage of the 0.25 acre of plot land, cleared up all his debt to the villagers and to the family of his wife, his economic position deteriorated even further. Now he only received the crops from 0.25 acre of his own land and half of the crops of 0.25 acres of the plot he sharecropped. Shortly after the mortgage, his debts to his brother started to accumulate again.

Eynuddin's economic position had gradually become better. A

rich peasant in a neighbouring village had given him a 0.50 acre plot for sharecropping, and from his wife's family, who lived in the neighbouring village, he also managed to get a short-term sharecropping contract. It was thus easier for him to finance his brother's debts. After a couple of years the debts had reached 2000 Taka, and this time Eynuddin insisted on purchasing the 0.25 acre plot. In addition to the 2000 Taka, Eynuddin promised that he would give Joinuddin 1500 Taka in instalments over a couple of years either in cash or in paddy. Thus Joinuddin would have received about 6000 Taka over a 5–6 year period for half of his original 0.50 acre of land. By a similar gradual loan and mortgage to a non-related rich peasant, he probably could have obtained 8000–9000 Taka, he figured.

Joinuddin managed to stretch the 1500 Taka to cover his deficit for a couple of years. Joinuddin realized that if he did not cut his expenses, he could be a landless man within another 5 years. He adopted some of the strategies of Mosum Ali and the landless, the most important one being that he entered the labour market. He was careful about the persons he approached to ask for employment, since he did not want to work for people whom he previously had considered to have similar or inferior status to him and his brother in the village. In the years after the sale of his 0.25 acre plot, he was employed for 80–90 days per year. In addition, he sent his son, when he reached the age of 12 years, to work as a seasonal servant in the home of a rich person in the neighbouring village for whom also Joinuddin worked in the peak season. Joinuddin also cut down on his expenses for food and clothes. His annual budget started to look more like that of Mosum Ali, although he would refrain from adopting many of the earning and saving techniques used by Mosum Ali's household. He would not let his wife work for others, except in his brother's household; he still would not send his daughters away to work as domestic servants, and he would not let any of his household members collect cow dung and sell it as fuel to others. He would also have felt it degrading if the rich *samaj* leaders had started to consider him eligible for charity-gifts from the *samaj* at the *Eid* festival.

Joinuddin had expected to incur great expenditure in connection with the marriages of his two daughters, and he turned to his brother to ask for loans. Eynuddin realized, however, that as the richer brother he had certain obligations towards his brother in this situation. A loan to cover expenses for a dowry and the marriage ceremony is a different type of loan from one for covering daily consumer needs. It would be more difficult to demand repayment of this type of loan. Therefore Eynuddin covered most of the expenses, which altogether amounted to 500 Taka, as a gift for the marriage of the eldest daughter of Joinuddin. The remaining money Joinuddin financed by loans from others, more distant *gusti* people and from the family of his wife. Eynuddin also gave substantial support to Joinuddin's second daughter, who married a few years afterwards. The large contribution from Eynuddin earned him much goodwill in the *gusti* and in the village and of course from his brother. Thus Joinuddin was spared a large amount of money which he otherwise could only have raised by mortgaging out a part of his last 0.25 acre plot of land.

With his daughters married off, his son working as a seasonal labourer and earning a small monthly income which he gave to his father, some of the expenses of the household were reduced. During this period his wife has given birth to another boy and girl who were 'unproductive' household members. Joinuddin still took regular loans from his brother, but the amount was less. The deficit on his yearly budget had been reduced to 500–600 Taka.

For some time Joinuddin had hoped to receive a 0.30 acre plot on a sharecropping basis from Halim Kahn, one of the richest landlords in the whole union. (The story of Halim Kahn is narrated in case 4.) His son worked for Halim Kahn as a seasonal labourer, and Joinuddin himself worked for him occasionally. Halim Kahn regularly employed many people to work on his estimated 30 acres of land. A condition, not however explicitly stated, for getting the land on a sharecropping basis was that Joinuddin would change over to Halim Kahn as a source of credit to cover his deficit. Halim Kahn also promised Joinuddin and his sons employment on his land. Joinuddin was in a dilemma as he realized that he would receive a higher price for the land, which he eventually would have to mortgage and sell to Halim Kahn. In addition, he and his sons could be employed for more days per year on Halim Kahn's land than on his brother's land, and the possibility of obtaining a 0.30

acre plot on a sharecropping basis was also tempting. Joinuddin grasped that many of these immediate benefits might be withdrawn as soon as he had sold the rest of his land to Halim Kahn. Joinuddin had observed that one of the techniques Halim Kahn used to obtain land gradually from poor people was to offer them employment, land on a sharecropping basis, and political protection in the period during which they established debt relationships to Halim Kahn. Joinuddin therefore chose to continue the relationship with his brother.

At present, 15 years after the separation, Joinuddin owns a 0.10 acre plot of agricultural land. Gradually he has mortgaged and sold his agricultural land except for this plot. He has also sold half of his homestead plot to his brother. Joinuddin has also sold his cattle and his iron-sheet roof. Since he has no cattle to plough his land, he has sharecropped out his 0.10 acre plot to his brother, who owns the adjacent plot. Sometimes when he is employed by his brother, Joinuddin finds himself in the paradoxical situation that he works as a wage-labourer on his own land, which he has leased out on a sharecropping basis.

Thus the decline of Joinuddin has been gradual. The 0.10 acre plot he still possesses can be sold for about 3000 Taka. Such a sum would cover Joinuddin's deficit for about 5 years. This means that the gradual mortgage and sale of 0.50 acre of land will have covered the deficit of Joinuddin's budget for about 20 years. Joinuddin, himself, in all probability, will not suffer and have to turn to begging when, as an old man, he has sold all his land. Because he has contributed to keeping the land within the *gusti,* Eynuddin and his sons are expected to give him and his wife some support when they are old.

It is not difficult to predict what will happen to Joinuddin when he gets old. He will have difficulties in obtaining employment and his wage will be reduced. His sons will establish their own households when they are married and have enough problems in providing a livelihood for their own families; only occasionally will they be able to give substantial support to their parents.

At present there is a striking difference in the standard of living between the households of Joinuddin and Eynuddin. Their two houses are situated next to each other. Eynuddin possesses several houses, which are well kept and all have iron-sheet roofs. Joinuddin's house is small and the bamboo mat walls are torn and have not been changed for years. Also the homestead plots are different. One is big and clean and contains separate houses for the kithcen and the animals. The other homestead plot is small, with an open kitchen and inexpensive clay-pottery.

Joinuddin and Eynuddin started off, from an economic point of view, on an equal basis. Their sons, when they take over the property from their fathers, will belong to different 'classes', Joinuddin's sons being landless wage-labourers, Eynuddin's sons being landowners.

Before describing the debt relations Eynuddin is involved in, a general discussion of economic strategies of households owning agricultural land but with deficits will be presented.

The other households owning agricultural land but with deficit budgets in Bhaimara

In our survey of all the households in Bhaimara we wanted to find out the extent of the mortgage and sale of land between brothers and *gusti* members. Table 4.2 gives information on the agricultural land the households in Bhaimara had mortgaged (in 1980).

The table shows that 19 households mortgaged land: 9 households in the 'poor' category mortgaged land (41 per cent of the households in that category); 6 'small category' households (75 per cent) and 4 'middle category' households (50 per cent) also mortgaged land. Altogether 32 plots were mortgaged. Only one plot was mortgaged between brothers, but 12 were mortgaged between households belonging to the same *gusti.* Although we do not possess exact information on when the plots were mortgaged, the great majority of the plots were mortgaged during the last 5 years. It is also clear that not all the mortgages are the result of a long credit relationship which accumulated and ended in mortgage. Some of the mortgages, particularly among the 'small and middle' category peasants are methods for raising a large sum of money quickly for a specific purpose. The debt will later be repaid, and the land will be released.

Table 4.3 gives information on the households that have sold land over a period of 20 years. Thus, most of the households that sold land many years ago had a very different composition from what they have today and could have belonged to a different landowning category. (The same households could also have purchased land during this period.) Therefore, for our purpose the table is only of interest for obtaining information on the relationship between the seller and the purchaser of land.

The table shows that 35 households report that they have sold land. Altogether 15 acres of land have been sold, comprising 64 plots. Fifteen plots (24 per cent) were sold between brothers and 18 plots (29 per cent) between households belonging to the same *gusti*. This implies that more than half the plots were sold between households that belonged to the same paternal lineage. Seventeen plots (27 per cent) were sold to households in the village that were not members of the same *gusti*. Only 13 plots (21 per cent) were sold to households living outside the village.

Table 4.2. Households having Mortgaged Land in Bhaimara.[3]

		Acres mortgaged			Relation to mortgagee			
Group[4]	No. of households mortgaging land	Size	Plots	Average size of mortgage per household	brother	gusti	villager	nonvillager
Landless	0	0	0	0				
Poor	9	2.26	14	0.25		3	7	4
Small	6	2.31	11	0.39		5	2	4
Middle	4	2.88	7	0.72	1	4	1	1
Rich	0	0	0	0				
Total	19	7.45	32		1	12	10	9

What these figures about mortgage and sale of land tell, is that in Bhaimara the closest relatives, brothers and *gusti* members, are the most important sources of credit. The reason for the development of credit relationships between close kin was mentioned above. There is a certain ignominy involved when a *gusti* member, because of poverty, sells his land to 'outsiders'. It can reveal that the material resources in the *gusti* are small, or that there is little unity and solidarity among the households in the *gusti.* Lack of these assets in a *gusti* has negative effects for the prestige *(izzat)* of all the households in the *gusti.* However, in the case of Joinuddin and Eynuddin, each of them will consider the economic advantages and disadvantages of their relationship. The *izzat* of their patrilineage will only be a part of their considerations. We noticed in their case that Joinuddin reckoned that he could have received a 30–40 per cent higher price for his land if he had sold it to the highest bidder on the open market. It is generally accepted that land is sold at a lower price between relatives. A sale well below the accepted market rate confers the advantage we saw Joinuddin enjoyed: a general economic, social and political support from his brother. It would have been an interesting task to estimate the costs and benefits of the relationship Joinuddin had with his brother over the years and compare it to what open market transactions would have given him. With all the different goods and services, employment and sharecropping contracts involved in the relationships, this would be an impossible task. Neither Joinuddin nor Eynuddin would have the detailed knowledge of the 'balance of their accounts', to assist us in such an endeavour.

With these conditions favouring transfer of land within the *gusti,* how can it then be explained that a fairly large amount of sale and mortgage of land takes place outside the *gusti?* Some main reasons for this have already been mentioned above. All the other members of the *gusti* could be so poor that they could not afford to finance the deficit of one of their relatives. It could also happen that none of them are able to supply regular credit to any of the others. It could also be that the brothers or the *gusti* members do not have a friendly relationship, and therefore will not deal with each other. It is not unusual for there to be a very poor relationship between some brothers due, for example, to disagreements about the division of the inheritance property. When the relationship between a more

Table 4.3. Households that have Sold Land in Bhamaira.

Group	No. of households	No. of acres sold in acre	plots	Relationship between seller and buyer of land				
				Brother	Gusti member	Villager	Non-villager	Total no. of plots
Landless	8	2.5	19	6	8	3	2	19
Poor	15	7.9	23	9	6	5	3	23
Small	6	1.0	7			5	2	7
Middle	6	3.7	15		4	4	6	14
Rich								
Total	35	15	64	15	18	17	13	63
Missing information	1							
	64							

well-to-do brother and a poorer one is bad, it is very easy for an unrelated rich peasant to exploit this situation and offer the poor brother better credit terms than the brother will.

Characteristically, when a credit relationship that will eventually end in a sale of land develops between a peasant with a surplus and one with a deficit, both parties have an interest in establishing a broader type of relation than the purely credit relationship. The peasant who intends gradually to sell his land realizes that he possesses such a scarce and valuable asset, which many well-to-do and rich people will compete to obtain, that he can demand certain favours in addition to the money he receives. Which favours he can demand depend on the value of his land and on his own political and economic position in the village society. Employment for household members, sharecropping contracts, political protection are favours which he can ask for when he is in the process of selling his land. For his part, the well-to-do man who is supplying credit can demand that the poor household that receives credit shall support him 'politically' and take his side in issues and cases which are brought up in the village. This type of relationship approaches and resembles in several aspects the relationship which ideally should exist between households of the same patrilineage *(gusti)*. Both parties in the relationship have the opportunity to raise demands and expect support in many spheres of life. Thus the credit relationship develops into a broader type of *patron-client* relationship. It is, however, the flow of credit which is the core of and the 'raison-d'être' for the relationship.

This type of credit relationship stands out in great contrast to the single-purpose traditional 'moneylender' and also 'pawnbroker' relationship. Thirty years ago there were many rich moneylenders and pawnbrokers operating in the neighbourhood of Bhaimara. Almost all these moneylenders and pawnbrokers were Hindus. In Bhaimara itself, there has been no Hindu population for the last 60–70 years, but for the population of Bhaimara the moneylenders and pawnbrokers were in the past a main source for large sums of credit. At present there are a couple of traditional Hindu moneylenders operating within an area as large as two unions. Very few of the villagers of Bhaimara have recently gone to them for loans. These moneylenders, like the former Hindu moneylenders, are purely economically oriented. They demand a higher rate of interest and a collateral for all loans. They have no other connections or relations with the households they supply credit to.

Above two very different ways of mobilizing credit have been described, the one type all-embracing, the other as business-like and as impersonal as a bank relation. In practice many of the credit relationships which are established between rich and poor in a village setting are a more intermediate type of relation in terms of rights and obligations in the relationship. It is obviously in the interest of a poor man to obtain sharecropping rights, political protection and employment from the more well-tó-do man who supplies him with credit. If the poor man can possibly turn to many people for credit, he has a chance of negotiating better conditions for the gradual sale of his land. In many cases, however, it is not possible for a poor man to choose between persons who will supply him with credit. If a poor man, for one reason or another, is considered to be in the 'domain' of a specific well-to-do person, the other potential suppliers of credit will not compete with this man and offer better credit terms. In such a situation, which is quite normal, the supplier of credit often takes advantage of his position and will not give sharecropping rights and employment possibilities in the slack seasons of the year. The well-to-do supplier of credit, if he has 'control' over his client and the other persons who have the ability and the willingness to be suppliers of credit, can then impose strict conditions on his credit. Already after the loan has reached only a few hundred Taka, he can demand a piece of land on mortgage terms. If the supplier is a rich and powerful man whom none of the other suppliers of credit wants to displease, he can even cheat the poor landowner and take his land without having paid the proper price for it.

There are two main types of mortgage practised in Bhaimara and in the surrounding areas. The most common type is when the supplier of credit takes over the *usufruct* rights of the land which is the security for his loan. The supplier of credit has thus, within certain limitations, the right to use or rent out the land to anyone he likes. It is very seldom that people who borrow money for consumption purposes are able to return the loan and release their land from the mortgage. Normally the sum of the loan which is paid to the landowner is one-third of the market value of the plot of land. This type of mortgage is almost always the first step towards selling the land. Since so much fear is connected with the sale and loss of land, many people often act irrationally in relation to their land property. It was found in several cases that households owning 1 to 2 acres of land had mortgaged all their land. Instead of mortgaging one plot and then selling the plot when the debts continued to accumulate, the households had, for fear of losing their land permanently, mortgaged out all their plots. In a few particular cases this had additional disadvantages in that the grown-up male persons who could work on the land became unemployed when the land was mortgaged to other households.

As regards consumption loans leading towards a mortgage, we did not find the creditor demanding interest on all the small loans which accumulated gradually. Rather than insisting on interest on the petty loans, he could at an early stage insist on taking the plot on mortgage terms. Similarly, as a compensation for not having taken any interest, he would ask to purchase the plot for a lower price than the market value. If the poor landowner at that stage should attempt to sell his plot for a higher price on the open market, the creditor would be certain to demand sufficient compensation for the loans he had made over the years. For loans for which there is a declared intention to pay back within a stipulated period, for instance the seasonal loans of rice before harvest, there is a very high rate of interest.

The other type of mortgage is called *khai-kalashi,* and this system of mortgage resembles more a rental system for agricultural land. A sum of money is paid to the landowner. This sum of money can be paid in one instalment or over a longer period. The security for the money is the right to cultivate the land and harvest the crops. The maximum period for which the land can be cultivated is spelled out in the contract. The duration of a normal *khai-kalashi* contract will vary between 5 and 10 years. For each year the loan is not repaid a deduction of part of the loan is made, since the creditor has used the land. For every year in a 5-year contract 20% is deducted and for every year in a 10-year contract, 10% is deducted. For a *khai-kalashi* contract which lasts for 10 years it is normal in the area of Bhaimara to borrow 1000 Taka for a plot of land which has a market value of about 10,000 Taka (1980 prices). 100 Taka will be deducted every year, and if the loan has not been repaid earlier, after 10 years the land is returned to the owner. If money can be raised to return the land after 3 years, 700 Taka is repaid and the land is taken back by the former owner. If the *khai-kalashi* contract is between a well-to-do and a poor person, the rich man can, if he is powerful, make efforts to prevent the poor man repaying the loan, in order to be able to cultivate the land as long as possible.

All poor people prefer this type of loan as they are certain to get their land returned. However, in Bhaimara and the neighbouring villages this type of mortgage was not common. This type of mortgage contract seemed to occur in circumstances when well-to-do people needed to help each other with a loan for a particular purpose. Seldom did the mortgage of the land last longer than a few years. Poor people would be able to make such a mortgage contract if they had an especially good relationship with their creditor, or if the creditor realized that he would have little chance of acquiring the land on the normal mortgage terms. In a few cases in the neighbouring villages of Bhaimara it was found that a *khai-kalashi* mortgage had been transformed to a 'normal' type of mortgage. This had happened when the landowner had to take up new loans from the same creditor who possessed his land on *khai-kalashi* terms. Among the 32 plots which the households of Bhaimara had mortgaged (see Table 4.2), 4 plots were mortgaged on *khai-kalashi* terms.

In most cases of either type of mortgage no deed or written agreement was made between the creditor and debtor. Only when the mortgage relationship took place between a rich man and a poor man who had no kinship relation to each other and the rich man wanted to have a document, was a document set up. Poor people were afraid of having their mortgaged land registered in a Government Registry Office, as registry was often considered identical with sale. For mortgaged land which had been registered only half of the value of the land had normally been paid.

Mortgage and sale of land are dealt with, to a greater or lesser extent, in all the village monographs from rural Bangladesh. To what degree are the kinds of mortgage, as we found them practised in Bhaimara, representative of other areas? The *khai-kalashi* system we found in Bhaimara is reported from many areas. Particularly

Arens and Van Beurden (Kushtia district)[5] and Van Schendel (Bogra district)[6] give detailed descriptions of the rights and obligations of the landowner and creditor which resemble the mortgage system we described above.

From Bogra, Kirsten Westergaard reports on a *khai-kalashi* system which differs from what we found in Bhaimara. Poor households, with a small surplus, could invest their money by obtaining a *khai-kalashi* contract from a more well-to-do person.[7] Ann-Lisbet Arn reports of a mortgage system *(girbi)* in a village of Mymensingh, which shares some features with the system reported by Westergaard:[8]

> This system functions as a 'banking-system' for landowners who give out land on *girbi* when they need money for other expenditures, mainly to buy land, or for consumption needs during a difficult period (sickness for example) or to pay for the higher education of a son.
>
> The general trend within this kind of land transaction is that the richer and middle peasants give out more land on *girbi,* and the small, poor and landless peasants take in more land. For these last categories the *girbi* system is one way of acquiring land to cultivate under circumstances where land for sale is rather scarce and expensive. When land is for sale they can seldom compete with the richer peasants who will give out some of their lands on *girbi* in order to be able to buy.

Arn notes that although poor and landless peasants are technically the moneylenders in this type of mortgage, they are unable to charge interest and the land is returned within 12 years, though it is usually redeemed earlier. For the great majority of households in Bhaimara this way of obtaining land is beyond their means.

From Goborgari in the district of Rangpur, Van Schendel reports a phenomenon concerning the practice of mortgage, which we did not observe in Bhaimara:

> It would appear that mortgage *not* leading to sale is a mechanism of far greater weight than is usually realized. Our data on mortgage in Goborgari show that land is sometimes kept in mortgage for a generation or longer without legal transfer.

The only circumstance in which we found that the mortgagee did not make any efforts to take over the ownership rights of land occurred when he had obtained a registration document of the mortgaged plot. Otherwise mortgage was only regarded as a necessary step towards obtaining full ownership rights. We have shown that very few peasants were in a position to go in for a direct purchase of a plot of land. The only way they could obtain land was through the cumbersome extension of credit and piecemeal mortgaging. This information on the role of mortgage as a major way of eventually transferring ownership rights of land is confirmed by other studies: G.D. Wood[9] reports this as a main transfer mechanism from the district of Comilla, and B.K. Jahangir[10] from Dhaka District.

Case 3. The economic strategies of a household with a small surplus

Already much has been said about the economic background of Eynuddin and some of the loans he has both taken and given out. The household of Eynuddin is one of about ten households in Bhaimara which has a surplus on its budget. This means that the household has the possibility of investing a small amount of money for productive purposes.

The first 6–7 years after Eynuddin and Joinuddin established separate households, Eynuddin's standard of living was almost as low as that of his brother. His only 'investment' in this period was the loans he gave to his brother, which eventually led to purchase of some of his brother's land. In order to be able to make this investment, he had reduced the expenses for his own household to a minimum. In some periods he even had to take up loans to be able to continue to cover his brother's deficit.

For a couple of years in the period after separation, the crops on Eynuddin's plots partly failed, and it was under these circumstances he had to take up loans. Two months before the *aman* harvest he went to a rich man and asked for a loan of 5 *maunds* of paddy. This amount of paddy (unhusked rice) would, together with some wheat he could purchase gradually, carry his family through to the harvest. After the harvest Eynuddin would return the 5 *maunds* of paddy from his own crops. In addition he would have to pay, in 1980 prices, 100 Taka for each *maund* as interest for the loan. The paddy and the money had to be returned shortly after the *aman* harvest. It is difficult to estimate the exact rate of interest on such a loan, since the price of paddy 2 months before the *aman* harvest is considerably higher than right after the *aman* harvest. (In 1980 prices a *maund* of paddy would cost 80–90 Taka after harvest, and before the harvest the price can vary from 130–160 Taka per *maund.)* For this particular loan, however, we calculated that the rate of interest would be 175 per cent per annum. Eynuddin realized that if there was anything that would drain his resources, it was this type of loan. The most secure way to avoid such loans was to make the paddy from the *aus* season last longer by consuming less of it. In order to pay back the 500 Taka interest, he mobilized his best sources of credit: the brother of his wife and a *'dost'* friend (a man he had a particularly close and supportive relationship with). He took 250 Taka from each of them. Since both the suppliers of credit were closely linked to him, he received the loans on easy terms. Both loans were considered as 'gift' loans, and there was no interest on the loans nor any fixed period within which they should be repaid.

In addition to these major loans Eynuddin, in the 6–7 years after separation from his brother, also gave and took some small loans, which were all settled. The only major credit relationship he established was with his brother. The situation changed, however, when Eynuddin's son finished his schooling and after training got a job in the police department in Dhaka as a police constable. Every month his son was able to send home several hundred Taka to his father. The son would not marry till his late twenties, and this would give him 5–6 years with income which he did not have to spend on a wife and children.

With the steady inflow of cash from his son, Eynuddin's household had a considerable surplus on their budget. More money was spent on consumption goods, and there were no difficulties in catering for the credit needs of Joinuddin. People realized that Eynuddin's situation had changed, and more people approached him for loans and gifts. Distant relatives came on visits and spent many days in his home, being freely provided with food. Even with these new expenses Eynuddin had a surplus. In addition to giving regular loans to his brother, Eynuddin started to give loans to two other peasants with deficit budgets. The loans to one of the peasants, a distant member of Eynuddin's *gusti,* accumulated very fast, and after a 2-year period, Eynuddin insisted on taking a plot of 0.20 acres on a mortgage basis as a security for the loan, which had reached 1500 Taka. Eynuddin started to cultivate the plot himself and continued to supply the man with credit.

Eynuddin also gave regular loans to a villager, Tomser Ali, who occasionally worked for him. After a 2-year period his debt had accumulated to 900 Taka, and Eynuddin asked for a 0.12 acre plot on a mortgage basis. Tomser Ali belonged to a small and poor *gusti,* and there was no one there who had sufficient surplus to cover his deficit. Tomser Ali was in a dilemma, however. He realized that he had small chances of obtaining valuable favours from Eynuddin in the future. In the household of Eynuddin there were several male members who worked in the fields on their land and only in the peak season, when there were no difficulties in getting employment, would Eynuddin ask people to work for him. Halim Kahn, the rich landlord in the area (case 4 below), was well aware of the advantages he had vis-à-vis Eynuddin in acquiring land. When he came to hear of Tomser Ali's debt to Eynuddin, he told Tomser Ali that he and his sons could be employed on his land in the slack seasons if he mortgaged the land to him instead. Halim Kahn also argued convincingly that he would be able to give Tomser Ali better political protection and more general support than Eynuddin would. Tomser Ali accepted the offer, and received 900 Taka from Halim Kahn to cover his debt to Eynuddin. Eynuddin also demanded another 150 Taka, money which was not interest but money he had given as gifts and small loans which had not been included in the sum of 900 Taka. Tomser Ali refused to pay this sum. The local court was summoned and decided that Tomser Ali should pay 50 Taka. Without the support of Halim Kahn in the court, Tomser Ali definitely would have had to pay more money. The relationship between Halim Kahn and Tomser Ali on the one side and Eynuddin on the other deteriorated and there were, as from then, no economic transactions between them.

With the sum of money returned from Tomser Ali, Eynuddin was in an even better position to offer loans, and soon he found himself supplying regular credit to two other deficit peasants. Eynuddin's economic position and his prestige improved considerably after his son was employed. The other well-to-do villagers and influential peasants in the neighbouring villages realized that the position of Eynuddin's household would only become stronger in the future. A well-to-do absentee landlord in a neighbouring village gave Eynuddin a 0.40 acre plot on a sharecropping basis, and later he also received two 0.30 acre plots from an absentee landlord in Bhaimara and from a resident landlord in the neighbouring village. There are many reasons for people to establish good relationships with Eynuddin through sharecropping contracts. One reason could be that the landowners who let out the land would be interested in marrying off one of their daughters to Eynuddin's son, the police constable.

During the period 1972–1980, Eynuddin was able to purchase another 0.60 acres of land apart from the land he bought from his brother. In addition by 1980 he had acquired on a mortgage basis from two different poor peasants two plots of land of about 0.25 acre each which he cultivates himself. Thus in 1980 Eynuddin owns 2 acres of land, is mortgagee for one acre, and sharecrops in 2½ acres of land. He is thus cultivating 5½ acres of land. With 3 sons to help in the field and a seasonal labourer Eynuddin uses his labour force almost optimally. He estimates that he and his sons would be able to cultivate about 7 acres, given that they hire a few extra labourers in the peak seasons. From 1978 Eynuddin has had four cattle and two ploughs, which has meant that he could have two plough-teams in operation at the same time.

One investment alternative not yet mentioned for Eynuddin concerns investment in intensive production of the land he already owns. To what extent does he use his surplus to purchase fertilizers and insecticides and grow profitable crops? In chapter 2 of this study we emphasized that modern inputs must be used carefully and coordinated if an increased yield per unit of land is to be achieved. Eynuddin does not own any land under the deep-tubewell scheme established in Bhaimara. Therefore the possibility of increasing the yield of his land is limited. During the dry season he cultivates tobacco and purchases the necessary inputs for this crop. It is very clear, however, that his investment is directed towards obtaining more land.

During the last 5 years Eynuddin's expenses have increased. With an improved economic situation, many people — from beggars to relatives — have turned to him for help. Some of the loans he gives out he can later benefit substantially from by obtaining land on mortgage. Some loans and gifts cannot be considered as profitable investments from an economic point of view. A peasant with a clear surplus on his budget will be confronted with various types of demands for material support which it is difficult to escape: gifts to the *Eid* festival, gifts to poor relatives and *samaj* members, gifts to beggars, donations to the villagers, the school, the *madrasa* school, etc. If the villagers consider a well-to-do person is trying to escape what would be considered his share of such 'public' obligations, or if he underpays his labourers, he will be labelled *'kripon',* which means he is a stingy person.

There are thus many *redistributive* mechanisms in the rural areas. Eynuddin and people in his position are often caught in a dilemma: on the one hand they want to minimize expenditure and use their surplus productively in giving out loans and thereby investing in land, on the other hand they have a need to live up to expectations about supporting 'good' causes and poor persons. They want the esteem and influence which they can derive from being 'patrons' in the community, and they fear being labelled *'kripon'.*

Five years ago Eynuddin also incurred a great expense. He married off his daughter to the son of a well-to-do peasant in a village some miles away from Bhaimara. The father of the bridegroom owns 8 acres of land. Eynuddin paid a substantial dowry and paid the cost of the wedding arrangements. Altogether the expenses amounted to 5000 Taka. In order to raise the money Eynuddin sold one of his best cows and mortgaged a plot of 0.20 acre of land to a rich peasant with whom he had a good relationship. There was a clear understanding between Eynuddin and the rich peasant that Eynuddin would return the 2000 Taka loan he received from the mortgage of the plot when he had accumulated a surplus again. For a period Eynuddin was thus in the position that he was both mortgagor and mortgagee at the same time.

Half a year prior to the wedding of his daughter, Eynuddin managed to get a loan of 1000 Taka from a Government bank in Manikganj. He offered one of his plots of land as a security against the loan. He continues, however, to cultivate the land and use all the crops from it as previously. The interest rate on the loan is only 7 per cent.

At present, in 1980, the household of Eynuddin has 13 members. Two of his sons (one is the police constable) have married and have small children. Eynuddin received several thousand Takas when his son, the police constable, married, and he also established ties with the influential family of his daughter-in-law. Eynuddin and his wife have three unmarried children — one daughter and two sons. The police constable sends several hundred Taka to the household every month. His wife and children are living in a separate, well-equipped house in the homestead yard of his father. All the household members eat from the same 'kitchen', and together they constitute one economic unit.

What is likely to happen to Eynuddin's household in the next 20 years? To-day Eynuddin is 50 years old. The police constable, living most of the year in Dhaka, needs someone to look after his family. His father and brothers work in the fields and provide food for the whole household. The household as a whole benefits from the money the police constable sends. There is a good chance that the household in the next 10 years can increase their landholdings by another 1–2 acres. The amount of land that will be bought will depend to a large degree on how much the police constable earns. It will also depend on expenditure the household will incur on costly events like marriages and sickness, and it will depend on the general consumption pattern the household will adopt. Another factor influencing the ability to purchase land will be the political and social status the household will enjoy in the village. If Eynuddin soon starts to be regarded as one of the *matbars* (a local judge who participates in the local courts), he has a better chance of lending against a mortgage and buying up land. Clever management of economic and social resources will thus be a decisive factor for the amount of land the household will acquire.

It could well happen that the extended household with several nuclear families will continue to exist for another 10–15 years. The situation would have been different, however, if there had been many sons with separate families living in the same homestead compound and working on the same land. Then the possibilities for disagreements on the division of labour and products would increase. Under no circumstances will Eynuddin and his wife suffer in their old age. In the event of a splitting of the household they will live with one of their sons. When the land is divided between the sons, a separate plot will be set aside to cover the needs of the old couple.

Eynuddin for his part will, however, make every effort to keep the family united as long as he is alive. He has at his disposal an important and effective apparatus of sanctions, since he controls the land the household possesses.

Some general features of the economic strategies of households with a small surplus

Of the 62 households in Bhaimara we noted that about 10 households are in the situation of Eynuddin with sufficient surplus on their budgets to invest in productive ventures. Only 3–4 of these ten households are in the same promising situation as Eynuddin in having a son with a satisfactory and regular income from employment in the urban area.

The main criteria for delineating this group of peasants with a surplus are that they are mortgagees and/or that they have purchased land since their households were established. Being a mortgagee or a purchaser of land is a good indication that the household has extra money left over to spend after the basic needs are catered for. The household may have taken up loans, but the total sum of incomes in cash and in kind is large enough to invest in land. Given such criteria, the households in the surplus group may well fall in different categories as regards amount of land (Table 1.2). Some households with 2.5 acres of land and a relatively high standard of living are not included in the surplus group if the households are in an overall deficit budget situation and in the process of selling their land. Households with only one acre of land but with relatively large incomes (from wages of the household members) and lower consumption can be in the process of acquiring more land and are therefore included in the surplus group. With these criteria for delimiting the households with a surplus, some households may belong to this group only in certain phases of their life cycle, when there are many income-earning and net-producing members of the household. On the other hand, the few households with a balanced budget or some households with a small deficit may in a certain phase of their life cycle acquire a surplus.

In accordance with the information we presented in chapter 1, Joinuddin and Eynuddin should each be representative, in terms of size of landholding and in terms of deficit and surplus 'budgets', of millions of peasants in the rural areas. We believe that the opportunity situation we have outlined in detail for each of them shares many common features with most deficit and 'small surplus' peasants, and that their credit relationships are typical and found all over Bangladesh.

On the basis of the description of the relationship between Joinuddin and Eynuddin, it should be clear that there hardly can be a development of 'class enmity' between the two brothers, although Eynuddin from a Marxist point of view 'exploits' his brother in major and different ways. The pattern of social organization which develops on the basis of millions of relationships similar to those described in cases 2 and 3 is more an encompassing, many-stranded *patron-client* relationship between peasants. We shall also see in cases 4 and 5 that the more well-to-do peasants become patrons to more clients than we saw Eynuddin was. Even Marxist scholars will readily concede that patron-client relationships are a major organizational feature of the rural areas. They would maintain that Marxist class analysis does not require that the objective conditions of exploitation will always involve a corresponding subjective awareness. G.D. Wood states: 'Vertical solidarities of the patron-client type become the form of class relations under the conditions of agrarian underdevelopment in Bangladesh.'[11] In chapter 9, section 3, we shall discuss some of the factors which hinder the development of collective class consciousness and thereby also collective action based on it.

A question we raised in chapter 2 concerned the incentives for effective mobilization of labour in agricultural activities. The story of Joinuddin and Eynuddin can throw some light on this issue. As long as the client (Joinuddin) operates in a *'protected labour market'* where he has priority of employment on a wage-labour basis, his input of labour will be affected. We heard many bitter complaints about lack of effort by employees from landowners who felt obliged to hire relatives or specific clients for weeding, ploughing and harvesting. The consequence of not being able to obtain the best man on the free market was that they could not afford to pay for the sixth round of ploughing and the third round of weeding. An aggregate effect of this is naturally that production becomes less than it could have been with a 'free labour market'.

Another general and significant feature which emerges from the case of Eynuddin is the redistributive system we indicated. It would be of great interest to have quantitative evidence as to the extent of this system. This is of course very difficult to obtain, and we do not know of any study that has attempted to assess the importance and the percentage of a given population which survives owing to petty gifts, 'charitable' employment opportunities, begging, etc. This system obviously has a 'levelling' effect on the polarization process, and should it collapse, the consequences would be dramatic for the group concerned, i.e., the poorest of the poor.

Rich peasants in and around Bhaimara

There are only three households in Bhaimara possessing more than 5 acres of agricultural land each. One household lives in Bhaimara. The second household lives in Dhaka, while the wife and children of the third household live in Bhaimara. The husband works in an urban area. The male heads of the second and third households derive substantial incomes from several sources. Both have good Government jobs with excellent opportunities for earning extra income in connection with their jobs, and both of them have also established small businesses in urban areas. In addition to this, their children are getting university education. Some aspects of the credit relationship and investment strategy of one of these two men will be dealt with in case 5. Within the boundaries of Bhaimara there are no households which are very rich. On the border of Bhaimara, however, lives Halim Khan. He is, as we noted earlier, one of the four most well-to-do peasant in the whole union. Halim Khan is counted as a member of the neighbouring village, but he belongs to the *samaj* (village association) of Bhaimara. Halim Khan is thus very much present economically and politically in the village affairs of Bhaimara. His credit relationships and investment policies distinguish him in some respects from the 'small surplus' peasant discussed in case 3 and from the two absentee landowners in Bhaimara, mentioned above.

Case 4. The economic strategies of a rich peasant

Halim Khan was the only child of his father's first marriage. His half-brothers and half-sisters are all 10–20 years younger than he. His father had worked as an assistant in the *Tahsildar's office,* an office which deals with registration and recording of land and tax-collection. Halim Khan was taught this work by his father, and when he was grown-up, in the 1930s, he was also employed at the *Tahsildar's* office. One of his duties was to collect taxes from the peasants in the area.

His father owned 5 acres of land at his death. Although the intention was that all the children should share the property according to the traditional rules, Halim Khan took all the land away from his step-mother and younger half-brothers and half-sisters. He registered all the land in his own name and established a separate household after his father's death leaving his step-mother and her children landless except for a household plot. Already from the time of establishment of his own household, Halim Khan had a considerable surplus on his 'budget'. Because of his work in the Tahsildar's office he had detailed knowledge of the 'status' of the different plots of land in the area. He knew which plots of land possessed or lacked the proper documentation papers and tax receipts. This information he used to his own advantage, and through coercion he acquired land belonging to poor and powerless peasants who lacked the necessary documents. When the Hindus left East Pakistan after the Partition in 1947, he also managed to buy parts of their land at a very low price. In 1960, 20 years after he established his own household, he owned 20 acres of land and he was one of the most powerful men in the whole union.

All the time Halim Khan has cultivated most of his own land with seasonal and yearly labourers and with hired wage-labourers on a daily basis. He leased out 5–8 acres on a sharecropping basis. A substantial part of the money he received from the sale of his surplus crops was spent on purchasing other peasants' agricultural crops and on money-lending. One of the main sources of income for Halim Khan has been hoarding and speculations in the seasonal prices of agricultural goods. After the harvest he would store his own crops of rice, jute, spices and buy up the same items from the local markets when they were at the lowest prices. He would sell the crops when the price was at the highest point. Jute he could store for several years and postpone the sale until the price was good. He would sell his crops both through the local *haats* (market places) and to individual persons who came to his home.

Another important source of income for Halim Khan has been money-lending to people who wish to use the loan for *productive* purposes. He has financed many labour migration trips for poor villagers who leave for the northern districts of Bangladesh. He can also lend to men who want to purchase a transport boat or establish themselves in trade. There are religious restrictions in the Muslim law about charging interest on loans, and since Halim Khan considers himself to be a deeply religious person, he would not accept such a practice. He receives, however, money for loans for productive purposes in the name of *'labh'*. *Labh* means profit, and the money he demands in addition to the repaid loans is therefore considered to be part of the profit which the man who borrowed the money makes.

But Halim Khan can also be engaged in petty lending of money for consumption purposes where the interest rate is 10 per cent per month. How he manages to define the 10 per cent interest he receives for the loan every month, we do not know. Another type of loan Halim Khan gives out is advance payment to his labourers. As compensation for these loans, he pays less than the market rate in wages. Also many of his labourers who are employed in the slack season have to pay for this favour by accepting a lower wage in the peak season.

Since Halim Khan is one of the leaders of a major *faction* in the area, he may lend, free of interest or on easy terms to his best supporters and members of his patrilineage. (The faction has not been very active for important purposes during the last 15–20 years, except for mobilization around specific candidates for political elections.) He himself estimates that he has outstanding claims for such loans on 20–30 persons. Although he gets no economic advantage from such loans, he can count on the people for support in village affairs, on their voting for his candidates in local elections, and on their working for him in the peak seasons. The poor people he gives most favours to he would also expect to act as *lathials* (fighters and physical protectors) for him when needed, and to do certain, occasional errands, free of charge.

Another source of income for Halim Khan is the services and advice he can offer people in connection with land dispute problems. Intimate knowledge about the various transfer mechanisms of land, e.g. the details of the Hindu and Muslim inheritance laws, is a scarce resource. He knows by which transfer mechanism all the plots in the surrounding villages have changed ownership for the last 50–100 years, and he remembers the decisions and arguments which have been used in *shalishes* over the years dealing with disputes about the ownership of the plots. He can therefore supply useful arguments to people who already are in or will be starting a dispute. If his 'clients' succeed in their efforts, he can expect to receive a good compensation.

Halim Khan's main investment object since he established his own household has been agricultural land. The whole time there will be 5–10 deficit peasants whom he supports regularly with loans. Normally it takes between one to four years from the time the deficit peasants start to receive loans to the time Halim Khan takes the land over. His main assets on the credit market are the employment possibilities and sharecropping contracts he can offer a man who mortgages or sells the land to him. Thanks to these assets, he can snatch away mortgage contracts from under the noses of less wealthy peasants who gradually and painstakingly have managed to supply a poor peasant with so much credit that they were on the verge of getting a compensation for their efforts (see case 3). He can also alienate a creditor and a debtor. He can convince a poor peasant that he is being cheated if he sells a plot of land for 4000 Taka which according to Halim Khan has a value of 5000 Taka. After conflicts and quarrels have terminated the relationship between the former creditor and debtor, Halim Khan can step in and pay 4200 Taka for the plot.

Halim Khan occasionally also takes loans from people in the rural areas. The marriages of his daughters have been very costly events, and so were the costs he incurred in a big land dispute he was involved in for a long period. Sometimes he needs to raise many thousand Taka very fast when there is a chance of making a quick purchase of a plot of land. He will always be able to raise a large part of the sum himself, but instead of mortgaging a plot of land, he will approach a well-to-do or rich peasant to obtain cash. On several occasions Halim Khan and Mohiddun Molla, who is also among the four richest landlords in the union, have in such situations borrowed 5000 Taka from each other. These loans are without interest. (Halim Khan's youngest daughter recently married one of the sons of Molla.) Halim Khan could also approach Razzak, the most well-to-do resident landowner in Bhaimara, for a loan of several thousand Taka. Razzak, whose household owns 5.2 acres of land, would feel honoured by such a request from Halim Khan, and he would make a great effort to collect the money. Razzak could expect many favours from Halim Khan for doing such a service. Halim Khan would never take away a mortgage contract Razzak was in the process of obtaining from a poor man. He could also support the nomination of Razzak to the Union Council or to the board of one of relief committees which the local Government offices often set up. Such positions are valuable both for economic and political purposes. Razzak would never think of demanding any interest or money compensation for such a loan to Halim Khan. He would, however, expect to receive loans on easy terms when he approached Halim Khan.

One effect of possessing so many economic and political resources as Halim Khan does, is that many people depend on him for the favours and resources he can distribute. Under such circumstances it is possible for him to take advantage of especially poor and isolated people. Although the community can condemn what they see and feel solidarity with the victim, they will not dare to oppose Halim Khan publicly. They would then lose his political protection and access to the resources he distributes.

For a rich landlord like Halim Khan it is easy to obtain credit from commercial banks and established institutions. Halim Khan has a loan, in kind, from the local tobacco firm, which supplies him with fertilizers and pesticides. During the last years he has cultivated tobacco on about 4 acres of land. The tobacco firm provides him with as much pesticide and fertilizer as he needs, but he asks for more inputs than he can use himself. What is left over he sells to small peasants who are not able to acquire the fertilizer and pesticides from the tobacco firm. The price he sells the inputs for depends on the type of relationship he has with the small peasants, but since there is a strong demand for the inputs, the sale provides an easily accessible source of income for him.

Halim Khan also has easy access to Government loans, for which the interest rate is low. He has received many loans of several thousand Taka each from the various Government banks. The interest rate has been very low, 7–20%, and the bank officials have not pressed him to repay the loans. The security for the loans has been land which Halim Khan has mortgaged to the bank. He continues to cultivate the land and dispose of the crops in the same way as prior to the mortgage. The reason for asking for the loans was that money should be spent on productive investment in inputs to increase the agricultural crops. Some of the money he may have used for this purpose, but when he has obtained loans in cash they have often been put into his general 'purse', to cover wedding expenses, gifts, expenses in connection with land disputes etc. The money borrowed from the bank has also been lent out again to poor peasants either against high rates of interest or as a regular and increasing loan which will lead to mortgage. The cash loans from the banks have not influenced the amount of fertilizers and pesticides Halim Khan has used. The amount he uses he would have purchased with his own money, if bank loans had not been available.

Nobody knows exactly how much land Halim Khan owns today. A guess is that he has close to 33 acres (= 100 *bighas)* of land registered in his own name, which is the legal maximum any household can own. Halim Khan fears nationalization and redistribution of land, and during the last 10 years he has started to register some of the land he has acquired in the name of his children. He has also tried to diversify his investments, but this has been difficult for him, since his skills, knowledge and passion centre around land. His main other 'investment' has been the education of his children and grandchildren. All his sons have completed Secondary School and one is a University graduate. Two of these six sons are already established in urban areas, one in a Government job and one in private business. With the help of their father two other sons may also eventually end up with jobs in the towns. He has not invested in ventures which other rich people in the union and surrounding unions have gone into: brickfield production, transport business, large country boats, trucks or buses, shops in the urban areas and houses for rent in the towns. Nor has he managed to 'invest' in smooth and easy relationships with the educated Government officials of the urban areas. For the educated, urban-oriented Government officials Halim Khan is nothing but an illiterate, though rich, peasant. He therefore has to pay the full price for the services and favours of the Government officials. In his attitude, manners and behaviour Halim Khan definitely belongs to the rural scene.

At present Halim Khan is about 75 years old. All his children, daughters-in-law and grandchildren are living in the same household, except for the two sons who live permanently with their families in the urban areas. (The household has at present 22 members.) His sons have taken over much of the money-lending business, crop stock-piling business, and land investment strategies of their father. Halim Khan has prepared his sons well for what could happen to many of the plots of land he has acquired during his life-time. He has furnished them with arguments and documentation papers which will help them in defending the land he has obtained by 'questionable' means.

The main aim for Halim Khan during the remaining part of his life is to go on a *Haj* trip to the holy city of Mecca. Together with Mohiddun Molla he has explored the possibilities for making such a trip. For many of the well-to-do and religious people this pilgrimage is one of the most important events in their lives. To perfom a *Haj* trip can also be regarded as a kind of 'investment'. He and Mohiddun Molla would undoubtedly gain prestige in the community after returning from Mecca.

Another plan Halim Khan wants to pursue is to move his house to Manikganj town. Already two of the four largest former resident landlords in the union have moved to Manikganj town, and also members of well-to-do and rich households in the nearby unions have done the same. They only visit their homes in the villages during the day and very seldom spend the night there. The reason for moving to the town is the feeling of insecurity and fear of losing their lives from which many rich people in the rural areas suffer. Most of them have been involved in serious crimes during their lifetime and therefore have numerous enemies. Some of the old rich people only move around in the rural areas with a group of loyal followers. The group of followers underlines the status and importance of the rich man, but also at the same time protect the rich man against a quick, physical assault by people seeking revenge for misdeeds committed in the past.

General features of the economic strategies of rich peasants

Not all villages will have among their population a landlord of the economic strength of Halim Khan. In a union covering 15–20 villages, there will normally be only a handful of landowners who possess as much land as he does.

Many of the credit relationships and methods of earning an income in which the large landowners are involved, are of the same type as the 'small surplus' peasants are engaged in. The difference between the two categories of peasants, however, is the number of cases they are involved in. As regards purchase and sale of food crops, however, the market involvement of landless and deficit households, 'small surplus' peasants and rich peasants differs greatly. One of the main sources of income for the rich peasants, which enables them to finance the loans they give out, is, as we noted, the profit they obtain from speculation in the price variation of food crops over the year. 'Small surplus' peasants who are close to having a balanced budget are much less involved in the food market. They only have enough food and money to finance one or two deficit peasants regularly. Deficit peasants on the other hand are, of necessity, deeply involved in the food market both as sellers and buyers, their transactions being to a large degree with the rich peasants. Deficit peasants sell crops at the time the price is low in order to pay back some of their debts in money, or they return the amount of paddy they borrowed before the harvest together with the money interest due on the loan. Thus most of the crops a deficit peasant with half an acre of land can obtain from a harvest are spent on repaying loans and interest in cash and in kind. When the remaining part of his crop is consumed, the household will have to enter the market as buyers at a time when the price of the crops has increased.[12]

One would expect the deficit households to be able to anticipate that their supply of food will be inadequate, and that they would therefore purchase rice when the price is low and store the rice until their own crop is finished. If this was done, they could at least avoid the increased cost of rice. There are several reasons why it is difficult for most deficit peasants to pursue such a strategy. First, they have to take up loans to finance a purchase of many *maunds* of paddy. Supposing they were able to get a loan for such a purpose, they would at any rate have to pay a high interest on the loan. Even if they had the necessary money, it could be difficult to buy many *maunds* of paddy. The rich landowners would not sell from their stocks, knowing that the price would increase considerably after a few months. But even given that the deficit peasants were able to purchase some *maunds* of paddy in order to avoid the increased cost, they would soon find themselves surrounded by people who would ask for loans or ask for debts to be repaid. Thus it is very difficult for deficit peasants to escape the adverse food market relations they are involved in, in which they become the losers and the rich peasants the gainers.

The rich landowners realize that if deficit peasants can organize their relations to the food market in such a way that they can reduce their deficits and come closer to a more balanced household budget, the chances of earning an income on money-lending are reduced. They also know that this would imply that they eventually would have to wait longer before being able to take over the land of the deficit peasants. The bigger the imbalance is on the budget of the deficit peasants, the more certain the rich landowners can be of earning an income through credit relations and profitable involvement on the food market. These are some of the important activities and relationships which confirm the main thesis of our study, i.e. that the rich people improve their economic position at the expense of the poor people.

Since many rich peasants make their most profitable investments from the credit relations they can establish with the poor, they have vital interests in maintaining this system of extracting money from the poor. They have an effective apparatus of sanctions which they can apply if the deficit peasants show tendencies to escape and get out of the credit relationships. These sanctions we noted, were of different types: refusal to give employment as a wage-labourer, thereby reducing the income of the household, withdrawal of sharecropping contracts, refusal to sell rice except when the price is at the highest level, not giving any 'gifts', etc. Rich peasants can also use sanctions of a 'criminal' nature when deficit peasants make efforts to free themselves from the grip of the exploitative exchange relations they are involved in.

It is also clear that there are other fields of exploitation available, and other methods which rich peasants use to exploit and impoverish peasants with deficit budgets. One method is to find excuses for disputes over the ownership rights to specific plots. The intention is not necessarily to take over the land, only to drain the resources of a deficit peasant in costly land disputes. (See chapter 7.)

Another general and widely accepted aspect of the credit situation of rich peasants is the ease with which they can raise loans on good terms. The more well-to-do a peasant is, the more certain he can be of obtaining a loan easily and on favourable terms. This is the case whether it is a matter of asking for a loan on the unorganized village 'market' or applying to the Government banks or cooperatives for a loan. They tend also to get institutionalized loans on better terms than the less wealthy peasants, even if the terms for those loans (interest rate, security, period of the loan, repayment plan) ought, according to the rules, to be uniform.

The rich peasants are the only persons who have the opportunity, economically, of investing in other fields than the agricultural sector and the related activities of usury, hoarding and market speculations. Ninety to ninety-five per cent of the rural population, including people like Eynuddin, can never venture beyond or depend on anything else than the agricultural sector. Only the most well-off households in this large group can be profitably involved in petty money-lending, petty trading, and at most increase their landholding by a few acres.

With multiple inheritance this large group can only offer their children less land and fewer employment opportunities than they themselves have experienced. In almost all the households we visited where we interviewed the parents about their children's future, we received a strong impression of their gloomy attitude and the deteriorating prospect they envisaged for their children. It is only the rich peasants who can hope that their children will not live in abject poverty. What are the ways by which the rich can ensure a proper livelihood for their children? The material from our investigation of the rich in the union showed them diversifying their investment to other sectors than agriculture. Several rich landowners had investments in a large brick-field next to the main highway. Some had invested in the transport sector, in large boats or in trucks, or buses for passengers. Other had bought houses in urban areas which they rented out, or owned small shops in the towns and bazaars. All seemed to have invested in their children's, particularly their sons', education. However, some rich peasants invested capital also in the agricultural sector, mechanized irrigation equipment and rice mills. It is not the intention at this stage to explore the implications which follow from these investments. Here we want to emphasize that the children of the rich will be able to acquire sources of income other than the land they are to inherit.[13] We found that there was a large variation in the ways agricultural land and the different investment objects were divided between the children when a rich household splits. The division depended on the skills and interests of the heirs and the nature of the objects which were passed on.

One topic we have discussed only briefly is the nature of relationship which exists between well-to-do and rich peasants. Although they have many common interests and privileges to protect, they also compete for the same scarce resources. We showed how enmity could develop when they compete to obtain the same plots of land from poor peasants. Case 3, chapter 7, narrates how rich peasants can be involved in disputes over large properties of land. There is also competition for access to Government favours (credit, tubewells, agencies for distribution of agricultural inputs, political offices, jobs in the urban areas for their sons). When factions *(dals)* are active, it is often the interests of the rich which are at stake and their supporters, the poor and 'small surplus' peasants, rally behind their leader.

However, the competition between the rich is not of such a nature that the rich are dependent for their continued position on the fall of one of their rich enemies. The rural landscape can easily be conceived of as a place where many patrons, with their separate groups of clients, can co-exist and live next to each other and only clash over limited and specific events.

Case 5 gives a description of Shamsul Huq. Halim Khan lives a few hundred yards from him and considers him his main enemy.

Case 5. The economic strategies of a rich absentee landowner

Shamsul Huq is one of the most wealthy men in the whole union. However, most of his wealth is invested in various ventures in urban areas and his main economic activities take place in Dhaka. Shamsul Huq and his family live permanently in Dhaka.

Shamsul Huq was born in Bhaimara and had four brothers and two sisters. Their father owned 8 acres of land and had a job as a junior official in the subdivisional headquarters of Manikganj. He educated two of his sons, and one of them, Shamsul Huq, even became a University graduate. After he had completed his education Shamsul Huq was employed in the Customs department in Dhaka with a fair chance of earning much more money than his salary. After the father died the four sons established separate households and divided the 8 acres. One of the brothers remained in Bhaimara while the other three were employed in urban areas. Because of his high income, Shamsul Huq was able to invest in various fields. Over a long period he purchased several small houses in Dhaka which he rented out and made much profit on. He also opened up a shop, which he gradually made larger. For a long period he did not make any investments in agriculture in his home village. He leased out his land on a sharecropping basis. After he was well established as an owner of several houses in Dhaka and owner of a profitable shop, Shamsul Huq directed some of his surplus towards investment in land in the rural areas. Over a 15-year period he increased his holding of land from the 1.3 acres he inherited to 5½ acres. Two acres of this land he purchased at a very low rate from a few wealthy Hindu landowners in a neighbouring village who were leaving for India. He managed quickly through bank loans and other loans to raise the money he needed for this purchase. Since he had close contacts with the police officers and other influential Government officers both in Dhaka and in Manikganj town, he could threaten the Hindu households with severe sanctions if they did not sell the land to him at a low price. One acre he also purchased at a low price from two of his brothers. None of the brothers was as clever as he was, and both had substantial deficits on their yearly budgets. The land he purchased from his brothers was paid for through loans which the brothers never managed to repay.

The remaining land which Shamsul Huq bought was obtained from 8 different people. Almost all the plots were purchased direct. The mechanism of transfer was thus different from the gradual consumption loans by which Eynuddin and Halim Khan normally, bit for bit, acquired their land. Since Shamsul Huq lived permanently in Dhaka and only visited Bhaimara some days each year, he did not have the opportunity to cater for the regular, often daily and weekly, credit needs of deficit peasants. Shamsul Huq was interested in buying land, and one way he could obtain land was by offering a good price immediately before the land was transferred between a creditor and debtor. Shamsul Huq's servant, who guarded and cultivated some of his plots and his house in Bhaimara, was well informed on the land situation of the different peasants and of plots which were in the process of being transferred. Shamsul Huq's advantage was that he could go in and offer to pay the debts of a poor landowner who was about to mortgage or sell his plot because of large debts. Shamsul Huq would also give him a better price, and in addition he would, if necessary, offer the indebted peasant a sharecropping contract on the land he had purchased from him. He obtained many of the plots in this way. In the future direct mortgage or purchase would also be his main method of obtaining land.

There were many reasons for Shamsul Huq's interest in investing in the agricultural sector. One was that he regarded diversifying his investments in different fields as a safety measure. Should one field fail, he would have security from the others. Investment in agricultural land was also a good way to hide much of the 'black money' he had earned through his job, and which was more difficult to conceal in other types of investments. Lately, agriculture in Bhaimara has also become an investment object with the possibility of a good return on the investment. Through his vast net of contacts Shamsul Huq realized that he would be able to acquire modern infrastructure and inputs to increase the agricultural output on his land. He has obtained a deep tubewell and necessary inputs, and he has also purchased a hand-tractor (motor cultivator), which cost 25,000 Taka. He uses the hand-tractor on his own land and rents it out to others. Shamsul Huq received loans from Government banks to purchase the hand-tractor. He also managed to get loans from Government banks on easy terms for the deep tubewell, which was obtained in the name of a local cooperative, organized and controlled by himself.

He runs the deep tubewell as his private property and demands payment for the water that is allocated to the plots within the command area of the deep tubewell.[14] Thus, investment in modern agricultural equipment not only increased the amount of crops from his own land, it has also opened up possibilities for earning an income by renting out the modern equipment. The deep tubewell also became a major political asset for Shamsul Huq. He could decide how the groundwater should be allocated. The plots Halim Khan, his enemy, possesses under the command area of the tubewell lie strikingly barren and brown next to plots where the green *boro* rice plants thrive in abundance. Thus Shamsul Huq is not only a landlord, he has also become a *waterlord!*[15]

The investment policy of Shamsul Huq follows a much more varied pattern than that of the rural rich. The agricultural sector will always only be one of many 'legs' Shamsul Huq and his household members will try to stand on. Continued and diversified business investments, rental of houses, advancement in the Government job for himself, and education of his sons with subsequent well-paid and prestigious jobs in urban areas will all be important in his household's strategy. All his sons, except one, will obtain University degrees, and Shamsul Huq is making efforts to arrange for further studies abroad for one of his sons.

There is a possibility that one of his sons, probably the one with the least formal education, will settle and establish himself in Bhaimara and run 'the farm'. Shamsul Huq's further plans for investment in the agricultural sector will be to obtain more agricultural land, especially within the command area of the deep tubewell. He will also try to make the homestead plot larger and build a solid and comfortable brick-house, where his family can live when visiting the village. He has plans for getting electricity to the area, and he considers he has a good chance of obtaining it, since rural electrification will in the next years be a major Government programme. The deep tubewell will then be run on electric power instead of the more expensive diesel oil. He would also establish a rice-mill, run on electricity, and earn money on that. Shamsul Huq's own house and maybe the houses of some of the well-to-do peasants will be supplied with electricity. His son would probably make such comforts a condition for establishing himself in the rural areas.

Some general features of the economic strategies of rich absentee landowners

The rich absentee landowners are to a varying degree involved in the social, political and economic affairs of the rural areas. Some rich absentee landowners in the village next to Bhaimara were less active in their home village than Shamsul Huq. They were well established in Dhaka and other urban areas and obtained a comfortable livelihood there. The land they owned in the rural areas was sharecropped or leased out. They did little to supervise and control the production of their land, and most of the crops were reaped by poor relatives in the village. Years could pass between the short visits they made to their village.

Although Shamsul Huq only spends 5–10 days in the village every year (and hardly any nights), he is very important and active in political, social and economic affairs of the village. In many respects, Shamsul Huq acts as a *broker* between the urban and rural areas. Partly through a distant relative who has been the Parliamentary representative for the area, he has managed to have the Government initiate a Rural Works Programme in the area and allocate money for the development of fish ponds. Across the river adjacent to the highway, he has obtained Government money to construct a wide and solid concrete bridge. On the fence of the bridge is an impressive plate clearly telling the passers-by who provided them with the comfortable bridge.

Many absentee landowners who want to increase their agricultural investments pursue strategies similar to those of Shamsul Huq. There is little doubt that it is people like him and not persons of Halim Khan's background, who can introduce some technical and organizational innovations in the rural areas. The effects of some of these innovations is another topic which we shall discuss in detail in chapter 8.

Notes

1 The Union Bhaimara belongs to contains 15 villages with a total population of 17,000 inhabitants.
2 For a comprehensive study which explicitly attempts to unravel the social and economic consequences of seasonality, see: *Some Aspects of Seasonal Dimensions to Rural Poverty in Bangladesh,* by Rafiqul Huda Chaudhury, Bangladesh Institute of Development Studies, Dhaka 1978.
3 Both for mortgage and sale of land there is some under-reporting. Since mortgaging land and sale of land is normally connected with 'shame', many people we interviewed refused to admit such land transactions. We present the table, however, in order to obtain information on the relationship between the households in these transactions.
4 See Table 1.2 for the amount of land owned by each category.
5 Arens and Van Beurden, *op.cit.,* p. 114.
6 Van Schendel, *op.cit.,* p. 330.
7 Kirsten Westergaard: *Boringram — An Economic and Social Analysis of a Village in Bangladesh,* pp. 9–13, Rural Development Academy, Bogra, Bangladesh n.d.
8 Ann-Lisbet Arn: *A Case-Study from Bangladesh: An Integrated Village in Mymensingh District,* Centre for Development Research, Copenhagen, Dec. 1978, p. 11.
9 G.D. Wood in M. Ameerul Huq (ed.): *Exploitation and the Rural Poor,* Bangladesh Academy for Rural Development, Comilla, 1976.
10 B.K. Jahangir, *op.cit.*
11 See G.D. Wood, 'Rural Class Formation in Bangladesh, 1940–1980', *Bulletin of Concerned Asian Scholars,* Vol. 13, No. 4, 1981, pp. 3–5.
12 For a more general discussion on the involvement in the market of different groups of peasants see: A. Bhaduri: 'A Study of Agricultural Backwardness under Semi-Feudalism', in *Economic Journal,* Vol. 83, No. 1, 1973, and *The Economic Structure of Agricultural Backwardness,* DERAP Working Paper A 172, Chr. Michelsen Institute, Bergen, 1980. Bhaduri explores the fields of investment (mainly usury) rich peasants direct their surplus towards, given the nature of this market involvement. He discusses the implications this investment pattern has for agricultural stagnation. Although spelled out at a much more empirical level than Bhaduri's studies, this is also an issue which is central for our study.
13 For a general discussion of how the rich manage to avoid a decline in the material standard of living when the children are to inherit from their parents see G.D. Wood in A. Huq (ed.), *op.cit.,* and B.K. Jahangir, *op.cit.* Both authors argue against a viewpoint and concept introduced by P. Bertocci, *op.cit.,* of *cyclical kulakism,* implying that rich families rise and fall, mainly due to the multiple inheritance system.

14 For a detailed discussion on the introduction, organization and consequences of the deep-tubewell in Bhaimara see: Eirik G. Jansen 'Choice of Irrigation Technology in Bangladesh: Implications for Dependency Relationships between Rich and Poor Farmers', *Journal of Social Studies,* Vol. 5, 1979, pp. 61–84.

15 See Jansen, *op.cit.* for how irrigation water is used as a political weapon and differently allocated to supporters and enemies.

5

The Sharecropping System in Transition

Introduction

A main aim of the presentation of the five detailed case studies in the previous chapter was to show the different factors the peasants considered when pursuing their economic strategies. We wanted to convey an impression of the complexity of their opportunity situations and to underline that credit and mortgage relationships could not be studied in isolation. We emphasized that most credit and mortgage relationships were not *single-stranded.* There were other types of rights and obligations which were also an integrated part of the relationship. Both in the case studies and in the general discussion following each case we mentioned that employment and sharecropping often were part of the 'whole relationship'. In this chapter we shall focus on the sharecropping of land.[1] A main aim will be to explore the different types of sharecropping relationships and to discuss the circumstances under which they occur. We shall find that the traditional conception of sharecropping, in which a rich landowner lets a poor peasant cultivate his land on a 50–50 share arrangement basis, accounts for only a small proportion of the sharecropping relationships we found in Bhaimara.

This chapter is organized as follows. First the households that rent out land on a sharecropping basis (the landowners) are identified. Then the households that sharecrop the land (the tenants) are presented, and an attempt is made to assess the economic importance of sharecropping for the tenants. Then follows a section which discusses some aspects of the terms and conditions of the sharecropping contract. After this come two sections which explore how various forms of credit and opportunities for employment can be linked to different types of sharecropping relationships. The following section focuses on some of the points landowners may consider when choosing their tenants. After this comes a section which discusses more concretely some terms and conditions of the sharecropping contracts as they were observed in Bhaimara, with special reference to the duration of the sharecropping contracts. We then briefly raise the question of the economic efficiency of the sharecropping system. Finally some factors which will influence the nature and extent of the future sharecropping pattern are mentioned.

In our presentation and discussion of the sharecropping system, we shall use linguistic expressions which are commonly used in the Bangladesh literature on sharecropping. The renting out of land by landowners on a sharecropping basis will be referred to as 'sharecropping out' and, vice versa, the taking over of land by tenants will be referred to as 'sharecropping in'.

Households renting land out on a sharecropping basis

Table 5.1 shows the extent of the sharecropping system in Bhaimara. The table states how many households sharecrop land out and the 'landowning categories' (Table 1.2) these households belong to:

Table 5.1. Households Renting Land out on a Sharecropping Basis in Bhaimara in 1980.

Group	No. of households	% of households in each group	Total acreage sharecropped out	No. of plots sharecropped out	Average size pr. plot in acres
Poor	10	48	5	15	0.3
Small	4	50	4	13	0.3
Middle	3	37.5	2	4	0.5
Rich	3	100	7	21	0.3
Total	20	49	18	53	0.3
Total no. of households, agricultural land and plots in Bhaimara	41	100	58.8	195	0.3

Of the 41 households in Bhaimara that own agricultural land, 20 households sharecrop land out, either all of their agricultural land or parts of it. Of the 58.8 acres of agricultural land which the 41 households own, 18 acres are sharecropped out (31%). In terms of number of plots, 53 of the 195 agricultural plots which the 41 households in the village own are sharecropped out (27%). For comparative purposes later in the chapter we should mention that 32% of the total number of households in Bhaimara (62) sharecrop land out.

It is surprising to see that as many as 10 of the 22 'poor group' households, which all own less than one acre of land, rent land out on a sharecropping basis. Nine of the ten households in fact sharecropped out all the agricultural land they owned; only one of the ten households cultivated approximately half of the land it owned. This finding contradicts the conventional conception of which landowners sharecrop out land. Half of the landowners with less than two acres of land, the households in the 'small group', sharecropped land out. Only one of these households, an absentee household, sharecropped out all its land. Three of the 8 households in the 'middle category' sharecropped out land, 7, 22 and 57 per cent of their total agricultural land respectively. All the rich households, of which two have absentee landowners, sharecropped out part of their land.

What are the various reasons for renting the land out on a sharecropping basis? In many cases there will be a combination of motives, particularly when the households are sharecropping out several plots. The main reasons for sharecropping out land were stated by the villagers to be as follows:

- 'We have traditionally been landlords and are not used to cultivating the land.'
- 'The plot(s) are far away from where we live.'
- 'We have not manpower or not sufficient manpower in the household to cultivate the land.'
- 'Other jobs in rural areas (teaching, small-scale business) are more lucrative and suitable for us than farming.'
- 'We live in urban areas and we cannot therefore cultivate the land ourselves or manage wage-labourers to do it.'

— 'We own so little agricultural land that it is not economical to cultivate the land.'
— 'We have no cattle and plough to cultivate the land.'
— 'Too much land to cultivate by own household members.'
— 'We sharecrop out land for the winter season only.'

The nature of the information makes it difficult to give the 'exact' reason why the 20 landowners sharecropped out their land. On the basis of our interviews we assessed that the distribution of the 'different reasons' was roughly as follows.

For 7 of the 20 households that sharecropped out land the main reason for renting the land out on a sharecropping basis was that they were absentee landowners living in urban areas. (Of these 7 households, three belonged to the poor group, one to the small group, one to the middle group, and two to the rich group.) Only one of the resident landowners showed some resemblance to the traditional landlords in that he owned more land than he and his only son could cultivate.

Four of the 20 households sharecropping out land owned little land but had available manpower to cultivate this land. These households would obviously have benefited from cultivating their land. The reason they did not do so was that the men in the households had never been used to cultivating land, since they descended from forefathers who traditionally claimed to belong to non-cultivating 'aristocratic' lineages. Instead of cultivating their land, these men have taken up work as small-scale businessmen or, in one case, as a private teacher giving reading and writing lessons to primary school students. The income they earn from these occupations is small compared to what they could get from cultivating their own land. But with the types of jobs they have they are able to maintain their positions as 'non-cultivators'. It is worth noting, however, that some of the brothers of the men in these four households, who share the same 'aristocratic' background, have given up this claim and cultivate their own land. Some of them obtain land on a sharecropping basis from others, which gives them a balanced or even a surplus annual 'budget'.

The motives for the remaining households to sharecrop out land seem to be various. Two have no male members to cultivate the land; three households sharecrop only for one season and will take the land back and cultivate it later. Two of these three households have also obtained land on a sharecropping basis and are full-time cultivators. Two households mentioned that they sharecropped out land because it was far away, but that they cultivated all the land they owned in the village and even sharecropped in land when this was possible. The other households, owning little land, sharecropped out the land because they did not have a plough and cattle for cultivation.

One can speculate about the alternative ways the 53 plots rented out on a sharecropping basis could have been used. Each of the households owning them had more than one gainful option. That these alternative opportunities for utilizing the plots are real can be confirmed when one investigates the former ways of utilizing the plots. Some years ago many of the 53 plots owned by the present owners were not sharecropped out. For some households the alternative method of utilization can be self-cultivation. For other households the plots could be cultivated by hired wage-labourers. Utilization of the plots against fixed rent on a seasonal or yearly basis is not yet a method that is practised in Bhairama or the neighbouring villages. In some villages a few miles away, however, we found some rich absentee landlords who leased out their land on a yearly basis. For each *bigha* of land they demanded 200–400 Taka per year, depending on the quality of the land. The money was demanded in advance. Although the return to the landowner for his land was less than he would obtain through sharecropping, this system required minimal involvement on his part.

Households that have obtained land on a sharecropping basis

Table 5.2 shows the groups of households that have obtained land on a sharecropping basis (sharecropped in). Seventy-seven plots of agricultural land are sharecropped in by the villagers of Bhaimara; about a third of these plots are obtained on a sharecropping basis from households living outside Bhaimara.

In the previous section we saw that 18 of the 58.8 acres of agricultural land were given out on a sharecropping basis. This means that 40.8 acres are cultivated by the owners of the plots or by wage-labourers. With the 27.2 acres sharecropped in, this means that the villagers of Bhaimara cultivated altogether 68 acres, *40 per cent* being worked on a sharecropping basis. Ten acres of this are located outside the village (see Table 1.2).

Table 5.2. Households that have Obtained Land on a Sharecropping Basis (tenants) in Bhaimara in 1980.

Group	No. of households that sharecrop in: No.	No. of households that sharecrop in: % of households in each group	Size of land sharecropped in: Size	Size of land sharecropped in: No. of plots	Average size pr. sharecropper in different groups
Landless	4	19	2 acre	9	0.5 acre
Poor	8	36	9 acre	24	1.1 acre
Small	5	63	8 acre	22	1.6 acre
Middle	6	75	8 acre	21	1.3 acre
Rich	1	33	0.2 ac.	1	0.2 acre
Total	24	39	27.2	77	0.35 acre

There is also a great variation in the economic background of the households that obtain land on a sharecropping basis. Households from all groups sharecrop in land, including the only rich resident household of the village. This rich resident household, however, sharecrops less land in than it lets out on a sharecropping basis. Except for this household, all the 23 other households that sharecrop land in are in the position of being active cultivators and owning less land than they are able to cultivate with their own household members, except in the peak season, when wage-labourers are hired. Almost all these households stated that they would like to sharecrop more land if additional land were available. The upper limit of land a household with 3–4 able-bodied male members, and wage-labourers in the peak season, could cultivate was set at 6–7 acres. Most households clearly cultivate less land, owned and sharecropped combined, than this amount. This means that except for one rich resident household, which only possesses 2 male labourers, all the other well-to-do households in the middle category are dependent on obtaining land on a sharecropping basis for maintaining their material level of living standard.

The 24 households of the village altogether sharecrop in 27.2 acres of land, which on the average means a little more than one acre per household. The importance of the sharecropped land varies among the households of the different 'land-owning' categories. For the landless households, naturally, all the land they cultivate is sharecropped land. On the average the landless households sharecrop in 0.5 acres each. This amount of land is normally sufficient to provide food for a small household for a couple of months a year. A main part of the income of these households will therefore come from wage-labour.

Households in the 'poor category' that obtain land on a sharecropping basis own, on the average, 0.5 acre of land and sharecrop in 1.1 acres. This means that the average household cultivates 1.6 acres, and consumes the crop of about 1 acre if the division of the crop of the sharecropped plot is 50–50. Such an amount of land would make a normal size household self-sufficient in rice for approximately half a year.

The households in the 'small category' that sharecrop in land own, on the average, 1.25 acres of land each and sharecrop 1.6 acres. This means that the average household would cultivate 2.8 acres and consume crops from 2 acres, which should enable the household to be self-sufficient or even have surplus rice production. The average 'middle' category household owned 2.6 acres and sharecropped in 1.3 acres, thus cultivating altogether 3.9 acres and consuming the crops of 3.3 acres. The only rich resident household in the village owns 5.2 acres. This household sharecropped in 0.2 acres and sharecropped out 0.9 acres, thus cultivating 4.5 acres.

For the households who have obtained land on a sharecropping basis (except for the rich household) the sharecropped land constitutes an important source of income. If the sharecropping contracts are lost, wage-labour is the most realistic alternative for the members of the 'poor' and 'small' category of households.

It should be mentioned that both renting land out on a sharecropping basis or obtaining land on such a basis is closely connected and correlated to the amount of cattle the household owns. The 24 households that sharecrop land in own in total 53 cows and oxen, while the 20 households that sharecrop land out only own 14 cows and oxen.

How does the extent of sharecropping vary between different villages where surveys have been conducted? In Table 5.3 we have selected a few studies and compared the percentage of households sharecropping land in and out.

Table 5.3. Sharecropping in Villages of Different Districts.

Per cent of households	Share-cropping out	Share-cropping in
In Jhagrapur (Kushtia district)[2]	15.0	37.6
In Bondokgram (Comilla district)[3]	11.8	22.4
In Boringram (Bogra district)[4]	8	35
In Bhaimara (Dhaka district)	32	39

We feel very uneasy about making this comparison. Our experience of comparing quantitative information regarding landownership and land tenure is sad. At the same time as we carried out our village survey in Bhaimara, other researchers made a similar investigation about the same issues. The percentages of landless households, mortgages and sharecropping varied by as much as 10–20 per cent. See Appendix 2 and a separate article for a discussion of why this could occur.[5] Many of the factors causing the variation in the results of the different surveys in Bhaimara will also pertain to the four different village studies compared here. Therefore we shall limit our comparison to only one feature: a larger percentage of the households in Bhaimara 'seem to' sharecrop land out. This 'impression' is confirmed in the discussion by each of the other authors on sharecropping. In these villages 'poor' and 'small' category peasants only rarely sharecrop land out, while our survey shows that in Bhaimara about half of the 'poor' and 'small' category households sharecropped out their land. There may be many reasons for this significant difference (including the small number of units being interviewed both in our and the other village studies). We do not, however, dare to speculate about the difference, partly because we think that if *one* and the same researcher had conducted the surveys in all the four villages over a short period of time, the results would have been different.

Terms and conditions of the sharecropping contracts

The traditional terms and conditions of the sharecropping relationship were that the landowner should receive half of the crop while the tenant received the other half. To some extent this traditional concept of what was a fair division of the crop influences the present terms.[6] The social and economic relationship between the landowner and the tenant was, however, in the past much more uniform than in the present pattern. In the past the traditional landowner owned much more land than he could cultivate himself and gave out plots on sharecropping basis to different poor tenants. In Bhaimara it is only the three rich households (of which two are absentee landowners) that conform to this pattern, while we have noted that many poor peasants sharecrop out their land to peasants better off than themselves.

It is obvious that there is a great difference between the bargaining strength of a rich peasant sharecropping out to a poor tenant and a poor household sharecropping out to a surplus household which owns 3 acres of land. Along with the varied pattern of households involved as landowners and tenants, many more types of sharecropping contracts have been introduced. In the following we shall explore how the sharecropping relationships have been linked to new types of terms and conditions.

Firstly, however, we discuss briefly some very concrete issues as regards the sharecropping terms. These issues are part of any sharecropping contract, and decisions will have to be made on how they shall be resolved between the landowner and his tenant.

These issues are:

— How shall the costs of production be divided between the landowner and his tenant (labour cost, fertilizers, seed, insecticides, possible expenditures for irrigation, plough and oxen)?

— In what proportion shall the crop be divided and where shall it be divided; shall the division take place in the field when the paddy is still attached to the straw or after the paddy has been husked in the homestead plot?
— How shall the by-products, mainly paddy-straws, be divided?
— Will the tenant be allowed to cultivate for his own use a few vegetables between the rice straws in the field?
— Who makes the decisions about what crop shall be grown and how the production process shall proceed (when the seeds shall be planted, time and amount of weeding, time of harvesting, etc.)?
— What is the length of the sharecropping contract and the 'security' and conditions for keeping the contract?

The terms about the division of costs and product must be set against other aspects of the relationship of which the sharecropping contract is only one part. The 'whole relationship' between a landowner and tenant also includes credit and employment relations.

Sharecropping and credit

Different types of credit are often linked to obtaining or maintaining a sharecropping contract. We noted that all the resident 'poor' and 'small' category households that rent out their land on a sharecropping basis are in a clear deficit budget position and have a constant need for money to purchase rice. In a few cases we observed that when they received loans from the more well-to-do tenants and the loans accumulated and reached several hundred Takas, the collateral for the loans became the sharecropping contract itself. This meant that the tenant would keep on sharecropping the land until the money was paid back. If the poor landowner giving out his land on a sharecropping basis was in a clear economic deficit position and could not manage to raise the sum of money he had borrowed, the tenant's bargaining position vis-à-vis the poor landowner was obviously stronger. We found this increased strength in the bargaining position could be used for different purposes. In some cases we were informed that the tenant with such a tied contract took the opportunity to provide for himself a larger part of the crop than had been negotiated. In other cases we were told that this did not happen, but that the well-to-do tenant tried to establish an even better relationship with the poor landowner and convince him that he could continue to rely on him for credit. His aim with this approach naturally was in the end to obtain a mortgage and purchase the plot he had worked on a sharecropping basis. In this way the sharecropping contract is linked via a credit relationship to the transfer of ownership of land. (See case 2 in chapter 4.)

The credit relationship between the landowner and his tenant is of a different character when it is the landlord who is economically the strong party in the relationship and it is the tenant who is in a deficit position and needs credit. Also the credit in such a type of relationship can take various forms. The landowner can provide the tenant with production loans (for fertilizer, seeds, insecticides, etc.) and also with consumption loans to cover the deficit of the annual budget. The landowner has a very good collateral for his loans, whether they are for production or consumption purposes. He can demand that the loans shall be repaid from the share of the harvest which belongs to the tenant. If he is in any way dissatisfied with his tenant, either for his production performance or for poor 'repayment record' of loans, he possesses a strong sanction: withdrawal of the sharecropping contract. The consequences of the loss of a one *bigha* plot of land could be, as we have observed, that the tenant's household will have rice for 1–2 months less per year.

Also this type of sharecropping relationship between a well-to-do landowner and a poor tenant is linked to transfer of ownership of land. If the poor tenant cannot repay his loans, the landowner will eventually demand to have a mortgage on parts of the land which his tenant owns. In fact, a major consideration of well-to-do landowners when renting land out on a sharecropping basis is to gain other advantages than half, or whatever portion is negotiated, of the crop. This wish is reflected in their choice of tenants (see cases 4 and 5 in chapter 4). Since many poor peasant households will compete over getting plots for sharecropping, the landowner will choose very carefully among potential sharecroppers. One main concern will be connected with eventually acquiring ownership over more land. A sharecropping contract is in many cases the necessary 'bait' for this to happen.

In Bhaimara we found that many sharecropping relationships between well-to-do landowners and poor tenants led to the result that the poor tenants through long credit relationships had mortgaged and sold their own land to the landowners from whom they had sharecropped land. However, we also found in many cases that a sharecropping relationship had not preceded the mortgage of land, but followed after the mortgage. This is often an expression of the fact that the poor households mortgaging land have demanded a sharecropping contract on the plot they mortgage or more likely that the mortgagee has offered the plot for sharecropping, as he understands he otherwise will not be able to obtain the land (see cases 2, 4 and 5 in chapter 4).

Table 5.4 gives some information about the 32 plots the landowning households in Bhaimara reported that they mortgaged. Here we are only concerned with households that cultivate the land which is mortgaged. The table shows that nearly half of the plots (44%) which are mortgaged are still cultivated by their owners. This percentage may cover both of the two situations referred to above.

In other parts of this study we have briefly criticized much of the abstract and general Marxist literature of the rural areas for not being able to depict the complexity of the opportunity situation of the actors and the *whole* relationships the actors are involved in. However, in a debate that has lasted for a dozen years in the Economic and Political Weekly (EPW) on the modes of production in Indian agriculture, an important question concerns (in our words) the relationship between sharecropping and credit.[7] Many of the issues we deal with in this chapter were brought to our attention through this debate.[8]

Here we shall only comment on one of the issues which has been discussed in this debate. A. Bhaduri has in his works stressed that an important part of the landowner-tenant relationship (rich landowners — poor tenants) is the usury which has become a main method of extracting advantages from the tenants. This method of 'surplus appropriation' has become so significant that the landowner's consideration for this income restrains him from increasing his production on the land, since part of the benefits of the increased production will be drawn by the tenant. The more the tenant can become independent of his credit relationship to the landowner the

Table 5.4. Land Mortgaged and Cultivator of Mortgaged Land in Bhaimara in 1980.

		Acre mortgaged			Who cultivates the land				
Group	No. of house-holds mort-gaging land	Size	Plots	Average size mortg. per house-hold	Owner cultivating the land on a share-cropping basis	The land is share-cropped out to other than owner	The land is culti-vated by mort-gagee	No in-formation available	
Landless	0	0	0	0	0	0	0	0	
Poor	9	2.26	14	0.25	3	6	2	3	
Small	6	2.31	11	0.39	8	2	1	0	
Middle	4	2.88	7	0.72	3	1	1	2	
Rich	0	0	0	0	0	0	0	0	
Total	19	7.45	32	0	14	9	4	5	32
					44%	28%	12.5%	15.6%	100%

less there is to earn on usury for the landowner.[9] It is difficult to test this hypothesis. On the basis of observation from Bhaimara, however, we shall agree that a landowner, if he sees chances of obtaining his tenant's land, will make efforts to get the tenant as deeply into debt as possible so as to take over his land on mortgage. (This is consistent with the main thesis of this study.) We did not find any material to support the hypothesis that the landowner deliberately refrained from increasing the production output on the plot he sharecropped out in order to impoverish his tenant and thereby take advantage of that situation. It is, however, possible to speculate on the circumstances under which this could be a likely strategy. If the landowner has little chance of obtaining or controlling his share of the crop (e.g. because he lives in an urban area or is a close relative), he would make no effort to increase the crop, since it would be the tenant who would benefit from the gain, and thereby also become less dependent upon him for credit.

However, the more likely way for a landowner to exploit his tenant through usury with the object of obtaining his land is to reduce his tenant's share of the crop. Through such a method the landowner can gain both from his share of the crop and by keeping his tenant poor and dependent upon him. In fact, we found many cases in which the landowner provided production loans to the tenant and regained his credit with high interest when the crop was divided.

Sharecropping and employment

The sharecropping relationship between a landowner and a tenant is also in many cases linked to the employment of people in the agricultural sector. The type of linkage between employment and sharecropping depends, naturally, also on the different economic positions and the bargaining strengths of the landowner and the tenant. In the 'traditional' sharecropping relationship of the past, it was not unusual that labour services were provided free of charge by the tenant. In the literature referring to the 'feudal' relationship between a landowner and his tenant, one central feature of the relationship was the 'appropriation of surplus' in the form of unpaid labour services. In Bhaimara we found some cases of employment contracts being linked to the terms and conditions of the sharecropping relationship. We did not find, however, that the labour services were free of charge. Under some circumstances, we were informed that a tenant would provide a limited number of services free of cost, especially if he was in a situation where he was about to lose his sharecropping contract. Normally, however, the tenant would receive the same pay as other wage-labourers when he worked for the landowner on the plots the latter had not sharecropped out.

For most of the year some tenants and wage-labourers compete in order to obtain employment, while for short periods in the peak season, some of the landowners can have trouble in finding available wage-labourers, especially in situations when natural events (flood, insect attack) can threaten the crop. In such situations the portion of the tenants who are also wage-labourers are expected to give priority to work on the land of the landowner they are sharecropping from. It is not unusual for members of a poor household enjoying a good relationship with a well-to-do peasant, whether this is due to kinship-connections or 'political' support, to both sharecrop land and work as wage-labourers for the landowner.

Employment is also linked to sharecropping when the landowner is the weak partner in the sharecropping relationship. We found that the households that had rented their land out on a sharecropping basis to more well-to-do peasants could be employed by their tenants (see case 2, chapter 4). Normally, however, the poor landowner will not work on the land he has sharecropped out, and he will only work for his tenant in the harvest season, since obtaining land on a sharecropping basis is most often an expression of the fact that the tenant has available manpower in his household. For very poor households that sharecropped out land and had no able-bodied male person, we found that the women of the household could be employed by their tenants in post-harvesting activities.

Other factors considered by landowners when choosing tenants

There is undoubtedly a strong demand for obtaining land on a sharecropping basis. Many of the landowners as well as landless households that did not sharecrop land would have wanted to obtain land on sharecropping contracts if they were available. What are the factors, apart from credit and employment relationships, the landowners who sharecrop out land will consider before making their choice of tenant? We have already argued that the considerations will vary with the type of landowner-tenant relationship, and maintained that these considerations must be understood on the basis of the total opportunity situation in which the landowner finds himself.

Sharecropping and kinship relationship: For transactions concerning both mortgage and sale of land, we saw in chapter 4 that kinship relations were important. About half of these transactions took place between members of the same *gusti* (patrilineage). Do landowners consider kinship relations when they choose their tenants? It can of course be difficult to distinguish between 'kinship' considerations, on the one hand, and credit and employment considerations, on the other. Often there is a combination of motives when choosing a tenant. In our village survey we found that of the 77 plots which are sharecropped in by tenant households of Bhaimara only 16 plots (21 per cent) are sharecropped in from brothers and *gusti* members.

The 20 households that sharecrop out land in Bhaimara sharecropped out altogether 53 plots. Of these 53 plots only 12 (22%) are rented out to brothers and *gusti* members. Also this is a small portion, especially when it is taken into account that 10–20 per cent of the households of the village that sharecrop in and out land are probably related to each other as *gusti* members. (See Appendix 3 for tables with more detailed information.) There is, of course, a large 'overlap' in the relationships of the plots sharecropped in and out.

Unlike mortgage and sale of land, the sharecropping relationship is not strongly correlated with *gusti*. This means that in Bhaimara patrilineal relationships are not the most important factor landowners consider when choosing their tenants. In fact, several times we heard statements that close relatives were poor tenants, since they felt entitled to a good share of the crop and disliked being evicted by their relatives from the plots they sharecropped. We were told that this was one reason why the absentee landowners in some villages a few miles from Bhaimara preferred to *lease* out their land on a fixed rent basis rather than let their rural relatives obtain the largest share. In another study, carried out in the northern districts of Bangladesh (Dinajpur and Mymensingh)[10] M. Hossain found that for 36 per cent of the area of land which was sharecropped, the transaction was between relatives. He, however, included relatives both of the patrilineage *(gusti)* and in-laws.

Although the sharecropping transaction normally expresses that a good relationship exists between the landowner and tenant, or at least existed when the transaction was initiated, it is a less 'serious' transaction than transfer of ownership of land. In other words, a household is allocating a more valuable asset to another household when it mortgages or sells its land to the household than when it only sharecrops the land out.

Sharecropping relationships and political patronage: Another consideration landowners make in their choice of tenants is of a political nature. Often the landowner recognizes that he can gain political support from his tenant. The political support may be support in village affairs, *shalishes* (local courts), or perhaps physical protection from attacks by enemies. We were informed that in some cases a sharecropping contract obtained by a tenant is a result of such favours.

Sharecropping and available labour in tenant's household: We have a strong impression that one criterion the well-to-do landowner almost always regards as important is the availability of several able-bodied and hard-working men in the tenant's household for whom there are few alternative employment opportunities to working on the land they sharecrop. We do not have statistical material to confirm our impression about this consideration, but we heard the argument about the importance of the labour supply in the tenant's household in many of our interviews. Also from a purely logical point of view this would seem to be sound judgement by the landowners.

Other terms of and conditions of sharecropping in Bhaimara: Above we have elaborated on the whole relationship of which sharecropping is a part. What are then the concrete obligations and rights in the sharecropping relationships in Bhaimara? For the sake of simplicity, we shall only consider the type of sharecropping relationship which exists between a well-to-do landowner and a poor tenant.

The normal pattern of cost-sharing in Bhaimara is that the tenant provides the fertilizer and insecticides he uses. He is also responsible for the plough team and all the costs of labour if he has to hire wage-labourers in critical periods of the work operations. The tenant also has to provide the seeds; if he receives the seeds from the landowner, their value is deducted at the time of the division of the crop. The place of the division of the crop depends much on whether it is the tenant or the landowner who processes the paddy. If both the landowner and the tenant process the paddy in their separate homes, the crop is often divided in two halves in the field. In this case, the by-products of the crop, the paddy straws, are also equally divided. If it is the tenant's household that carries out all the post-harvesting operations, this household would normally get all the by-products and a compensation for the various post-harvesting tasks.

We found that normally both the absentee landlords and the well-to-do resident households that rented out land on a sharecropping basis participated in the decision-making about the production as much as was possible for them. They decided what crop was to be grown and often encouraged their tenants to use fertilizers, which they supplied on favourable credit terms. We did not notice any instance where the landowner had refused to let the tenant also make other sharecropping relationships with other landowners. The fact that 20 tenants sharecrop in 77 plots should indicate that the landowners do not monopolize their tenants, even if some tenants sharecrop several plots belonging to the same owner. Neither did we find the situation where the tenant was forced to market some of his half share of the crop through the landowner. However, when the tenant was in debt to the landowner, the landowner could demand repayment of the debt immediately after harvest when the price of the crop was low.

There is of course great variation in the decision-making, the degree of monopolization, and the control which the landowner exercises over his tenants, which can only be understood from the economic position and the wider opportunity situation the two parties to the sharecropping relationship find themselves in. It is, however, our general observation that the tenants of the 'small' and 'middle' category peasants cannot be considered as 'serfs' as in the traditional 'feudal' relationship.

An important feature of the sharecropping contract is the duration of the contract. In our village survey we investigated the length of the sharecropping for the 53 plots which landowners in Bhaimara had sharecropped out. We encountered several difficulties in obtaining a correct answer to our question. Even so, it is clear that more than half of the contracts had lasted for less than five years. (See Appendix 4 for a table which provides more detailed information.)

The short duration of the sharecropping relationship is also found in Hossain's study referred to above. About 52 per cent of the sharecropping relationships he had recorded had lasted less than three years.[11] The Land Occupancy Survey of 1978 found that the duration of tenancy relationship, as reported by tenants, was as follows: 26 per cent of the tenants had a sharecropping contract lasting for less than 1 year, 20 per cent a contract lasting between 1–2 years, 16 per cent a contract lasting between 2–3 years, 8 per cent a contract lasting between 3–4 years, while 12.5 per cent of the tenants reported that they had a contract that had lasted for more than 10 years.[12]

For our purpose the interesting issue is not whether the average length of a sharecropping relationship is 3 or 6 years, but what the circumstances are which make some contracts last for many years while others last for only one year. (We are not here concerned with the prearranged 'duration' of short-term contracts.) Through interviews with the older men in the village we received a clear impression that the sharecropping contracts lasted much longer a few decades ago, and that the present pattern was that a typical sharecropping relationship only lasted a few years. According to the villagers, the reasons for the shorter contracts are the increased competition for sharecropping contracts and also the increased poverty of tenants and landowners, which results in conflicts over the division of the crop and division of input costs. The consequence of the shortening of the sharecropping contracts is that more plots for sharecropping are on the 'market', given that they are not cultivated in another way. Shorter sharecropping contracts also mean less security for the tenants and increase the possibilities for the well-to-do landowners to take advantage of the insecure situation. The contracts that lasted for many years, we were told, indicated that there existed a good and solid, *many-stranded* relationship between the landowner and tenant.

Features of the sharecropping system at a national level and aspects of the economics of sharecropping

Above we have in the main referred to our own findings on the sharecropping system in Bhaimara. Through the large and comprehensive national survey, the Land Occupancy Survey of 1977 and 1978, information exists about many of the features we have discussed on the basis of our village study. Jannuzi and Peach have summarized the findings of the Land Occupancy Survey of 1977 and 1978 with regard to tenancy relationships. (Tenancy relationships, besides sharecropping, also include lease of land.)[13]

In sum, the data of the 1977 and 1978 surveys suggest the following conclusions regarding tenancy relationships in contemporary Bangladesh:

1. More than 35 percent of all farm households are either tenant or owner-tenant households.
2. These tenant and owner-cum-tenant households cultivate more than 22 percent of the land of rural Bangladesh excluding homestead land.
3. The extent of tenancy varies widely from village to village and district to district within Bangladesh.
4. The average size of tenant holdings is small — generally less than one acre of tenant land.
5. The most common form of tenancy relationship in Bangladesh is sharecropping.
6. Sharecropping terms are generally 50 percent of the crop at harvest time, although
   a. some sharecroppers are required to make additional cash payments or pay a a higher share of the crop to the owner of the land, and
   b. almost one-sixth of all tenant and owner-tenant households have cash-only agreements.
7. Sharecropping and other forms of agreements are almost exclusively oral agreements.
8. Landowners generally do not provide agricultural inputs (seed, fertilizers, pesticides, irrigation facilities, etc.) or share in the cost of inputs.
9. Tenants generally do not remain tenants on the same agricultural land for long periods of time.

All these conclusions concerning the terms and conditions of the sharecropping relationship seem to fit in and be consistent with what we found in Bhaimara. Even the 'average' nationally based quantitative figures on the extent of sharecropping are not very different from what our information tells us about Bhaimara (see points 1 and 2 above). In Bhaimara we noted that 24 of 62 households (34%) obtained land on a sharecropping basis, i.e. were tenant and tenant-owner households, and that 18 of 58.8 acres of agricultural land owned by the villagers were given out on a sharecropping basis (31%). The fact that the 'average' extent and some of the conditions of sharecropping show similarities to our own findings should make some of the conclusions and speculations we shall make in the rest of the chapter more interesting and of greater relevance.

In chapter 2 we stated we would discuss the effects of the land tenure system on productivity and in relation to the under-utilization of labour resources. For more than two centuries agricultural economists have been engaged in arguments and discussions concerning the effect of sharecropping. On a general and theoretical level many approaches and 'schools' have put forward arguments in the debate.[14] For our purpose much of the theoretical and abstract debate is of little use when attempting to assess whether sharecropping depresses productivity in the rural areas of Bangladesh. Some schools base their theories on the owner and the tenant having alternative employment possibilities and the tenant being a pure tenant possessing no ownership right to land himself. This is very rarely the case in Bangladesh. A common conclusion all the different approaches arrive at, as summarized by Jannuzi and Peach, is:

> All of the theoretical approaches, however, have one implication in common. Unless input costs are shared between landowner and sharecropper in (at least) the same proportions as the rental share, then a sharecropper will tend to use less of any given variable input than an owner-cultivator.[15]

Many researchers have conducted studies with particular reference to the efficiency of sharecropping in Bangladesh. A conclusion which many researchers reach in these studies is that the productivity per unit of land is higher for an owner-cum-tenant on his own land than on the land he is cultivating on a sharecropping basis.[16]

We have no quantitative evidence on the productivity of the sharecropped versus the owner-operated land in Bhaimara. We think, however, that regarding the level of productivity of the land as being dependent on whether the land is owner-operated or sharecropped makes too simple a distinction and conceals important aspects which influence the efforts of the tenants. More especially through our case studies in the previous chapter we have attempted to convey an impression of how important it is to have an understanding of the full opportunity situation people are in when we attempt to explain their behaviour. On the basis of our case studies, it should be obvious that there are many factors which will influence tenants to put in different amounts of efforts and inputs on the plot of the landowner. The amount of labour efforts and inputs which are put in by the tenant must be viewed in relation to the other aspects which are part of the relationship between the landowner and tenant (credit, mortgage, employment, kinship-relationship). There is little doubt that a tenant who feels he is competing hard on an open market to obtain a plot for sharecropping, will increase his efforts to produce a good crop. On the other hand, an owner-cum-tenant, who for different reasons may have a more long-lasting sharecropping contract, will put more labour efforts and inputs into his own land. A variety of conditions affect the amount of effort made by the tenants. In our opinion many of these conditions have escaped due attention by the economists conducting studies on the efficiency of sharecropping.

On the whole, however, we think it is reasonable to conclude that the terms of tenancy relationships encourage the owner-tenants to put more labour effort and inputs into their own land than into plots they sharecrop. On the other hand, for most tenants, the differences between the output of their own land and the sharecropped plots cannot be very great. With the existing strong demand for sharecropping contracts, the landowner who sharecrops his land out on an 'open market' will naturally want to have a tenant who can provide him with as much agricultural product as possible.

Sharecropping and social organization

Sharecropping is important both because this land tenure system involves so many people and because it is of economic significance, particularly for the tenants (in the traditional rich landowner — poor peasant relationship). How is the practice of sharecropping related to the social organization of the rural areas? In order to discuss this issue we have to reiterate that the sharecropping contract is a dyadic relationship between two households. These two household 'choose' each other as counterparts in the sharecropping relationship. In the traditional sharecropping relationship it is the landowner who picks a poor tenant among many willing and potential tenants. Normally there is no pressure on the landowner as to whom he shall take on as a tenant. However, domination of the village affairs by faction politics can set boundaries for his choice of tenants. Also, under some circumstances, more powerful households on whom the landowner is dependent can narrow his range of choice or single out households as tenants for him.

Another feature we have to bear in mind is the great demand for land on a sharecropping basis. The landowner who wants to give out land on a sharecropping basis has command over an asset for which many tenants are willing to offer other achievements than half of the crop they produce. A dyadic relationship entered into on this basis contributes to develop and maintain a many-stranded patron-client relationship. The rural areas are 'filled' with these relationships in which poor peasants try to align themselves with well-to-do peasants. We saw in the different cases of chapter 4 that the number of clients a patron could have would vary from a few to many.

What are the factors which generate these patterns and types of patron-client relationships? We have indicated some conditions: the individual property rights to land, the multiple inheritance system and the non-corporate character of the patrilineage, the scarcity of sources of livelihood and their unequal distribution. This leaves each person and each household to fight for its own survival. For people who possess less than they can subsist on are forced to enter into relationships with the minority who possess adequate means. Sharecropping, as we have shown above, is only one element in this patron-client relationship. In chapters 7 and 8 we will see how other factors and conditions also contribute to generating and maintaining the patron-client relationships. In chapter 9 we shall assess the strength of some of the conditions which could break down the patron-client pattern of relationships.

The system of sharecropping in the future

In the introduction to this chapter we mentioned that during the last decades the sharecropping system had undergone a change. A much more varied pattern of different types of sharecropping relationship has developed. Is it possible on the basis of the material we have presented in the study so far to predict any trends along which the sharecropping system will develop in the future? Will the practice of sharecropping become more dominant and/or will the terms and conditions of the contracts change? We shall not attempt to give full answers to these questions but only indicate some factors which could influence the nature and the extent of the sharecropping market in the future.

Owing to the increase in population and sale of land among the poorest landowners, the underemployment and unemployment situation will almost certainly become worse. This will lead to a downward pressure on wages. Some landowners would be induced by the lower wages to use wage-labour to cultivate their land instead of sharecroppers. Another factor which strengthens the use of wage-labourers at the expense of sharecroppers is labour migrations. In the past there were no labour migrants working in Bhaimara and the neighbouring areas. Today there is a limited number of migrants, and the number will no doubt increase in the future and lower the level of wages. We shall discuss these issues in the next chapter.

A different type of occurrence which could play an important part in the future is the change of technology in agricultural production. In Bhaimara we observed that many sharecroppers were evicted when the plots they worked on came under deep-tubewell irrigation. The cultivation of HYV-crops under irrigation caused the amount of crop per unit of land to double and triple. The landowners found it more profitable to cultivate these plots with wage-labourers than with sharecroppers.[17] Also other types of technology, like hand-tractors (mechanized power tillers) may be introduced in greater numbers, with the consequences that the machines handled by skilled manpower adversely affect the opportunities for tenancy contracts for the sharecroppers. From a nearby area we were given information on what was considered to be new conditions for sharecropping. Various tenants were competing against each other in order to get plots under irrigation for sharecropping. It appeared to be the person who could offer the landowner most money who obtained the plot for a definite period for sharecropping. We were informed that it was necessary to pay several hundred Taka to obtain a small plot of about 0.15 acres, for one year only. This system of cultivation combines features of the fixed rent system of land and the sharecropping system.

Stefan de Vylder discusses another way the sharecropping system can be adapted to HYV-technology:

> Considering the effects of share-tenancy on innovation and growth, there is some evidence that the landlords are quite aware of the disincentive aspects of share-tenancy. A new pattern in the landlord-tenant relationship seems to be emerging: in order to make the sharecroppers adopt the H.Y.V. technology, the landlords are slowly beginning to accept a rental arrangement involving a partial cost-sharing. Sometimes this cost-sharing simply assumes the form of a credit — the landowner provides all inputs, except labour, but deducts his costs from the gross harvest before output is shared. The tenant's risks are thereby reduced, but certainly not eliminated.[18]

For the 85–90 per cent of the land which is not under HYV-cultivation, lease and fixed rent could, as we noted under certain circumstances become a more prevalent practice. On the other hand the well-to-do landowners have so many means at their disposal to reduce the share of their tenants that the system could continue but on more onerous conditions for the tenants. Mahabub Hossain has calculated that the average tenant hardly gets more, and sometimes even less, return on his labour than he would get alternatively by selling his labour on the market at the prevailing wage rate.[19]

The extent of the practice of sharecropping in the future also has to be assessed in relation to the increasing polarization of the ownership of land. Many of the 'poor' and 'small' group households that now for different reasons sharecrop out land will no doubt in the course of one or two decades become landless. Some well-to-do households which sharecrop out land will split up, and the newly established households will need all their plots of land for self-cultivation. On the other hand, some rich households will acquire more land through purchase and will be in the position that their landholdings become too large for physical cultivation by themselves. Therefore they will have to make use of tenants/labourers for cultivating their land.

One policy issue discussed at national level which may have consequences for the extent of sharecropping concerns the terms and conditions of the sharecropping contract. Several Government Committees have recommended legislation to secure the tenants a larger share of the crop and more permanent contracts. According to the week-end newspaper Holiday,[20] the 'Land Reforms Commission has proposed five year tenancy rights for the sharecroppers and the *Tebhaga*[21] model for sharing the produce.... The sharing will be done on the basis of one-third for the land, one-third for labour and one-third for input.' The recommendations of the Commission have not yet been adopted by the Government. Although it would be difficult to enforce such legislation, the fact that the issue is discussed at national level and that this is known may encourage some landowners to think of alternative ways to cultivate their land.

The practice of sharecropping will also in the future depend on what other transactions are involved in the whole relationship of which the sharecropping contract is only one part. There are many 'benefits' a combined 'tenant-client' can offer and provide a landowner. Some of the benefits, or requirements of the landowner, could, maybe, better be met in a sharecropping relationship than in a wage-labour relationship and fixed rent relationship. It is difficult to predict what new requirements and services big landowners in the future would need from their clients. It could happen that the need for physical protection from clients will increase in the future, and the security issue could best be met by offering land on sharecropping basis in a tight patron-client relationship.

Notes

1 Sharecropping also occurs in relation to objects other than land: cattle, goats, hens, ducks, and different types of fruit trees may be rented on a sharecropping basis. The sharecropper then tends the animals or the trees and receives half of the products.

2 See Arens and Van Beurden, *op.cit.,* p. 109.

3 G.D. Wood conducted a survey in Bondokgram and is cited in Arens and Van Beurden, *op.cit.,* p. 109.

4 See Kirsten Westergaard, *op.cit.,* p. 16.

5 E.G. Jansen, B.K. Jahangir, B. Maal and N. Rahman, *op.cit.*

6 The Land Occupancy Survey, 1977: Tables VI & VIII reported a 50–50 arrangement in 93 per cent of the cases of sharecropping. In 99 per cent of the cases the inputs were provided by the sharecropper. See *Land Occupancy Summary Report of 1977,* Bangladesh Bureau of Statistics.

7 For a comprehensive overview of the debate see Alice Thorner: 'Semi-Feudalism or Capitalism? — Contemporary Debate on Classes and Modes of Production in India', *EPW,* Vol. 17 (1982), No. 49, 50, 51.

8 See V.M. Rao: 'Village Lease Markets for Agricultural Land: Some Approaches for Analysis', *EPW,* Review of Agriculture, June 1974; K. Bharadwaj and P.K. Das: 'Tenurial Conditions and Mode of Exploitation — A Study of Some Villages in Orissa', *EPW,* Annual Number February 1975; Pranab Bardhan and Ashok Rudra: 'Terms and Conditions of Sharecropping: An Analysis of Village Survey Data in India', *Journal of Development Studies,* Vol. 16, No. 3, April 1980, pp. 287–302.

9 See A. Bhaduri, *op.cit.,* 1973 and 1980.

10 Mahabub Hossain: 'Nature of Tenancy Markets in Bangladesh', *Journal of Social Studies,* No. 3, 1979.

11 Hossain, *op.cit.*

12 See Tables of the 1978 Land Occupancy Survey, in Jannuzi and Peach, *op.cit.,* p. 113. The table is quoted in Appendix 5.

13 Jannuzi and Peach, *op.cit.,* pp. 21–29.

14 For overviews of this debate see: Jannuzi and Peach, *op.cit.,* pp. 121–131. Clive Bell: 'Alternative Theories on Sharecropping: Some Tests Using Evidence from Northwest India', *Journal of Development Studies,* Vol. 13, No. 4, July 1977, pp. 317–346; N.K. Chandra: 'Farm Efficiency under Semi-Feudalism — A Critique of Marginalist Theories and Some Marxist Foundations', *Economic and Political Weekly,* Special Number, August 1974.

15 Jannuzi and Peach, *op.cit.,* p. 128.

16 See: Mahabub Hossain: 'Farm Size, Tenancy and Land Productivity: An Analysis of Farm Level Data in Bangladesh Agriculture', *The Bangladesh Development Studies,* Vol. V, July 1977, No. 3, pp. 285–349, and Md. Abdus Sattar Mandal: *An Economic Analysis of Resource Use with Respect to Farm Size and Tenure in an Area of Bangladesh;* unpublished dissertation, Wye College, University of London, August 1979.

17 See E.G. Jansen, 1979, *op.cit.*

18 See Stefan de Vylder: *Agriculture in Chains, Bangladesh: A case Study in Contradictions and Constraints,* Zed Press, London 1982, p. 120.

19 Mahabub Hossain: *Foodgrain Production in Bangladesh, Performance, Potential and Constraints,* BIDS, Dhaka, 1980, mimeo.

20 See article by Mahfuzullah: 'Sharecroppers' rights', *Holiday,* December 25, 1982, Dhaka, p. 1 and 8.

21 During the 1940s many sharecroppers revolted, demanding better terms and conditions. The movement has become known as the *Tebhaga* Movement.

6

Competition for Employment and Wages

There is a tendency among some researchers to reformulate the question of unemployment as a problem of poverty and low productivity:

> More important, perhaps, than unemployment and underemployment is the low productivity and occasionally low intensity of work arising from the poor motivation, poor health and injustice that is found in most rural areas. The exploitation and inequality to which the majority of the rural population is subjected is demoralizing, engenders resentment and stifles initiative and creativity. The effect is not only to lower current output below its potential but to reduce the capacity and willingness of the population to innovate.[1]

On the basis of our fieldwork experience in the rural areas, we agree to a large extent with these viewpoints, but nevertheless we want to emphasize that unemployment is a very real problem in rural Bangladesh. We have emphasized in this study that apart from scarcity of land there is a lack of remunerative employment opportunities. This chapter will consider aspects of the organization of the wage labour market in the rural areas and discuss some of the implications of the worsened terms and conditions for the wage labourers.

In the first part of this chapter we shall see who the employers and employees are and take up the duration of the different employment contracts. We shall emphasize that the available employment is unevenly distributed, and we shall discuss some factors the employers consider when they pick their employees. We shall make some comments on the fixation of the wage rate, and we shall go on to explore in detail methods applied by employers to reduce labour costs. We shall then proceed to discuss what the present wages can buy and outline some social and economic effects of the lowered wages. Finally we shall allow ourselves to speculate on some future aspects of the organization of the wage labour market.

Who are the employers and the employees in the village?

The wage-labour market we shall discuss here will mainly be the market for male persons. As we noted in chapter 3, men and women are, and have traditionally been, engaged in different sectors of agricultural work. Owing to the restrictions of *purdah,* women have been confined to work within the *bari* compound and have not carried out any work in the fields. Even today it is extremely rare to come across women who participate in any of the field operations: land preparation, sowing and transplanting, weeding and harvesting. The post-harvesting processes of the crops which take place in the *bari* are, however, regarded as the responsibility of the women, and it is this work which constitutes the main area of wage employment for women. Therefore, the labour market for males and females is segregated. Under some circumstances men do participate in the post-harvesting activities. When they are employed on a wage basis, their wages are higher, by 35–50 per cent, than women performing the same jobs.[2] Children may under certain circumstances represent competition for male labour for some of the less physically hard tasks in the field.

In Bhaimara all the 62 households are more or less involved in the labour market either as employers or employees. For all the households without agricultural land wage-labour is the main source of income, except for six households in which begging and gifts seem to be the main sources of income. We noted that many of the households with agricultural land but deficit budgets depend on the income one or more of their households members can provide through wage-labour. Among the 27 households owning agricultural land, but which have been classified as deficit households (see Table 1.3), about 15 were found to have one or more members who were regularly employed as wage-labourers in agriculture activities. We noted in chapter 5 that some of these, out ot consideration for their *izzat,* would not enter the labour market, or only work within a very protected market which would not cause loss of status. Some of the 27 households would also for short periods in the peak seasons be employers and hire wage-labourers for work tasks which have to be finished over a short period. The main employers are, however, the rich absentee landowners, and the well-to-do or rich resident landowners. The permanent servant of Shamsul Huq, case

5, in chapter 4, will in the absence of Shamsul Huq be vested with the task of hiring wage-labourers on the land his master does not sharecrop out. Halim Khan, case 4, chapter 4, who cultivates more than 20 acres of land by wage-labourers, is undoubtedly the largest employer of landless and poor peasants in Bhaimara.

Length of employment contracts

The available amount of wage-labour employment in Bhaimara is divided in different ways among the people who are seeking labour contracts. Some persons are able to secure employment every day throughout the year, while others, who would be willing to work every day except for the 2 days of *Eid* celebration, i.e. 362 days per year, are only employed for 30–40 days per year. According to rough survey estimates made on the basis of our data from Bhaimara, the grown-up male persons in a landless household would on an average be employed for 200–220 days a year. We do not have exact information about how much time the landless would spend on agricultural wage-labour work versus non-agricultural wage-labour work. (The division would depend on the skills of the particular persons; some landless persons have a reputation for being clever in specific non-agricultural tasks, for instance, housebuilding, fence-making, roof-thatching, etc.) In the following we shall limit our discussion on wage labour to the agricultural sector.

Many surveys have been carried out on the extent of unemployment in the rural areas. Khan, Islam and Huq comment on a survey they carried out on two villages in Bangladesh:

> First, the average number of days worked per worker is very high, 275 days per year in Bhatpara and 262 days in Bhabanipur. This would appear to contradict the widespread belief, based on a number of surveys, that the average number of days of employment in rural Bangladesh is below 200.[3]

We shall not here discuss the extent of unemployment and underemployment; we only want to stress that the employment opportunities are so unevenly distributed. What are the factors causing this?

One reason for the big difference in the amount of time people are employed is the type of labour contract they have obtained with their employers. There is great variation in the length of the periods these contracts last. A few labourers in Bhaimara are attached to their employers on permanent work contracts. In one of the rich absentee households of the village the yearly labourers have for two generations been recruited from the same family. Only the two rich absentee landlords in Bhaimara have a servant's household permanently attached to them. These two servants' households both live on the compound of their employer, and both male and female members of their household would work for their employer's household. The men work in the field and they are in charge of the daily management of the 'farm'. The women are employed in the post-harvesting activities.

Another type of long-term labour contract extends for a period of 10 months. We found that three of the well-to-do, surplus households in the village employed wage-labourers on a 10-month contract. The wage-labourer would live in the household of his employer and be regarded as a servant who could be asked to do any kind of work his employer needed him for. The servant would normally be a young man who had not yet established his own household. The reason for the 10-month period of the contract is that for two months of the year, September to November, very little agricultural work can be carried out owing to inundation of the agricultural land.

Wage-labourers can also be hired to work for from a few weeks to a couple of months in one stretch. In this case too it will be peasants with a surplus and rich landowners who hire people for such shorter periods. Both for the 10-month period contract and seasonal short-term work the employers would feel no obligation towards providing the labourers they hire with so much money that they can also cover the needs of the non-productive members of their households.

The normal length of a labour contract is often only one day; sometimes it can even be as short as half a day. The length of the employment contract will thus be an important factor for explaining the large difference in the amount of time people are employed. The attractiveness of the various long-term contracts varies. By many landless households permanent employment with a rich landowner would undoubtedly be regarded as an ideal situation. The security of such employment would last as long as the household has members able to carry out the necessary working tasks satisfactorily. The 10-month contract and the seasonal short-term contracts are not as attractive and rewarding as a permanent contract. A wage-labourer for whom there is a high demand would earn more by taking on daily contracts than through a seasonal short-term contract.

Considerations when hiring labourers

What factors does an employer consider when he chooses between the available wage-labourers? One is the skills and the physical strength of the labourers. Among the labourers who enter the labour market there are great differences in working capacity. Some can weed, transplant and harvest two to three times as much as less strong labourers. This difference is to some extent compensated for in terms of the amount of wages paid.

In the other chapters we have continuously emphasized that very few economic relationships are purely single-stranded. The employer therefore considers other factors than skill and capacity for hard work when he hires labourers. All the surplus peasants and the rich landlords mentioned that they under 'equal circumstances' would feel obliged to prefer a *gusti* member to a *non-gusti* member and secondly a *samaj* member and a villager to a *non-samaj* member and non-villager.[4] We have also seen in the two previous chapters that employment can be a 'bait' or an exchange favour for credit and mortgage relationships entered into and plots sharecropped out.

Another consideration the employer will have in mind when employing workers is the relationship he has to his poorer neighbours. Most often a well-to-do household, in the area Bhaimara belongs to, will have a poor neighbour living in a house only 20–40 yards away. In the village it is important to have a good relationship with neighbours. Theft and other crime are constant threats to the villagers. Large robberies and cattle theft carried out by armed robbers in the dark of the night and petty thieves operating during day-time are not uncommon and unknown incidents. For these types of crime it is necessary to have alert neighbours who will give support and at least try to inform the owners of the identity of the thieves. If a well-to-do man has a bad relationship with some of his poor neighbours, the poor neighbour can be non-supportive when the crime takes place or even be 'agents' or silent supporters of the thieves. In all crimes in the rural areas the role the neighbours may have played in the offence is automatically speculated upon. Silent or active support in a crime can thus become a sanction poor and dissatisfied neighbours can use against their more well-to-do and rich neighbour. One of the best things a well-to-do landlord can offer a poor neighbour is employment, and one of the worst things he can do is to deny him employment when the poor neighbour asks for it and feels he has a certain 'right' to it. Owing to the necessity of having a good relationship with the neighbours, a landowner will in some circumstances feel forced to hire an older neighbour instead of a young hard-working, unrelated person.

In periods when faction politics are important in village affairs this has consequences for the employment market. Twenty years ago there were three factions in Bhaimara, due to a certain dispute between some rich peasants. All the villagers belonged clearly to one or other of the three factions. The three factions were headed by the most well-to-do in each of the groupings. All faction-leaders and members who needed wage-labourers would approach or be approached by those in their own faction seeking employment. No one who did not belong to the faction would be employed by the faction-leaders. When the issues that had caused the split between the three factions gradually were resolved and faded away, this was also reflected in the employment pattern in the village. There were no longer moral sanctions involved in employing wage-labourers who belonged to other factions. For a period, though, all available employment had been allocated on the basis of faction-membership.

Not only the employers will be selective in their choice of wage labourers. Some of the wage-labourers, as we have noted (see case 2, chapter 4), will not be willing to work for just any employer. This is particularly relevant for some of the households that have recently slipped down the scale economically but still have a certain prestige attached to their household. The members of these households would never work for a household which they previously considered to have less status, *izzat,* than themselves. The members of such a household would have a much more limited number of potential employers to approach than members of households which have little status to defend vis-à-vis the village community.

The labour market is therefore far from being an 'open' market where all the wage-labourers compete with each other to obtain work from any employer. Even for the labourers who are working on daily contracts and willing to work for most of the employers, the choice of employers is limited. The rough survey we made on employment patterns in Bhaimara showed that most wage-labourers worked for only a limited number of employers. We found that the wage-labourer who on the average worked 200 days a year would for 150 days be employed by only 3–4 different employers. Only for about 50 days would he work for employers with whom he did not have a regular working relationship. During these 50 days he could be employed by as many as 10–15 employers living both inside and outside the village. For these 50 days he would have entered the 'open' labour market and have succeeded in getting a job. He would, of course, also for the period when he is unemployed, try to get employment. The effort he puts into his hunt for employment would depend on the chances he felt he had of being hired. The extent to which a wage-labourer is employed on a daily, regular basis by an employer will naturally vary with the need for work his employer has and how closely he is attached to his employer. If there exists a close patron-client relationship between the two and the patron owns much land, the client will spend a large proportion of his working days on his patron's plots.[5]

In Bhaimara there is no formal system for allocating employment to wage-labourers who are willing to work for any employer. There is no place in the village where all the available labourers meet with landowners who need to hire labourers in the morning before the work starts, and where the employers will pick out the labourers of their choice. There are many obvious reasons why employing short-term labourers is not managed in such a way. A characteristic feature of interpersonal relations in the village is that public confrontation between persons in conflict is minimized, and it would be against all such notions for employers to pick some labourers and reject others in public. Daily contracts are made directly between the employer and the employee without intervention from other persons. Often the contract will be made in the evening when the employer or employee will meet at the home of one or the other. The work tasks to be carried out the next day will be decided and the terms of the contract agreed on.

Under some circumstances employment is not obtained through negotiations between employers and employees buth through *contractors.* Sometimes when rich landowners will need 5–10 people to work for a certain period, they can contact a contractor who will collect the wage-labourers. Negotiations about wages will be left to the landowner and the contractor. This method of employing wage-labourers takes place especially when the place of work is some distance from the homes of the wage-labourers. Almost all labour migration trips from the area around Bhaimara are organized between a resident contractor and the rich landlord in one of the northern districts of Bangladesh.

But also in the village area rich landlords can approach contractors and ask them to organize 10–15 labourers for a few days' period. From the employer's point of view the system of hiring wage-labourers has some advantages. He does not have to spend time on negotiating wages and output of work with a large number of individual wage-labourers. The contractor alone will be responsible for the output and quality of the work. It will be easier to give the blame or the credit to one identifiable person. The labourers will have to negotiate and if necessary complain to the contractor about their terms and conditions and not to the landowner. On the other hand, using a contractor means that the employer forgoes the advantages he could obtain from his relationship with the individual labourers.

Some comments on the fixation of wage rates

There are different ways of paying wage-labourers. The different methods are influenced by the type of labour contract which exists between the employer and employee, by the social relationship which exists between them, by the working capacity of the employee, and by the seasonal scarcity or abundance of wage-labourers on the labour market.

Permanent wage-labourers working on an around the year basis for a rich landlord, and living in their employer's *bari* would receive both food, house, clothing and money as payment. On certain occasions they also receive small gifts. Since several of the family members may be working for the employer, the wage is normally sufficient to cover the basic needs for all the household members, productive as well as non-productive. Also the seasonal labourer, whether he is on a 10-month contract or for one season only, will have a wage consisting of several items. He could receive lodging in the house of his employer, he will eat all his meals with his employer's family, he will receive clothing (a *lungi* (loin cloth) every six months at least) for the period he is working for the family and normally a fixed salary in cash money every month. For the wage-labourer on daily or short term contracts, the modes of payment are cash money, cash money and food, share payment (a certain share of the crop which is harvested), and fixed payment for doing a certain amount of work.

In Bhaimara payment in cash only, or a combination of cash and in kind payment, are the most normal modes of payment. We observed very few cases of share payment between the individual employer and employee. Share payment took place between a rich landowner and a contractor who would collect and organize a number of labourers to carry out a certain task, most often harvesting, for the landowner. Then 1/10 or 1/15 or more recently 1/20 of the crop which is harvested is paid as wage. Fixed payment for weeding would be applicable when a contractor negotiates a certain amount of cash payment for weeding a specified area of land with a group of labourers. Fixed payment can also be the type of contract between an individual employer and a labourer, especially if the employer is old and weak.

On the 'open' market for contracts on a daily basis the wages vary throughout the year, and both the size of the wage and the 'mode of payment' are an expression of supply and demand and the strength of the relative bargaining positions of employers and employees. In the 1979–1980 season the money wage in Bhaimara varied from 5 to 12 Taka per day. The amount of 12 Taka was only received for a period of a few days by some strong, hard-working labourers when the crop had to be harvested very fast in order to save it from attacks from insects. The normal peak season wage was 10 Taka.

Normally, in an area of the size of a few villages, there will be a uniform wage rate of, for example, 7 Taka or 9 Taka. This wage rate will be referred to and used as a yardstick when wages are negotiated. Even if the actual wages paid to workers are lower or higher, depending on the strength of the workers or the social relationship between the employer and employee, the existing 'average' rate will be used as a reference point for the payment which is negotiated. According to the views of the labourers, the wage should be the same on the 'open market' for old as well as for hard-working young men. In the peak seasons, with no unemployment, we found wage-labourers obviously contributing differently as regards the amount of work done but being paid the same 'top rate'. In non-peak seasons, many of the physically weaker and not so hard-working men would not be hired unless they had a special relationship with their employers.

The fixation of the reference wage rate revealed some signs of group solidarity among the wage-labourers on the open market. Employers who offered less pay than the accepted rate to able-bodied men were regarded as *'kripons'*, stingy persons. Under certain circumstances the labourers could at the height of peak seasons, when everybody was employed, decide to boycott them. The people who decided not to work for a *kripon,* would, however, be careful not to boycott, or make other types of sanctions against employers they would be dependent upon for off-season employment.

Similarly, fellow wage-labourers who were found to accept lower wages than the reference wage rate were frowned upon. In Bhaimara and neighbouring villages stories circulated of how labourers who, maybe clandestinely, had accepted a lower wage and thereby displaced other wage-labourers had been beaten up. They would also be discriminated against by not being invited along by other wage-labourers when the latter were introducing friends to work for their employer. The period when wage-labourers would accept a lower pay than the 'reference wage rate' would be at the end of a peak season, when employment was becoming more difficult to obtain. The more people who succumbed and accepted a lower rate, the more the going peak-season wage rate would be undermined, and a new and lower one established as the new 'reference wage rate'. The fixation of the wage level is an issue where the wage-labourers, on the one hand, and the employers, on the other, clearly see that they have contradictory interests. The wage-labourers collectively take measures with the few means they have available against those employers who are most active in reducing wages, and they also react against those colleagues who accept payment below the reference rate. The employers, as we shall see below, make many efforts to find methods to set the market mechanism out of operation, and create an imperfect market, particularly when the wage rate is at its highest point.

Methods by which employers may reduce labour costs

The amount a household would have to spend on wages when hiring labourers will to a large extent depend on the amount of land owned by the household and the number of male persons who can work in the field. Peasants with less than 2 acres of land and with 2 male workers and a pair of bullocks and a plough will in a normal year only have to hire wage-labourers for a few days for weeding and harvesting each season. The number of days for which such a household will need to hire wage-labourers depends on how many plots of land the household has and to what extent the crops on the plots need to be worked on simultaneously. Households with more land depend much more on hired wage-labourers.

Table 6.1 is based on information from a survey conducted in Barkait village in 1976 in Comilla.[6] The table shows how much time is spent on the different working operations in the production of rainfed *aus* and *aman* on one acre of land, and it shows what the market price would be to hire wage-labourers to carry out the different work tasks. No such detailed survey was carried out in Bhaimara. If surveys had been conducted, they would probably have reached fairly similar results to those in Barkait village in Comilla, since the amount of time spent on each work task, the wages and price of fertilizers and the price of the grain seem to be close to the rates observed in Bhaimara in 1979-80. Even if there had been fairly large differences, however, the point to be made in this connection would still be valid. A household depending on hired wage-labourers to carry out labour tasks in agricultural production would have to be prepared to pay a substantial part of the value of the paddy[7] grown in wages to the labourers. Labour accounts for about 70% of the total production costs needed to produce paddy on one acre of land, provided that labour for all the different work tasks has to be purchased at the market (which very rarely happens). The 70 per cent constitutes in this case 635 Taka and 715 Taka respectively for the *aus* and *aman* seasons. (The production cost does not include any expenses for land. Most cultivated land has not been bought but inherited.)

A small peasant will, maybe, spend 100–150 Taka on hired labour, since most of the work will be carried out by his own family members. A more well-to-do peasant may have labour costs of 300–350 Taka per acre. For the peasants this is a considerable expense, and they are naturally very concerned about reducing the cost as much as possible. What are the strategies they could use to reduce their expenses?

One strategy is to use the family labour to the maximum point, both in the fields and in the post-harvesting operations inside the homes. It is easy to observe that all households in which there are no 'moral' or 'social' inhibitions about doing manual labour follow this strategy. Production plans are made for the different plots so as not to create more employment in peak periods than can be met by the family members. The owners will be working harder and longer hours than would be required of them as wage-labourers; in the peak season the boys will even stay away from school and work in the fields. Many people living in the urban areas will return to the rural areas during the harvests. According to observers, as many as 15 per cent of the industrial work force returns to the village at harvest-time to help relatives with their work.[8] In the *bari* the care of small children will in part be made the responsibility of non-productive family members — other children or old persons so that also the women can work full time with the paddy. Self-employment to the fullest extent, including exchange of labour services with other households, is thus the main method for reducing the costs paid to

Table 6.1. Statement Showing Costs and Returns for *Aus* and *Aman* (per acre) (Man-day = 8 hrs.).

A) COSTS	Daily Wage Rate (Taka per day)	Number of days reqd. *Aus*	Total wages costs paid (Taka)	Number of days reqd. *Aman*	Total wage costs paid (Taka)
Human Labour:					
1. Land preparation	10.00	16	160.00	13.5	135.00
2. Manuring and fertilizing	8.00	1	8.00	1	8.00
3. Sowing/transplanting	10.00	1	10.00	12.5	125.00
4. Weeding	8.00	18.5	148.00	2.5	20.00
5. Harvesting	10.00	13.5	135.00	19	190.00
6. Threshing	10.00	Approx. 6	60.00	Approx. 8	80.00
7. Cleaning and winnowing after threshing (done by females)	4.00	Approx. 2	8.00	Approx. 3	12.00
8. Boiling of grain	3.00	4.5	13.50	Approx. 6	18.00
9. Drying of grain	3.00	3.5	10.50	Approx. 4.5	13.50
10. Husking and winnowing	6.00	13.5	81.00	19	114.00
Total cost of human labour			634.00		715.50
Animal Labour (for land preparation and threshing):	10.00 per pair	Approx. 22 animal pair days	220.00	Approx. 21.5 animal pair days	215.00

Total labour costs (human and animal)			854.00		930.50
Other Costs (including costs of seeds, fertilizer, pesticides, etc.)			80.00		100.00
Total costs			934.00		1030.50
B) RETURNS	Price (Taka)	Yield *Aus*	Value of Yield (Taka)	Yield *Aman*	Value of Yield (Taka)
1. Paddy grain	75.0 per maund of *Aus* and 70.00 per maund of *Aman*	18 maunds	1350.00	25 maunds	1750.00
2. Paddy straw	6.0 per maund	27 maunds	162.00	37.5 maunds	225.00
Total value of of return			1512.00		1975.00
Balance (Total return minus total costs)			578.00		944.50

Source: Barkat-E-Khuda — *The Use of Time and Underemployment in Rural Bangladesh,* University of Dhaka, 1982, pp. 59–60.

wage-labourers. These mechanisms naturally have effects on the extent of the demand for wage-labourers and thereby also on the level of wages. Despite the efforts to reduce labour costs, most of the households would need to hire wage-labourers. Of the 41 households in Bhaimara with agricultural land, 30 said that they used labourers outside their family to work on their land. For about 10 of the 30 households, the households with the least land, we got the impression that the labour they had used had been on an equal exchange basis with other poor households. Only about 20 households had hired labourers and paid wages to them, and only 10 of the households regularly hired labourers for many days at a stretch each season for agricultural activities.

What other strategies could these households use to reduce expenditure on hired labour? Some strategies have already been mentioned. For a household that owns a fair amount of land it could be advantageous to have a seasonal labourer staying in the *bari* instead of paying out wages on a daily basis. For the rich landowner, whether he resides in the village or not, it could be beneficial to have a permanent caretaker family living in his *bari*. Then both the activities in the field and the post-harvesting tasks would be carried out by the male and female members of the servant's family.

To participate in undermining the prevailing 'reference wage' is one way of reducing labour costs. The more well-to-do and rich a landowner is, the easier it can be to use this method in order to pay a lower wage. The method is often coupled with another method of reducing the payment: a promise by the landowner that he will employ the labourers also in the slack season when there is competition for obtaining employment. Furthermore, the employer can create an imperfect market situation when the employee is in debt and has 'labour obligations' to the employer. In chapter 4 we saw that the security for many loans was labour services to be rendered at a later stage. The employer is in a good position to impose his own terms and conditions for the type of work and the level of the wage for this type of contract.

We observed many times in Bhaimara that weeding tasks were undertaken by young boys and even girls working in a group. Normally it would take about 7 man-days to carry out a one time weeding on a one *bigha* plot. With a 10-Taka wage per person, it would cost 70 Taka to hire able-bodied men. In order to reduce this expense a landowner could offer a sum of 40–50 Taka to the children to finish the plot. In the weeding operation both children and old men, too weak to do ploughing or harvesting, would participate and would thereby compete with the healthy and strong wage-labourers and cause a depression in the level of wages. This method of reducing labour costs resembles the contractor approach we mentioned, when a fixed payment is made for a specific work task.

Another method which has been used to reduce wages is to compensate the labourers with the left-over straw from the paddy they have harvested. This mode of payment is a fairly recent phenomenon and illustrates clearly the deteriorating living conditions of people. Many middle-aged and old wage-labourers remembered well the days when they could bring home free paddy straw, with no deductions being made in their wages. According to the villagers of Bhaimara, it is only during the last 10–20 years that there has been a market for paddy straws. Paddy straws used for cattle fodder can reach a price of 4–5 Takas per *maund.*

In order to clear the land the remaining paddy straws will have to be removed. This is part of the preparation of the land for the next season. Children and poor women will sometimes do this work and as compensation receive the straws they have cleared. The straws can be used either for their own cattle or sold. Also in the first processing of jute when separating the fibres from the wooden stems, jute palings are sometimes the only wage for the work. The jute palings are used for constructing house walls and fences. This mode of payment also reveals a new development in the rural areas. Items that were traditionally considered free and available to all have become resources with a price attached to them. This is a very beneficial mode of payment for the landowner if he himself has sufficient jute palings and paddy straws for fodder. He will be saved the job of selling it, and normally with this type of wage the labourers get an incentive in that the more jute they process the more palings they get, and the more paddy straws they clear, the more straw they obtain. In Bhaimara we also observed children, with the permission of the landowners, going into the fields and picking big weeds which they gave to their own cattle. In this way free labour was given to the owner of the land.

A different method of reducing labour costs is to get as much work carried out by the wage-labourers as possible. If the employer has no definite idea of what should be achieved and if he does not supervise the work, the speed of the work carried out may be slow. If there is close supervision and especially if the landowner himself is working in the field, the labourers can be incited to prove their abilities and by that means hope to be considered for future employment by the employer. Another way to get as much work out of the labourers as possible is to feed them well if food is part of the payment. The wife of an employer explained to us that when fish was provided as part of the meal, the labourers would work harder.

Food as payment can also be used the other way; as a method of reducing expenditure on wages. When food has been the wage or part of the wages for men and women (carrying out post-harvesting tasks for other households), it has been an unwritten rule that the labourers get a well-cooked meal and that they can eat sufficiently. Many of the labourers have obviously taken advantage of this 'uncontrolled wage' and eaten more than is expected of them. (Old women informed us that in earlier times they would always bring their small children along when they worked in somebody else's *bari,* and the children would be properly fed as well.) Over the last years many women and some men reported that they were not paid their food in prepared meals in the home of the employers, but only received a small amount of uncooked rice to bring home, less than they would have eaten if they had received a prepared meal. This is also a new mode of payment reflecting the pressure on labourers to accept a wage of less value than previously. In many cases this mode of payment also shows the deteriorating economic conditions of the employer's household, i.e. that it cannot even afford to feed its labourers properly.

Maybe the most blatant example of manipulation of the wage system is a mode of payment called *magna kamla* which means labour without payment. This institution has long traditions in the rural areas, and we were informed that it existed and was practised in various parts of the country. *Magna kamla* was traditionally called a few times every year by the big landlords of an area. All relatives, neighbours and *samaj* members were called on to participate, and there was a moral obligation to attend. All the people who participated worked together for a day to finish a certain work task, weed a large plot or harvest it. The occasion was more than work, however; it was turned into a community event. The best available food would be served, a goat would be slaughtered, and sweets and plenty of rice would be served not only for the workers, but for family members of the workers as well.

According to information about how this institution is practised now, the rich landlords can nowadays call a *magna kamla* whenever appropriate and convenient for themselves. If insects have attacked their crops or their fields are flooded, they can at short notice call a *magna kamla.* Wages under such natural disasters, when the crops will have to be saved within a day, are often doubled. By calling the occasion a *magna kamla,* the rich landowner can get away with only giving a good meal to the labourers (not to their household members any more). The labourers will be left with a full stomach after a day's *magna kamla* work, but they will have nothing to bring to their families. These are without doubt hard terms, for the *magna kamla* coincides with one of the few days when the wage-labourers could have fed their whole families well and even saved a little. By not participating in the *magna kamla* when summoned by a rich landlord, a person would define himself as outside the community or group, and he cannot then expect support and favours from the person who calls the *magna kamla.* It was difficult to judge the extent of the practice of *magna kamla.* In Bhaimara we were told that many of the poor labourers a few times a year, when wages were at their highest level, would have to participate. Only the very rich and established landlords of an area would call a *magna kamla* today. In Bhaimara only a couple of landowners could call a *magna kamla* and be expected to be taken seriously and get a response, however, reluctant, from the participants.

A common and very different way to save expenses on labour costs is to reduce the amount of work to be carried out in the fields. Instead of weeding the *aus* crop three times, it will be weeded only twice or even once. Also in the preparation of land, clearing it, ploughing and harrowing, many labour days can be saved. The result is, of course, a poorer crop. The owner of the land will, however, make a calculation over how much he will save in expenses for labour versus the value for him of the reduced amount of paddy.

Also in the harvesting operation, a point is reached where the owner has to balance how thoroughly he will harvest his land with the cost he is incurring by hiring labour. It is striking to observe after each *aman* harvest, how all the old women and divorced women with their small children go to the fields and glean up the little left-overs of paddy grain.

A fairly new phenomenon in Bhaimara is the *labour migrants* who come to the village in the harvest period, especially the *aman* harvest. Bhaimara village, the surrounding villages and unions have always been considered as surplus labour areas, and poor peasants and landless labourers have left in large numbers for the northern districts of Bangladesh to participate in the *aman* harvest there. The number of migrant labourers coming to Bhaimara is small, however, only 5–10 people in the harvest season. The big landowners have allowed them to put up small huts adjacent to the landlords' homestead plot. The migrant labourers do not feel obliged to keep to the unwritten rules which the local labourers of Bhaimara and the surrounding areas stick to. Lack of solidarity between the migrant and local labourers about the level of wages they will work for has several times resulted in clashes in which attempts have been made to chase the migrant labourers away.

An article by Clay[9] shows how the system of payment for agricultural wage labourers has changed. This change could partly be attributed to the increased number of migrant labourers who have entered the labour market in the peak season. Instead of a system of payment where share payment was the mode, more employers have adopted cash wages on a daily basis as the wage system. The effect of the change in the mode of payment is that the link that existed in the share payment system between income of the wage-labourers and labour output of work is broken. The result of this is that the wage level is depressed. The employers' invitation to migrant labourers is thus one of the many strategies which can be used to reduce wage costs.[10]

There is little doubt that many of the employers, through the variety of methods mentioned above, have managed to lower their expenses on labour. It is especially the 'high' peak season wage which the employers have endeavoured to erode. The effect of lowering the wage level in peak seasons has been that after the peak season is over the wage-labourers have less left to sustain them through the slack seasons when low wages and unemployment and underemployment are common. This means that the poor and landless households depending on wage-labour will have to get into debt, with land or homestead plots as collateral for the loans.

The mode of payment and the value of the wage will, of course, also depend on whether there exist job opportunities outside agriculture in the area. For the poor and landless people in Bhaimara and its neighbouring areas job opportunities exist to a certain degree during the winter season when hard work in the brickfields is, for some, an alternative to agricultural employment. For some, short-term migration to the northern districts is also a possibility. In the winter season, except for the peak *aman* harvest period, rough estimates showed that 20–30 per cent of the wage-labourers in Bhaimara were employed or looked for employment outside the village area (as unskilled labour in Manikganj town, as migrant labourers, as rickshaw-pullers, and in the brickfields). Some wage-labourers who did not go outside the village searching for jobs were trying to find income-earning activities outside agriculture in the village area. Some work as housebuilders and masons, while others venture into petty trading and small-scale business or work in the transport sector. It is, however, difficult to judge to what extent these alternative sources of income have consequences for the wage level and mode of payment in the agricultural sector. Probably the wages, at least in the peak season, would have been lower for agricultural wage-labourers than the present rates.

What can a wage buy?

The essential commodities a poor and landless household must buy on the market are rice, wheat flour, salt and chillies. Of non-food items clothes and kerosene (for the small lamps at night) would be important. On the basis of a random sample survey of some of the landless and deficit households in Bhaimara it was found that 70–90 per cent of the expenditure on goods bought in the market was on rice or its substitute, wheat, alone. The poorer the households, the more they would spend on rice only.

The development of the real wage for the poor and landless

household is closely connected with the amount of rice a daily wage can buy, or the amount of paddy paid as wage, if the payment is in kind. However, before discussing the purchasing capacity of the present wages, it would be of some interest to try to get an idea of the value of the agricultural wages (in terms of the capacity to buy rice) as they were many decades ago. The oldest information we have from the village of Bhaimara was collected from the Revenue office in Manikganj. According to these sources the daily wage in Bhaimara in 1857 was reported to be:

For *ploughing*	3 *annas* + 2 meals
For *weeding*	3–4 *annas* + 2 meals
For *aus-crop harvesting*	4 *annas* + 2 meals
For *aman-crop harvesting*	4 *annas* + 2 meals
For *jute harvesting* and *jute processing*	8 *annas* + 2 meals

One *anna* is 1/16 *rupee.*

This information does not bring us much further, as we did not manage to obtain reliable knowledge on the price of rice at that time. (In 1920 reliable sources said that paddy was sold for one rupee per *maund* after the *aman* harvest.)[11] It is interesting to note the fairly large difference in payment for various types of work. It is difficult to make a considered judgement on whether it is supply and demand in the seasonal labour market which caused these differences or whether the differences are related to the physical hardships connected with the work tasks.

The oldest man in the village, about 90 years old, but with a very clear memory, could relate that when he was young, around 1910, the daily wages would be the equivalent of 5–6 *seers* of rice + 2–3 meals on a normal work day. Other old villagers who could report about the wages in the 1920s and 1930s estimated that the average wage would be 4–5 *seers* of rice every day in normal years, including meals. It is of course difficult to know to what extent these statements are correct. The information, however, from many sources seems consistent enough to say that real wages in normal years were much higher than at present.[12]

More recent and more accurate estimates are, however, available. According to information from the Bangladesh Bureau of Statistics,

Economic Indicators, the real wage in agriculture in Bangladesh was 30 to 40 per cent lower in the years of the mid 1970s compared with the early years in the 1960s.[13] Table 6.2 quoted from The Second Five Year Plan 1980–85 shows the trend in the real wage index.[14]

Table 6.2. Trend in Real Wage Index (1969–70 = 100).

Year	General Wage Index	Agricultural Wage Index
1972–73	67.6	66.5
1973–74	64.5	63.2
1974–75	57.4	60.7
1975–76	66.9	76.6
1976–77	71.2	75.6
1977–78	66.7	74.3
1978–79	75.7	81.0

Source: *Second Five Year Plan 1980–85,* Planning Commission, Dhaka, May 1980, p. 1–15.

Some of the comments the Second Five Year Plan makes about this table are presented below:

pp. 1–15, 1.52:
Inflation plus short supplies of essential consumer goods severely affected the standard of living of the mass. Both industrial and agricultural wages failed to keep pace with inflation. Real wages as a result declined and remained substantially below the 1969–70 level throughout the entire decade. The little progress that took place in this respect following the good harvest of 1975–76 also could not be steadily maintained. Though the situation was much better in 1977–78 than it was in 1974–75, the working class has still a real income which is one-fifth to one-fourth below the 1969–70 level.

pp. 1–15, 1.54:
Because of decline in real income of the working population, over four-fifths of population continue to be below poverty line, which is defined by the minimum caloric requirement of 2122 cal. The percentage is sligthly higher in the rural sector (86.7 per cent) against the national average of 84.6 per cent. The percentage of population below the extreme poverty line (1805 cal.) is estimated to be 53.6 per cent.

In the 1979–80 *aman* harvest in Bhaimara, the average peak season wage was 10 Taka without any meals. The price of rice was at the same time 4½ Taka per *seer* of rice. Later in 1980 the wage was down to 6–7 Taka and one *seer* of rice was costing 6–7 Taka. In

Bhaimara we found no rules linking the size of wage to a certain amount of rice which could be purchased directly with the wage. In the slack season we found that for some periods a full day's wage could only buy ¾ of a *seer* of rice, while in the peak season as much as 3 *seers* of rice could be bought by a top wage. All these wages are without food. When two meals are given as part of the wage in the peak season, the money part of the wage is down to 6–7 Taka, and in the slack season down to 2–3 Taka. Thus in the slack season a wage labourer, eating ½ *seer* of rice per day is only able to sustain himself and ½ another grown-up person.

Our information about the relationship between the level of the wage rate and the price of rice is contradictory to what Arens and Van Beurden observed in Jhagrapur.[15]

p. 98
We know of a few fixed rules in Jhagrapur which are applied when the wage rate has to be fixed. We will mention them briefly. Throughout the year labourers are paid three or four pounds of unhusked rice (paddy) or its equivalent in cash per day.

and p. 100
It is self-evident that a relationship exists between the wage rate and the prices of essential commodities. Therefore we shall devote some attention to prices. In Jhagrapur and surroundings average daily wages are equivalent to ¾–1 *seer* of husked rice. If the price of rice changes, the wage rate changes accordingly.

Our information, which is confirmed in many rural studies, shows the wages to be highest in the harvest season when the price of grain is at its lowest, and vice versa. In the slack season several months after the harvest, the price of rice is at its highest and wages at their lowest. As we shall elaborate on later in this chapter, we do not think there is a close connection between the wage level and the needs for survival of the wage labourers. Arens and Van Beurden also note, however, that the real wages in Jhagrapur have declined; the 'real wages in 1975 were about 40 per cent of what they were in 1969' (p. 104, *op.cit.)*.

Economic and social effects of lowered wages

What are the effects of lower real wages in agriculture for the poor peasants and the landless households? It seems obvious that their material standard of living has deteriorated during the last 10–20 years. It is not only the statistical data presented above that show this; the poor people's own view of how their situation has developed clearly supports this assumption.

According to interviews, the landless and poor households now eat less rice per day than they did 10–20 years ago. Some women told us that 10 years back they would live on a starvation diet, by which they meant eating rice only once a day, for two months every year. In the last years this period has been extended to 4–5 months every year. Often they will substitute wheat for rice and sometimes even the inexpensive sweet potatoes. The persons interviewed said that 10–15 years ago they never substituted sweet potatoes for rice. Chillies, salt and vegetables are now hardly bought from the market at all, whereas these items, at least in the peak seasons, were regularly purchased 10–15 years ago.

Clothes which were previously bought new at least once a year by the poor and landless households are now either purchased second hand or received used from well-to-do persons. The poor and landless households interviewed also related that their general health conditions had deteriorated, and they clearly attributed this to the lack of a proper diet. Wage-labourers confront the dilemma of either feeding themselves properly, so that they are able and fit to work, or feeding their unproductive family members a little better. The wage has now become so depressed that they cannot manage to do both. We observed and were told of many cases in which household supporters had lived on so little and poor food (for example sweet potatoes instead of rice) that they became sick and were unable to work. (See case 1, chapter 4.)

The decline in the material standard of living has also had implications for the social life of the poor and landless households. The material standard of living is now so low that the viability of the traditional household is threatened. Since unproductive members cannot be fed from the income of the productive members, unproductive children, both boys and girls, are often sent away to work as servants in more well-to-do households. Unproductive, old household members are also in pressed situations separated from the productive household members. We noted in chapter 3, how old parents may be separated and each placed in the household of a different child. In this way the material burden is shared by the children. It is not uncommon among the landless and poorest households that none of the children can afford to feed the old parents. The old parents will then be left on their own to starve or to the humiliation of becoming beggars. The events preceding splitting of households are degrading; quarrelling and fighting over the sharing of food occur between the household members, and jealousy, suspicion and enmity are created. The material base that should foster the traditional supportive and warm family relationships has been undermined for the poor and landless households.

Development prospects for the wage-labour market

Which of the present patterns on the labour market will be strengthened or weakened in the future? All the evidence indicates that the number of people who will depend on wage-labour in agricultural activities will increase in the years to come. This is due partly to the population growth and the 'demographic profile' of the population in Bangladesh. The percentage increase in the labour force is larger than in the population as a whole, 4 to 4½% each year, as we noted in chapter 2. The expansion of the labour force will also increase, because more people will become landless or have less land than they can subsist on. The growth in the labour force will partly be off-set by the growth in employment opportunities. High-yielding varieties and more intensive cropping will create more jobs in agricultural activities, and the estimates show that there will also be an increase in employment opportunities in non-agricultural activities in the rural areas and in urban employment. But the growth in the agricultural labour force will be much larger than the expansion in employment opportunities.[16] We shall discuss the employment effects of the new HYV (High Yielding Variety) technology in detail in chapter 8. Unemployment and underemployment will thus become even more rampant in the future. What effect will this dismal macro-perspective have at the village level? A higher number of unemployed people in the village areas would probably mean that there will be more migrant labourers also going to villages that are characterized as surplus labour areas. An increased number of both local and migrant labourers will compete for employment in the villages. The effect of this will be that the bargaining position of the wage-labourers will be weakened, and this will in turn lead to changes in modes of payment advantageous to the employers and the ultimate consequence of this is lower real wages.

How low can the wages drop? It should be clear from the above discussion that the standard of living of the agricultural wage-labourers will depend not only on how much they are paid when they are employed, but also on how long periods of a year they are able to secure employment for. The standard of living of the wage-labourers will further depend on the extent to which they depend entirely on wages for their total income. We have seen that many of the wage-labourers also have a little bit of agricultural land; some may be both landowners and sharecroppers. Most of the landless households will have a homestead plot (14 out of the 21 landless households in Bhaimara have one). Even a small homestead plot will normally constitute a source of livelihood. This means that most of the households of the wage-labourers are sustaining themselves from resources additional to the wages the household members may earn. Since so many of the wage-labourers have additional resources they can pool with their wages in order to survive, many are willing to accept that their wages only partly cover their household's basic needs. Since the level of wages for the wage-labourers is not dependent on or connected with the amount of other resources which the wage-labourers' households have at their disposal, the completely landless, without agricultural land or a homestead plot, are the ones who suffer most from the low wage level. (Households with unfavourable ratios of productive/non-productive members are also, of course, more vulnerable to low wages.)

Thus the unequal economic position of the wage-labourers as regards alternative income sources has very negative consequences for the wage-labourers who depend entirely on their income from employment. We think that economic inequality among the wage-labourers and the implications this has for lowered wage rates have escaped due attention in many village studies. In the future too the economic position of the wage-labourers will vary. It is very clear, however, that over the next decades there will be many more wage-labourers dependent on wages *alone* for their survival, but the category of wage-labourers will remain heterogeneous. Many households that today are composed of 'middle-class' peasants will during the next decades slide downwards and end up in a situation where they partly depend on incomes from wage-labour for their livelihood. Therefore a group will still exist which has other resources to depend on. The households in this group will accept lower wages and press down the wage level for the households without any resources but their labour to depend on.

One theme we stated in previous chapters we should address ourselves to is the effects of lowered real wages on agricultural production. Erich Jacoby has described a 'vicious circle', which in many respects is relevant for Bangladesh.[17]

> It is obvious that the increase in rural unemployment, which is not balanced by additional employment possibilities in urban areas, will have serious repercussions on the domestic market and price developments. The multiplied supply of marketable food crops will be met by a declining effective demand for food due to the rising unemployment. This will cause declining food prices which ultimately will further impair the rural labour situation: on the one hand, the large producers will try to defend their profits by reducing labour costs through an increased use of modern farm machinery and often even by cutting down the actual area under cultivation; on the other, the small farmers, who cannot afford to rationalize, will be forced to market their surplus at prices which will reduce their main source of cash income, with the result that in the end they may have to sell their land cheaply and join the ranks of the unemployed.
>
> The vicious circle of unemployment, declining food prices and new unemployment must inevitably lead to a deterioration of the social stratification in the rural areas.

There are many issues brought up in the description of this 'vicious' circle. It is obvious that unemployment and low wages lead to a reduced purchasing capacity for a large and growing part of the population. This lack of demand naturally has consequences for the efforts the peasants with a surplus make to increase agricultural production. We have noted in previous chapters that the technological and organizational difficulties involved in adopting HYV-technology and the profits to be gained by hoarding and price speculation of agricultural products and money-lending have made many 'surplus' peasants opt for the more secure investment of expanded land property. The low level of purchasing capacity, closely related to these issues, only strengthens the 'surplus' peasants' interest in the alternative of investing in increased holdings of land. In chapter 8, when describing the Food Rationing System, we shall see that there are several ways of increasing the price of rice. We shall see, when discussing the Food Rationing System and the employment effects following the adoption of HYV-technology, that the implications of an increased price of rice are complicated, the outcome being dependent on a variety of factors.

A final comment should be made on the relationship between increased unemployment and the pattern of social organization in the rural areas. We believe that, given the present framework of economic and political conditions, the easiest way for underemployed wage-labourers to secure employment is to align themselves with well-to-do and rich landowners. The social organization which emerges from this adaptation will be numerous *patron-client* relationships in the rural areas. Such relationships will naturally undermine the possibilities for creating a 'class' solidarity among the wage-labourers. We shall return to this issue in chapters 9 and 10.

Notes

1 See K. Griffin and Khan, A.R., 'Poverty in the Third World: Ugly Facts and Fancy Models', *World Development,* No. 3, 1978, p. 298.

2 See Azizur Rahman Khan, Riawanul Islam and Mahfuzul Huq: *Employment, Income and the Mobilization of Local Resources — A Study of Two Bangladesh Villages,* ILO, 1980.

3 A.R. Khan, R. Islam and M. Huq, *op.cit.,* p. 15.

4 Arens and van Beurden, *op.cit.,* found the patrilineal group playing a much less important role for economic relationships than we found in Bhaimara. Patrilineal relationships are unimportant compared to the strength and skills of the workers when an employer is to hire a wage-labourer, they maintain, see pp. 89–93.

5 Arens and van Beurden, *op.cit.,* pp. 94–104, also emphasize the importance for wage-labourers of attaching themselves to *patrons.* They do not consider whether a patron can also be a *gusti* member, a patrilineal relative of the client, a phenomenon we often found in Bhaimara.

6 Barkat-E-Khuda: *The Use of Time and Underemployment in Rural Bangladesh,* University of Dhaka, 1982, pp. 59–60.

7 Paddy is rice in the husk.

8 See Area Handbook for Bangladesh, *op.cit.,* p. 135.

9 Edward J. Clay: 'Institutional Change and Agricultural Wages in Bangladesh', *The Bangladesh Development Studies.* Volume IV, Oct. 1976, No. 4, pp. 423–440.

10 The implications of labour migrants for the wage level and for solidarity among the labourers are also discussed by G.D. Wood in A. Huq (ed.), *op.cit.,* and Arens and Van Beurden, *op.cit.*

11 A *maund* of paddy is equal to about 27 kiloes of rice.

12 Van Schendel, *op.cit.,* p. 226, provides some information on the development of the daily wages in relation to the price of rice:
The money component of the daily wage expressed in kg of rice at contemporary price: 1.7 (in 1789), 6.8 (1850), 9.0 (1859), 3.6 (1866), 5.2 (1870), 5.8 (1894), 3.7 (1910), 2.3 (1970), 1.3–2.5 (1978). Food was probably always added to this. The reliability of the earlier figures is unknown and could not be checked. Sources: Thompson, 1918: 285,295; Browne, 1866: 3.7; Hunter, 1876: 396,397; Cumming, 1894: xxviii. 48; Webster, 1910: 40–41; N.I. Khan, 1977b: 110–113; 1978 field-notes (Qadir (1960) did not give information on this point). Introduction of HYVs in the 1960s did nothing to stop this decline, let alone reverse it. (Cf. R. Islam, 1979: 397–398).

13 E.J. Clay, *op.cit.*

14 *The Second Five Year Plan 1980–85,* Planning Commission, Dhaka, May 1980.

15 Arens and van Beurden, *op.cit.,* pp. 94–104.

16 For a more precise discussion on this topic see E.J. Clay and Md. Selkandor Khan, *Agricultural Employment and Under-employment in Bangladesh:* The Next Cecade. Dhaka: Bangladesh Agricultural Research Council, October 1977.

17 Erich H. Jacoby: 'Effects of the "Green Revolution" in South and South-east Asia', *Modern Asian Studies,* Vol. 6, No. 1, 1972, p. 260.

7

Disputes over Ownership of Land

Introduction

Land disputes are common and well-known incidents all over rural Bangladesh. Social scientists who have conducted field work in rural areas are well aware of the frequent occurrence of land disputes. Yet in almost all the sociological and anthropological literature published about rural Bangladesh, the issue of land disputes has been dealt with only peripherally or incidentally, focusing on the effects land disputes have had on other events. A land dispute will often be briefly described in the sociological literature because, for example, it has caused a split in a traditional faction of the village; or a land dispute may be given as a reason why some poor people have become landless. Little effort has been made to go into a deeper description and analysis of the land disputes.[1]

We believe that a closer study of land disputes is important for several reasons. Maybe more than any other events land disputes throw light on how essential it is to have support in the community. If it cannot mobilize aid from an important *patron* or a faction, a household is very much exposed to attacks. We described in chapter 3 how vulnerable Durzon Ali, a poor immigrant to Bhaimara, was when for dubious reasons he was expelled from his homestead plot and the village. An analysis of land disputes is therefore also a study of local level politics. Disputes over ownership rights can also be regarded as a mechanism of transfer of land. In the previous chapters we have emphasized inheritance and sale of land as the two most important mechanisms for transfer of ownership rights. (In chapter 3 we also mentioned that land could be transferred as a gift and later in this chapter we shall discuss possession of *khas* land (Government land) as a method of obtaining land.) Compared with the amount transferred through inheritance and sale, the amount of land transferred as a consequence of disputes is very small. Yet most plots of land may, in certain circumstances give rise to disputes. Disputes as a method of competing for land must be understood in the light of the scarcity of land and the difficulties involved in obtaining land through legal ways.

There is great variation in the background of land disputes and in the types of claims a plaintiff can make against a landowner. The different types of land disputes have a certain pattern in which the actions and counteractions by the litigants can be anticipated. This chapter does not aim at trying to capture the specific and inner dynamic of the various forms of disputes. It will, however, indicate the variety of reasons for land disputes and present some case studies to illustrate some characteristic features of the specific types of disputes. The case studies do not claim to be 'representative' of the type of dispute they are listed under. A common feature of all the case studies presented is that they are oversimplified. A land dispute is often a complicated and long-lasting affair in which the issues and claims that are brought into the dispute are in many cases matters that at first sight seem irrelevant to a dispute over ownership to land. For each of the case studies presented many more steps have taken place in the strategies of the litigants than we mention. In many of the case studies more people are also directly and indirectly involved as supporters of the parties to the disputes. For the sake of simplicity we have to a large extent omitted many of the persons involved and the arguments they have put forward.

Most of the case studies presented in this chapter have been collected from Bhaimara and the surrounding villages. A few have, however, been recorded during shorter field-trips to other districts in the southern and northern parts of Bangladesh. It was very difficult to get quantitative measurements as to how many households had been involved in land disputes. Few households mentioned that they had been engaged in land disputes, even households we, who collected the information, knew very well had been deeply involved. It is thus very difficult to judge the extent of the phenomenon on the basis of superficial surveys. Through the case studies we want to convey a picture of the complex opportunity situation of the parties involved. The cases presented in chapter 4 emphasized particularly the wider economic aspects of people's opportunity situation. Through the cases in this chapter weight will be put on the alliances people can call on for support.

The first 'type' of dispute we discuss concerns division of inherited property. This type of dispute will often not involve many other parties than the relatives themselves.

Disputes due to division of inherited land

In chapter 3 we saw how the rules of inheritance gave detailed instructions on the proportion of land to be inherited by sons, daughters, wives and under specific circumstances other family members. We noted, however, that despite the clear rules there are often conflicts about division of land.

There are many reasons for the conflicts. One common reason for the disputes is connected with the contribution the brothers have made to the family when they lived in a joint household. In many cases one or two of the brothers have produced and contributed much more to the 'common pot' than they have consumed. Younger brothers and sisters can have consumed much more than they have produced. In many cases elder brothers have financed the education of their younger brothers, and they feel they should be compensated when land and property are divided. In some cases, as explained earlier, they will already have provided for themselves by having, for instance, saved or invested clandestinely in land while they lived in a joint household. Some brothers will, however, demand a larger or better share when the land is divided. Some brothers may also have tried to influence their father to set up a will where special plots are set aside for them because they have produced more or have been 'favourite' sons. All these forms of unequal distribution can at a later stage lead to disputes.

Another ground for dispute is the land that is inherited by the sisters. We noted that normally sisters do not claim their land, in order to maintain a good relationship with their brothers. In some cases they take the land they are entitled to according to the Muslim law of inheritance, and this can cause disputes between brothers on the one side and sisters and their husbands on the other. Sometimes sisters can sell their land or give it to one particular brother, and this may again cause conflict between the brothers. (Disputes over sisters' land can be started even 20–30 years after the division of the land.)

There are no detailed regulations for giving land to adopted children who may have lived in the household for many years. Grandchildren whose father is dead before the death and division of land of their grandfather are not entitled to any inherited land property. Both adopted children and fatherless grandchildren may through the written will of the head of the household inherit land. Disputes over land they inherit at the expense of other heirs are common. Also in households where the head has, or has had, several wives disputes over land can arise among the children of the different wives. Situations also occur when land which should be inherited by a group of brothers and sisters is snatched away from them. Especially when the head of the household dies at a time when his children are young and not able to protect their property rights, an opportunity may be found and a claim fabricated by others in order to take the land. These children can at a later stage, if they become powerful, start disputes.

It can also happen that an elder and unscrupulous brother can take all the land for himself and leave his younger and maybe defenceless brothers and sisters without land. (See case 4, chapter 4, the story of Halim Khan.) When conducting interviews in the village we were struck time and again by the often great disparity in wealth and standard of living between brothers. It is not uncommon that within the same compound where brothers live with their separate households, one brother may live in a comfortable well-built brick house and own several or many acres of land, while a poor landless brother and his family live next to him in a small grass hut. Individual skills play an important role in deciding how much property a person may accumulate, and disparity in the standard of living between brothers may be due to the fact that one has been more skilled in managing the resources he has been allocated. The difference in the standard of living can also be attributed to the fact that one brother started at a different economic level by having inherited more land. Although there is no quantitative data on the types of relationships which exist among litigants in land disputes, it should be clear that for a large proportion of the land which is disputed, members of the same family are the litigants.

Case 1. Dispute in connection with the division of inherited land among three brothers

The following story illustrates a conflict between three brothers which arose when dividing the property they inherited. The conflict was not over the ownership rights to land but about the right of one of the brothers to use a specific plot of land in order to compensate him for certain expenses he had incurred when the brothers lived in a joint household.

The three brothers, Samad Khan, Shadjahan, and Shuva Mia lived in a joint household for a few years after the death of their father. They inherited altogether 5 acres of land from their father. Shadjahan, the second oldest brother was the only one of the brothers with a formal education. He had received a medical degree which allowed him to practise as a village doctor. In order to buy medicine which he could give to his patients, he needed money in cash. With the agreement of his two brothers he obtained a loan of 2000 Taka from a Government bank. A large plot of land was given as security to the bank, but the brothers continued to cultivate the plot in the same way as before.

Some years after this money was raised the brothers broke up from the joint household and established separate households. There was no quarrel when the different plots were divided except about the plot that had been mortgaged to the bank. Shadjahan wanted all the three brothers to pay one-third of the loan each to the bank in order to release the plot from the mortgage. He claimed that much of the 2000 Taka had been spent on joint consumption for the three brothers and their families, for food, travel, clothes, education of children. The money he had used for medicine, he maintained, had been returned to the joint household from the income he earned on the sale of medicine. He said therefore that if he alone had to pay back the 2000 Taka, he would farm the whole plot by himself and take the whole crop for his own use. His brothers refused to pay and Shadjahan returned the 2000 Taka to the bank alone. Under the protests of his brothers he started to cultivate the whole plot. The brothers maintained that they had received little of the 2000 Taka and that Shadjahan had much unsold medicine which he had bought with the 2000 Taka. When Shadjahan harvested his first crop from the plot, Shuva Mia was so annoyed that he went into the field and demanded his share. When he did not get it, a fight started between the brothers. The brothers were armed with sticks, but no one was seriously injured in the fight.

After this fight, the dispute was brought before a *shalish* (local court) in the village. The case lasted for a long period and many *matbars* (respected elder persons who can participate as judges in the local courts) were consulted. Other issues which were not directly linked to the use of the disputed plot but which were connected with other parts of the inherited property were brought in. Shuva Mia told the *shalish* that the wife of Shadjahan had taken a good grinding stone for paddy from the joint household without giving any compensation to his wife. Shadjahan for his part said that Samad Khan had taken a bed from the joint household without compensation to the others. Many other items were also disputed. The final verdict of the *shalish* was a compromise whereby the different items and the plots were divided among the brothers. The *shalish* decided that Shadjahan would cultivate the whole plot for which he had secured the loan and consume all the crops for three years, after which the land should be divided among the three brothers.

The brothers accepted the verdict and for the three years Shadjahan cultivated the plot. When the three years had passed, Shadjahan complained that for two years the crops had failed completely. He would therefore continue to cultivate the land until he felt he had been adequately compensated. Again there was a quarrel and during the first harvest of the fourth year there was a fight in the fields. The case was taken to the *shalish* and debated there, but before any final decision was taken a situation arose which seemed to provide an opportunity to resolve the dispute. Shadjahan decided at this time to stand for a seat in the Union Council. He needed all the support he could muster, and he told his two brothers that if they helped him in the campaign he would drop his claim to cultivate the plot any longer. The brothers agreed to this proposal and assisted Shadjahan in winning support in the village. This dispute seems to have ended after this.

This type of dispute is quite common. In many cases the brothers and family settle the dispute themselves without bringing it before the local court. A large patrilineal group will often, especially if they have a strong, recognized leader, feel that it is rather shameful not to be able to settle smaller types of disputes themselves. Even if inheritance disputes are brought before the *shalish,* the dispute seldom involves many people. Therefore factions are seldom created or mobilized on the basis of this type of dispute. It is also typical that when local courts settle a dispute like the one mentioned above they want to establish a compromise between the litigants.

The case we present below is a 'classic' story of how an older brother can exploit his younger, illiterate and powerless brother.

Case 2. Illegal acquisition of land which did not result in a formal dispute in the local court

In case 1 in chapter 4 we outlined the economic strategies of Mosum Ali, one of the landless wage-labourers of Bhaimara. Mosum Ali was cheated by his half-brother at the time the inherited land was divided. When he was younger Mosum Ali lived in a well-to-do household. He was the only son of his father's second wife. The first wife of his father had one son, Shiraz, and two daughters, who were all much older than Mosum Ali. On the father's death, Shiraz managed to get 3 acres from his father while Mosum Ali who was then only a boy received 20 decimals (0.2 acres) of agricultural land. (The father had expressed this division in his written will. Villagers later claimed that Shiraz had at the death-bed of his father managed to obtain his thumbprint on a piece of paper he himself had written.) Shiraz has expanded his farm since the death of his father and now owns 3.8 acres.

Although Mosum Ali was entitled to inherit much more than he did, he has not been able to bring his case before a recognized *shalish.* He has talked to all the *matbars* in the village. All of them realize that he has been cheated, but none are willing to bring the case before a *shalish.* There is very little to gain from fighting for the rights of Mosum Ali. Nobody who sided with him could expect to obtain bribes, and they would first of all have to fight against Shiraz who has become one of the most powerful men in the village and is aspiring to become a *matbar* himself. (Already some people address him as Shiraz *matbar*.)

The only way Mosum Ali could have managed to start a dispute against his half-brother was to gain the support of a powerful man who had interests in destroying Shiraz. Although Mosum Ali should have excellent evidence for his claims, no dispute is launched because of his powerlessness. His situation is further disadvantaged by the fact that he is dependent on Shiraz for employment, credit and gifts. Should Mosum Ali try to start a dispute and attract the interest of a powerful person for his case, Shiraz would automatically demand his loans repaid and never employ Mosum Ali again.

The situation of Mosum Ali is not uncommon in rural Bangladesh, i.e., that the person on whom a poor man greatly depends is also the one who has exploited him most. Among brothers, in cases where one brother has expanded his property at the expense of the others, the ideal situation for the rich brother would be to create a relationship of *patronage* to his poor brothers. The poor brothers can be employed, receive credit on good conditions, receive gifts as long as they acquiesce in a subordinate position. As soon as they act against their richer brother's interests, the richer brother will withdraw all these benefits, which at least give the poor brothers a minimum degree of security. We have seen in the cases in chapter 4 that this unequal relationship not only exists among brothers: it is also a very frequent relationship between any rich and any poor man in the village.

Land disputes over Hindu land property

For a long period in this century Hindu landowners owned and controlled the largest land estates in what today is rural Bangladesh. After the partition of India and Pakistan in 1947, many Hindus left for India. In the 1950s much of their land was declared 'enemy' property and considered as *'khas'* land, Government land, which could be given out on lease. The land that was taken from them by the Government and declared *khas* land has often been the subject of disputes. In the case of *khas* land and also for other types of disputes over Hindu land property, the litigants are often not the former owners, but various people who compete against each other in order to acquire the land. Disputes may have started between the former sharecroppers of the Hindu landowner and the persons who managed to acquire the land after the Hindus had left the country. The Hindus, having been in a very difficult position for the last 35 years, have often tried to sell their land, usually at a price much below market rate. Such sale has created many problems and disputes. The Hindu landowners may have given a title-deed to the buyer of the land which has not been accepted by the Government.

The case we narrate below started at the time of Partition, when many Hindus sold their land. The main opponents in the case are two rich Muslim peasants. The case is a very simplified version of what actually happened. (In our first description of the case, we went back to events which happened in the 1920s. Our records showed that 34 persons had been actively involved in the case of the last 60 years and countless actions and counteractions had taken place. Our chief informant on this matter, however, when we read him our original 15 page typed version of the case complained that we had not been able to capture the whole story and appreciate the complexity of the case!)

Case 3. Disputes among rich peasants over former Hindu land

For our simplified version the starting point for the dispute was that the son of a rich Hindu landlord, 35 years ago when he was about to leave for India, sold 10 acres to another Hindu person named *Dash Bhandu.* (The main participants all live in the neighbouring villages of Bhaimara.) The land he sold also belonged to his younger brother, who knew nothing about the sale at that time. *Dash Bhandu,* realizing the illegal aspect of the sale, soon sold part of this land to *Mohuddin Molla.* Later the younger brother sold 'his' half of the land to *Rashid Khan,* a rich and powerful landowner. *Rashid Khan* soon took possession of parts of the land which belonged to *Dash Bhandu* and *Mohuddin Molla* and started to cultivate the land with his sharecroppers and wage-labourers. He also built a large house next to the land in order to protect his crops. Bhandu and Molla filed a cased in the Government civil court and won it. With help from the police, Bhandu and Molla tore down the buildings of Rashid Khan and reclaimed the land. The incident was a big defeat for Rashid Khan. Some years later Rashid Khan had managed to become Chairman of the Union

Council and became closely connected with the MP (Member of Parliament) for the area. His position was strengthened, and he again started a dispute over the land. This time Rashid Khan had fabricated a document which showed that the land belonged to him. The case was brought before the courts without any final decisions being made. Both parties spent large sums of money on bribes, and both parties hired groups of 'fighters' *(lathials)* in order to fight and evict the other from the fields. Both parties also hired 'professional' people to murder the other. As a consequence of his insecure position Rashid Khan moved his home to the district town, where he bought a house very close to the police station. Rashid Khan only went to the village area during daytime and when he moved around he always had several strong, armed men close to him.

The case lingered on for many years and several levels of courts were involved. Finally the case ended at the High Court in Dhaka. During the dispute Dash Bhandu died and his sons left for India. His daughter with her family continued to stay in the area, but she was unable to fight against Rashid Khan. Gradually Mohuddin Molla took over and represented both the interests of the daughter of Dash Bhandu and himself against Rashid Khan. Mohuddin Molla had been able to buy up much land during the 1950s and 1960s, and he was able to get 'his man' elected to the Union Council Chairmanship during the 1960s. Mohuddin Molla had thus accumulated great resources with which to fight Rashid Khan. Molla also won the final verdict in the High Court of Dhaka, and the 10 acres were registered in his name and the name of the family of Dash Bhandu. Molla estimated that over the 20 years the dispute had lasted he had spent between 15,000 and 20,000 Taka to hire lawyers and give bribes to different people. As a compensation for working for the daughter of Dash Bhandu he received one acre of her land.

Rashid Khan died a few years after the verdict, and his eldest son took over his position as head of the household and the patrilineage. The eldest son, who for a period also was Chairman of the Union Council, still lives in a joint household with his younger brothers and their separate families. He will not revive the dispute with Molla, who has steadily become more powerful.

This dispute has not only been between Mohuddin Molla and Dash Bhandu on one side and Rashid Khan on the other. Molla, Bhandu and Khan came from three different, but neighbouring villages. Most of the people in these villages have in one way or the other participated in the dispute and taken sides with one of the two parties. Bhandu, Molla and Khan each have many persons who depend on them for sharecropping rights, seasonal and daily labour, credit, gifts and other favours. All these people with their families have sided with their 'patron', supported him when physical protection was needed, and voted for him or 'his' candidates in the Union Council elections. During the 20 years the case lasted the main factions of the whole union were formed on the basis of this particular dispute. A method the three rich peasants applied to implicate their supporters was to let them buy small parts of the disputed land cheaply or give out parts of the disputed land on easy sharecropping terms. Both the sharecropping market and the labour market were to a large degree affected and structured by the two main factions. Even the choice of marriage partners took place along faction lines. During the dispute Halim Khan (case 4, chapter 4) became a main supporter of Mohuddin Molla, and we noted earlier that these two rich peasants cemented their relationship by their children being married to each other.

What issues does this case bring up? It shows that a dispute can go on for decades and that the children of the persons who started the dispute can 'inherit' the dispute from their parents. A dispute in which a verdict has been reached can be started again if the other party sees that there is chance of reversing the decisions. Arguments, dates and reasons for starting a dispute can be found in events which date 30–40 years back. The case also spells out different techniques of acquiring land, e.g., by making false documents (this can be done in various ways) or by taking forceful possession of the land. One way to take forceful possession of land is to have a physical fight where both 'real' supporters (sharecroppers, seasonal labourers) and hired fighters, *lathials,* are mobilized. The role of the Union Council can be important in large land disputes. The members and Chairman of the Union Council may play a part in influencing decisions in the dispute. When disputes over large areas of land go on for years, huge sums of money are spent on paying lawyers and bribing people. Much surplus which has been produced in the rural areas where the litigants have their economic assets is thus in this way transferred to urban areas where the lawyers, government officials and judges reside. Criminality and murder often occur as a consequence of land disputes, and such incidents have of course far-reaching repercussions in the villages. We were told about and also met a few people for whom the land dispute they had been involved in had absorbed and obsessed them completely. No other issue was of importance, and they reacted irrationally in relation to the land they had lost. They spent the rest of their money and all their energy in trying to reclaim the land they would have no chance of getting back, regardless of the objective merit of their case.

The 'official' reason for the dispute narrated below is connected with the implementation of the inheritance rules of Hindu-owned land. This is, however, not the real cause of the dispute. The way the inherited property was divided can only be considered as a pretext for starting the dispute. If the plaintiff could not have used this argument, he would have invented another strategy in order to obtain the land.

Case 4. Dispute due to the Hindu rules of inheritance

The two persons involved in this dispute were Kashem Ali and Mohuddin Khan, who lived several miles away from each other in different villages. The disputed plot of land was 0.3 acre in size and belonged to Kashem Ali. The plot was situated very close to the homestead compound of Mohuddin Khan. Kashem Ali's father had cultivated the plot for 20 years, and after his death Kashem Ali had used the plot for 10 years. Khan was very anxious to get hold of the land, which was so conveniently situated in relation to his home, but since the plot was very fertile and Kashem Ali was not a poor man, there was little chance that he would sell it at a reasonable price.

Khan thought up many ways to get the land. Through investigations he discovered that it was Kashem Ali's father who had bought the land from a widowed Hindu woman, Saudamani, 30 years before. Before Kashem Ali's father bought it he had sharecropped the land for many years. Khan consulted the Hindu law of inheritance and found that Saudamani had no right to sell the land, which was registered in her father's name. The land should according to the Hindu law of inheritance have been inherited by her two sons, who were very young 30 years ago. Khan found here a possibility of fomenting a dispute. For a long period he pressed one of the sons of Saudamani to draw up a document and sell the land to him. The son knew, of course, that it was his mother who sold the land 30 years ago. Saudamani, who was still alive and lived in her son's home, told him not to sell the land a second time. The son was physically threatened by Khan and 'forced' to sell the land to him. He probably received a very small sum of money for the sale. The dispute between Kashem Ali and Khan started after this sale. Khan took over the land by force. Kashem Ali immediately called a *shalish* with *matbars* from different villages. The verdict was in favour of Kashem Ali. One argument Kashem Ali used in the *shalish* was that the two sons of Saudamani had, according to Government law, the opportunity to protest against their mother's sale of the land for a period of up to 18 years. During these 18 years the sons would have been able to buy the land back. Since 30 years had passed, this opportunity was lost. Next season Kashem Ali again went to the plot, but as soon as he had planted, the plants were uprooted by Khan. Again there was a *shalish,* which decided that Kashem Ali was the owner of the plot. Khan, however, continued to occupy and use the land. Several more *shalishes* were held, all of which reached verdicts in favour of Kashem Ali. The *shalishes* had, however, no power to enforce the decisions.

There are several reasons why Khan can continue to use the land. The land is far away from Kashem Ali's home, and he will have difficulties in protecting the crops on it. Khan also belongs to and has support from a village that is situated next to a main path which is the only way to reach a ferry quay at a riverside. People from different villages, including the village Kashem Ali belongs to, have to pass along this path to reach the ferry quay and from there the main town of the area. The people of Khan's village are well-known in the area for being dangerous and threatening physically people they dislike. When people they consider as 'enemies' pass along the path at night, they can easily be attacked and injured. Kashem Ali and his supporters are therefore afraid to enter into a fight with Khan's people because they know that they can be punished when they walk through Khan's village at night alone or in small groups. This sanction of physical harassment has also scared some of the *matbars* and judges on the *shalishes.* Although Kashem Ali has raised his case many times, he has gradually got less influential *matbars* to sit in the *shalish.* The fact that the *matbars* know that there is very little chance of implementing the verdict leads the most influential of them to refrain from participating in the *shalishes,* in order to maintain their reputation.

Why then has Kashem Ali not taken the case to the Government court? There are several reasons for this. One is that it can be difficult to implement even a Government decision in this case. A more important argument is all the expenses which will be incurred by bringing the dispute before a Government court. For only 0.3 acre of land, which he estimated was worth 6000 Taka, the expenses and time spent on the dispute could soon exceed the value of the land. The dispute seems for the time being to have ended by Khan having started to cultivate the land. Should Khan become poor over the next decade, or even if Kashem Ali's children should rise and become powerful, they could start a dispute again.

This case illustrates several points. If a rich man wants to have a certain plot, he will fabricate any type of claim to the land; in this case, some doubt about the correct implementation of the Hindu law of inheritance was the starting point for the dispute. If he cannot manage to produce a logical claim with at least some reasonableness attached to it, he can of course occupy the land by force. There are, however, barriers involved in the use of such a method. For a rich household, however, honour, *izzat,* and respectable behaviour are also important features to consider. The behaviour and actions of everyone have an aspect of honour/dishonour attached to them. The criteria for evaluating the level of honour and respect is relative, depending on specific circumstances and people's economic position. While everyone taking forceful possession of land belonging to Hindus who have fled to India can be accepted, such action would not be regarded a s proper in the case above. Even if the reasons for the claim are not strong, at least a claim has to be put up. The weaker the arguments for the claim, the greater is the chance that the plaintiff can suffer loss of reputation and respect.

Another issue which highlights the case above is the way threats of physical violence may restrain people's actions. It is not uncommon for people in rural areas to fear and avoid conflicts and confrontations with groups of people who are either living in strategically important areas and/or are known for not being scrupulous in physical confrontations. A final, general feature of this dispute we shall mention here, concerns the lack of confidence in the Government courts. Many people have experienced that it is in the interest of lawyers and judges to prolong land dispute cases and squeeze bribes out of the litigants at each step. Also, in many cases one of the litigants may know that even if he wins in the Government court, there may be difficulties in enforcing the decision. Or even if he obtains the land, he knows that he may be threatened in other ways by his more powerful opponents.

Disputes over khas land

In all areas of Bangladesh there are plots which are owned by the Government and not by private people. This land is called *khas* land. Altogether 1.4 million acres of land, that is about 6 per cent, of a total of 24 million acres in Bangladesh, are estimated to be *khas* land.[2]

There are several ways in which land can become *khas* land. If a person has not paid taxes on the land, the Government can declare the land to be *khas* land and evict the owner. We noted that large parts of the land property the Hindus left behind when they moved to India have been declared *khas* land. *Char* lands, the areas of agricultural land which arise from deposits along the edges of many rivers, are also often taken by the Government and given *khas* land status. Certain ponds and small bamboo-forests having no clear private ownership can also be declared *khas* land. All *khas* land which is agricultural land is being cultivated by private persons. The Government can lease the land on a yearly basis to peasants and in this way generate revenue. The Government can also auction the land for sale.

Khas land is, however, very insecure land, since it can be claimed back by the original owners if they pay outstanding taxes or can substantiate a claim that they were the original owners of the land. Despite the insecurity of obtaining permanent rights in *khas* land, there is much competition to get it. The competition is generally between the rich people of an area, who try to make private arrangements with the revenue officials to get the land allocated to themselves. A whole group of intermediate persons whose main task is to collect information on the status and degree of security of land has developed. This group of people consists both of Government officials and of villagers who are clever and have means of obtaining such information. (We noted in case 4, chapter 4, that this was a main method used by Halim Khan.) They can either use the information about the security of the land and of the possibilities of obtaining it to their own advantage, or they can pass the information on to people they know would be interested in buying the land. One type of land they are on the look-out for is *khas* land or possible future *khas* land (for example land for which tax has not been paid for almost the length of the period which is required before the land can be declared *khas* land).

We recorded many land disputes which concerned the ownership rights and the usufruct rights to *khas* land. One story, told us while we took a bath in the village pond, impressed us particularly. The two parties in the dispute were on the one side a powerful and rich landowner and on the other side almost 50 households of a village in Pabna district. The disputed *khas* land was a pond, 2 acres in size (the one we took a bath in), which had for generations been used by the villagers. If the water were pumped out of the pond, the site would be excellent agricultural land during the winter season. Owing to the close ties he had with important political leaders and Government officials after Independence, the rich landowner obtained the *khas* land on a lease basis. Against the wishes of the villagers he pumped out the water and started to cultivate the land. When the national political situation changed dramatically in 1975, his best supporters were removed. The villagers took revenge on the rich landlord for the misdeeds he had committed by killing him. During the following monsoon the pond was again filled with water and has since then again been a public pond.

Land disputes over boundaries between plots

The agricultural plots are divided by small borderlines which demarcate the boundaries of the plot a man owns. The borderlines take different physical shapes. Sometimes the boundaries can be demarcated by a strip of soil only a few inches high and a few inches wide, and sometimes there is not even a visible line to indicate the boundary. The type of borderlines constructed will depend on the level of the land. Big borderlines can be made when soil needs to be removed from the land in order to make the land level. Also big borderlines may be constructed and maintained when they are used for paths for the public. Disputes over where the borderline runs between two plots are very common. If there is no clear borderline between the plots, a plot owner will often at the time of ploughing try to make one or two extra furrows on the borderline of his neighbour's plot. The exact measurement of the size of each plot is kept in the local Government office. It is a common occurence to find officials from the local Government office coming to the fields to measure the size of the plots in order to draw the current boundaries.

The following case about a change of borderlines between two plots was observed and followed over a long period in Bhaimara.

Case 5. Dispute over borderline between plots

A rich absentee landowner and Government official in Dhaka, Shamsul Huq, had managed to get a deep tubewell to Bhaimara. (See case study 5 in chapter 4.) The deep tubewell was sunk on his land, and canals were dug in order to conduct the pumpwater to the fields. One of the large plots Shamsul Huq owned was demarcated with a solid foot-high boundary between his plot and the plot of his much poorer neighbour. A canal for the irrigation water needed to be made.

In connection with work on the canal Shamsul Huq wanted to make sure the big boundary line, which for more than a decade had been used as a public path, was placed 'correctly' as a demarcation line between the two plots. Shamsul Huq called a Government official to measure his plot, and the Government official found, after probably having received a bribe, that the correct borderline should be made three feet in on Huq's poor neighbour's plot. The length of the borderline was about 50 yards long, thus Shamsul Huq enlarged his plot by about 50 square yards, or a little more than one decimal (0.01 acre). The value of this decimal would, since it now was going to be irrigated land, be about 300 Taka. As soon as the Government official had said where the new borderline should be made, the servant of Shamsul Huq hired labourers and the old solid borderline was torn down and moved 3 feet into the neighbour's plot. The poor neighbour was well aware of what was going to happen when the Government official appeared with *Mouza* maps on his plot. (*Mouza* is the smallest administrative unit in Bangladesh. For each *Mouza* there are maps which show the exact position and size of each plot of land.)

No dispute started because of Shamsul Huq's seizure of a small portion of his neighbour's land. People in the village do not expect the poor neighbour to make any claims and call for a *shalish* or go to a Government court with the case. Some people guessed that Shamsul Huq took the land not only to get more agricultural land. His poor neighbour is a client of Halim Khan (case 4, chapter 4). We noted that Shamsul Huq has been on hostile terms with Halim Khan for many years, and that he has much better connections with Government officials than Halim Khan. By taking land from his poorer neighbour, Shamsul Huq also showed his powerful position in relation to Halim Khan. Halim Khan did not want to face the economic and political costs connected with defending his client.

One can speculate on why Shamsul Huq did not cut deeper into his neighbour's plot. This fact must be understood in light of the type of claim he made. Shamsul Huq's reason for moving the border, was that the former borderline had been wrongly measured. It is possible to place a borderline a few feet on one or the other side of the real border, but not several yards. If Shamsul Huq wanted to move his plot several yards into his neighbour's plot, he could not have used the same argument with the same degree of 'reasonableness'. It would affect his 'izzat' if, on the basis of such a claim, he took a large part of his neighbour's plot. The poor neighbour and his patron Halim Khan have by their non-action lost some prestige. They have not even been able to make an attempt to defend the land, and this is taken as an expression of powerlessness.

Land disputes over char land

Land disputes over *char* land are very common. Much agricultural land is lost every year owing to the overflowing rivers and floods in the monsoon periods which inundate and break down the land. Many years later, when the rivers may change their courses or become smaller, land can again arise from the silt deposits along the edges of the rivers, or as islands in the rivers. Since the land which re-emerges has been under water for years and even decades, and since also the lost land of a village can emerge in a different area, there are many disputes about the ownership rights to *char* land. The land lost by inundation or gained through *char* land may be much or little. Shapnan Adnan[3] has described the conflicts that arose between two villages which both lost substantial parts of their agricultural land owing to floods. When the level of the land rose again many years later, a dispute broke out between the people of the two villages, which lasted for years and caused much violence. In the case Adnan describes, local village leaders of each village organized the people as corporate groups with opposing interests.

We collected many stories of disputes over *char* land which had occurred between individual persons. We found in these cases that it was 'objectively' difficult to find the 'right' owner of the re-emerged *char* land. More than for other types of disputes we got the impression that it was the strongest and most powerful party who won the case. Physical fights over the ownership rights to *char* land were common we were told.

Land disputes due to false registration and recording of land

In chapter 3 we mentioned the three different types of documents it was necessary to have in order to prove ownership to a specific plot (registration document, land-recording documents, and tax receipts). If all these documents are in the name of one person, the land can be considered to have a very secure status, and it will be very difficult to make a claim for it with reasonable arguments. A crucial period for the ownership rights to land is when the plots are being re-registered, as they sometimes are after the death of the household head when the land is divided between the family.

Powerful members of the family often get more land registered in their names than they are entitled to according to the inheritance rules. When land has once been registered in a powerful person's name, it is not impossible to obtain the real or faked tax receipts and the land-recording papers.

Since ownership to land plots changes and plots are divided, Government officials go to the rural areas every 10 to 15 years to record the latest owners of the different plots. For the villagers it is an important event when the Government officials come to measure the size of the plots and record the names of the owners. It is normal for a Government official to measure and record the ownership of 5 to 10 plots every day. Many people are aware that land ownership and the size of the land can be recorded wrongly. Therefore people who are having their plots registered try to stay close to the Government official all the time in order to prevent anybody from giving false information. However, well-to-do peasants can manage to keep people away from the Government official and bribe the official if they want to have another man's land recorded in their own names. Often Government officials come twice to the village to check the records. People who are not aware of the second check can sometimes find their land recorded in another person's name.

We were told of many cases in which clever people over decades had paid and collected tax receipts on land they did not own or use. They also had managed to have the land recorded in their own names. When the real owner of the land who possessed the registration documents was in a weak position, they started a dispute backed by the documents they had been able to acquire. Particularly illiterate and poor people with little knowledge about the various documents were vulnerable in such situations.

Conclusion

As will have become apparent in the discussion of the different types of land disputes, the disputes share many common features, and in many cases the reason for a land dispute is a combination of several of the causes dealt with separately above. The background for disputes will vary both with respect to geographical area and the existing political and economic conditions of the country. A dispute over *char* land has a geographical dimension attached to it and is more common in the southern parts of Bangladesh. Disputes over former Hindu property have a historical dimension in that they are connected with specific political events after the Partition in 1947. In periods of political instability when the judicial system is more or less out of operation, the ways used to obtain land and for settling disputes involve even more forceful means and illegal methods than normally. It is, however, fruitless to attempt to estimate the extent and frequency of the various types of disputes. We noted that the causes for a claim by a disputant might only be a pretext for starting the dispute.

A perspective which we believe is rewarding for understanding land disputes is that all agricultural plots only have a certain degree of security. We have in the course of our discussions and case studies delineated four important elements which are decisive both for whether a dispute over a plot does arise and for the outcome of such a dispute if it is taken to a court:

(i) The forms of documentation the claimants to the disputed land possess, and the mechanism by which the land was transferred to the claimants (through inheritance, purchase, gift, *khas* land possession and through dispute),

(ii) The degree of local support the claimants can mobilize,

(iii) The economic and political position of the claimants,

(iv) *Izzat* (honour) considerations for claimants presenting patently faulty cases.

On the basis of these elements it is possible to make a simplified model of land disputes and speculate on the outcome of the disputes. In a very informal and implicit way these were the elements and the perspective we adopted in the cases we could present above only very briefly.

We noted that as a mechanism for the transfer of land, the amount of land gained through disputes is very small compared with the amount which is transferred through inheritance and sale. Nevertheless land disputes are an important and integral part of rural society. We have through the case studies and discussions in this chapter wanted to conjure up a picture of how insecure many people feel their land possessions to be. The effect of this insecurity on the individual peasant is that he seeks 'political support' through individual friends, *patrons,* alliances and factions. We noted that also the supporters often become in one way or the other implicated in the disputes. The aggregate effects of all these efforts to protect one's land is that millions of alliances and patron-client relationships in rural Bangladesh are established. (We have also shown other factors which contribute to creating and maintaining these relationships in other chapters of this study.) Thus the social organization which emerges in the rural areas can partly be understood against the background of the problems people face in relation to the security of their land.

In what circumstances may disputes over land become more prevalent and become an alternative mechanism to inheritance and sale for the transfer of land? We have indirectly indicated part of the answer to this question by pointing to some 'macro'-factors influencing the rural areas. During periods of national instability when lawlessness prevails more easily, *izzat* considerations become of less significance for many ruthless people. People with arms and the necessary support, whether based on local, regional or national levels can exploit the situation. Also the availability and possibility of obtaining land through legal ways will affect the number of disputes. The role of the courts and the amount of the costs incurred in bringing a dispute to court will to a certain extent decide whether a dispute will be started or not. From the point of view of the individual peasant, however, the chances of a successful outcome to a dispute will be related to the four elements we presented above.

Notes

1 The only village studies we are aware of which have treated disputes over land as a separate theme is 'Jhagrapur' chapters 16 and 17, *op.cit.,* by Arens and Van Beurden and *The Net: Power Structure in Ten Villages* by A. Jenkins et al., Bangladesh Rural Advancement Committee, Dhaka 1980.

2 See Kamal Siddiqui, *Journal of Peasant Studies,* Vol. 6, No. 3, April 1979.

3 Shapnan Adnan, and the Village Study Group, *Land, Power and Violence in Barisal Villages,* University of Dhaka, 1976.

8

Political and Economic Integration of Villages into a Wider Society

Introduction

In more than one chapter of this study we have stated that we wanted to describe as fully as possible the framework within which the competition for land and employment in the villages takes place. In chapter 2 we saw how ecological and technological factors shaped the relationships and the economic activities of the peasants. Chapter 3 outlined how a framework of certain cultural factors and social institutions put restrictions on people's behaviour. This chapter will focus on the wider political and economic context of which the villages are a part.

It struck us, at first, when we lived in Bhaimara that the village appeared in many respects to be a fairly independent unit and that the outside political and economic influences on economic activities were not of great importance. Almost all the villagers gain a livelihood from the land belonging to the area, either as owner-cultivators, tenants, and/or as wage-labourers. The basic necessities are produced by the villagers in the village and its neighbourhood. Also the basic services and crafts are provided for within the village and its neighbourhood. For most of the households only a small part of the income goes on the purchase of goods that are 'imported' to the market in the village area (salt, kerosene oil, clothes). The village thus appears to have many 'self-sufficiency' features. Also from another viewpoint the village seems untouched by the outside world. Most of the inhabitants of Bhaimara very seldom leave the village and its neighbouring area. Although Dhaka is only 1½ hours away by bus, many of the villagers have never been to the city, and most of the old male persons have only been to Dhaka a few times in their lives. The sub-divisional town and the Thana headquarters located in this town are within 45 minutes walking distance of Bhaimara village. Also a trip to this town is a yearly event for some people in the village. The great majority of the grown-up women in the village have never been to Dhaka and only very occasionally travel to the sub-divisional town. (The households in which one or several of the members regularly work in an urban area are of course an exception.) The apparent isolation of the resident villagers is also expressed in the small number of 'strangers', outsiders, visiting the village. Many months pass between the visits of Government servants dealing with official business in the village (health work, agricultural extension service, registering of land plots, etc.). An exception is the Government-supported school placed on the outskirts of the village where a few teachers from outside are working.

It would, however, be very misleading to conclude on the basis of these superficial impressions that external political and economic conditions have limited influence on what goes on in the villages. For our purposes we shall describe and discuss how outside determinants influence the economic and political position of the peasants. We want to show how rich peasants are able to take advantage of the political and economic system operating beyond the boundaries of the villages and the rural areas. One effect of their strong position is that it enables them to purchase and obtain more land. For the poor peasants and the landless we want particularly to explore to what extent employment opportunities are created through external determinants.

The external factors we are referring to are in the main activities for which the Government of Bangladesh is responsible. Our focus is therefore on how policies implemented by the Government integrate the villages into a larger political and economic context. In this chapter we shall first give a very brief characterization of certain aspects of the State and the Government of Bangladesh. We shall point to certain basic features of the State and Government which set strict limitations on the policies the Government can pursue towards the rural areas. We shall then go on to describe some policies which, mainly indirectly, influence the population in the rural areas; the allocation of Government funds to the rural sector, the food-rationing system, the system of domestic procurement of food grain, and the agricultural tax system.

We shall then discuss the actual policies which the Government carries out in the rural areas. The main policy the Government implements is a 'production-oriented' agricultural strategy. We shall attempt to assess some of the employment effects of this strategy and the effects the strategy has for the rich peasants. After this discussion we describe the organizational context through which this strategy is implemented and point to some implications this context has for the policies which are executed. In a separate section we then go on to indicate very briefly the role and the functions of the political elections in the rural areas. The last section of the chapter discusses how the villages are economically integrated into larger systems through goods going out of the rural areas. An attempt is made to make a rough assessment of the quantity of food grains going out of Bhaimara village and to identify the mechanisms by which the goods are transferred to the urban areas. Finally, a very brief note will be made on how the villages are linked to a wider society through the labour market. The discussion of all these issues will be both general and specific, presenting material from Bhaimara.

The outside determinants, however, do not pull in one direction only. Processes going on in the rural areas also have a feedback effect. We shall explore in particular the mutually beneficial link which is created between the urban and the rural rich and indicate the flow of goods and services in this relationship. We shall also concern ourselves with the social processes which are being generated in the villages through the urban-rural relationships, and indicate the implications these processes have for the social organization in the rural areas.

Aspects of the State and Government of Bangladesh

The past and present dependency relationship to which Bangladesh has been subjected by foreign countries and international organizations has contributed towards forming the character of the State. Also the concrete policies implemented by the Government of Bangladesh in the rural areas are influenced by forces operating outside the country. Foreign aid has in the last years accounted for 75–80 per cent of all development expenditure in Bangladesh.[1] Much of the aid is tied, and donor organizations also impose other constraints both on the nature of aid given and on the use of it.[2]

The Government policies and the way they are implemented are also a result of the past history. The structure of the existing legal, administrative, and educational systems are very much influenced by the British colonization, tradition and presence in the area. During the 1950s and 1960s the earstwhile East Pakistan was exploited by West Pakistan and various devices were invented for the transfer of resources from the East to the West. The Government consistently discriminated against East Pakistan while it attempted to industrialize West Pakistan with the resources extracted from the East. This process has been dealt with extensively in many studies, and it is beyond our aims to discuss this issue here.[3] For our purpose the point is that a set of policies was pursued in different fields which gave a very high priority and allocation of funds to urban areas at the expense of the development of agriculture.

In many respects, although under different political circumstances, aspects of the urban-oriented policies pursued by the Pakistan Government in the 1950s and 1960s have been perpetuated by the Bangladesh Government in the 1970s. A SIDA report[4] has dealt with Bangladesh Government agricultural policies under the headings: the urban bias, the foreign bias, the bureaucratic bias, the capital bias, the production bias, the landlord bias, the rice bias, and the private bias. We shall, in this chapter refer to many of these 'biases' and explore the impact these policies have on the economic position of the different groups of households in the villages.

Another part of the framework within which the Government policies have been and are formulated is the established laws concerning the ownership of land. During the 'Ayub regime' in the 1960s the ceiling for the ownership of land was set at 375 *bighas*. In their study Jannuzi and Peach summarize how the ownership to land has been modified by law since independence in 1971:[5]

> Following independence in 1971, the government of Bangladesh has continued to recognize the body of law affecting rights in land that had been applicable to the region of East Pakistan. That is to say, the provisions of the East Bengal State Acquisition and Tenancy Act, 1950 (later known as the East Pakistan Acquisition and Tenancy Act, 1950) have the force of law in contemporary Bangladesh. The only modifications in this body of law have been in the form of ordinances issued in the 1970s. These ordinances have

1. exempted landholdnings of 25 standard bighas (approximately 9 acres) or less from payment of land revenue,
2. lowered the ceiling on the size of landholdings to 100 standard bighas (33.3 acres), and
3. provided a *de jure* means by which landholders can re-acquire lands sold in distress following unprecedented floods and the destruction of crops in Bangladesh in 1974.

Land reform, implying a more equitable distribution of land, has many times been discussed by politicians. The fact that no major land reform has been passed and that even the existing ceiling of 100 *bighas* is not enforced, reveal important aspects of the nature of the state and whose interests the state cannot afford to violate. The Government has not yet passed any legislation dealing with the security and length of tenancy contracts in connection with share-cropping relationships. This has, however, as we noted in chapter 5, been an area where there have been discussions about whether the Government should intervene and 'protect' the interests of the tenants.[6]

Government policies which in indirect ways influence the rural areas

Many of the Government policies only indirectly influence the economic situation of the population in the rural areas. In this section we shall discuss some of these policies. The discussion will mainly be general and 'macro-oriented'. In some cases, however, we shall, on the basis of our material from Bhaimara village, attempt to explore the effects of these policies for the village population. It should be mentioned that the various policies are not necessarily consistent and 'pulling' in the direction of advantages for one population group only. Some of the policies are contradictory in nature and affect the economic position of the various groups of households differently.

a) Government allocation of funds to the rural sector
An indicator of the priority which the Government gives to agriculture is expressed through the size of public development expenditure on the agricultural sector and rural development. The amount

must be considered in relation to the role agriculture plays in the national economy. More than 90 per cent of the total population of Bangladesh live in the villages in the rural areas of Bangladesh, about 80 per cent of all employment is in agriculture, 60 per cent of the national product originates in agriculture, and 90 per cent of the exports are agricultural products or goods which are manufactured from agricultural products.[7]

Despite the size of the agricultural sector only 10–15 per cent of public expenditure on the average was allocated to the agricultural sector in the period 1973–1977. If the expenses for rural development, water and flood control are included, the total share of expenditure on the rural sector varied between 28 and 30 per cent in the annual budgets for 1976/77–1978/79.[8] In 1978/79 17.2 per cent of the funds of the annual development budget went to the industrial sector, mainly as support to large scale manufacturing in the large urban centres; 14.3 per cent went to the development of power and natural resources and scientific research, and 7.8 per cent to the transport and communication sector. Physical planning and housing accounted for 7.7 per cent, education for 5.3 per cent, health for 3.7 per cent, and population control (family planning) for 3 per cent, while social welfare, public administration and miscellaneous received 3.4 per cent.[9]

Of bank credit only 9–11 per cent in the period from 1973–1977 went to the agricultural sector and only 7–9 per cent of private investments.[10]

From the above figures it should become clear that in relation to other sectors of the economy the importance of agriculture is not reflected in public and private development expenditure. In one particular field it becomes clear how the Government policies favour the urban population at the expense of growth in agricultural production; the food-rationing system. It is difficult to discuss the effects of the food-rationing system and relate it specifically to Bhaimara. It will be discussed generally, and some more common and general effects on how this system affects the economic position of rich and poor households will be described.

b) The food-rationing system and domestic procurement of food grain

After the disastrous famine in Bengal in 1943, in which an estimated 1.5 million people died, a public food-rationing system was organized to feed the destitute. Since the middle of the 1940s this has continually expanded, partly with the help of imported food. The system was originally intended to cater for the poorest segment of the population, but as the food-rationing system grew in terms of quantity of food, a middle-class urban population has increasingly managed to take advantage of it. A large part of the food is given on weekly and bimonthly ration cards to 'statutory' recipients in the six largest cities of the country. A modified rationing system operates in the smaller cities and towns. There are many different categories of people and institutions eligible for ration cards. The largest portion of the food, however, ends up in the urban areas in the hands of groups who already are among the well-to-do segments of the population. Only about ten per cent of the food channelled through the rationing system ends up with the very poor.[11] An estimated 4.5 million people are covered by this rationing programme.[12]

The food distribution through the food-rationing system has in recent years been around 2 million tons, which represents about 12–15 per cent of the total food grain consumed by the population in Bangladesh. The food distributed through the rationing system mainly comes from foreign countries through food aid. In fact, food aid constitutes about a third of the total foreign aid given to Bangladesh. It should be mentioned that the value of the food aid received is larger than the total development expenditure in agriculture. Almost all the food aid Bangladesh receives is channelled through the rationing system. In addition Bangladesh has bought food from abroad on a commercial basis, and in recent years food acquired from domestic sources has also been distributed through the food-rationing system. The size of revenues earned through the sale of food aid has in some years been almost equal to the amount the Government has spent on domestic procurement and on food grain imported on a commercial basis.

Many authors have discussed the effects on agricultural production of the two separate food markets in Bangladesh: one urban food market supplied with 'inexpensive' food grain through the rationing system and another food market in the rural areas where the price of food grain is considerably higher than the grain obtained through the rationing system.

One effect of the fact that two million tons are provided at a low price for a population which has a relatively strong purchasing capacity is that the price of rice in rural areas is reduced. If the rural area had been given the task and the opportunity of supplying the food grain for an urban population, this reduction would have led to a stronger demand and higher price. The higher price obtained by the producers, mainly the peasants with a surplus, would have provided incentives for increased production — at least for a part of the producers. Some researchers have maintained that the approximately two million tons of food grain which in recent years have been imported annually have caused the price of food to become so low that it has acted as a disincentive to further production.[13]

It is problematic to assess the effects which would follow if prices were increased for the peasants through e.g. Government policies abolishing the food-rationing system or through export of food grain abroad. For the 'surplus' peasants increased prices would mean that they had more money after the harvest. Instead of investing in traditional fields like money-lending, mortgage of land, hoarding of food stocks, etc., it could mean that they would make efforts to increase production on their land by using more inputs and more labour, provided that the necessary inputs were made available to them. For whatever purpose they used the money, the economic position of the 'surplus' peasants would seem to be bettered by an increase in the price of food grain. It is more difficult to assess the effects of higher prices of rice for other groups of the rural population. The great majority of the rural population purchase more food grain than they produce themselves. Their situation need not deteriorate if the higher prices for rice lead to increased production and better opportunities for wage employment. A higher total income through wages over the year (not necessarily higher wages per day, since price of rice and size of wage are not 'indexed', see chapter 6) may lead to increased purchasing capacity. For households, however, with few wage-labourers in relation to consumers, the higher prices of rice would most likely lead to a worsening of the economic position.

In this connection it should be emphasized that the incentives higher prices for rice may provide as regards increasing production may also have several consequences for the amount of agricultural employment which is generated. In a later section of this chapter we shall describe how a specific amount of rice can be produced with varying labour/capital inputs. If capital-intensive technologies are applied in the production, fewer people will be employed. The large groups of landless and near landless households will be the losers if a higher price of food grain in the rural areas does not in one way or another lead to increased employment and correspondingly increased purchasing capacity for them. The different methods through which production can be increased thus make it difficult to assess the net effects of increased prices of rice for the poorest groups. Rao[14] concludes a discussion on this issue for India with:

> It is clear, therefore, that for the rural poor, the negative real income effects of the rise in food prices outweigh the possible employment and income effects.

We shall not here try to draw any conclusions as regards the net effects of possible increased prices of food grain for the poorest groups in the villages of Bangladesh. It seems obvious, however, that the 'surplus' peasants would benefit from a rise in the price of food grain. As a general point one could say that the food-rationing system's effect on food-grain prices is that the economic positions of the poor and rich households in the villages are affected differently. At present the poorest households with few or no wage-labourers benefit from the low prices for food grain.

Rehman Sobhan discusses some of the issues we have raised above. He outlines the effect imported food has on the price of grain in the rural areas and also shows how the economic position of the poor is dependent on and linked to a political and economic system beyond the rural areas:[15]

> ... some three-quarters of rural households in Bangladesh are now dependent in all or part on the market economy, as opposed to subsistence cultivation, for their basic staple diet. This large category of the rural population is now directly touched by the world economic system to the extent that the market regime for foodgrains in Bang-

ladesh has over the years become critically dependent on imports. Today some 12–15 per cent of foodgrains consumed in Bangladesh are imported, but at least 50 per cent of domestic output is not marketed. Of the grain entering the market, imports account for 30–50 per cent, depending on the size of the domestic crop and the marketable surplus derived from this. The availability of grain imports has a crucial importance for the volume of marketed grain and consequently the market price of grain. Both factors are critical to the level of consumption of the rural poor, for whom scarcity of grain on the market, operating through the price mechanism, may make all the difference between starvation and subsistence. This was made apparent in 1974 when the delay, for political reasons, by the US government in sanctioning US PL. 480 food aid, precipitated a severe famine in Bangladesh where some 30,000 perished.[16]

We mentioned that part of the grain allocated to the food-rationing system was obtained through domestic procurement. Government policies in connection with procurement of domestically produced food grain have effects for the population in food-grain-supplying areas. Many dilemmas arise when establishing a procurement system, and one important problem concerns the price which the Government establishes for the rice to be procured.

For long periods in the 1960s and 1970s the price of procured rice was set lower than the market price. The effect of this naturally was that the 'surplus' peasants, who were in a position to sell rice, managed by various devices to avoid having some of their crops procured by the Government officials. The amount of food grain procured on a national basis remained very low in the 1960s and the first half of the 1970s, normally less than 100,000 tons annually.

After the good harvest of 1977–78, the Government raised the price for rice, and managed to procure 0.5 million tons of food grain. In Bhaimara and the surrounding areas the Government procurement price was well above the local market price. In Bhaimara we observed in 1977 and 1978 that both 'surplus' peasants and poor peasants (with an annual food deficit) wanted to sell paddy to the Government procurement dealers. However, we found that many of the sellers, especially the poorer ones, received a much lower price than the official rate. The Government dealers created difficulties for direct sale between them and the peasants. The poor peasants were obliged to sell the rice to intermediate businessmen who operated between them and the Government buyers. In some cases there could be several or many levels of intermediaries through whom the food grain passed before it eventually reached the Government officials at a rate below the official one, so that the Government officials too could take their share. The losers in this procurement drive were the poor peasants, who benefited little from the increased prices, and the landless, who had to pay a higher price for the food in the local markets, since also the price on the local market increased a little owing to the Government procurement market. (The price on the local market would, however, have increased much more if the Government procurement price had been given to all who wanted to sell rice.)

It became very clear to us that it was the rural 'power structure' which gave shape to the Government procurement drive in the area around Bhaimara. Halim Khan, the rich peasant we have now referred to so many times, and the other rich peasants of the union had no difficulties in obtaining a very good price for their grain. They also were able to avoid some of the intermediaries and sell direct to the Government dealers. Some of the rich peasants themselves turned into businessmen and intermediaries. In this field too they established themselves as patrons and would distribute favours to their supporters and clients by giving them a better price for their grain or helping them to avoid the clutches of the middlemen.

There are many other implications and interesting aspects of the food-rationing system and its operation which it is outside our scope to deal with here. We shall refrain from entering into the discussion about whether the availability of food aid can act as a disincentive at Government level to increase and give priority to agricultural development.[17] Another issue which we shall only mention is that food aid also has given international and foreign donors opportunities to exercise leverage on the course of the development policies Bangladesh should follow.[18] This leverage eventually has also had consequences for the type and nature of the development policies which are implemented in the rural areas.

Given the critical comments with which it has been confronted both from people within the Government and from foreigners, one may wonder why the food-rationing system has continued in its present way. J. Parkinson has provided the following explanation for perpetuation of the food-rationing system:[19]

However, even seven years after independence and after dramatic changes in Government structure and personalities, a basic change in food policy in Bangladesh has yet to be made. The overriding reason for this is quite simply that the policy of providing subsidised food to all Government employees (including those in the armed forces) and to the whole urban population, irrespective of income, reflects the realities of politics and power in the country. The urban middle class, the industrial workers, the officers and men in the army and administration constitute vocal, volatile, and organised groups which would create disorder, incite dissatisfaction and threaten the political status quo if estranged. These governing elements of the population, minuscule in number but overwhelmingly powerful, have grown accustomed to their privileged position, including the supply of cheap rations of food. By contrast, the rural poor remain unorganised and as a silent majority in the political structure constitute no immediate threat. The Government's policy is not designed to help the poor at the cost of eroding the positions of power and privilege of the few; it is designed to meet the Government's strongly felt need to secure its political position. This was the situation in the early years of Bangladesh; it could hardly have been otherwise. It remains the situation under the successive Governments in the post Mujib era.

This explanation shows which important groups the Government cannot afford to undermine. In the next sections we shall see how difficult it is for the Government to interfere with the interests of other strong groups.

c) Agricultural taxes

Traditionally the agricultural sector has been taxed heavily. First, the Mughals and then the British were able to levy heavy taxes on agriculture and to thrive on this important source of revenue. A complicated revenue system in which there could be as many as ten levels of intermediate revenue collectors between the cultivator and the *zamindar* developed.[20] Thus a large population living both in the rural and urban areas managed to prosper on taxes collected from the agricultural sector.

The contribution of taxes to the central authorities declined sharply after the British withdrew. An important political aim of the Awami League was that only the largest holdings should be taxed. When the Awami League came to power after Independence in 1971, the lower limit for taxation, we noted, was set at 25 *bighas*. The holdings below were to be exempted from tax. In practice it proved very difficult to tax even the peasants owning more than 25 *bighas,* since these well-to-do and rich peasants found many ways of escaping taxation. The agricultural income tax which has been practised recently has mainly been confined to the tea estates in north-western Bangladesh.[21] In 1975–76 the direct tax on agriculture represented only 0.25 per cent of total agricultural income, and agricultural taxes constituted less than two per cent of the entire state revenue. The land tax is so low that the revenue earned from it does not even cover the cost of collecting it.[22]

Various authors and policy-makers have stressed the contribution agricultural taxation could make towards raising resources for the public sector. 'If taxes on land and income generated from land had been progressively applied to farms above 25 *bighas* tens of *crores* Takas could be raised.'[23] (One *crore* is 10 million.) The fact that these relatively large farms remain untaxed in spite of official policy must be understood in the light of the Government's unwillingness to become alienated from and lose the support of the powerful rural rich. The nature of the Government and the interests it caters for is thus also reflected in its practice of agrarian tax policies.

Government policies in the rural areas

The Government also formulates rural development policies which are more directly felt in the villages. In contrast to the operation of the food-rationing system and tax system these policies can be 'physically' observed in the village, and their influence has very concrete consequences for the economic position of the different households. Also when assessing the effects of these policies, we have to bear in mind the important role the rural power structure plays in changing any good intentions the central Government may have had with the policies.

Before describing and analysing these policies, it should be said that there is great variation in the way Government policies affect the different rural areas. Distant villages to which there are poor routes of transport and villages which have few or no absentee landowners are much less influenced by Government policies than Bhaimara, to which access is fairly easy.

Bhaimara also has several rich and influential absentee landowners who have been clever in attracting Government support for agriculture and other rural development projects (see case 5, chapter 4). In this respect the village is therefore not an 'average' village, and it would only be 'representative' of villages (of which there are many thousands) which have some proximity to urban areas and Government offices.

The organizational context for the implementation of the Government policies varies. The same 'policies', e.g., agricultural credit, or an agricultural input, can be delivered by different institutions: a cooperative, a bank, a Government ration dealer or by dealing directly with Government *Thana* officials, etc. Here we shall discuss the Government policies more or less independently of the organizational context through which they are provided. In a later section of the chapter we shall discuss briefly the practice and functioning of some of the institutions which implement the policies.

a) The government production-oriented agricultural strategy

We have already observed that the agricultural sector is a neglected field as regards the allocation of funds compared with other sectors. Even so, public involvement in this sector is important, since little private accumulated capital is available for the sector.

The present Government's agricultural policies have been and are continually announced publicly. During the Second Five Year Plan, 1980–1985, the aim is to increase food production from 13 to 20 million tons of food grain. It has, however, also been officially announced that within the same period the goal is to double the food production from 13 to 26 million tons so that Bangladesh will become not only self-sufficient in food production but also be able to export large quantities of food grain abroad and in this way earn foreign exchange.

A vital part of the Government's efforts to increase production is the introduction and spreading of HYV-technology into new areas. We shall not here discuss technical aspects of the HYV-technology. As we emphasized in chapter 2, the HYV-technology is part of a large packet of agricultural inputs which will have to be used and adopted in a concerted manner, otherwise agricultural production may suffer and the potential of the new seed technology will not be realized. The main technical inputs in this packet consist of the

HYV-seeds, fertilizers and pesticides in balanced quantities. Water is also essential, and it is necessary to be able to control the level of the water in relation to the growth of the rice plant. Another item of the packet is credit, which is intended to be used for the purchase of the technical inputs.

Properly applied the HYV-technology has a great potential for increased production. It is possible to produce on the same area of land 2–3 times more grain than with local varieties of seed and traditional techniques. While the local varieties in the different seasons *(aus, aman, boro)* in one particular area were found to produce 9–16 *maunds* of rice per acre, the high yielding varieties produced from 23–40 *maunds* of rice per acre. (The great variation in the range of the amount produced is related to the different years the survey was conducted in and to the different seasons of the year.[24]

There is no doubt that the potentials of the HYV-technology look promising. At best the 'Green Revolution' introduced by the HYV-technology could not only increase the production of food grains sufficiently for deficit peasants to obtain a balanced or even surplus budget, it could also imply that the rural areas would be able to supply urban areas with more food than at present. (The possibility of this happening would, of course, depend on the nature and extent of the operation of the food-rationing system.) In the rural areas, the landless and poor peasants who depend exclusively or partly on employment for an income could increase their purchasing power by being employed more.

b) Possible employment effects of the HYV-technology

The employment effects of the introduction of the HYV-technology are important for the landless and poor peasant households who depend on wage-labour. Here we shall discuss this issue first from a general point of view and then on the basis of what we discovered about the employment conditions in Bhaimara when the new technology was introduced.

The number of people employed can vary greatly both for the production of local variety food grain and HYV grain. In theory mechanical labour can replace human labour in many of the work tasks connected to the production process. Ploughing of the field, which is very labour-intensive, may be mechanized by power-tillers and tractors; herbicides and other chemical and mechanical methods of weed control can replace the very labour-intensive weeding operations. The harvesting of the crop can also be carried out by the use of mechanized methods, and it is argued by some that mechanization of the harvesting operation must be encouraged, especially for the HYV crop, as it is important to harvest the crop quickly. The HYV crop also needs to be processed and dried very fast. This encourages the use of electric rice mills.[25]

We mentioned that irrigation was an important pre-condition for the successful growth of HYV crops. Irrigation can also be carried out in different ways. In many areas of Bangladesh it is technically and ecologically possible to choose between irrigation technologies having very different implications for the quantity of labour needed to operate the irrigation equipment. There are, thus, innumerable combinations of degrees of mechanization and amounts of inputs applied, each resulting in different levels of labour requirements per acre.

In Table 8.1, E.J. Clay has estimated the annual crop labour requirements of selected traditional varieties and HYV crops.[26] The table clearly shows that the demand for labour can vary a great deal when a 'new' HYV crop is introduced. This variation could have been shown to be even bigger in the above table if the other labour-saving devices (herbicides, tractors, mechanized harvesting, rice mills) had been included and compared with the corresponding traditional labour intensive methods.

Generally, however, it can be concluded that the introduction of a HYV crop will normally expand the opportunities of employment. The opportunities created must, however, be considered in relation to not only the degree of mechanization applied in the different work operations, but also the place of the HYV crop in the annual crop rotation. If the new HYV crop demands much labour in periods which prior to the introduction of the HYV crop were slack seasons without employment opportunities, then the new crop will have a positive effect for the people who depend on wage and sharecropping contracts.

Table 8.1 Annual Crop Labour Requirements of Selected 'Traditional' and 'New' Crop Rotations in Bangladesh

Rotations		Annual Labour Requirement (man-days/acre/year)		
A 'Traditional'	B 'New'	A	B	% Change
Local *Boro*-Fallow (trad. irrigation)	Modern *Boro*-Fallow (low lift pump)	111	109	- 1%
Ditto	Modern *Boro*-Fallow (doan irrigation)	111	144	+30%
Boro-Aman-Fallow	Modern *Boro* (low lift pump)	85	109	+28%
B. *Aus*-B. *Aman*-lentils	Modern *Boro* (low lift pump)	125	109	-13%
Ditto	B. *Aus*-B. *Aman*-*Dwarf Wheat*	125	156	+29%
Local T. *Aman*-fallow	Late *Boro* (low lift pump)-Local T. *Aman*	64	173	+170%
Local T. *Aus*-Local T. *Aman*-Fallow	Modern late *Boro*-Modern T. *Aman* (deep tube-well irrigated)	142	215	+51%

Note: T. stands for transplanted, B. for Broadcast

However, the adoption of a HYV crop is not necessarily only a switch from one type of seed to another; sometimes it is necessary to alter the entire cropping pattern over the full year as a result of the introduction of the HYV-technology. Under some circumstances one crop less can be grown in a year through the introduction of one HYV crop.[27] If the HYV crop replaces a crop that is cultivated by labour-intensive methods, the demand for increased labour may not be significant, and if one HYV crop replaces two traditional crops, the employment impact may be negative.

Many researchers take a very pessimistic view of the effects for the poor groups of the introduction of HYV-technology into Bangladesh. H. Brammer has estimated that the landowner's share of the agricultural output increased from a ratio of 2.4 to 1 for traditional varieties, to 3.5 to 1 for HYVs.[28] Other studies also confirm that when production increases with HYVs by 100 per cent, the total payment to labour increases by only 31 per cent.[29] Stefan de Vylder discusses the employment elasticity when introducing HYVs:

> A shift from local varieties grown with traditional techniques to H.Y.V.s plus mechanization would give an employment elasticity of 0.20 — that is, output grows five times as fast as demand for labour. Or, put another way, a 10% increase in production implies only a 2% increase in labour requirements.[30]

and later he summarizes the effects for the rural poor of the introduction of the HYVs

> In a balanced growth strategy, with both big and small farmers investing in agricultural production and where any tendency to a decline in crop employment was offset by a rise in demand for labour in other activities, it would be possible to take full advantage of the H.Y.V. potentials without impairing the workers' situation. Under such circumstances, the fall in labour requirements per unit of output would be matched by an increase in effective demand for foodgrains and for non-agricultural products, producing an overall rise in wages. This has not been the case in Bangladesh where, on the contrary, rural unemployment has increased and institutional changes in the labour market have depressed agricultural wages beyond the effects of the rise in unemployment. Hence, the decline in labour-intensity in additional foodgrain production is likely to aggravate the situation of labour more and more. The Green Revolution in Bangladesh has been much more effective in reducing average costs per unit of output for a minority of farmers than in increasing the overall level of production.[31]

c) Effects of introduction of HYV-technology in Bhaimara

In the sections above we have discussed and referred to literature which in general economic terms assesses the effects of HYV-technology. We did, however, obtain a much more 'anthropologically oriented' perspective on the complex set of events which were set in motion in the rural areas when HYV-technology was introduced. Fortunately for *us* a deep tubewell was sunk on the outskirts of Bhaimara while we were staying there. Thus the picture we obtained when the 'Green Revolution' occured on our doorstep became much more vivid than the descriptions and abstract analysis conveyed through the distant and macro-oriented reports of the Dhaka-based economists.

The deep tubewell, which is the central and most costly 'input' of the HYV-technology packet, was far from 'given' to the villagers. There was strong competition and a 'fight' to acquire it among people from different villages. We noted in chapter 4, case 5, that Shamsul Huq was the important person who finally managed to have the deep tubewell allocated to Bhaimara. After the well had been installed, a series of events which affected most households started. The processes which were generated in the village concerned almost all of the 'themes' which we have dealt with in this study. Land disputes were started, sharecropping arrangements were renegotiated, labour-saving technology was introduced, new employment relationships were created, new alliances between people were made, and old relationships of enmity were revived. Patronage became even more vital in the village. Below we shall go chronologically through a series of events which happened when the 'Green Revolution' came to Bhaimara.

We were told that for a couple of years Shamsul Huq had indulged in a cumbersome process of giving bribes and favours to various Government officials engaged in distributing deep tubewells to the rural areas. In all, he paid many thousand Takas (nobody knows exactly how much) to obtain the deep tubewell for the village and to locate it on one of his plots of land. Although Shamsul Huq mostly made contacts on his own with the Government officials, he acted 'officially' on behalf of a cooperative. No village was to receive a 100 per cent subsidized deep tubewell, worth several *lakhs* (one hundred thousand) Takas, unless a cooperative had been formed and a scheme for water distribution had been approved by the Government officials. Shamsul Huq was elected President and Secretary of the cooperative and the other members on the board were all his loyal, hand-picked supporters. After the deep tubewell had been sunk, Shamsul Huq took full charge of the deep tubewell through his resident caretaker. (Shamsul Huq, we remember, was an absentee landowner.) He started to behave as if the deep tubewell was his private property. He felt he had a right to recover the expenses incurred in acquiring the deep tubewell from the peasants who were to have their land irrigated. He charged an amount equivalent to 25 per cent of the crop grown for the water allocated to the peasants. A peasant who managed to produce a 20 *maund* paddy crop in the *boro* season would have to give 5 *maunds* to the 'owner' of the deep tubewell. This amount of paddy could have a market value of 500 Taka (1980 prices). Many peasants with land under the command area of the deep tubewell hesitated to participate, and some of the persons to whom the new 'waterlord' had a hostile relationship were not given any water at all, even if they were willing to pay.

The two first seasons, *boro* seasons, were not successful. The first year the engine of the deep tubewell broke down for a week and the transplanted rice was destroyed. Since water canals had not been completed after the installation, the deep tubewell only irrigated a small fraction of its technically potential command area (50 acres). Because of this failure many peasants chose to grow winter crops on their plots the next *boro* season. For the last couple of *boro* seasons, however, the performance has improved. When we visited the village briefly in the winter of 1982, the deep tubewell irrigated some 30 acres. When walking on the narrow paths and trails between the plots we could clearly distinguish the land belonging to some of the enemies of Shamsul Huq; their land was brown and barren, next to plots filled with bulging, green rice plants. From the top of the engine-house of the deep tubewell the command area of the well resembled a chessboard, where the plots were spread about in green and brown squares.

We have noted that along with access to water also other inputs are part of the Green Revolution packet. Fertilizers and pesticides are essential ingredients for the success of the HYVs.[32] Both through the cooperative in Bhaimara and through the Government-appointed fertilizer dealers the demand for fertilizers increased as more land became irrigated. Since the fertilizers were heavily subsidized and in scarce supply, most peasants had to purchase this input from the black-market.[33]

Therefore dealing in fertilizers also became a source of income and an opportunity for the fertilizer dealer to build up a following of supporters. (For many of the poor peasants who do not obtain sufficient fertilizers the effect naturally is that their yields suffer.)

We noted that Shamsul Huq had acquired a small power-tiller with which we estimated he could plough 8 to 10 times as much land during a day as with the traditional cattle-pulled plough. Fortunately for the wage-labourers, the power-tiller has broken down so many times that many peasants who might rent it do not rely on it. Others maintain that the furrows it makes are not deep enough. With a skilled technician to operate it, however, Shamsul Huq may in the future own another capital investment on which he can make money. According to the Far Eastern Economic Review, many rich peasants will follow in the path of Shamsul Huq:

> An acute labour shortage is likely to develop during November and December (1980). Arrangements are being made to make power tillers available to the farmers to prepare the soil for sowing wheat.[34]

Credit is also an essential part of the 'Green Revolution packet'. The deep tubewell cooperative in Bhaimara has not yet been given the task of distributing credit. With Shamsul Huq as President and Secretary, the distribution will not, in practice, deviate much from the Government allocation of this scarce resource. It will end up with the rich even if the target group is the poor peasant with less land than 2.5 acres.[35] We have outlined the effects of this disbursement of credit in case studies 4 and 5 and in the general discussions of chapter 4.

On our last visit to the village, poles for electricity had been erected on the main path of the village leading up to the houses of Shamsul Huq and to his deep tubewell. Besides supplying the deep tubewell with electricity, instead of oil, Shamsul Huq has decided to establish a rice mill run on electricity. When rice mills, run on electricity, are set up, some of the lessons and effects are very clear. Such rice mills employing only a dozen workers each can replace the work which several hundred women carry out. The women who are engaged in the post-harvesting operations for other households belong to the poorest strata of society. Thus the poor women in Bhaimara and the surrounding villages may soon lose their best source of income. Many of these women are the main income-earners in their households.

How has the introduction of the deep tubewell in Bhaimara affected employment among the male wage labourers? After the command area of the deep tubewell was expanded, the employment opportunities seem to have increased. The irrigation water from the deep tubewell was used for growing a *boro* crop. This *boro* crop substitutes a winter crop of pulses, which was not a labour-intensive crop. The *boro* crop, we were informed, would be followed by a jute crop and then an *aman* crop instead of a pattern of winter crops, *aus*/jute and *aman*. If this cropping pattern can be established, the demand for labour will increase in Bhaimara, despite the variation in the need for labour attached to HYV-technology which we referred to above. With a changed cropping pattern, the situation, however, could be altered. Many of the wage-labourers feared, however, that their daily wage would not increase much. The employers have already, as we noted in chapter 6, invited in some labour migrants, and they would have no difficulty in finding more wage-labourers from the nearby areas where there are no *boro* crops grown. Also we noted in chapter 6 the variety of the methods by which the employers can erode the peak seasong wage rate.

The 'Green Revolution' thus provided many subsidized items from outside, which were available for grabbing by the few rich peasants. Besides their strengthened position through the new inputs they acquired command over, the rich also made efforts not to let the wage-labourers and poor peasants gain anything from the increased output. Attempts were made to keep wages low, and the terms for the sharecropping contract changed. The estimated 25 per cent charge for the irrigation water had to be paid by the sharecropper. In addition the owner of the land would obtain money from the sharecropper prior to confirming the sharecropping contract. With the strong demand for land on a sharecropping basis on rainfed land, there was no point and no need for the landowner to leave the sharecropper with a higher net gain from irrigated land unless the sharecropper was a particularly good client. In the wake of the 'Green Revolution', land disputes followed. We narrated one case, the borderline dispute, case 5, in chapter 7. There were disputes about other plots in the command area as well, and several landowners, we were told, had their registration documents confirmed by the Government Land Registration office in Manikganj.

What happens to the money and net profit gained by the well-to-do peasants as a consequence of the deep tubewell? Some peasants obviously use part of the money for purchasing more fertilizers. Many use their profit for developing credit relationships with poor peasants which they anticipate will end in purchase of the poor peasants' land. Part of the money is also spent on increased consumption both for food and for other basic needs. Shamsul Huq's plans are to purchase more land, to obtain one or two shallow tubewells, and to establish a second rice mill next to the market place in the neighbouring village of Bhaimara. A substantial amount of his gain is, no doubt, transferred to Government officials and businessmen in the urban areas in order to obtain the capital goods he is after.

On our last visit to Bhaimara we also found a very different, but new, type of irrigation equipment for the crops. On the agricultural land next to some homestead plots a few hand-pumps had been installed. In a separate paper we have discussed some of the effects of these hand-pumps, by UNICEF named MOSTI (Manual Operated Shallow Tubewell for Irrigation).[36] This pump is inexpensive (US$ 70), labour-intensive, and can only irrigate ½–1 acre. Even so the pump offers a good rate of return.[37] The point we want to emphasize here, however, is the very different organizational implications which follow from the use of a hand-pump and a mechanized deep tubewell. There is no need to form and maintain a co-operative around a manual hand-pump. If credit is provided, even the poorest landowners could become owners and operators of a hand-pump. In Bhaimara, in fact, it was two peasants in the 'poor' category who had obtained one pump each. They expected to regain their investment after the first *boro*-crop season. While we found the effect of the deep tubewell would be to increase and strengthen the patron-client relationships in the rural areas, the hand-pumps, as we assessed the effects of them on the poor peasants, would function as a means to break up this pattern. A relevant question to pose in this connection is why the Government has not been more active in encouraging and promoting this labour-intensive technology. There are many reasons for this, and we believe the nature of the Government and of important donor organizations, and whose client groups they support, are reflected in the choice of imported capital-intensive technology.[38]

d) Some conclusions on the effects of the production-oriented strategy

Despite the attempts for the last couple of decades to introduce HYVs to Bangladesh, the HYV-technology has not yet been adopted to the extent the Government had envisaged and hoped. In the period between 1970 and 1978 the acreage covered by HYVs varied between 7 to 19 per cent of the total agricultural land. It is outside the scope which we have set for this study to attempt to explore and follow all the implications of the production-oriented strategy in the agricultural sector. Above we have mainly been concerned with the direct effects the HYV-technology has on the economic situation of rich and poor households. In short we have shown that it is the well-to-do and rich who gain both by the increased output and by obtaining access to the scarce resources of the inputs. We have shown how large sums of money in the form of bribes for the allocation of subsidized inputs are transferred from the rural to the urban areas.

We have not dealt with the role and effects of subsidized agricultural inputs. It is obvious that the Government policy on agricultural subsidies affects poor and rich differently. R. Sobhan states that an important policy objective of the World Bank and IMF has been to phase out subsidies by raising prices on agricultural inputs (including mechanized irrigation equipment). He is, however, inconclusive on the effects of the subsidies:[39]

> Suffice it to say that simplistic notions that all subsidies are bad and that the market mechanism will ensure optimal resource allocation does not alway hold good in Bangladesh. Thus raising fertilizer price as well as grain procurement prices may compensate the 10% of farm households who have a marketable surplus. But for the remaining households made up of subsistence farmers and/or those who are net buyers of grain, the rise in prices represents a net deterioration in their terms of exchange. Such a policy is thus potentially regressive and will need to compensate low income households through alternative sources of earnings. A policy on subsidies can therefore only be meaningful if it is formulated within the context of a national incomes policy which aims to distribute the gains and losses from public policy and allocates the costs of a strategy of self-reliance on a more rationally determined strategy for realising more equitable income distribution.

Less subsidized inputs could, however, lead to a much more economic utilization of the inputs, e.g. better utilization of irrigation equipment. It would also set barriers to the high profits to be earned on the black market. We shall not pursue this discussion here.[40]

One type of aggregate effect which is often lost sight of by the village-focused anthropological studies concerns the implications of the lack of purchasing capacity for the large groups of poor. If the increased production of the 'Green Revolution' does not meet with a corresponding demand to absorb the increased agricultural output, the success of a production-oriented strategy will automatically be barred. What many researchers on rural Bangladesh point to now is that the purchasing capacity of the great majority of the population has been declining (see chapter 6 for discussion and references). This large population group who desperately need to consume the additional food grain produced by the HYV-technology are unable to do so for lack of purchasing power. Stefan de Vylder states on this issue:

Demand tends to generate its own supply, but the opposite is not equally true, and the key success in a production-oriented strategy in Bangladesh is to concentrate on efforts to increase effective demand, i.e. to reduce the poverty of the masses.[41]

Lack of demand leads to low profitability in agriculture, which in turn implies that investment is canalized into other activities. These activities, usury, investment in land, trading, business, are generally non-productive. We have discussed these investment patterns in detail in chapter 4. Lack of a domestic market for grain has sometimes made politicians and bureaucrats in Bangladesh raise the question of whether the 'surplus rice' should be exported abroad. (We think 'surplus rice' is a ridiculous and meaningless concept in the context of Bangladesh given that three-quarters of the population eat less rice than they need because they cannot afford it.)

e) Food grain for export?

In 1980 a new Government policy of exporting grain was discussed. That this could be an option has been indicated many years ago. One book that discusses some possible effects if the new HYV-technology is successful for well-to-do peasants states:[42]

With greater supplies [of food grain, E.G.J.] development will also open up opportunities for improved diet. Unless, however, there is parallel development in other sectors in town and country, success of agriculture will increase income inequality and unemployment will rise, it seems, very rapidly. Rice production would be a highly profitable market-oriented activity for relatively few; it would tend to become an export industry (through smuggling and economic and political pressures to allow sales abroad) like jute. The rice producer would want to sell to whoever could pay the most, which is not likely to be his unemployed and poverty-stricken compatriots.

Export of food grain was publicly announced as a policy, and rice was exported from Bangladesh in 1980. According to the Far Eastern Economic Review:[43]

> Although the country has yet to become self-sufficient in food production, it has decided to export at least 100,000 tons of rice this year, and possibly 300,000 tons if the main aman crop is harvested in November and December without any setback.

The Government also affirmed in 1980 that it planned to develop the infrastructure facilities, especially the mechanized river transport sector, so as to make transport of food grain to the export harbours smoother and easier.[44] However, later in 1981 and 1982, Government officials have stated that Bangladesh will not export any food grain. We shall not here attempt to pursue this issue further.

Some organizational aspects of the Government's rural development strategy

So far we have not discussed the organizational context within which Government policies take place. There is a variety of channels through which the 'Green Revolution' input package is distributed to the villagers. It can come through organized cooperatives, through resources channelled to the Union Council, or through individual contacts between peasants and Government officials at various levels. Special programmes can also be organized, e.g. 'credit programmes' provided through banks. Almost all the literature referring to this 'top-level approach' to distributing inputs to the villages has concluded that even with the best intentions on the part of the cooperatives and the programmes, these approaches have eventually become elite-dominated. We have already described that this was the pattern we found in Bhaimara.

To explain how and why the rural rich always draw the advantages from the Government policies, we must discuss shortly the linkage between the rural and urban elite, here particularly represented by the bureaucracy and the Government officials. National policies and programmes are eventually carried out and implemented by local level officials. These officials are responsible for allocating the resources which have been canalized through the Government system down to the different levels. These officials participate in deciding who are eligible for credit, who shall be appointed as ration dealers in different commodities, which cooperatives shall receive deep tubewells, who shall receive power tillers, which areas shall receive a 'food for work' programme, electrification, rice mills, small-scale industry projects, etc.

In order to understand why the Government officials allocate these resources to the rural rich, it is necessary to be aware of some aspects of the livelihood situation of the officials. Most of the Government officials at local level earn between 500–1000 Taka per month (1980). If they live in an urban centre, it can be very difficult to manage economically on such a salary, especially if they also have to maintain a family there. Since the central authorities have entrusted the officials with the power to make decisions about the allocation of the inputs, it is very tempting for them to add to their meagre incomes by levying a charge on the recipients of the inputs. There are very good opportunities for this, since the market price for these scarce, subsidized inputs is, as we noted, much higher than that actually charged for the inputs. The rich peasants can afford to pay the additional price, and it is advantageous for the local Government officials to provide services for this group.

When it comes to the allocation of credit, the Government officials can with some justification argue that the scarce supply of credit at favourable interest terms should benefit the rural rich. This group satisfies the 'objective' criteria of 'credit-worthiness' in having sufficient land as collateral for the loan, and having the ability to repay the loan. From a 'risk' point of view the officials can defend themselves against attacks of misallocation when they allocate the credit to this group of borrowers. The fact that many loans given to the rich are defaulted on is not the issue; the Government officials can maintain that they have made responsible allocations, giving credit to those who according to accepted criteria and considerations should best be able to repay the loans.

H.W. Blair has discussed the role of the bureaucracy in rural development in Bangladesh.[45] A main point he makes is that if the central authorities let the administration at local level implement the Government policies, the local officials will take advantage of the situation. Regardless of any good intentions the central Government may have for the implementation of their policies, the local officials will exploit the situation when they gain control over the resources channelled down to them.

To give this decision-making authority to officials at the local level is almost inevitably to invite corruption, i.e. bribes and personal contacts rather than merit become the criteria for allocation of resources.[46]

Allocation of inputs is also made through other structures and organizations, and theoretically it should be possible to avoid the direct relationship between local level officials and the rural rich by channelling the resources to a cooperative. The cooperative should obtain the inputs from the Government as a unit and then allocate the inputs to its members on the basis of criteria such as the trustworthiness and industry of the members. For a short period the 'Comilla cooperatives'[47] managed to allocate inputs and credits to all its members, poor and rich alike, with very good and productive results. A main reason for this success was that there existed close supervision and good knowledge of the economic situation of the individual members of the cooperatives. When the cooperative programme expanded to new areas of the country, this close supervision ceased, and the cooperatives were soon taken over by the local rich. Several studies have documented that the existing cooperatives are dominated by the big local landowners, who allocated the inputs and credit given to the cooperative mainly to themselves. The poor are subjected to obtaining credit on the local credit market with much higher interest rates. They have to purchase inputs allocated through the cooperative on the black market at high prices, if they can afford it.[48]

The *Rural Work Programme* and the *Food for Work Programme* are other structures through which the Government implements its policies. These programmes have two main objectives. One is to improve the physical infrastructure in rural areas e.g., by making roads, canals, ponds and embankments etc., the second is to implement these projects in the dry season, when there is little employment. Thereby the rural poor can be employed and either earn money or receive wheat or rice as their wage in the season when employment is scarce. Many have argued that at least these work projects are beneficial to the poor. According to the Director of the

Food for Work Programme, in the period 1975–1979 the Programme was responsible for clearing nearly 2000 miles of silted-up canals and rehabilitating 3000 miles of embankments. The main input for this was 480,000 tons of wheat supplied by the Programme to be used as wages to the workers. In some periods more than two million men and women were employed on the project, and the work carried out is expected to increase the country's rice yield by 200,000 tons annually.[49] In 1979–80, a peak year for the Rural Public Works Programme and the Food for Work Programme, 547,000 tons of grain were made available for the poorest part of the population. 'This in theory could provide work for about 1.49 million people for 100 days in a year at a rate of 6.6 lbs. a day, which would permit a diet of 2 lbs. a day for a working adult and a little over a pound for a family of four.[50]

For many of the poor employed by the Rural Work Programme and the Food for Work Programme the projects are no doubt of some immediate use. The rich are, however, the main beneficiaries on a long-term basis. It will mostly be the rich who will draw advantage from the improved infrastructure. There is little doubt that much of the 200,000 tons extra food grain will be grown on the land of the rich, who choose the sites and places for the projects and organize them. In a more direct and concrete way officials of the Programme and the rural rich also draw advantage from the Programmes. There is no doubt that a large proportion of the 480,000 tons of wheat did not end up as wages for the labourers of the projects. Many projects for which wheat was allocated were never implemented, and the wages of the labourers were distributed among the local influentials on the project committee. Often, especially when there is competition for work on the projects, the wage rates are lowered and the committee and its friends take for themselves part of the available resources intended for wages to the workers.

Government and institutional rural development efforts have come to Bhaimara through all the structures described above. Our observations and information about the practical effects of these efforts from Bhaimara and the surrounding villages are in agreement with findings from other ares of the country. Many of the planned rural work projects for which money was allocated and spent were never executed, and the rural rich in Bhaimara and its neighbourhood benefited from this. Two big ponds on the land of two landlords in neighbouring villages of Bhaimara were excavated by rural work projects. It is, of course, only the rich peasants and their nearest family members who have access to these ponds.

Some of the poor peasants and landless wage labourers know about the official and good intentions of the cooperatives, the credit programmes, the Rural Works and Food for Work projects. Many times we asked them, (like a UN bureaucrat!) what benefits they felt they gained from the various Government Rural Development Programmes. The strong impression we received from them was that they were not at all surprised to see that it was in the main the rural rich who benefited from the Government programmes. They seem to take it for granted, and as an inevitable fact of life, that it would be the rich who were the first to reap any benefit from Government programmes, and that they themselves had to be satisfied with whatever was left over. This pattern of allocation only confirmed their deep-rooted suspicion that the Government would not do anything for them — at least not directly. Many, however, were very glad to be employed in the Rural Works Programmes.

The knowledge and understanding which the poor have of the nature of the Government is based on the experience they have from meeting Government officials in the rural areas. These meetings have generally resulted in their being exploited and discriminated against by the officials. Their jute and rice (on procurement) have been classified as low grade, despite good quality, and thereby been marketed at a lower price; they are harassed for not having paid *haat* (local market) tax when selling a few vegetables or fruits; they do not obtain the full wages they are entitled to in the Rural Works Projects, etc. From their own experience or from other poor people they know how Government officials have sided and been aligned with the rich in cases of conflict. In short, they believe that there is nothing they can gain from the Government officials and that the best thing is to avoid them. The allocation of privileges to the rural rich therefore only confirms their experience of the Government officials and reminds them of their own low position in society.

Under some circumstances the poor can react in a concerted manner to some types of misallocation and abuses by the Government officials and local rich on the Government committees. These cases relate to experiences where the poor themselves are directly affected. We were informed that, a few years ago, some women who participated in a Food for Work Project had only received half of the pay they were entitled to. It was one of the well-to-do peasants in Bhaimara who was on the committee and paid the women. He kept, however, a large part of the sum allocated for himself. In a large group the women together lodged their complaints to other people on the committee and other local influential persons. They did not manage to obtain their full wages, but they managed to damage the reputation of the particular person who had cheated them. Actions have also been taken against certain appointed members of relief committees and corrupt Government officials who have exploited them badly. The outcome of these efforts by the poor people depends a great deal on whether they can mobilize support from powerful persons who are in a competitive relationship to, or an 'enemy' of, the persons who are the targets of the poor people's complaints.

It was under such conditions, with defined and concrete cases in which the poor have been exploited, that protests were made. The poor are, however, to disorganized and split through alliances with their different rich patrons to be able to unite and protest against misallocations in general.

Political elections in the rural areas

Another way in which the villages are integrated into a larger society is through elections of people from the rural areas to institutions of elected representatives set up by the Governement. Such elections take place at various levels. In Bhaimara we were able to observe both an election to the Union Council in 1977 and the campaign of candidates for the Parliamentary elections in 1979.

There are many issues which could be raised and discussed in relation to these elections. Our intention in this section is briefly to indicate how these institutions of elected people function in relation to strengthening the economic position of the different groups of people in the rural areas.

The role the Union Council plays will vary in different parts of the country according to both the ability of the various elected bodies and the Union's closeness to a large administrative centre. A Union consists of 15–20 villages. The Union Councils have been given several tasks to work with. In the Union to which Bhaimara belongs, 9 people are elected to the Council. The budget of this Union Council was in the late 1970s very small. We were informed that the Council would only dispose of about 20,000 Taka annually, which means that it can only spend on the 'average' about one Taka per inhabitant of the Union per year (17,000 inhabitants). Only very limited development efforts can, of course, be made with such a small amount of money. The Union council, however, has more important functions than the projects it can implement through its own budget. It or its elected representatives can compete for having projects and resources channelled to the Union from the Thana level.

The development efforts made by the Union Council to which Bhaimara belonged were limited. A fish pond was dug near the home of the Chairman, some bamboo bridges were constructed over canals, some facilities at the market place were improved, and a few village roads were made better. The main function of the Council, from this study's point of view, is its role in providing advantages to the people and their allies who are elected as members. Although the 9 members of the Union Council do not get any financial compensation, except the Chairman (who receives about 100 Taka per month), it is advantageous both for economic and political reasons to be a member. The members do very often provide material benefits for themselves when projects are implemented, and they can gain political respectability if they manage to steer 'projects' and benefits to the people of their constituency. The Council also makes it possible for the members to obtain contact with the Government administration and to acquire information about future Government projects likely to be implemented. In many cases the Union Council members can act as information agents and as middlemen and 'brokers' to the people in the villages.

Our material from Bhaimara shows that most of the members who are elected were rich or well-to-do landowners. Only a couple of the members owned less than 3 acres of land. They had, however, economic interests in other fields (business) and were also backed by rich landowners who did not want to run for office themselves. (In chapters 4 and 7 we noted that two of the four rich landlords of the Union, Halim Khan and Mohuddin Molla, would never run for office themselves. They would, however, have their own candidates whom they supported and could rely on.)

It is fairly costly event to participate as a candidate in Union Council elections. One important method of gaining supporters and votes is to provide supporters with 'material gains' either in direct cash, parties with good meals, or other favours (credit, land on sharecropping and employment). The 'goods' offered will, of course, depend on the needs of the potential supporters and the ability of the candidates to provide for these needs. Elections thus have some *'redistributive'* aspects from which also the poor and landless can draw some advantage. The voters will evaluate the candidates according to various criteria. Their closeness to them in terms of kinship and neighbourhood, their ability to provide concrete benefits for them, and their assessed political ability, toughness, and cleverness in the Council and among Government officials to attract projects and support from outside.

From Bhaimara there was one 'serious' candidate who participated in the election in 1977. This man owned two acres of land and was the medical doctor of the area (see case 1, chapter 7). The man had the reputation of being an honest, uncorrupt person. He lost the election in his constituency (three villages) to a rich landowner. The reasons why he was not elected to the Union Council, people maintained, were that he had not been able to provide non-villagers with sufficient material benefits and had not convinced them that he had the ruthless and shrewd qualities needed to operate among Government officials and among the members of the Council. Election campaigns for the Union Council are events which often have consequences for the rearrangement of factional politics in an area or which confirm old rivalries or alliances. This we also observed in Bhaimara. In factional politics there can be material gains to collect for poor, but loyal supporters.

We also observed part of the election campaign for membership to the National Parliament in Dhaka. In fact, the successful candidate in the election came from a neighbouring village. The villages were much less affected by the Parliamentary election than the union Parishad elections, since the candidates mostly belonged to villages miles away. On the list of 'local level' promises made by the successful candidate were electrification, more deep tubewells, rice mills, better roads, more development projects, in short, 'modernity and development'. A very visible sign of the candidate's promises was a cement bridge connecting the main tarmac highway with the village road network. The bridge has an inscription showing its date of opening by the MP and his name. (This bridge is very close to a bridge provided by Shamsul Huq, case 5, chapter 4, showing clearly that there are several important people in the area.)

The successful candidate also brought up national issues in his campaign. Since he belonged to President Zia's party, Bangladesh National Party, he vigorously attacked the Awami League candidate.[51] A few of the main supporters of the successful MP came from Bhaimara. These supporters were the two absentee landlords and a couple of other well-to-do people. They each 'controlled' the votes of many men and women. There is little doubt that the MP, if he hopes to be re-elected, will have to provide services to these main supporters both in terms of inputs in the agricultural sector and attempts to provide jobs for their relatives in the urban areas.

Flow of rice out of the village

The above description of the Government policies towards the rural areas has shown which group of people benefit from these policies. This description has at the same time shown important aspects of how the rural population are economically integrated into a larger society through the subsidies on inputs, the food-rationing system, the lack of land reforms, the small agricultural taxes, and the production-oriented agricultural strategy. These policies, along with the Government bureaucracy which implements the projects and programmes, have, as we showed, implications for the flow of resources between urban and rural areas and for the nature of economic and political integration between the two areas.

The themes discussed in the previous sections relate mainly to the way in which the Government has determined the extent and type of flow of goods and values into the rural areas. From a different angle, one can ask the question: What are the mechanisms which integrate the villages into a larger society through the flow of goods that go out of the village? (We have already emphasized how money has been transferred to urban areas in the form of bribes and purchases of goods from businessmen in the towns.) In colonial times the Mughals first, then the British and the Zamindars, appropriated a substantial surplus produced in the rural areas and managed to provide a good livelihood for a large urban population. We have noted that the State has not taken over this role as direct 'appropriator' of the agricultural produce, since taxes on agricultural products and land are negligible. What is the amount and nature of the flow of agricultural products between rural and urban areas?[52] In order to answer this question it is necessary to have information about many patterns of this flow: how much of the goods which are produced (rice, jute, tobacco, milk, fruit, vegetables, cattle, chicken) are consumed by the household members themselves; how much of the goods produced has to be used to compensate for former loans in kind; how much of the goods produced is sold in the local market and purchased by local traders who take the goods to urban centres or to other rural markets; how much is sold direct or given as wages (in kind) to villagers (mainly landless and deficit peasants); how much of the goods produced by the surplus farmers is transported and sold direct in the urban areas. Does any rice come back to the rural market in periods before harvest when the supply is small?

These are questions which would have to be answered in order to give a precise estimate of the flow of goods in and out of the rural areas. We were not in a position to make any surveys of these flows. The only flow we attempted to make some 'guesstimates' about, based on some rough assumptions, was the flow of rice out of Bhaimara village.

However, before discussing the flow of rice in Bhaimara, we will briefly mention one village study, where the authors have been in a better position than we to quantify these flows. This study, which estimated the agricultural production in a village and showed how the agricultural goods were distributed, was conducted in a village close to Madras city in southern India.[53] The authors estimated that 20,000 bags of paddy were produced in this village annually. Of this amount of paddy 64 per cent entered the market. About half of the paddy that was sold in the market was exported out of the area to the urban centres. The other halv of the paddy sold in the market was purchased by the villagers themselves (mainly by deficit peasants and wage-labourers and non-agriculturalists). Thirty-six per cent of the paddy did not enter the market; of this amount 14 per cent (of the total produce) was spent on harvest wages to agricultural labourers and 22 per cent (of the total produce) was retained by the farmers for their own consumption. The authors state that the poorest part of the population received so little of the produce that they could not even be ensured a minimum food standard. Below follow two paragraphs which partly explain why and how the village is integrated with the market economy:[54]

> But the purchasing power of the people in Thaiyur is not so high that they can buy the whole marketed surplus. Nearly 7 000 bags, i.e. about 1/3 of the net produce permanently leaves the panchayat and is exported, mainly to Madras City. After having passed through the hands of a number of middlemen, they end up with the urban consumers. That is the price which Thaiyur has to pay for being 'integrated with the market economy'.
>
> In the pre-colonial mode of production the non-agrarian sector was fed via the tax levied by the king on the village community. He had his local agents who, in return for collecting the tax, were granted certain privileges. Their 'modern' counterparts are (mainly) the rich farmers, the landlords, and the money-lenders. But the basis for their position is not political supremacy, but the agrarian class structure (and basically their control of the land). The mode of distribution is also fundamentally different: They do not deliver grain to the store-house of the king; they sell the exportable surplus for cash, which they can use, either as money-capital in further exploitation of the rural proletariat, or in luxurious and conspicuous consumption.

The authors go on to discuss the contribution to the paddy production (in terms of work-days) which the various categories of the population make, and they then compare the distribution of income obtained from paddy production by the various groups of the population. What becomes very clear is that the labourers and the poorest peasants contribute a large proportion of the work-days in production but receive a small part of the paddy which is produced (roughly only half of the value which they contributed).[55]

On the basis of our information from Bhaimara it is possible to speculate on some aspects of the flow of the rice. In chapter 1 we estimated that 48 of the 62 households produce no paddy (landless households without sharecropping contracts) or less paddy than they consume. This implies that these households for the whole year or part of it enter the market as buyers. A few households were considered to have a balanced budget and about 10 households to have a surplus budget. In Bhaimara a large number of the households are involved in selling paddy at the market. Most of the ten surplus households have more food grain than they consume, and they sell their surplus at the market. Also most of the deficit peasants, we noted in chapter 4, sell part of their harvest in order to repay debts and cover some of their cash requirements. We would estimate that about 30 out of 48 food-growing households enter the market as sellers for every season of the year. The households that do not enter the market as sellers are either those which receive a very small harvest from their own little land or the land they have sharecropped, or those which have almost a balanced budget.

Although it is difficult to give exact estimates of the flow of paddy, it is possible to obtain a rough estimate of the production of paddy in the village. The villagers cultivate 68 acres of land. We noted in chapter 5 that the households in Bhaimara sharecropped in more land than they sharecropped out. For this land they only receive about half of the crop. This means that all the households in this village obtain the harvest of about 65 acres of land, which is almost equal to 200 *bighas.* The size of the total paddy production will of course vary from one year to another according to natural and ecological conditions, individual ability and efforts, and with the annual crop pattern. All households cultivate *aman,* and the peasants themselves have estimated the average yield per *bigha* to be about 5–6 *maunds. Aus* is cultivated on roughly 70–80 per cent of the land (the rest of the land is used for *jute* cultivation). The *aus* crop normally is less than *aman,* 4–5 *maunds* per *bigha*. Only about 15 *bighas* of the total land have, up to 1980, been under *boro* cultivation. For this crop, the yields are higher, about 15 *maunds* per *bigha.* This means roughly that the average yield per *bigha* per year is 10 *maunds* of paddy. This figure is not very different from estimates that have been obtained from areas with similar ecology and technological equipment in the production.[56] This means that 2000 *maunds* of paddy are produced by the households in the village. It would have been very illuminating for obtaining a picture of the difference in standard of living among the 62 households to know how much the different households, and the 311 individuals the households contain, each acquire of the 2000 *maunds* of paddy.

If the production of paddy is 2000 *maunds,* this means 1400 *maunds* of rice (the weight of rice is about two-thirds that of paddy); 1400 *maunds* of rice is equal to 56,000 kgs of rice. For the 311 inhabitants of the village this means on the average 180 kg per year or almost half a kilo per day. According to nutrition studies this amount of rice should be sufficient if it were distributed to the villagers according to their physical needs.[57] Thus, if the 56 tons of rice had been distributed 'equally' to the needs of the population, all the inhabitants of Bhaimara would have received an adequate amount of rice. This would also imply that if a substantial amount of rice is exported out of the area, the village as a total entity would be in deficit, unless rice is also imported into the village area.

We cannot say how much of the 56 tons of rice leaves the village for outside markets. That some rice does leave the area we observed after the harvest when traders going to urban areas each carried many *maunds* away on their donkeys or in vehicles. The 'surplus' peasants of Bhaimara would definitely not sell as much rice as the village referred to above in south India. We have already observed that the 'surplus' peasants in Bhaimara only own between 3–5½ acres of land. Many of the families are large in size, and after a proper amount of rice is consumed within the household there can sometimes only be 20–50 *maunds* left annually which can be sold on the market. Some of the rich, however, will, as we have discussed, purchase paddy elsewhere immediately after the harvest, or have paddy repaid to them in return for loans in kind given before the harvest. Some of this paddy, not obtained from their own production, will also be marketed to the urban areas. Even so the role played by the rich in Bhaimara in the transfer of rice to the urban areas is less important than in areas with big landlords who own a hundred acres of land each. But also for Bhaimara the 'surplus' rice is transferred by the rural rich via the market to the urban areas.

Also from the point of view of the landless and poor peasants it is obvious that the 56 tons of paddy are not distributed equally. The majority of these households, we have emphasized, cannot provide a sufficient diet for their members. We have mentioned elsewhere that some of these households are not viable units and not able to sustain themselves; they split and let the old, unproductive, members take care of themselves. Some of the poorest people also sell rice at the local market after the harvest, and some of this rice will end up in the urban markets. We are, however, not in a position to say whether 5 or 10 or 15 tons of rice of the 56 tons (assuming this amount to be fairly correct) end up in the urban markets.[58]

If we had accurate information on how much went out of the village (paddy, jute, vegetables, fruits etc.), it could have been interesting to make a comparison with the value of goods coming in (agricultural inputs, consumer goods). This we are in an even weaker position to assess, and the matter becomes even more complicated by the fact that many of the goods entering the village come in under the circumstances we described above for the agricultural inputs: subsidized by the Government but heavily bribed for by the rural rich. Thus we are unable to make any estimate of quantities of the 'exchange relation' and 'direction of the exchange' between the village and the urban areas. It should, however, be very clear from the description in this chapter which groups benefit from the integration with the outside world as the exchange relations operate today.

Finally we should mention that the village is also integrated into the larger society through a labour market. This integration takes place in different ways. In chapter 6 we noted that the labour market to which the area of Bhaimara belongs is a labour surplus area, where for large parts of the year it is difficult for the residing male persons to obtain sufficient employment. For most of this labour force the urban areas do not provide any opportunities for employment. Many of the unemployed men will, however, go on seasonal migration trips to the northern area and participate in the harvest operations there. The absentee landowners and the households that live in the village but have individual members working in urban areas are also, but in different ways, integrated into a larger society. There is little doubt that some of the absentee landowners extract resources from the area (e.g. Shamsul Huq), and that the resources they invest in the village have the effect of creating a differentiation and polarization among the households in the village. The few households that have members working as unskilled labourers in the urban areas may receive a part of the wage of their absentee household member, but they may also subsidize him (and thereby indirectly the industry or institution he works for) by sending him food grain from the land of his household. The reason the urban wage labourer can accept the low pay he receives is that his other household members can sustain themselves through their own resources and efforts in the village.

Although this chapter has emphasized the important role the Government plays in the rural areas, we have also wanted to convey the point that the policies of the Government are only one factor, among many, which give shape to the social relationships which exist in the villages. The patron-client relationships which are the dominant feature of the rural social organization are, as we have shown in the other chapters, generated by many other factors (the scarcity of credit, land, tenancy contracts, employment opportunities and the need for political protection). The State of Bangladesh sets a legal framwork for many of the activities which occur in the rural areas, but the Government policies which are implemented only strengthen a pattern of relationships and social organization which would already be there.

Notes

1 There are several methods of estimating and measuring the percentage of development expenditure covered by foreign aid. The different estimates depend on which expenses are included and which left out.
2 The major sources we have used when discussing the role donor organizations play in development planning in Bangladesh are: J. Faaland (ed.): *Aid and Influence,* Mac Millan Press, 1981, and Rehman Sobhan: *The Crisis of External Dependence, The Political Economy of Foreign Aid to Bangladesh,* University Press Limited, Dhaka 1982.
3 See Mahbub-ul Haq: *The Strategy of Economic Planning: A Case Study of Pakistan,* Oxford University Press, 1966.
4 See Asplund and de Vylder, *op.cit.*
5 Jannuzi and Peach, *op.cit.,* pp. 12–13.
6 A book that puts land reform legislation into a historical perspective and discusses a number of issues and dilemmas connected with land reform and the difficulties of implementing land reform is: *Land Reform in Bangladesh,* edited by Muhiuddin Khan Alamgir, Centre for Social Studies, Dhaka, September 1981.
7 Asplund and de Vylder, *op.cit.*
8 *Ibid.*
9 *Ibid.*
10 *Ibid.*
11 FAO/UNDP/Government of Bangladesh: *Agricultural Mission. Selected Policy Issues and Working Papers,* Dhaka 1979.
12 Zahir, S. and Kamel, A.: *Urban Rationing System in Bangladesh,* Dhaka, BIDS; draft 1981.
13 For a discussion of this issue see J. Stepanek, *op.cit.,* Chapters 5 and 6.
14 C.H.H. Rao: 'Urban vs. Rural or Rich vs. Poor.' Review article in *Economic and Political Weekly,* 7 October, 1978.
15 Rehman Sobhan: 'Bangladesh and the World Economic System: The Crisis of External Dependence', *Development and Change,* Vol. 12, No. 3, July 1981, pp. 327–347.
16 Rehman Sobhan: 'Politics of Food and Famine', *Economic and Political Weekly,* 1 December 1979.
17 For a discussion of this issue see McHenry, D.F. & Bird, Kai: 'Food Bungle in Bangladesh', *Foreign Affairs,* p. 79, No. 27/1977, and Rehman Sobhan, 1981, *op.cit.*
18 This topic is treated in a chapter on 'Food Aid' by J. Parkinson in *Aid and Influence,* MacMillan Press, 1981, edited by J. Faaland. See also Rehman Sobhan: *Food Politics and Famine in Bangladesh.* DERAP Working Paper No. 158, Chr. Michelsen Institute, Bergen, Norway, and R. Sobhan, *op.cit.,* 1982.
19 J. Parkinson, *op.cit.,* p. 94.
20 See Philip B. Calkins: 'Stability and Change in Landholding and Revenue System in Bengal', pp. 9–28, in *Rural Development in Bangladesh and Pakistan,* edited by R.D. Stevens, Hamza Alavi, Peter J. Bertocci, The University Press of Hawaii, 1976.

21 J. Faaland and J.R. Parkinson, *op.cit.,* p. 49.

22 See M. Hossain, A. Rahman and M.M. Aksah, *Agricultural Taxation in Bangladesh,* Bangladesh Institute of Development, 1978.

23 See J. Faaland and J.R. Parkinson, *op.cit.,* pp. 48–50.

24 The information is obtained from various reports from the Bangladesh Rice Research Institute.

25 For a discussion of this issue see Asplund and de Vylder, *op.cit.*

26 E.J. Clay, *Employment Effects of the HYV Strategy in Bangladesh: A Rejoinder,* Dhaka, March 1978 (a), table 6, p. 30. (Quoted from Asplund and de Vylder.)

27 Asplund and de Vylder, *op.cit.*

28 H. Brammer, *Costs of Production, Profits and Returns for Paddy and Wheat Cultivation at New Fertilizer Prices,* Soil Survey Department, Dhaka 1976 (mimeo).

29 N.U. Ahmad, *Cost of Production of Aus Paddy and Jute Cultivation per Acre,* U.S.A.I.D., Dhaka, August 1976.

30 Stefan de Vylder, *op.cit.,* p. 91.

31 *Ibid,* p. 122.

32 Jannuzi and Peach, *op.cit.,* have estimated that 69 per cent of 'farm households' reported the use of chemical fertilizer on their *boro* crop, (61 per cent for their *aman* crop and 62 per cent for their *aus* crop), p. 117. (We noted in table 2.4, chapter 2, that the quantity of fertilizers used on the *boro* crop was much larger than the quantity used on the *aus* and *aman* crops.)

33 40 per cent of public expenditures on the rural sector are subsidies on fertilizers and pesticides alone, see Asplund and de Vylder, *op.cit.*

34 *Far Eastern Economic Review,* 24 October, 1980, p. 62. 'Basket Case to Bread Basket' by S. Kamaluddin.

35 An ambitious credit programme was the 100 Taka Crore (1 *crore* = 10 million) Credit Programme launched in 1977. The programme's main target group was the poor peasants; however, the main beneficiaries were the top 20 per cent of the peasants, see de Vylder, *op.cit.,* pp. 111–114.

36 E.G. Jansen, *op.cit.,* pp. 61–84.

37 For a discussion of the economics of MOSTI-pumps see Biggs, Edwards and Griffiths, *op.cit.,* and L.M. Hannah, *op.cit.*

38 For a discussion of this issue, as pertaining to import of deep tubewells, see E.G. Jansen, *op.cit.,* pp. 82–83 and Biggs, Edwards and Grittiths, *op.cit.,* and J.W. Thomas, 'The Choice of Technology for Irrigation Tubewells in East Pakistan: An Analysis of a Development Policy Decision', in the *Choice of Technology in Developing Countries,* by Timmer, Thomas, Wells and Morawetz, *Harvard Studies in International Affairs,* No. 32, 1975.

39 R. Sobhan, *op.cit.,* pp. 218–221.

40 For a discussion of these issue see J. Faaland and J.R. Parkinson, *op.cit.,* chapter 7.

41 Stefan de Vylder, *op.cit.*, p. 101.
42 J. Faaland and J.R. Parkinson, *op.cit.*, p. 145.
43 *Far Eastern Economic Review, op.cit.*
44 See E.G. Jansen: *Possible Socio-Economic Implications of Norwegian Assistance to Bangladesh's Inland Waterways Transport Sector.* DERAP Working Paper A 197, Chr. Michelsen Institute, Bergen, February 1981 and E.G. Jansen: 'The Development of the Mechanized River Transport Sector in Bangladesh. Aid to the Poor?' In: *Poverty and Aid,* edited by J.R. Parkinson, Basil Blackwell, Oxford 1983, pp. 163–168.
45 Harry W. Blair: 'Rural Development, Class Structure and Bureaucracy in Bangladesh', *World Development,* 1978, Vol. 6, No. 1, pp. 65–82.
46 *Ibid.*, p. 72.
47 Experiments with developing cooperatives were made in Kotwali Thana, Comilla district from the end of 1950s and through the 1960s.
48 For a thorough discussion of these issues see Asplund and de Vylder, *op.cit.*, pp. 133–162.
49 Garson Vogel, 'Overseas Development', UK Overseas Development Ministry, September, 1978, p. 4. Quoted from Michael Scott: *Aid to Bangladesh — For Better or Worse,* p. 22, Oxfam of America, The Institute for Food and Development Policies.
50 See R. Sobhan, 1982, *op.cit.*, pp. 53–54.
51 See R. Jahan: *Local Power Structure and the Mobilization of Vote: A Study of the Bangladesh Election 1979.* DERAP Working Paper A 155, Chr. Michelsen Institute, Bergen, August 1979. The election campaign in the area showed many of the features discussed by Rounaq Jahan in her analysis and description of a parliamentary election campaign in a constituency in the district of Comilla.
52 For a general discussion of the flow of resources in Bangladesh and South Asia between the rural, urban and external sectors, at different historical stages (pre-colonial, colonial and post-colonial) see J. Faaland and Mosharaff Hossain: 'Structural Transformation and Rural Development', in *European Studies on Development,* edited by Jacques De Bandt, Péter Mándi and Dudley Seers, The MacMillan Press Ltd., London 1980, pp. 281–290.
53 Göran Djurfeldt and Staffan Lindberg: *Behind Poverty — The Social Formation in a Tamil Village.* Scandinavian Institute of Asian Studies. Monograph Series No. 22, 1975.
54 *Ibid.*, pp. 160–161.
55 *Ibid.*, p. 163.
56 See Haroun Er Rashid, *op.cit.*
57 See discussion in chapter 2 and reference to the work of L. Chen on estimate of rice needed per person per day.
58 Kirsten Westergaard in her study from Bogra states that an estimated 20–25 per cent of the rice produced in the Thana is exported primarily to Pabna district, south of Bogra. Some of this rice is then transported further to Dhaka. See K. Westgaard, *op.cit.*, pp. 36–38.

9

Analytical Approach to the Study of Competition for Scarce Resources

Introduction

This chapter will outline the analytical approach which has underlain our study. It will explicitly refer to and discuss concepts and elements which have structured our description and analysis. In our presentation of the material in this study this analytical approach is, for the most part, implicit. In outlining the analytical approach we shall directly relate our discussion of the concepts to the empirical material we have presented in the previous chapters.

First, however, we shall give a brief summary of the main points and issues which we have raised in this study. In the last section of this chapter we shall outline some of the main features of the social organization of rural Bangladesh and discuss why a class-based social organization has not developed in rural Bangladesh.

Brief summary of main points of the study

We set out our problem as being a study of competition for scarce resources. We documented how heavily the population in the rural areas depended on income and employment from agriculture and showed that both land and opportunities for employment in agriculture were scarce. Our departing point for unravelling the story of the competitive relationships was the 'budget' situation of households in different economic positions. Most households have insufficient land to subsist on and too few possibilities of supplementing their income through work as agricultural wage labourers. How do the households manage when their expenses are greater than their incomes? The answer to this question, we maintained, must be seen in relation to the economic activities of the households that are able to acquire a surplus from their resources. All through the study we have shown that peasants who produce more than they consume are not content with the amount of land they own, no matter how much land they possess. To a large degree the economic expansion of these 'surplus' peasants occurs at the expense of the households who are in a deficit budget position. From one point of view the main body of this study can be read as an account of how poor peasants attempt to cope with their deficit budgets by interacting in economic relationships with 'surplus' peasants who strive to expand their possessions. We noted how deficit peasants were compelled to take up consumption loans in order to survive. When the loans accumulated, the land of the poor peasants, whether agricultural land or homestead plot land, was demanded as collateral for the loans. Competition due to credit leading to mortgage and sale of land took place in several relationships. 'Surplus' peasants will often struggle among themselves in order to finance the deficits of poor peasants whose economic positions are fast deteriorating. From the 'surplus' peasant point of view it is the land of the poor peasants, soon to change ownership, which is the scarce resource. The deficit peasants, for their part, naturally try to keep their land. They are involved in a number of economic activities of a competitive nature with creditors in order to postpone the mortgage and sale of land.

We gave a detailed account of one of the areas in which most of the deficit peasants compete: contracts involving land on a sharecropping basis. The best way poor peasants can cope with their deficits is to obtain favourable terms for sharecropping. We saw that almost all landowning households in the village were involved in sharecropping, either as tenants or as landowners leasing land out on sharecropping contracts. We found that even relatively well-to-do 'surplus' peasants sharecropped land, and in this respect became tenants if they possessed sufficient and available manpower for agricultural activities in the fields.

Another major way of coping with a deficit budget is to enter the agricultural wage labour market. We noted that almost all the households of the village were involved in the labour market either as employees or employers. In the labour market too these strong competitive relations exist both in securing an employment contract and in negotiating good terms for it.

The most fierce and disruptive way of competing for scarce resources we found in illegal land possession. Disputes over the ownership rights to land often preceded or followed transfer of land in this way. In this type of competition normal rules of proper conduct were set aside.

We described how many of the factors causing this scarcity and the competition for the resources are clearly evident in the village: a very high man-land ratio, very poor utilization of land and manpower, little Government assistance to increase agricultural growth. The origin and major dynamics of some of the factors contributing to the poverty take place outside the village boundaries. We have discussed some of these factors in detail. We showed how ecological and technological factors became part of the framework for economic activities and influenced the nature of competitive relationships. We also discussed how different types of cultural values influenced economic activities and how Government relations with the rural areas sustained the interests of the most well-to-do and rich peasants. In fact, a major portion of this study has been devoted to a description and analysis of the wider framework within which the competition for scarce resources in the rural areas takes place. We emphasized, however, that there was no simple one-way direction of the influence of the exogenous factors on the rural areas. The exogenous factors were in turn, to a varying degree, modified by processes going on in the rural areas.

Concepts and approach needed to capture the real life situation of the people in the rural areas

No matter what analytical approach is chosen by social scientists when interpreting social and economic activities in the rural areas of Bangladesh, the scarcity of land and of opportunities for employment are facts which cannot be disputed. It has been a contention of this study that the competition around scarce resources permeates almost all social intercourse and dominates and shapes the lives of the peasants. Given the pervasive poverty most people face, there could, as we have shown throughout the study, hardly be anything else which from their point of view should receive higher priority and more attention.

In order to capture the essence of this competition, it is necessary to have sharp and adequate analytical tools. An analytical perspective lies behind the empirical material we have put forward in this study. We have felt strongly that it has been necessary to adopt concepts and an approach which, we believe, are compatible with the real world of the competition and struggle people are engaged in. Such an approach should also force and stimulate us to formulate questions and give reflective accounts of the interconnections which exist between all the observations we have made as regards people's struggle for scarce resources. An essential requirement of the approach ought to be that it enables us to capture the factors which structure and channelize people's behaviour. The approach should also assist us in discovering the implications of people's behaviour.

As we stated in Chapter 1, we have adopted the analytical approach and concepts developed by Fredrik Barth during the last decades. His main analytical contribution is *Models of Social Organization.*[1] Barth's approach has been elaborated on and restated in a number of subsequent works (F. Barth 1967, 1969, 1972, 1975). For the purpose of our study we have particularly referred to his latest works: 'Models reconsidered' and 'Swat Pathans reconsidered'.[2] This approach has influenced our study profoundly both when collecting information in the field and when analyzing and presenting the material. Below we shall be more explicit and go into more detail on the concepts and approach we have utilized. This is necessary both for showing the advantages which can be gained by such an approach and also for spelling out the conceptual basis we have for speculating about future tendencies.

The analytical approach presented below can, of course, be placed in relation to other anthropological approaches and schools. Barth's analytical contribution must be understood both in relation to and reaction to structuralist, functionalist and historical approaches and in the light of his extensive fieldwork in different societies.[3] This study has not aimed to trace historically the various arguments that have been put forward in the debate on the different modes of explanation and thought in anthropology, nor to place Barth's approach in such a context. Nor have we had any intention of challenging any of the concepts in Barth's model, as Paine, Evens and Asad have done.[4] Barth's model is encompassing and ambitious, since it claims to describe, analyse and explain a wide range of social and cultural phenomena. Our use of the model must be seen in relation to the problems we have focused on and the material we have collected. Therefore the potential of this analytical approach is only incompletely utilized.

We shall discuss, step by step, the different concepts and elements which have been used in our analysis. There are, however, problems connected with a separate, stepwise, discussion of our concepts, since these are related and interdependent. In our discussion of the concepts we shall refer to the empirical material we have presented in the previous chapters. At this stage we need to emphasize that the concepts we discuss must not be mixed and muddled up with the empirical reality we observed in the rural areas. The model we present and its concepts are only a symbolic representation of this social reality. The model and concepts we discuss are utilized in order to facilitate our analysis of the nature of this social reality. When therefore, for instance, we discuss the 'actors strategies', we *analyse* people's behaviour and actions as strategies, we do not *identify* behaviour as strategies.

Decision-making unit of study

For most of the issues we have dealt with in this study the individual household has been the decision-making unit. It is the household which has to manage scarce resources and which is involved in competitive relationships with other households. It is also the household which has to face and deal with the consequences of its activities. We have referred to the household in various ways. Often we have mentioned the economic position individual persons find themselves in. Sometimes we have mentioned the names of particular persons. On other occasions we describe certain aspects of the situation 'people' find themselves in. We have implied when referring to named or unnamed individuals or generally to 'people' that they all act on behalf of the household they belong to. Although the decisions, as we noted in Chapter 3, are not made by all the members of the household, all of the household members will directly and indirectly be affected by the decisions taken. It is therefore the household which is the unit when such references are made.

We have, however, also shown that there are other types of decision-making units than the household. These are of a more corporate character; the *patron-client* relationship, the *samaj* (local society), the *dal* (faction), the *gusti* (kin-group), the *shalish* (local court), the village, the Union Council, etc. These decision-making units operate for different and more specific purposes and normally, except for the *patron-client* relationships, contain many individual households. Here, in our characterization of the unit of our study, we shall only be concerned with the household unit.

In order to understand the decisions taken by a household unit it is necessary to have information both about the internal structure of the unit and the context and strategic position the household is placed in. We have in various chapters of this study given an account of these, but not in a systematic way. Here we shall separately and briefly summarize the factors we found important for understanding the choices for courses of action taken by the households. We have implicitly referred to these factors in various chapters, and in particular these factors should be easily discernible through the case studies we have presented in Chapters 4 and 7. Throughout the study we have emphasized that there is a variation in the behavioural solutions of the households. The factors we discuss below are of great significance for explaining this variation.[5]

(a) The Internal composition of the household: In Chapter 3 we showed that the internal structure of the household varied. Depending on its development cycle, the household consisted of incomplete elementary families, elementary families or extended families. We accounted for the degree of cohesiveness of the household and related that to the development stage the household found itself in. Internal conflicts in connection with decision-making and economic activities occurred when a household was on the verge of splitting. The household's behaviour towards other decision-making units, we maintained, must therefore be understood in light of the internal processes going on within the unit.

(b) The nature of the different assets of the household: We have emphasized that the most important asset a household possesses is its land. The amount of land a household owns defines to a large degree the household's economic, social and strategic position, and it also indicates the type of economic relationship the household is

engaged in. Other production factors like technical equipment, cattle and inputs for agricultural production are of minor importance compared to land. The labour force the household possesses can also be regarded as an asset. A high proportion of net producers and income-earning members as compared with net consumers naturally influences the adaptation of the household. We have also emphasized that the patrilineal kinship group, if it consists of many and well-to-do households, can be of significance for the support a household can mobilize and for its strategic position vis-à-vis other households.

A fairly unconventional type of asset which we have considered very important is the *political skills* of the members of the household. The ability of the members of a household to be attractive in alliances and factions in the villages can easily be converted into economic opportunities. Our case study of the two brothers, Eynuddin and Joinuddin, cases 2 and 3, Chapter 4, who inherited an equal amount of land, but ended up in very different economic positions, shows the importance of management skills and political connections.

(c) Institutionalized mechanisms for transfer of value of different types and cultural standards affecting these transfers. We have accounted for the inheritance system in detail, with specific reference to the important and valuable transfer of land. We also outlined in great detail the way land was transferred through sale, and how tenancy and labour contracts were established. In different chapters we pointed out how kinship obligations and cultural standards put restrictions on certain types of transfers. Joinuddin, case 2, Chapter 4, we noted, felt obliged to sell his land to his brother, and he also, at one stage, felt his social status would be lowered if he and his family members entered the open labour market.

(d) Relationship between households in terms of competition and symbiosis. The whole study has been an account of competition, conflicts and contradictory interests between households over sharing limited resources. Alliances are made between households, but seldom in order to augment the total amount of goods to be shared. The alliances are made to obtain a larger share of a given amount for the members of the alliance.

(e) The households' ability to articulate their interests to the outside world. We have shown important ways in which the village society is integrated economically and politically into a larger society. We have also emphasized that the ability of the households to articulate their interests to the outside world differed greatly, depending much on the economic position, political alliances and educational background of the household members.

On the basis of the above conditions, what conclusions can we draw when attempting to understand the direction of the behaviour of the households? It should have become clear that a household finds itself in a very *complex opportunity situation.* The household will often pursue goals which are conflicting, e.g., retaining social status and carrying out degrading economic activities, extracting economic advantages through marriage of a member of the household while at the same time maintaining the prestige of the household. Behaviour in one field cannot be understood with reference to that field alone, e.g., the negotiations about a sharecropping contract must also be seen in the light of possible political support following on the same relationship. Different statuses are mobilized between the same units; landowner-tenant, patron-client, employer-employee. The 'many-stranded' nature of the *whole relationships* the households are involved in must be captured if we are to understand their behaviour. In fact a main aim of this study has been to emphasize that complexity and 'many-strandedness' is the essence of these relationships. We believe that our strong insistence on this view, which is supported with extensive amounts of empirical material throughout the study, gives this monograph a different emphasis from that of many of the other village studies we have referred to.

Nature of decision-making strategies

Throughout the study we have maintained that a fruitful perspective for analysing social life is to apply a 'strategic perspective' to the behaviour of the decision-making units. It seems obvious that the households need to plan carefully in order to survive in an environment marked by scarcity. Here we want to identify the nature of some types of strategies, because each type of strategy has particular implications for the social organization which emerges.

We have shown that there is competition among households over obtaining a sharecropping and an employment contract and over purchasing land. When such a relationship is finally established between households, it is almost always of *dyadic* character, between two units who are employer-employee, landowner-tenant. We noted that there was much haggling involved in negotiating the terms of a contract. What is normally one party's gain in these contracts is the other party's loss. In our empirical presentation of the relationships in which the two households are involved we have also discussed the alternatives, or lack of real alternatives, each of the households has. Barth gives a general characterization of these types of relationships:[6]

If an actor is confronted with a reasonably informed, self-seeking other on the issue of dividing a limited good, it is good strategic sense to act so as to preclude the worst eventuality: a mini-max principle can serve *because* alter can be assumed — or feared — always to choose the option most favourable to himself and thus, in such contexts, least favourable to ego. If alter may be expected to seek to maximize his own net gain in a context where this does not need to entail maximal loss to ego, it makes good sense to present alter with the option of *transaction*. (My emphasis.)

In another work Barth elaborates on the content of transactions:[7]

They [the transactions] consist of a sequence of reciprocal presentations, which represent successive moves in the game. There must be a ledger kept of value gained and lost; and each successive action or move affects that ledger, changes the strategic situation, and thus canalizes subsequent choices. Many possible courses of action are ruled out because they are patently unsatisfactory, i.e. an actor must expect that value lost be greater than value gained. In such a model the incentives and constraints on choice are effective through the way they determine what can be gained and lost; and each actor's social adjustment to the other party in the transaction is depicted in terms of alter's possible moves, and how they in turn affect ego's value gains. The structure depicted in this model is a successional one over time — in other words, it is a model of process.

We believe that the concept of transaction elaborated above is a concept with a perspective which can very fruitfully be applied to understanding and illuminating the nature of an important process which is a dominant feature of many social relationships.

We mentioned that the household units are members of many corporate groups, and that it can also be strategically advantageous to make alliances with other units in order to ensure that their own interests are catered for. Barth has termed this type of relation *incorporation*:[8]

It is possible to define a relationship of incorporation as an analytical opposition to a transactional relationship — one where a value optimum, probably for a restricted range of values, is sought for the sum of partners, and not for a single party. Such partnerships can engage as units in transactions vis-à-vis other persons or groups; internally, their interactions will not be systematically governed by reciprocity. Yet there are limits in most cases to the losses, or inequalities of gains, which people are willing to bear through such incorporation.

Incorporation is also a concept which we believe can profitably be applied, providing insights to specifiable processes of the social relationships we have discussed in this study. It should be clear from the material we have presented that local organizations act as units for specific purposes, and that the individual household will from time to time assess whether it is worthwhile becoming a member of a particular corporate group. We saw how people threatened to leave the *samaj* (local society) and the strategic considerations involved in deciding whether one should quit a faction or a political alliance. The patron-client relationship we have referred to so often, has an aspect of corporate character. One way this was expressed was when the patron acted as a guarantor for the loan his client had taken. Vis-à-vis the creditor both the patron and the client had joint interests. We noted that patrons often considered dropping their clients or the clients thought of shifting to a new patron.

We mentioned another feature of a corporate nature when describing how wages were negotiated. Although there was no formal organization of the daily wage-labourers, a tacit understanding prevailed as to what should be the minimum level of wages acceptable to a wage-labourer. Sanctions could be applied by other wage-labourers to those in their ranks who started to acquiesce in lower wages.

Barth mentions a third type of strategy:[9]

If ego's choice will not affect the moves of alter, i.e. the contest is like a game against nature, then it makes sense to take chances if the probabilities are favourable — but within limits set by the amount of resources available to the actor which can buffer him against total destruction in the case of loss.

In our analysis in some part of this study we believe it makes good sense to apply this perspective for providing further understanding. A case in point is what we observed Shamsul Huq (case 5, Chapter 4) do when he snatched a bit of land from a poor peasant with whom he shared boundaries. This act is certainly not of a 'transactional' or 'corporate' type. Shamsul Huq realized that there was no chance that his poor neighbour would react. The only retaliation he might face was the silent disapproval of the villagers.

The relationships between the households are, however, often of a very complicated nature. In the relationship between the two brothers Joinuddin and Eynuddin, both transactional and corporate elements were involved. If we focus on a specific activity a household performs, for instance in agriculture, we find that the household will be involved in a strategy of chances against nature (when to plough, plant etc.), transactional relations when hiring wage-labourers, and corporate relationships in protecting its ownership rights to land. Barth comments on transactional and incorporate relationships.[10]

> We should think of them not as a partial (much less an exhaustive) typology of relationship, but rather as specificable processes which, under certain circumstances which we want to identify and explore, can dominate the shape people give to their acts, and thus also the emergent properties of social aggregates.

When focusing on the nature of relationships people are involved in, we were stimulated to explore the organizational implications which followed. We have not been explicit in the preceding chapters on the connections we have seen between the nature of the strategy households are involved in and the type of social organization which emerges. In the final section of this chapter we shall discuss this issue in more detail. For the moment we shall return to our discussion of actions of the decision-making units.

It is, of course, impossible for a household unit to be strategic and make plans for all the moves it makes. With the complex opportunity situation the unit finds itself in, it would be a frustrating and time-consuming task to make elaborate plans for all the acts it is involved in. Most of the activities a unit is engaged in are of *repetitive* nature. The employers and employees have almost daily experience in coming to an agreement on the level of wages.

Although sharecropping contracts occur more seldom, there are established rules which serve as a point of reference for negotiations. The same applies to credit and mortgage relationships. Many of the decisions concerning the activities we have described are without doubt taken on routines based on previous experience. Decisions made on the basis of established practices have many advantages: the outcome is fairly predictable, there will be no moral sanctions from the community for violating rules, and less time will be consumed. Although the households may not consider their routine actions very carefully, this type of action can nevertheless be analysed in a strategical perspective, since the results of the behaviour will be evaluated if they are unexpected.

However, there are occasions when minute plans are needed. When a person challenges routine solutions, he must be careful to assess his support in the village. We have described many cases which require strategy from the units involved; illegal possession of land can hardly ever become routine, and we saw how much effort and energy went into land disputes. Also breaking the wage level or performing any type of entrepreneurial activities needs planning and strategic considerations.

We felt and observed, however, that there also was a tactical element in many of the daily activities and relationships people were involved in. These tactical elements were not related directly towards obtaining a better deal for specific purposes, but more towards securing a more overall support and general concern from powerful persons. Throughout the study we have demonstrated what difference the availability or lack of such support means for survival. More than in other societies, not burdened with similar poverty, we found most people, almost as by a reflex, to be purpose-oriented and strategic in their general dealings and daily encounters with well-to-do and rich persons. This expressed itself through the way poor people made efforts to please and publicly support and adopt a respectful attitude towards the more powerful persons. We observed this behaviour daily in the fields, in the markets, and on the village paths. The almost institutionalized deferential attitude of the poor towards the rich, at least when meeting them face to face, is naturally linked to the view that one's economic interests are best served by becoming attached to a patron.

Social patterns

From one perspective it can appear as if our study has mainly focused on the decision-making and strategies of individuals. The many case studies could strengthen this view. Our aim has, of course, been broader than to discuss the considerations and dilemmas individuals like Mosum Ali and Joinuddin (cases 1 and 2, Chapter 4) are involved in. Our intention has been to describe the more regular behavioural patterns of households in different economic categories and to account for the more general features which structure their opportunity situations. What are the connections between the individual acts we can observe and the patterns of behaviour, and how have we accounted for this relationship between acts and social systems in our study?

One very simple way in which we have dealt with this relationship, is through our tables.

On the basis of our village survey we added the responses of the individual units to our questions and searched for what we thought to be interesting and important interconnections. We 'discovered' some clear patterns in our material for which we felt we had found plausible explanations; for instance, that about half of the mortgaged and purchased plots of land were transferred between members of the same kin-group. Our statistical universe is confined to only one village, and we have formulated hypotheses about the factors causing the specific patterns we observed. Our further generalization is that wherever these factors are operating, similar patterns will be generated; a generalization which clearly can be tested by further investigation. A departing point for understanding how patterns come about is obtained by focusing on the factors which induce repetitive acts. Above we discussed how many of the problems and issues people have to solve are of a regular, repetitive nature. When a person finds a solution to such a problem, then the chances are great that others who are in a similar opportunity situation, will act likewise. Certain quantifiable aspects of these acts can be added and considered as statistical evidence for the prevalence of a particular pattern. The tables alone naturally offer no explanations of the constellation of factors causing the pattern.

Merely adding and correlating the individual acts is, however, a very imperfect way of arriving at the aggregate pattern. The nature of the aggregate patterns is much more complicated. The aggregate patterns have their own 'properties' and generate their own dynamics. These dynamics have feedback effects on the opportunity situation of the decision-making units. This may in turn effect the choices of action and thereby lead to a changed behavioural pattern. A major aim of this study has been, on an empirical level, to follow this line of argument; in other words, to discover and discuss the implications which result from the dynamics of the aggregate patterns. For instance, a series of implications we have followed through is the effects of the transfer of ownership of land. The result of all these transfers is, as we showed, polarization of land holdings through which many households become landless and a small percentage of households accumulate land. With the existing high unemployment rate, this implies that an increasing number of landless households lose their purchasing power.

Lack of purchasing power has in turn consequences for the investment alternatives of the well-to-do peasants. Another series of implications we followed through dealt with the level of wages. We saw that employers had at their disposal a number of measures by which they could circumvent attempts by employees to maintain a high level of wages. We also indicated some of the implications which followed from all landowning households wanting to possess their own pair of bullocks for the ploughing seasons. One result of this wish is that there are 18 million head of cattle in Bangladesh, which is far too many for the grazing capacity of the country. An effect of this is that the great majority of cattle are very poorly fed and undernourished. Many other consequences also follow from the large number of cattle.

These series of implications have been oversimplified above; in the preceding chapters we presented their more complicated context. Also for many of the other patterns of behaviour we have described and analysed, the implications of their specific dynamics are only indirectly referred to. It should have become clear from our examples that the rationale which lies behind the individual acts cannot also be attributed to the outcome of the aggregate behaviour. The results of the aggregate patterns were, in the examples we gave above, contradictory to the interests of the individual actors.

People are very conscious of many of the implications which follow from their total sum of behaviour, and recognize that their behaviour may often lead to results against their own interests. An example of this recognition is the growth of population. From the point of view of the individual couple it is regarded as socially and economically advantageous to have many children (particularly boys). People see, however, how livelihood in a long-term perspective is undermined when everybody wants many children. On many occasions we heard the villagers pondering and worrying over the fast growth of population and the seemingly constant amount of land and resources.

Although we have not been explicit in our presentation of the relationship between individual acts and behavioural regularities and the feedback effects which follow, we, nevertheless, maintain that a main concern of this study has been to point to such interconnections. Some of the interconnections we have discussed are well-known and generally recognized. Other interconnections have we think, on the basis of the fairly detailed knowledge we possess, not been acknowledged or given proper attention in the other monographs on the villages or rural Bangladesh. In order to discover interesting interconnections, the interdependence of the individual acts and strategies, on the one hand and the aggregate behaviour and social system, on the other, must be recognized and not separated when the material is analysed.

A question we have posed about almost all the issues we have discussed is why there exist variations in the adaptations people make. We observed that wage-labour contracts varied, and the same applied to mortgage and sharecropping agreements. The way we explained variations was by focusing on possible differences in the opportunity situation of the actors. The factors we emphasized as important in people's opportunity situation were listed above (a-e) when discussing the individual properties, assets and environment of the household unit.

It is appropriate to bring in the 'modelling perspective' of our study at this stage when focusing on variation. The steps we have followed in the course of our study and analysis can roughly be summarized as follows.[11] During our fieldwork we made hypotheses about empirical factors which influenced the adaptational forms we focused on. Later, when we had collected information, we made models, not formalized in any sense, isolating the factors which we found to be important 'determinants' for the processes we observed. Finally we were concerned about the 'fit' between the form generated and explained by our model and the empirical cases. Our concern about the fit between the model and reality was expressed both in our investigations in the field and in our analysis of the material. A case we have dealt with in detail may serve as an example of our modelling operations: Our first impressions and early hypothesis on mortgage showed it to be a phenomenon which occurred between poor and well-to-do peasants. We specified a limited set of factors in connection with this process: characteristics of the actors involved, general features of their opportunity situation, and the transactional relationship between them. The 'modelling ' we thus performed was brief and schematic, but it helped us to depict linkages between empirical processes and events.

When we conducted surveys to discover the extent of mortgage relationships, we were made aware of mortgage cases which deviated from our model. We found that mortgages also took place between persons who both were well-to-do and on an equal footing. The social reality of this type of mortgage relationship was therefore incompatible with the first model we had constructed. In order to account for this varying type of mortgage, other factors and processes were essential, as we showed in our exposition in chapter 4.

In our opinion, one of the most fruitful properties of the analytical model we have adopted is its insistence that model and reality should be confronted. The model allows us then to argue for implications which can be tested against further observations. One advantage to be gained by this confrontation is that the models can be falsified. This fact should not be regarded as a tragedy; on the contrary it should provoke and force the researcher to do more detailed studies and construct new models. Therefore an insistence on a permanently critical attitude towards the model we make is our best guarantee for obtaining a more comprehensive picture of the complexity of social life.

This attitude to the relationship between model and reality has naturally had consequences for the way we collected information. In chapter 1 we elaborated on our field work situation and emphasized that during an extended stay in the village we learnt about the strategies of different groups of people. During our stay in the village we transcended to a certain extent our own 'western categories', and discovered the *izzat* value system and the stratification system which were part of the people's framework. Field work is normally a cumulative learning process: the picture of people's opportunity situation gradually becomes more complex and first impressions may prove too simple or wrong.

The analytical approach we used deviated on this point from other approaches which possess a more ready-made paradigm for interpreting information. The evolutionary, structuralistic and functionalist approaches have in their different ways more pre-established categories, structures or development sequences in which to order their information. We think on the basis of many village monographs of rural Bangladesh that this exogenous notion of what constitutes the important categories of analysis has prohibited many researchers from exposing themselves to a wide variety of information. Although many 'bold' statements on important interconnections may be made by these approaches, the insights seem often to be of a general, abstract character. The abstractions can be interesting and serve as a departing point for empirical investigations, but they provide little detailed knowledge on social life in rural Bangladesh. Barth, whose model we have elaborated above contrasts his approach with other analytical approaches on these issues:[12]

> 'Society' in this perspective is not a thing, of which you tell a history or for which you show the fitness of design in how each part functions to support the other; it is, on the contrary, an epiphenomenon (and no less interesting for that reason!), i.e. 'society' is how things happen to be as a result of all manner of activities and circumstances. The thrust of analysis is not to show that it must be like this, but to show what must be since it is like this — i.e. to discover the major determining factors and processes. An essential link in these models is the part played by real people going about their lives. My perspective does not allow any shorthand language whereby patterns, lineage-systems, exploitation and class, or any other macro-feature is described as 'reproducing itself': the social events that make up such patterns are all brought to pass by *people*. The key which secures this integrity of people as actors is the concept of choice. Not free choice — indeed that is precisely what makes an analysis of choice illuminating: choices are decisions which are constrained by the perceptions of the actors, the circumstances under which persons act, and the reactions of others.

Regional and historical variation of social patterns and the contextual framework of the villages

On several occasions we have referred to events and findings from different regions of Bangladesh. Although we have presented very little material fram Pabna district, the information we collected there, from the home village of our assistant, has nevertheless, been of value for us. We continually contrasted our material from Bhaimara with the patterns we knew to exist in Pabna. This comparison proved to be a fruitful exercise in assessing the importance of influential and determining factors. Some of the factors which explained differences in adaptations were of an exogenous nature; the ecological conditions of Pabna were different in certain respects and the penetration of Government activities seemed less strong. Within the village the polarization of landholdings was greater than in Bhaimara; several rich landowners possessed more than 30 acres of land. This had clear consequences for the nature of employment and sharecropping contracts and credit relationships and mortgage patterns.

Another type of variation we have referred to is of a historical nature. On several occasions we have mentioned people's conception of the past. We outlined how old people had memories of times when there was less scarcity of resources and the agricultural wages could purchase more rice than today. For the old people these memories became a standard they often referred to and judged the overall present poverty against. Memories of the past, conveyed to the younger generation, also included, as we have noted, particular events like important court cases, floods, droughts, the status of the kinship lineages, etc. Local history is part of the consciousness of the people living in the village to-day. For many purposes, therefore, the past is made relevant for the present behavioural solutions and interpersonal relationships.

Another 'type' of history which also manifests itself in people's minds is the exogenous factors influencing their lives. History of this type is national events (1947, 1971), the changing role of the Government, the overall growth of population, different types of new crops and technical innovations in agriculture, etc. People are conscious about the past of these trends and speculate on what will happen in the future. The few well-to-do and rich people try to predict and prepare for the future. We mentioned how Halim Khan, the rich peasant (case 4, Chapter 4), feared a land reform. His and other rich people's response to this is to conceal and 'hide' their landholdings in the names of others. Education of children, attempts to migrate abroad, diversification of investments, were other ways to be better prepared for the future. These preparations are made on the basis of interpreting the likely course of 'historical trends'.

Professional historians would naturally have a much deeper understanding of the historical trends which have influenced the rural areas than the villagers themselves possess. In this study it has not been an aim to give a detailed historical account of the sequences of the various issues. We have referred to certain trends and events, but we have, for instance, not given an account of the rise and fall of the *zamindari* land holding system. Nor have we, in a systematic way, reviewed the different ways the rural society was politically and economically integrated into a larger society at various points of time in the past. Such a task would require a different focus and a different type of material. One aim we have pursued, however, is to see how history is made relevant and manifests itself as constraints on and opportunities for people's activities presently. For this purpose one does not need to outline the details of the Permanent Settlement Act of 1793.

We need, however, to have a rough understanding and knowledge of important events and the main trends. In a study on authority relationships in a Ugandan tribal society, D.W. Cohen states that he wants to catch 'the *moving context* [my italics] of the past and to allow those moving contexts to inform a discussion of authority'.[13] Throughout the study we have pointed to the change over time occurring in important variables. In Chapter 10 we shall speculate on how the dynamics in some of these factors will influence the future context for the lives of people.

We have given strong emphasis to the wider context of which the village is a part, and we have depicted how external conditions influence and give shape to the opportunity situation of the actors. In fact, a main portion of this study (chapters 2, 3 and 8) presents different aspects of the wider framework which influences the competition for scarce resources in the rural areas. We have also demonstrated, in most cases only implicitly, how activities in the rural areas in turn and to a varying degree, have feedback effects on these external conditions. Our guide in selecting the external factors we have discussed is whether they are relevant for rural people's economic, political and social activities or not. We have shown how these external conditions manifest themselves as constraints and opportunities for the villagers. In our selection of the external conditions we found relevant, we have not been influenced by preestablished schemes of what constitutes the important variables.

Dominant features of rural social organization

We have emphasized in this study that the patron-client relationships are a main feature of rural social organization. We have shown that the nature of the relationships people were involved in as regards credit, mortgage, sharecropping, employment and political protection are to a large extent of a patron-client nature. In the various chapters, we have discussed both directly and indirectly the factors and circumstances which we believe generate this pattern. Below we will summarize a limited set of factors which are crucial for the emergence of these patron-client relationships:

(i) multiple inheritance system with many heirs to an estate
(ii) individual property rights to land
(iii) scarcity of land and unequal distribution of land
(iv) scarcity of employment and other sources of livelihood
(v) need for political and physical protection
(vi) lack of access to resources made available by the Government for the rural areas.

The implications are numerous. We noted in chapter 3 how the inheritance system and the individual property rights gave the patrilineal descent group a very non-corporate character. In fact we showed that the competition around the main means of production, land, often occurred among brothers and close patrilineal relatives. The inheritance rules and the property rights are divisive in their implications, and therefore make it highly unlikely that significant and lasting corporate groups would emerge purely on the basis of patrilineal descent.

With individual property rights to land each household becomes basically responsible for providing a livelihood for itself. With the scarcity and unequal distribution of land there is naturally no possibility of a rural society consisting of self-sufficient subsistence households producing and providing a livelihood for themselves from their own land. The scarcity and unequal distribution of the resources are, as we noted in chapter 1, the basis for the relationships we have described and analysed in detail: credit, mortgage, sale of land, sharecropping and employment relations. These relationships are, in their nature, of a *dyadic* character, and the flow of goods and value in these relationships can from our point of view, be interpreted in a *zero-sum* perspective; what is one party's gain is the other party's loss. We have emphasized that the concept of a 'transaction', as we have defined it in this chapter, can fruitfully be applied to illuminate and describe the processes occurring in these relationships.

Thus the dominant organizational feature of rural Bangladesh is the many patron-client relationships. We have, however, emphasized in the study that there is a large variation in the type of patron-client relationships which exist. The 'small surplus' peasant like Eynuddin (case 3, chapter 4) with one or two poor clients, is a very minor and also in some aspects different patron from the large landowner, Halim Khan, who may have economic relationships with 50 clients. Many 'small-scale' patrons, we showed, were in their turn clients to more well-to-do patrons, or patrons in the urban areas (Government officials, businessmen). One feature we have pointed to is that patrons can easily live next to each other and prosper. There may be enmity and competition or alliances between the different patrons for specific purposes, but the livelihood of one patron does not depend on the downfall of another patron. Expansion of their properties, however, occurs, as we have shown, at the expense of their clients.

Yet we have noted that the concept of transaction is not applicable for illuminating all the processes which generate social patterns. The concept of *incorporation* also contains a structure which we believe can fruitfully capture and identify processes which take place between people. Despite the basic non-corporate character of the descent group, there are some limited rights and duties connected with descent group membership. The patrilineal descent group has, as we noted in chapter 3, an informal council of elders and normally a recognized leader. A main function of this council is to watch over the proper behaviour *izzat* (the honour) of the lineage members. The selection of mates for children ready for marriage has to be agreed upon by the informal council, and disputes occuring among the members of the group, should ideally be settled by the leaders of the lineage. We noted also that land changing owners should preferably be kept within the lineage. Thus, around moral issues and also around the land of their forefathers, the members of this unit have joint interests and may constitute a corporation for these limited purposes. The relationships between the individual members within such a corporation, we noted, may not be interpreted with reference to a transactional principle. The members of the corporate unit have joint interests as against other units for these specific purposes. We saw, however, how weak the corporate descent group was, how often it split, and how particularly the rich members of a descent group would disown their more distant relatives in order to avoid the responsibilities they had towards them. From the rich households' point of view it was also advantageous not to include their poorer relatives in the groups, so that behaviour and activities of the poorest members did not affect the *izzat* of the lineage.

We also noted that despite the fact that many of the patron-client relationships were permeated by processes of a transactional character, this relationship could also function as a corporate unit. We gave many examples of how patron and client had joint interests against other units and corporations. Case study 3 in chapter 7 showed how the members of a large-scale faction, led by a rich patron, had joint interests in winning a land dispute against a similar faction. On the whole, however, we found no large, lasting and significant corporations in the rural areas. Neither the *village,* nor the *samaj* (village association) was important for major corporate activities. In a neighbouring village of Bhaimara a religious leader *(pir baba)* had built himself up, and a large loyal flock of believers rallied behind him. This group was capable of corporate action in religious, economic and political fields. Although such a group may contain loyal supporters and can be mobilized for many purposes, it is of a marginal importance in the lives of most people living in the rural areas.

What are the factors, other than those we have already mentioned, which hinder the emergence of large scale corporations? We believe that the size of the ownership holdings is important. The many million small-holdings are the basis for the patron-client relationship through which a 'small surplus' peasant cultivates a many-stranded patron-client relationship with a handful of clients. Large, or larger, landholdings would have increased the number of people siding with the rich or influential on a permanent basis. We have shown that extensive factions are mobilized when the joint interests of a patron and his many clients are threatened. However, the corporate interests of a faction are specific, and as soon as the occasion or incident around which people have rallied disappears, the corporation withers away.

One form of corporation we have indicated we would discuss is the 'class-based' social organization. G.D. Wood has posed a question which no social scientists working in rural Bangladesh can avoid considering.[14]

> With the rapid rise in landless rural population and the relentless process of pauperization for many other poor peasant classes either through usury, changes in tenancy arrangements, the availability of land to lease and distress sales of goods and land, the obvious question to ask is why rural Bangladesh does not burst asunder in organized revolution or chaotic anarchy.

The issue we shall be concerned with here is what are the factors which hinder the development of class consciousness among the rural poor. A discussion of these factors also indicates the conditions which have to be changed in order to create class consciousness. This issue is also, of course, closely related to the conditions which sustain the patron-client relationships. Throughout the study we have directly and indirectly touched on various aspects of this issue. Below we will summarize and discuss some of the main factors which we believe hinder the development of class consciousness.

(i) There is no clear distinction between people on the basis of their rights to the main means of production, i.e., land. We have shown that the relationship of most households to land is not fixed; it changes continually, land is either in the process of being gained or lost. In chapter 4 we showed that the landless group of 21 households in Bhaimara was far from uniform, and the 'members' of this group did not conceive of themselves as being in the same economic position.[15] There is no doubt that in many circumstances they are discontented and feel exploited, and subjugated by the rich, but only under specific circumstances does this lead to joint collective action.

(ii) For the landless and poor it is difficult to define a common 'enemy' by whom they feel exploited. It is naturally difficult to feel that your brother or cousin, who in Marxist terms 'objectively' exploits you in all possible ways, is your 'class' enemy. The many-stranded, patron-client relationship, which can also be turned into a corporate unit for specific purposes, hardly shapes people's consciousness in class terms.

The moral precept of *takdir,* referring to Muslim ideology, stresses the predestined limits and potentialities bestowed by Allah on each individual life.[16] Many poor peasants obviously accept their abject poverty with reference to fate, and their interpretation of the Muslim ideology stops them from revolting against the status quo. (The rich peasant Halim Khan, case 4, chapter 4, told us that it was by the gracious will of Allah that he had acquired his properties.) Many will also interpret their economic position in life in relation to the numerous 'chance' factors which operate and which cause one brother to rise and another to fall.

In order to grasp the 'consciousness' of people we must, as we attempted in chapter 3, search for and investigate the various native conceptions of the groups and struggles people may be engaged in. Our research is not furthered by G.D. Wood's observation 'Vertical solidarities of the patron-client type become the form of class relations under the conditions of agrarian underdevelopment in Bangladesh...'.[17] Neither can the categories and ideals people harbour merely be ascribed to 'false consciousness'. The way traditional concepts about relations between groups are couched in the people's own language needs to be investigated further in Bangladesh. Our research, however, as we showed in chapter 3, did not reveal any categories referring to concepts of class in a Marxist sense.

We believe, however, that there is a large variation in rural Bangladesh in the way people define their own economic and social relations to other groups of people. In chapter 3 we described some native terms of classification. On this issue we agree with Barth's general observation that:[18] 'The 'consciousness' of a population is rarely consistent and of one piece.'

(iii) Linked to the lack of class consciousness is the issue concerning ways through which the jointly felt discontent of the poor can be articulated. None of the organizations we have mentioned, *village, samaj* (village association), *factions,* can provide a basis for the articulation of class interests. The *Tebhaga* movement in the late 1940s, demanding a better deal for the sharecroppers, was repressed, and the literature available to us does not reveal any similar major case of a peasants' uprising.

(iv) We were told of outsiders, often intellectuals, who had tried to organize the landless against the rich. This we heard had failed miserably.[19] Many of the development projects carried out by Non Government Organizations have had the poor and landless as their target groups and aimed at raising people's consciousness about their economic and social situation.[20] These projects are only carried out in a very small number of the 65,000 villages of Bangladesh and thereby, naturally, have limited impact.

(v) Even if the poor would want to articulate some of their interests and discontent against the rich, they fear the sanctions they may face. In several chapters we have discussed the immediate sanctions a client may be confronted with if he goes against the interests of his patron (withdrawal of sharecropping contract and employment opportunities, etc.).

All these conditions hindering the development of class consciousness and class-based actions contribute to the maintenance of the patron-client relationships. However, we have referred to some circumstances when collective action based on joint class interests may occur. The migrant labour groups normally have a purely economic, single-stranded, relationship to their employer. We were told that if they felt unjustly treated in any way, they might retaliate jointly in a forceful manner before leaving the area. Such options are seldom available for resident wage-labourers, even when they are conscious of their joint interests (see chapter 6 for a discussion on the fixation of the wage rate). A. Jenkins et al. give a detailed and vivid picture of how women and landless peasants in a number of cases have been successful in uniting and fighting against the powerful rural elite.[21] Although we consciously and specifically looked for instances in which the poor unitedly confronted the rich, we found only a few cases of such joint actions. No lasting organization or group developed on the basis of these encounters.

For very apparent reasons one would think that the landless and the poor would be able to predict their gloomy future and the even more miserable prospects for their children. If they do not to any significant extent unite in order to demand a better deal as regards their economic activities vis-à-vis the rich, could they not unite for some productive purposes in order to do something about their deteriorating prospects? A. Jenkins et al. provide a description of a number of cases where the landless cultivate land under a lease contract and of poor women who participate in and share the results of cottage industries.[22] In our area we hardly saw any such cases of the poor joining hands for a joint long-lasting economic activity. In fact the main efforts we observed poor people make in order to improve their conditions took the form of aligning themselves individually with potential patrons on whom they could rely for support.

The conditions sustaining the pattern of the patron-client relationships are not static in any sense. The adaptations which take place will depend, among other factors, on the growth of the population and on the mobility pattern which arises. By far the most explicit and thorough study on the mobility of peasant households in Bangladesh is the book written by Van Schendel, which we have referred to many times earlier in this study. Van Schendel has 'adapted' Shanin's model of peasant mobility to the conditions of rural Bangladesh. He isolates certain circumstances and factors generating *centrifugal* mobility (polarizing trends) and *centripetal* mobility (levelling trends).[23] The factors he isolates are to a large extent identical with the conditions we found in our study when explaining why certain households manage to improve their economic conditions and others fail to do so and become poorer. We are also ready, on the basis of our material from Bhaimara, to accept his conclusion:[24]

> The consequences of peasant household mobility in Bangladesh may be summarized as follows: mobility does not lead to equality within the peasantry but to the maintenance and, indeed, reproduction of intra-peasantry differences in relationship to means of production. These difference, however, have not yet crystallized into clearly recognizable 'objective' peasant (sub)classes on a national scale.
>
> Peasant mobility also contributes, among other factors, to the absence of 'subjective' class (class consciousness) among different peasant groups. In other words though there is considerable economic differentiation within the Bangladesh peasantry, this does not produce the political articulation one might expect.

We noted that the mobility pattern in Bhaimara had changed during the 1970s. A larger proportion of the households had become landless. In chapter 1 we saw that the villagers in 1970 only counted 7 landless households in the village (we do not know the exact number of households at that time, probably it was around 40). In 1980, 21 of 62 households were landless, and a few rich households were in a better economic position. By the year 2000, there could be close to 120 households in Bhaimara, and we would not be surprised if more than half of them were landless. We would also expect that some of the sons of the rich peasants will have consolidated and expanded their properties. However, there is little doubt that also many of the sons of rich peasants will gradually decline and fall into our 'poor', 'small', 'middle' categories of size of land holdings. What this implies is that when at some stage in the future there will be 600 people in Bhaimara (and not 311 as in 1980), comprising some 120 households, there will still be many households in the middle categories. If these predictions about tendencies prove to be correct, no clear-cut distinctions between 'haves' and 'have nots' will emerge during the next decades. In terms of social organizations this implies that there would still be a basis for the maintenance of many patron-client relationships. A problem we shall address ourselves to in the final chapter is that there may be too few patrons for the growing number of poor people who cannot even hope to achieve a client-status in relation to a patron.

Notes

1 F. Barth, 1966, *op.cit.*
2 F. Barth, 1981, *op.cit.*
3 F. Barth, 1981, *op.cit.* Vol. 1, pp. 4–8.
4 See R. Paine, 1976, T.M.S. Evens, 1977, T. Asad, 1972.
5 For a more comprehensive discussion of the factors we mention, see F. Barth: *Sociological Aspects of Integrated Surveys for River Basin Development.* Paper presented at the ITC-UNESCO Centre for Integrated Surveys, 4th International Seminar, 1969, and Gunnar Haaland: *Problems in Savannah Development,* pp. 30–33, Occasional Paper No. 19, Department of Social Anthropology, University of Bergen, 1980.
6 F. Barth: 'Models Reconsidered', *op.cit.* p. 98.
7 F. Barth: *op.cit.,* 1966, p. 4.
8 *Ibid.,* p. 4.
9 F. Barth: 'Models Reconsidered', *op.cit.,* p. 98.
10 F. Barth: 'Models Reconsidered', *op.cit.,* p. 85.
11 For a more elaborate account on the steps in model-building see F. Barth: 1966, *op.cit.,* pp. 31–32.
12 F. Barth: 'Swat Pathans Reconsidered', *op.cit.,* p. 129.
13 D.W. Cohen: *Womunafu's Bunafu — A Study of Authority in a Nineteenth-Century African Community,* Princeton University Press, Princeton, New Jersey, 1977, p. 17.
14 G.D. Wood, *op.cit.,* 1981, p. 4.
15 For a discussion of the heterogeneous economic conditions and the different occupations and sources of livelihood the landless have, see Abu Abdullah, Mosharaff Hossain and Richard Nations: 'Agrarian Structure and the IRDP-Preliminary Considerations', in *The Bangladesh Development Studies,* Vol. IV, April 1976, No. 2, pp. 212–216.
16 See Peter Bertocci: 'Structural Fragmentation and Peasant Classes in Bangladesh', *Journal of Social Studies,* No. 5, October 1979, pp. 43–60. Bertocci mentions another precept, *tabdir,* which has an opposite implication to *takdir,* referring to the obligation of each individual to realize via maximum effort the fullness of one's given potentialities.
17 G.D. Wood, 1981, *op.cit.,* p. 4.
18 F. Barth, 'Swat Pathans Reconsidered', *op.cit.,* p. 150.
19 B.K. Jahangir gives examples of the role of outsiders in the political affairs of the rural areas. See his case studies, *op.cit.,* pp. 240–278.
20 See various project plans for BRAC (Bangladesh Rural Advancement Committee (BRAC Printers, Dhaka); Andrew Jenkins et al. *Unite and Survive: Developing Landless Organization in Bangladesh,* Oxfam, 1980; Bangladesh International Action Group, *Oppressed People in an Aid Dependent Country,* London, April 1982.
21 Andres Jenkins et al., *op.cit.*
22 *Ibid.*
23 For a short overview over these factors see Van Schendel, *op.cit.,* p. 281.
24 Van Schendel, *op.cit.,* p. 297.

10

Future Prospects for Rural Bangladesh

Introduction

What are the prospects during the next decades for the population living in the villages of rural Bangladesh? We shall summarize some of our speculations on the basis of the various development trends we have identified in the preceding chapters. In previous chapters we have emphasized that the limitations on resources will become even more pronounced in the future. Many more will become landless, the competition for obtaining sharecropping rights and employment will harden. The scarcity of land will lead to disputes over ownership rights to land. Even direct 'land robbery' may, in given circumstances, become a more normal mechanism for transfer of ownership of land. We have emphasized that the way the great majority of poor people cope with their lack of resources is by aligning themselves with the more well-to-do peasants. The dominant feature of the social organization in rural Bangladesh is the many vertical relationships which exist between rich and poor peasants.

In our analysis of the scarcity situation in rural Bangladesh we have maintained that the development of a number of factors external to the individual villages will constrain the activities and the adaptations which people will make. In this chapter we shall examine the development trends of some of these external factors and indicate some likely implications. We shall then describe some further possible prospects of development and their consequences for the rural population. This chapter will also refer to prospects which have been presented by some of the authors to whom we have referred elsewhere in this study.

Growth of population and unemployment

The growth and density of the population in the rural areas will be a major factor constraining social and economic processes in the villages. Much will have to happen if the village of Bhaimara has to accommodate and sustain some 600 persons in year 2000, compared to the 311 individuals who in 1980 derive the major part of their income from the about 70 acres of land farmed by the villagers. Most of the population projections for the whole of Bangladesh estimate that the country will have a population between 130 and 160 million people at the turn of the century.[1]

Faaland and Parkinson have projected a population in the year 2000 of 150 million people.[2] On the basis of these figures they have made some calculations on how people will be employed in year 2000 compared to 1975.[3] (See Table 10.1.)

We note that the number of unemployed will increase from something like 8 million in 1975 to 20 million by the end of the century. In previous chapters we have emphasized and discussed why the increase in expected agricultural production will not augment correspondingly the numbers employed. Faaland and Parkinson state: 'It seems extremely doubtful if the amount of employment that the land can offer can be increased by more than one-third on the average, an additional 5 million jobs.'[4]

Table 10.1. Employment by Economic Sector and Total Labour Force 1975 and 2000. Illustrative Calculations of the Incidence of Unemployment.

	Million man-years	
	1975	2000
Employment in:		
Agriculture	15	20
Manufacturing	1	4
Commerce	1	2
Services	2	6
All other (including construction)	1	4
Total employment	20	36
Unemployment	8	20
Total labour force	28	56

Note: The figures for 1975 are rough estimates only, based on incomplete information. They must be considered only as indicative of the structure of occupations rather than absolute levels.

What options are open to the increasing population? Migration from the country whether across the border (Assam, India), to the Middle East, or to Europe/America is no alternative except for a very small minority. Bangladesh will have to cater for its growing population within its own territory. Some of the rural unemployed may migrate either to the urban centres or to Dhaka. Only a small part of them will be successfully employed there unless larger investment programmes are implemented, which at present seems very unlikely. We believe, that by the year 2000 (if not *that* year at least some few years later), there could well be 20 million people who will have to be provided for by the agricultural sector but who will not be remunerably employed by the sector. The situation thus envisaged forms the background for our further speculations about some of the social and economic processes which are likely to occur. The category of the population we shall particularly focus on is the '20 million unemployed'.

Economic strategies of the unemployed

What are the processes which are set in motion as unemployment gradually increases? In order to answer this question we have to focus on the micro-level situation. We believe that the main strategies which will be open to the unemployed are similar to the activities that the poor and unemployed pursue at present. Those who seek employment but very seldom obtain wage-labour contracts will belong to households that are in clear 'deficit budget' positions.

To cover their deficit, they will have to take up loans. They will have no difficulties in obtaining credit as long as they have an attractive form of collateral to put up (agricultural land, homestead plot land, iron-sheet roof, wife's ornaments, etc.). With the declining possibilities for obtaining an income through employment, a gradually larger part of their economic needs will have to be met through loans. During a period extending from a few years to 10–15 years, they may thus become totally landless (no agricultural land and no homestead plot). In chapters 4 and 6 we noted that since it is so scarce, the employer would often only offer employment to a person from whom he knew that he could eventually extract other advantages, including the establishment of a credit relationship expected in due course to lead to transfer of land. The people who will be totally landless will therefore also be disadvantaged on the wage-labour market. Thus, the process which occurred in the past, but which is gradually becoming more widespread, results in a larger part of the population becoming both totally landless *and* unemployed. In chapter 4 we described how some households in Bangladesh were obviously unable to provide an income from their own resources. They were completely landless and owned no items which could be used as collateral making them worthy of credit. It was also quite obvious that they could not survive on the meagre incomes which they obtained when they occasionally were employed. The main way in which they obtained food was through receiving gifts and through begging. We estimated that by 1980 such supportive mechanisms were the main source of livelihood for 6 of the 62 households in Bhaimara. The 6 households were small in size, three were only 'one-member household' while the remaining were two and three member households. Also about 10 other households, mainly incomplete families, received an important part of their income through gifts. Thus, a small percentage of the population in Bhaimara, roughly estimated at 10 per cent, would not be able to survive unless they were catered for through the benevolence of other villagers. As the population grows and employment becomes more scarce the group, landless *and* unemployed, will increase fast. It would appear to be a conservative estimate that by the end of the century 20 to 25 per cent of a population of 600 people in Bhaimara would be both totally landless *and* unemployed. The critical question in this connection is whether the supportive mechanisms operating in the village today will be able to sustain this increasing number of dependent and totally deprived people. On this score, it is difficult to be an optimist.

Provided that the above numerical implications are accepted *grosso modo,* we may speculate also on the consequences which this situation will have for the strategies and the situation of the deprived households. The strategies in the future are likely to share many of the features of those which the poorest few per cent of the population adopt today, for example: (i) Violence and robbery could easily follow in the wake of increased poverty. In chapter 6 we noted that conflicts and fights have occurred between local and migrant wage labourers entering the wage-labour market in a village. (ii) Many more households, or individual members of households, would attempt to migrate either to the urban centres or to other rural areas. (iii) Rich people would increasingly build houses in the urban areas and thus transfer the 'surplus' from agriculture and from the village economy. (iv) The traditional informal rule that women should not claim their part of the inherited land, may be undermined. In chapter 3 we showed how this could put the women in a very exposed position. They would not so easily be able to return to their fathers' and brothers' home in case of divorce and widowhood, and they would therefore be more vulnerable to maltreatment by the family of the husband. Many more women would also be forced out of *purdah* in order to obtain a livelihood. (v) For the most deprived households more severe starvation strategies are likely to be adopted in the coming decades. During the famine in 1974 some people in Bhaimara and other villages told us that they had to boil and eat the common water hyacinth found in all rivers and ponds in Bangladesh. This plant has little value from a nutritional point of view; people ate it only in order to fill their stomachs and to feel less hungry. We also heard that the water hyacinth had been eaten in other districts of the country. Such starvation strategies may thus become even more common in the future for many individuals, and the number of people living on a deficient and inadequate diet will increase. This naturally has consequences for the health of the community, and in severe situations also for the level of mortality in famine-hit areas. It will especially be the non-productive members of a household, the young and old, particularly the females, who will be most exposed to starvation. Within the poorest households there will be keen competition when dividing the food. Quarrels between spouses, which arise out of scarcity of food and may lead to divorce, are not uncommon today among the poorest segment of the population. Thus, for the most deprived household, the survival of the nuclear family will in many cases be at stake.

Some organizational implications of the growth in the numbers of landless and unemployed people

What further implications will follow when the numbers of totally landless *and* unemployed increase? Although members of this deprived group will only rarely be employed, many of them will at least attempt, or be willing, to enter the wage-labour market. In chapter 6 we distinguished between the 'protected' and 'open' wage-labour market. Many of the totally landless and unemployed would, if given the opportunity, be available on the open wage-labour market, that is they would work for anybody if they have the chance. This large reserve of unemployed naturally depresses the wage level.

We have previously also discussed another factor which depresses the wages, viz. the heterogeneous economic background of people who want to work as wage-labourers. A household that has income from some other sources (own land, tenancy contract, and/or homestead plot) may feel under pressure to seek any kind of employment for one or more of their unemployed members even at a very low and uncertain wage. However, accepting a wage below 'subsistence level' will naturally not be a viable alternative in the longer term for households which have no other sources of livelihood. We have noted in other chapters that although the main pattern of the economic and social change is one of polarization, there will also in the next decades be households in the 'middle' economic categories. Typically these 'middle' households will tend to find their economic position deteriorating over time, and eventually they will become landless. However, the members in this category of 'middle' households will for a while tend to be sustained by the entry of new households from the ranks of 'rich' households, whose property gets divided, in particular through inheritance.

Another consequence is that the problem of the deprived persons' lack of purchasing power will be more acute as their numbers grow. This means that this growing group of the population provides little stimulus to increased agricultural and other rural production. Thus the existing investment pattern of the rich tends to be conserved: viz. investment in more land or urban houses, in profitable credit relationships, and in hoarding and other market speculation.

How will the dominant patron-client type of social organization be affected by the increased number of deprived households? In Bhaimara we observed that the destitute households were not part of any patron-client relationship. As clients they had nothing to offer a more well-to-do patron. They were without any influence in the 'political sphere' of village life and nothing could be extracted from them, since they were without possessions. The only asset with which they could enter into an exchange relation was the provision of their labour. On the labour market, as we saw, however, others received priority. Thus it would appear that in the future many more deprived households will belong to a section of the community which has no important vertical relationships with the more well-to-do households of the community unless there are close kin relationships. However, many of the totally deprived will not be able to mobilize kinship relations for support, since their kin may be equally poor or simply unwilling or unable to support their poorer relatives.

It is difficult to envisage the consequences of 'non-alignment' between the rich and the poorest. We believe that 'middle' and 'small' category households who possess attractive assets will continue to enter into client relations with richer households. The landless *and* unemployed households will probably be too weak and too split to unite and constitute any threat to the existing order. Unless there is an unexpected and, in Bangladesh, unprecendented popular and revolutionary mobilization in the countryside, it is more likely that their energy will be spent on internal fighting for the few resources and gifts which may be available to them.

During the next few decades the social organization of the rural areas could well continue to be dominated by patron-client relationships, while at the same time a growing section of the village communities is unable to achieve a viable 'client-status'. It is this growing group of people who will be most exposed to food scarcity and famines in the future, whether these emerge from developments internally or abroad, whether they are man-made or caused by natural disasters. For an understanding of the ongoing social, political and economic changes in Bangladesh and as an early warning system for emerging stresses in the social fabric, it will be increasingly important to watch, describe and analyse the changing situation in which the growing number of households who are totally landless *and* unemployed find themselves, particularly as they find themselves falling outside the traditional system of supportive mechanisms still operating in the village.

Government policies — foreign aid

The situation described above will clearly be affected also by the development of other factors than growth of population and the situation on the employment market. In chapter 8 we emphasized the important role of the Government in the processes which occur in rural Bangladesh. If the character of the Bangladesh State and the policies of its government were to change dramatically in the next decades, the situation might be very different. Our predictions about the next few decades are made on the basis that the nature of the State and of Government policies will remain more or less the same as today and that the framework and the policies described in chapter 8 will be perpetuated: that the laws regulating land ownership will not in practice set any ceiling on the size of the landholdings an individual may own; that strict taxes will not be imposed on the rich peasants; that government policies in the rural areas will in the main continue to support the richest section of the rural population; that the production-oriented agricultural strategy pursued by the Government will not substantially augment opportunities for employment; even some of the policies which will be aimed at the direct benefit of the poor will often be circumvented owing to the nature of the organizational apparatus through which they have to be implemented. Given the perpetuation of this system during the next decades, the polarization process will clearly be accelerated.

In previous chapters we have also emphasized how important foreign aid has been for the economy during the last decades and how important it remains today. We have also indicated, particularly in connection with food aid, how politically important foreign assistance has been, and remains, for catering for the interests of the urban and rural rich. In several of his studies, Rehman Sobhan has discussed the role of foreign aid in maintaining and strengthening the position of the rural and the urban rich:[5]

... A powerful constituency has developed around the aid regime which has power, influence and depth in the society. We have seen that at the apex of this system a class of people in business, the state sector, the professions and amongst the rural elite, have directly identified their interests as a class and their personal advancement, with the perpetuation of the aid regime. Whilst this class may dominate state power they in their own right are not strong enough to sustain themselves in power in the face of the mobilised masses. Indeed any challenge from the masses, which cuts them off from access to the aid regime would immasculate this class and effectively neutralise their political power base. Cut off from their agency commissions, consultancy fees, state sponsored credits and subsidies from aid financed projects, the overwhelming bulk of this class will have to join the ranks of the wage earners, except for the few who are willing and able to seek their fortunes abroad.

It follows then that the dominant classes in Bangladesh do not constitute an autonomous ruling class. As a class they remain dependent on external patronage provided through the aid regime, to remain on top and to contain the pressures from below. The aid regime has therefore become an essential element in the process of class formation in Bangladesh and in ensuring the survival and dominance of the ruling elite.

If aid continues to pour into Bangladesh under the same type of conditions as in the past, and into a regime which in character will remain the same, there is little doubt that the small elite will be strengthened and take the necessary measures to protect its privileged position.

Thus, in our speculations about the future, we have taken the basic nature of the external variables as given and only extrapolated the existing trends of development of these variables. This is, of course, a questionable assumption. Most of the authors we have referred to in this study agree on one basic issue: the present system of agricultural production in rural Bangladesh is not a 'viable' system. Statements like 'Bangladesh society is very close to the edge of a precipice'[6] are common conclusions in most articles and books on the current situation of Bangladesh. Some other conclusions and predictions are: 'The basic issue must be squarely faced: The present institutional stucture must be altered if Bangladesh is to function as a nation',[7] or 'it may seem that if the problems of income distribution and access to work are to be solved, communal cultivation systems will have to be introduced',[8] or 'Government policies ... are doomed to failure unless and until the exploited majority manages to change the social structure within which they are living and within which these schemes get implemented'.[9] Our own experiences and analyses of the micro-level village situation are in line with these pessimistic views. Comprehensive land reforms or some other change to agricultural production on a collective basis is the recommendation of both students and policy-makers as the basis for both increased production and a more equitable distribution of the product. Unless such drastic measures are taken, new or reformed policies are unlikely to succeed significantly better than do present policies.

To implement effective and encompassing land reforms or to adopt a collective farming system would, of course, seem a hopeless task given the nature of the existing regime. The implication of such a change would be that the rural and urban elite would 'voluntarily' sacrifice their privileges for the 'common good'. We believe that as long as the Government is of its existing character, it would neither dare nor want to undercut the privileged position of its own members and main supporters.

In the literature available to us it is Rehman Sobhan who most explicitly comes up with detailed proposals for a policy for Bangladesh over the next decades.[10] He selects three main areas for urgent action:

> 1) Planning for utilizing indigenous resources for more self-reliant development, 2) Reforming the administrative system by bringing Government closer to the masses and involving them more closely in the planning and development process, 3) Changing the incentive structure with a view to rewarding productive effort and realising a more equitable social order.

We shall not review the concrete policies proposed by Rehman Sobhan, but only point out that it is the immediate interests of the rich which will suffer directly if the proposals for the 'socialization of the production and distribution system without the immediate socialization of property rights'[11] are actually implemented. In fact, what Sobhan proposes amounts to no less than a revolutionary change. Under the present conditions this seems far off, also in the opinion of Rehman Sobhan:[12]

> It is for those who are engaged in the tasks of revolutionary mobilisation, rather than for bourgeois academics, to really judge how far they have in recent years enhanced their political authority within Bangladesh. Whilst there may be parties operating outside the public eye who have acquired the necessary capacity to commit

themselves and the masses to revolutionary struggle, there is no public indication of the emergence of such forces. On the contrary the public image appears to be one of growing fragmentation amongst those forces which profess a commitment to revolutionary social transformation, whilst there is a corresponding increment in the confidence and authority of the reactionary forces within Bangladesh.

In light of the unlikely prospects for a radical change in the existing framework, development of the external factors may well continue along its present course. If this happens, the situation we have depicted above of a large, and growing, totally deprived and destitute group of people may well be realized. If the means of survival for this group cannot be catered for by the supportive system of benevolence in the rural areas, then aid from outside is necessary in order to keep people alive. Bangladesh in the future may, 'in effect, become the world's largest camp for destitute people'.[13]

Past experiences of famines in Bangladesh

With a growing population totally deprived of resources, the experiences and lessons of the past famines in Bangladesh are dangerously relevant: 1½ million people starved to death in 1943 and several hundred thousands died of starvation as recently as 1974. Amartya Sen has discussed the causes of these two famines in Bangladesh in a recent book.[14] His main thesis in explaining these famines is, briefly stated, that it is not a decline in the amount of available food which caused the famines (Food Availability Decline), but the fact that a large portion of the population in his terms lacked 'exchange entitlement' with which they could obtain food. Among the influences that determine a person's 'exchange entitlement' are the following:[15]

(1) whether he can find an employment, and if so for how long and at what wage rate;
(2) what he can earn by selling his non-labour assets, and how much it costs him to buy whatever he may wish to buy;
(3) what he can produce with his own labour power and resources (or resource services) he can buy and manage;
(4) the cost of purchasing resources (or resource services) and the value of the products he can sell;
(5) the social security benefits he is entitled to and the taxes, etc., he must pay.

As we found in our study, it is exactly in these respects that the growing group of deprived people in rural Bangladesh are becoming more deprived. A. Sen shows that food grain production was not reduced drastically in the years of famine. Food grain was available in the rural areas. B.K. Jahangir reports in his book how people starved quietly and silently to death outside storehouses filled with grain in Savar, 20 miles away from Dhaka.[16] Rumours of an expected famine, however, induced many rich peasants to withhold their stocks of grain and to speculate in increased prices. The prices for rice increased many-fold, and the poor who owned land sold it at low prices. For neither of the years 1943 and 1974 was the Government able to counteract this trend and to supply grain on the market in order to lower the prices.

Thus, as long as the Government has food grain in reserves (whether procured domestically or purchased or obtained as gifts from abroad) and the transportation system operates, famines of these magnitudes can be avoided. As long as the external factors we have mentioned are not altered, the picture of the future we have drawn in this chapter, however depressing, is likely to emerge; in A. Sen's terminology the rural population without 'exchange entitlement' will continue to grow. This group will be dependent on direct Government aid, obtained from foreign donors. However, foreign aid may not be continually supplied and expanded in the decades to come. Rehman Sobhan elaborates on the insignificant position Bangladesh occupies in the world, and the precarious position it has as receiver of aid:[17]

> ... To the extent that Bangladesh generates very little surplus for extraction or has few resources for exploitation and has limited strategic importance, its linkages with the world system are, somewhat uniquely, those of the taker. ... Bangladesh therefore appears to need the world system for its survival within its current social system. The world system does not need Bangladesh all that much and could cut it adrift without concern and perhaps even with feelings of relief.
>
> The only concern in the world system relating to Bangladesh arises out of the potential for endemic and proliferating social chaos, growing out of the unresolved contradictions and problems within this country and the possible incapacity of the existing political structures to mediate the crisis within the framework of the prevailing system. The fear that the crisis within the existing social order may not contain the repercussions of this upheaval of humanity within its national boundaries has found a place for Bangladesh in the concerns of the aid donors. In this situation the

> leverage of a regime whose survival, both as a regime and as a class, is dependent on external donors is nominal and must remain subservient to those who keep it alive.
>
> This uneasy relationship of dependency is however likely to prove increasingly unviable. The heightened instability of the world economy appears to be sharpening the internal crises within the DCCs [Developed Capitalist Countries, E.G.J.]. Aid donors from these countries are therefore likely to be less capable and inclined to undertake the apparently unrewarding task of keeping the social order in Bangladesh afloat.

The scenario to be feared is the one in which there is a *combination* of 'food availability decline' and tens of million people without any 'exchange entitlements'. We do not doubt that when Bangladesh again faces famine, the foreign donors would be ready with food shipments and medicines but possibly only after a costly delay causing tremendous human suffering. There are, however, limits to the number of rescue operations likely to be organized. It could well happen that in the long run the crises need to become more spectacular in order to capture the attention of the world. Neglect or lack of will could then cause the people of Bangladesh to wither away by the million. This process will continue until such time as the social system is transformed.

Notes

1 See *Population of Bangladesh,* Country Monograph Series No. 8, New York, 1981. See particularly Chapter 8, Population Projections, which reviews all major population projections that have been made for Bangladesh.
2 Faaland and Parkinson, *op.cit.,* p. 97.
3 *Ibid.,* p. 85.
4 *Ibid.,* p. 85.
5 Rehman Sobhan, 1982, *op.cit.,* pp. 202–203.
6 Rehman Sobhan: 'The Crisis of External Dependence: Some Policy Options for Bangladesh', *Journal of Social Studies,* No. 18, October 1982, p. 63.
7 J. Stepanek, *op.cit.,* p. 173.
8 Faaland and Parkinson, *op.cit.,* p. 87.
9 Stefan de Vylder, *op.cit.,* p. 156.
10 See Rehman Sobhan, *Journal of Social Studies, op.cit.,* pp. 17–61.
11 *Ibid.,* p. 45.
12 *Ibid.,* p. 23.
13 J. Stepanek, *op.cit.,* p. 173.
14 Amartya Sen: *Poverty and Famines. An Essay on Entitlement and Deprivation,* Clarendon Press, Oxford, 1981.
15 *Ibid.,* p. 4.
16 B.K. Jahangir, *op.cit.,* and personal communication.
17 Rehman Sobhan, The Crisis of External Dependence, *op.cit.,* 1982, p. 227.

Appendix 1

Size Distribution of Total Owned Land in Rural Bangladesh[a]

No. of acres	No. of households	Per cent of total	No. of persons	Per cent of total	Area (Acres)	Per cent of total
Zero	1,767,334	14,69	8,081,266	11,59	—	—
0.01– 1.00	5,375,887	44.68	27,561,648	39.54	1,733,233	8.33
1.01– 2.00	1,830,170	15.21	10,821,861	15.53	2,660,128	12.78
2.01– 3.00	1,045,072	8.69	6,706,826	9.62	2,556,850	12.28
3.01– 4.00	621,105	5.16	4,438,188	6.37	2,141,713	10.29
4.01– 5.00	370,799	3.08	2,811,716	4.03	1,651,046	7,93
5.01– 6.00	253,414	2.11	2,027,653	2.91	1,375,463	6.61
6.01– 7.00	173,661	1.44	1,520,481	2.18	1,123,908	5.40
7.01– 8.00	110,825	0.92	963,593	1.38	827,971	3.98
8.01– 9.00	94,944	0.79	835,505	1.20	803,505	3.86
9.01–10.00	66,979	0.56	581,056	0.83	636,690	3.06
10.01–11.00	60,764	0.51	568,972	0.82	634,253	3.05
11.01–12.00	38,668	0.32	378,394	0.54	444,388	2.14
12.01–13.00	36,251	0.30	358,024	0.51	451,674	2.17
13.01–14.00	25,894	0.22	276,200	0.40	350,779	1.69
14.01–15.00	19,679	0.16	215,091	0.31	285,006	1.37
Over 15.00	95,790	1.16	1,556,732	2.23	3,137,282	15.07
TOTALS[b]	12,031,272	100.00	69,703,206	100.00	20,813,879	100.00

a Total owned land is the sum of all lands to which legal title is claimed by any member of the household.
b Components may not add up to totals owing to rounding off.

Source: Jannuzi, F. Thomasson and Peach, James T., 'Land Occupancy Survey, 1977', in *The Agrarian Structure of Bangladesh, An Impediment to Development*, Appendix F, Table F.1 Tables of the 1978 Land Occupancy Survey, p. 107.

Appendix 2

Defining and Delimiting Households in Bhaimara[1]

We encountered methodological and practical problems when we wanted to set up a list of all the households in the village. That there were dilemmas involved in defining and delimiting the household units became obvious when during the winter 1979–80 we collected data on the state of landownership of all the households in Bhaimara. Shortly before, a similar collection of data had been undertaken in the village by several investigators who independently had arrived at varying totals for the number of households. We arrived at yet another total. The number of households in the different investigations varied from 42 to 62. The discrepant numbers of households had an obvious influence on the proportion of landless, the distribution of land, an on other important statistics from the village. There is obviously little purpose in aggregating village statistics and in making regional and time comparisons when the figures from the same village, collected by different investigators at the same point in time, can differ as much as they do. We think it is a striking characteristic of studies of Bangladesh villages that the methodological aspects of identification and definition of the household unit have been little discussed. In this appendix we shall briefly elucidate some problems of definition and limitation which crop up when the household unit has to be identified.

There can be several reasons why different investigators register a different number of households in one and the same village. We shall here discuss three different situations:

(a) Choice of definition of the household unit.
(b) Different methods of collecting information on the number of households in the village.
(c) Different opinions as to which households shall be included in the village.

These three situations will be separately discussed below.

(a) *Choice of definition of the household unit.* We have constructed analyses of social and economic conditions in the village using the following definition of the household unit:

The household is the basic unit of production, reproduction, consumption, and of social, ceremonial and political interaction.[2]

There is a series of social units at different levels in the village, and an outsider needs anthropological training in order to identify the household unit. In the village the social unit at the lowest level is the *ghor. Ghor* is the name of the hut in which the nuclear family sleeps and keeps its belongings. Those, then, who live in this same hut constitute a social unit. At the next level is the *chula,* which literally means the fireplace where food is prepared. Those who eat food from the same hearth constitute a social unit. Frequently, the unit *ghor* and *chula* are identical, i.e. those persons who share a hut also share their food. Ideally there are several *ghor* attached to one *chula;* that is to say that an extended family, consisting of several nuclear families, prepares and eats its food together. At an even higher level, a *bari* describes a collection of huts *(ghor)* within a circumscribed homestead. The last unit that should be mentioned is the patrilineal family *(gusti),* and this plays an important role for certain specific purposes in the villages of Bangladesh.

Of these four social units, we identified *chula* as the household, since this unit has the characteristics most closely associated with the above definition of a household. The group of persons belonging to the same *chula* constitute an economic unit, because what is produced by its members is put into a common pool for common consumption. *Chula* is the unit that decides on purchase and sale of land and on the use of capital. For many important purposes *chula* is also a political and a ceremonial unit. A *chula* may vary in number of members and in composition. It can consist of the nuclear family, an extended family, or of an incomplete family as, for instance, a single man, a widow or a divorced woman and her children.

There are some problems connected with deciding whom to include in the *chula* if the unit is to be defined as incorporating those who eat from the same fireplace. It is difficult to place servants on annual contract, since they eat with the *chula* where they work, whereas from an economic point of view, they really belong to another *chula.* In our delimitation of the households we put more weight on economic links between members of the same 'budget' unit when we group 'dubious' individuals than on the joint residential and cooking relationship.

We should also mention that when household definitions are made explicit for a survey, the definitions can vary and thereby make the produced statistics less reliable for purposes of comparison. The Bangladesh Fertility Survey,[3] 1975–76, applied the following definitions of the household:

> A group of persons usually *living and eating* together in a structure or dwelling. A household may also be formed within a shop, office, mosque or on a boat, in a tent as long as its members sleep and eat there regularly.

This definition implies that a household may be formed of members of different families. Both in its content and in its practical application, this definition would delimit households differently from the definition we have chosen.

(b) *Different methods of collecting information on the number of households in the village.* The method of data collection is also of consequence to the number of households registered. The grounds for claiming this are that there is constant change in the composition of a household. The methods and techniques needed for identifying the number of households must be suited to catching and interpreting the changes that occur in this composition. We shall discuss below some of the processes which take place when a household disintegrates and when members of the household unit are separated from it. Changes in the composition of the household must partly be seen in connection with the consumption and production patterns of its members, which alter at different age levels:

— first, as a child, one consumes more than one produces,
— then, one produces more than one consumes,
— and finally, as an old person, one again consumes more than one produces.

In a country lacking social security and where poverty is widespread, that group which consumes more than it produces is especially exposed during periods of extreme poverty when it is necessary to give food priority to those who produce most. Those groups which are particularly exposed are children and old people, and especially women.

It frequently happens in households owning no cultivable land, that the older people are excluded from the household because the young people of productive age are unable to support them. This means that the old people must find food and the means to live on their own. Support of one's old parents is a strong moral duty in Bangladesh, and it is a norm that the extended family shall live together. Exclusion of the old people is therefore one of the most painful aspects of poverty, both for the old people themselves and for the young who must exclude them. In interviews therefore this is a situation which the respondent tries to hide. Even using a precise definition of the household unit, the method of data collection can influence the number of households registered. When one is interviewing a household representative, most valid data are usually collected from the oldest member. In addition, observant participation, which in this instance involves interviewing at the homestead plot, affords control by counting the number of fireplaces in a *bari* and thus acquiring concrete evidence of the number of *chula* in the *bari*. Should one conduct the interview away from the homestead, this opportunity would be lost.

Separation of landless extended families into nuclear families or into incomplete nuclear families is a process that can take place very suddenly. This usually occurs because the one nuclear family 'subsidizes' the other. Such separation does not have to be permanent. If these nuclei decide that it would be economically advantageous, or if the stronger nuclear family considers that it is able to 'subsidize' the weaker part, they come together as an extended family or as a larger unit again. These changes over time can be the reason that inhabitants of a village often regard a household as being composed of other members than is in reality the case. This is a further reason for attaching importance to the source of information when one is determining the number of households in a village.

The large discrepancies in the number of households in a village can then be due to:

— old people, constituting an independent household, not being included.
— changes through time of landless extended families to nuclear and incomplete nuclear families.

(c) *Different opinions as to which households shall be included in the village.* The third main reason for household numbers from different investigators varying is the question of which households should be included among the village's households. This especially applies to households which have or have had close connection with the village but in which some or all of the household members live in an urban area. (Dhaka was the town to which most people from Bhaimara had moved.)

In the village there are two categories of household which we might have ignored if we had not been focusing our attention on economic activities and a study of land ownership:

— Households where all members live in an urban area and where the land they own is rented out on a sharecropping basis.
— Households where some members live in an urban area. Especially those in which the head lives in a town and where the land which the household owns is let out to sharecroppers.

The most important reason for the large discrepancies in the number of households given by the various investigators who worked in Bhaimara was that they included different numbers of absentee households having economic interests in the village. Even when it is decided to include absentee landowners and others with economic interests in the village, it is extremely difficult to draw an 'objective' line for each household defining which shall be included or excluded. We arrived at a figure of 62 households in the village, of which 12 were wholly or partly absent. Other investigators might have argued persuasively that a further 5–10 absentee households should also be included.

Conclusions

It will always be difficult to decide how many and which households constitute a village. Although the investigator operates with a useful and practical definition of the household unit and applies good methods and techniques in his efforts to find these units, he cannot avoid meeting instances where it is doubtful whether a household is independent or not, or where he is not sure whether to include or exclude a household in his study.

A Bangladesh village of average size has about 200 households. We believe that, even utilizing a useful and practical definition and a good interview technique, different investigators at the same moment of time will arrive at considerably varying figures for the number of households in the same village. It is evident that when the definition of a household unit is not explicit nor universally used and when interview techniques are poor, a situation which we believe usually applies to village studies in Bangladesh, the number of households will vary even more. It follows that the processed statistics will be even less valid and therefore less suitable or reliable for purposes of comparison.

Notes

1 This appendix is a shortened and partly rewritten version of E.G. Jansen, B.K. Jahangir, Bodil Maal, Nazibor Rahman, *op.cit.*

2 This definition is discussed in detail in: Benjamin N.F. White *Rural Household in Studies in Anthropological Perspective,* Revised version of a background paper prepared for the ADC - RTN Workshop in Household Studies, Singapore, 3–7 August, 1976.

3 Government of Bangladesh, *World Fertility Survey. Bangladesh Fertility Survey 1975, First Report,* Dhaka: Ministry of Health and Population Control, Population Control and Family Planning Division, 1978.

Appendix 3

Relationship between Landowners and Tenants in Bhaimara.

Table 1. Relationship between the Head of Tenant's Household and the Head of the Landowner's Household in 1980.

Group of tenants	No. of house-holds	No. of plots share-cropped in	From whom the tenant has obtained land on a sharecropping basis				
			Brother	*Gusti* member	Villager	Non-villager	No. of plots
Landless	4	9		1	6	1	8 (11%)
Poor	8	24	3	4	7	9	23 (31%)
Small	5	22	3	3	10	6	22 (29%)
Middle	6	21		2	7	12	21 (28%)
Rich	1	1			1		1 (1%)
Total	24	77	6 (8%)	10 (13%)	31 (41%)	28 (37%)	75 (100%)
			No information available				2
							77

Relationship between Landowners and Tenants in Bhaimara.

Table 2. Relationship between Head of Landowning Household and Head of Tenant's Household in 1980.

Group of land-owners	No. of house-holds	No. of plots share-cropped out	To whom the land is given out on a sharecropping basis				
			Brother	*Gusti* member	Villager	Non-villager	
Poor	10	15	5	1	7	2	
Small	4	13	2	2	5	4	
Middle	3	4		2	2		
Rich	3	21			14	7	
Total	20	53	7 (13%)	5 (9%)	28 (53%)	13 (25%)	53 (100%)

Appendix 4

Length of the Sharecropping Relationship for the Various Groups of Landowners in Bhaimara

Year when share-cropping relationship was established	Groups of landowners and amount of plots they rent out on a sharecropping basis in 1980					
	No. of plots	Poor	Small	Middle	Rich	No. of plots
Before 1970	1	1				1
1970–1975	10	2	6		2	10
1975–1978	14	6	2	2	4	14
1978–1980	9	3	3	1	2	9
1980	4	1	2		1	4
Uncertain	15	2		1	12	15
Total	53	15	13	4	21	53
% of total	100%	28%	25%	7%	40%	100%

Appendix 5

Duration of Tenancy Relationship as Reported by Tenants[a, b]

No. of years	No. of households (000's)	Per cent of total	Area (000 acres)	Per cent of total
1 and less	863.7	26.30	816.1	17.55
2	669.3	20.38	800.7	17.22
3	517.2	15.75	823.1	17.70
4	260.4	7.93	457.1	9.83
5	208.5	6.35	372.5	8.01
6	115.6	3.52	273.4	5.88
7	100.2	3.05	184.1	3.96
8	112.0	3.41	275.3	5.92
9	27.6	0.84	58.1	1.25
10 and above	409.5	12.47	589.7	12.68
Totals	3,284.0	100.0	4,650.1	100.00

a Components may not add up to totals owing to rounding off.

b Data are for both tenant and owner-cum-tenant households. When an individual respondent possessed multiple tenant holdings, the response recorded was for the holding(s) for which the tenancy relationship was of greatest duration.

Source: Jannuzi, F. Thomasson and Peach, James T., 'Land Occupancy Survey, 1977', in *The Agrarian Structure of Bangladesh, An Impediment to Development,* Appendix E, Table E.8, Tables of the 1978 Land Occupancy Survey, p. 113.

Glossary of Non-English Words

ajlaf	low-born of status (synonym in Bengal *atraf).*
aman	autumn (late summer) rice; autumn season.
anna	1/16 of a Taka.
ashraf	high-born of status.
aus	early summer rice; early summer season.
bari	homestead, usually consisting of an inner courtyard with huts around.
bayna	advance payment, the seller and the buyer are bound to complete the transaction after *bayna* has been made.
bigha	unit of land measurement, officially 0.33 acre, but with many local variations. (In Bhaimara one *bigha* equalled 0.33 acre.)
boro	winter rice.
boro-bou	first wife, wife of eldest male person.
chacha	father's younger brother.
chachi	father's younger brother's wife.
char	agricultural land which arise from silt deposits along the edges of rivers.
chula	oven, hearth; household.
crore	10 million.
dada	paternal grandfather.
dadi	paternal grandmother.
dal	faction.
dosto	friend.
Eid	There are two Muslim festivals called *Eid. Eid-ul-Fitre* falls on the first day following the month of *Ramadan, Eid-ul-Azha* occurs on the occasion of *Haj,* the pilgrimage to Mecca.
ghor	hut, room.

ghor-jamais	husband living uxiorilocally (in his wife's paternal household) lit.: 'son-in-law of the house'.
ginny	first wife, wife of eldest male person.
girbi	a type of mortgage system.
gusti	patrilineage.
haat	afternoon village market held twice a week.
haj	pilgrimage to Mecca.
imam	leader of a Muslim congregation; lineage title.
izzat	prestige, honour.
jamin	a person who will guarantee that his client will repay the loan.
jetha	father's elder brother.
jethi	father's elder brother's wife.
jolha	a Muslim weaver.
kamla	wage labourer.
khai-khalashi	a particular system of land mortgage.
khana	eating group.
khas	Government-owned land.
kripon	a stingy person.
labh	profit.
lakh	one hundred thousand.
lathial	fighter and physical protector.
lungi	men's garment, loin cloth.
madrasa	an Islamic school.
magna kamla	employment without payment in cash money but in food only.
maund	a measurement equivalent to about 37 kiloes.
matbar	village 'leader', 'leader' of *samaj*.
mehr	payment pledged by bridegroom's family to the family of the bride in case of divorce.
molla	head of a mosque; lineage title.
mouza	smallest revenue unit, a revenue 'village'.
mowlana	Islamic scholar and teacher.
palok	adopted child.
para	part of a village.
pir baba	religious teacher.
purdah	the seclusion of Muslim women from outsiders. Women are confined to their homestead and go

	veiled when they move outside the fences of their homestead.
samaj	Muslim congregation; village association.
sari	women's dress.
seer	a measure of weight (=0.9 Kg.).
shalish	local court, village court.
sheikh	common Muslim family title.
tahsildar	a revenue collector or revenue clark.
taka	the monetary unit of Bangladesh.
thana	administrative unit of Bangladesh (roughly a county).
zamindar	superior landlord/revenue collector.

Bibliography

Abdullah, Abu, Hossain, Mosharaff and Nations, Richard. 'Agrarian Structure and the IRDP-Preliminary Considerations', *The Bangladesh Development Studies,* No. 2, Vol. 4, April 1976.

Abdullah, T.A. *Village Women as I Saw Them,* Ford Foundation, Dhaka, 1974.

Adnan, Shapnan, et al. *Land, Power and Violence in Barisal Villages.* The Village Study Group, Dhaka, 1976, mimeo.

Adnan, Shapnan, et al. *Differentiation and Class Structure in Village Shamraj,* The Village Study Group, Working Paper 8, Dhaka, 1977, mimeo.

Adnan, Shapnan, and Rahman, H.Z. *Peasant Classes and Land Mobility: Structural Reproduction and Change in Rural Bangladesh,* The Village Study Group, Working Paper 9, Dhaka, 1978, mimeo.

Ahmad, Alia. *Some Important Features of the Agrarian Economy in Bangladesh,* Working Paper No. 3, Department of Economics, University of Lund, April 1980.

Ahmad, N.U. *Cost of Production of Aus Paddy and Jute Cultivation Per Acre,* U.S.A.I.D., Dhaka, August 1976.

Ahmed, Raisuddin. *Foodgrain Production in Bangladesh: An Analysis of Growth, Its Sources and Related Policies,* International Food Policy Research Institute, Washington, 1976.

Alamgir, Muhiuddin Khan. *Land Reform in Bangladesh,* Centre for Social Studies, Dhaka, 1981.

Area Handbook for Bangladesh. Foreign Area Studies, The American University, Washington D.C., 1975.

Arefeen, H.K.S. *The Concept of Castes among the Indologists,* The Centre Paper No. 2, Centre for Social Studies, University of Dhaka, 1977.

Arefeen, H.K.S. 'Muslim Stratification Patterns in Bangladesh: An Attempt to Build a Theory', *Journal of Social Studies,* No. 16, 1982.

Arens, J. and van Beurden, J. *Jhagrapur — Poor Peasants and Women in a Village in Bangladesh,* Third World Publications, Amsterdam, 1977.

Arn, Ann-Lisbeth. *A Case-Study from Bangladesh: An Integrated Village in Mymensingh District,* Paper A 78.5, Centre for Development Research, Copenhagen, December, 1978.

Arn, Ann-Lisbeth. *Mobilization and Development in Bangladesh,* Progress Report, Institute for Peace and Conflict Research, Gothenburg University, August, 1976.

Asad, Talal. 'Market Model, Class Structure and Consent: A Reconsideration of Swat Political Organization', *Man* (NS), Vol. 7, No. 1, 1972.

Asplund, Daniel and de Vylder, Stefan. *Contradictions and Distortions in a Rural Economy: The Case of Bangladesh,* S.I.D.A., Stockholm, 1979.

Aziz, K.M. Ashraful. *Kinship in Bangladesh,* Monograph Series, No. 1, International Centre for Diarrhoeal Disease Research, Dhaka, 1979.

Bangladesh International Action Group. *Oppressed People in an Aid Dependent Country,* London, April, 1982.

Bardhan, Pranab and Rudra, Ashok. 'Terms and Conditions of Sharecropping: An Analysis of Village Survey Data in India', *Journal of Development Studies,* Vol. 16, No. 3, April 1980.

Barth, Fredrik. *Models of Social Organization,* Royal Anthropological Institute, Occasional paper No. 23, London, 1966.

Barth, Fredrik. 'Economic Spheres in Darfur', in R. Firth (ed.), *Themes in Economic Anthropology,* London, Tavistock, 1967.

Barth, Fredrik. *Sociological Aspects of Integrated Surveys for River Basin Development,* Paper presented at the ITC-UNESCO Centre for Integrates Surveys, 4th International Seminar, 1969.

Barth, Fredrik (ed.). *Ethnic Groups and Boundaries,* Oslo: Universitetsforlaget, and Boston, Mass.: Little, Brown, 1969.

Barth, Fredrik. 'Analytical Dimensions in the Comparison of Social Organizations', *American Anthropologist,* Vol. 72, No. 1-2, 1972.

Barth, Fredrik. *Ritual and Knowledge among the Baktaman of New Guinea,* Oslo: Norwegian University Press, and Cambridge, Mass.: Yale University Press, 1975.

Barth, Fredrik. 'Models Reconsidered', in *Selected Essays of Fredrik Barth,* Volume 1, 76–104 and 'Swat Pathans Reconsidered', Volume 2, 121–181, Routledge & Kegan Paul, London, Boston and Henly, 1981.

Bell, Clive. 'Alternative Theories on Sharecropping: Some Tests Using Evidence from Northeast India', *Journal of Development Studies,* Vol. 13, No. 4, July 1977.

Bertocci, Peter J. *Elusive Villages: Social Structure and Community Organization in Rural East Pakistan,* Ph.D. dissertation, Michigan State University, 1970.

Bertocci, Peter J. 'Microregion, Market Area and Muslim Community in Rural Bangladesh', *The Bangladesh Development Studies,* Vol. 3, No. 3, 1975.

Bertocci, Peter J. 'Social Organization and Agricultural Development in Bangladesh, in R.D. Stevens, Hamza Alavi and Peter J. Bertocci (eds.). *Rural Development in Bangladesh and Pakistan,* The University Press of Hawaii, Honolulu, 1976.

Bertocci, Peter J. 'Structural Fragmentation and Peasant Classes in Bangladesh', *Journal of Social Studies,* No. 5, 1979.

Bhaduri, Amit. 'A Study of Agricultural Backwardness under Semi-Feudalism', *Economic Journal,* Vol. 83, No. 1, 1973.

Bhaduri, Amit. *The Economic Structure of Agricultural Backwardness,* DERAP Working Paper A 172, Chr. Michelsens Institute, Bergen, 1980.

Bharadwaj, K. and Das, P.K. 'Tenurial Conditions and Mode of Exploitation: A Study of Some Villages in Orissa', *Economic and Political Weekly,* Annual Number, February 1975.

Biggs, S., Edwards, C., and Griffiths, J. *Irrigation in Bangladesh,* Discussion Paper No. 126, Institute of Development Studies, University of Sussex, 1978.

Blair, Harry W. 'Rural Development, Class Structure and Bureaucracy in Bangladesh', *World Development,* Vol. 6, No. 1, 1978.

Brammer, H. *Costs of Production, Profits and Returns for Paddy and Wheat Cultivation at New Fertilizer Prices,* Soil Survey Department, Dhaka, 1976, mimeo.

Browne, J.F. *General Report on the Tipperah District,* Calcutta, Thaker, Spink, 1866.

Cain, Mead T. 'The Economic Activities of Children', *Population and Development Review,* Vol. 3, No. 3, 1977.

Cain, Mead T. 'The Household Life Cycle and Economic Mobility in Rural Bangladesh', *Population and Development Review,* Vol. 4, No. 3, 1978.

Cain, Mead T. 'Class, Patriarchy, and Women's Work in Bangladesh', *Population and Development Review,* Vol. 5, No. 3, 1979.

Calkins, Philip B. 'Stability and Change in Landholding and Revenue System in Bengal', in R.D. Stevens, Hamza Alavia, and Peter J. Bertocci (eds.) *Rural Development in Bangladesh and Pakistan,* University Press of Hawaii, Honolulu, 1976.

Chandra, N.K. 'Farm Efficiency under Semi-Feudalism: A Critique of Marginalist Theories and Some Marxist Foundations', Economic and Political Weekly, Special Number, August 1974.

Chaudhury, Rafiqul Huda. *Some Aspects of Seasonal Dimensions to Rural Poverty in Bangladesh,* Bangladesh Institute of Development Studies, Dhaka, 1978, mimeo.

Chen, Lincoln. *An Analysis of Per Capita Food Grain Availability, Consumption and Requirements in Bangladesh: A Systems Approach to Food Planning,* Ford Foundation Report, No. 24, Dhaka, 1974.

Chowdhury, Anwarullah. *A Bangladesh Village: A Study of Social Stratification,* Centre for Social Studies, University of Dhaka, 1978.

Clay, Edward J. 'Institutional Change and Agricultural Wages in Bangladesh', *The Bangladesh Development Studies,* Vol. 4, No. 4, 1976.

Clay, Edward J., and Khan, Md. Selkandor. *Agricultural Employment and Underemployment in Bangladesh: The Next Decade,* Bangladesh Agricultural Research Council, Dhaka, October 1977, mimeo.

Clay, Edward J. *Employment Effects of the HYV Strategy in Bangladesh: A Rejoinder,* Dhaka, March 1978, mimeo.

Cohen, D.W. *Womunafu's Bunafu: A Study of Authority in a Nineteenth-Century African Community,* Princeton University Press, Princeton, New Jersey, 1977.

Cumming, J.G. *Survey and Settlement of the Chakla Roshnabad Estate in Districts of Tippera and Noakhali, 1892–1899,* Bengal Secretariat Press, Calcutta, 1899.

de Vylder, Stefan. *Agriculture in Chains, Bangladesh: A Case Study in Contradictions and Constraints,* Zed Press, London, 1982.

Djurfeldt, Göran and Lindberg, Staffan. *Behind Poverty: The Social Formation in a Tamil Village,* Scandinavian Institute of Asian Studies, Monograph Series No. 22, 1975.

Dumont, Rene. *A Self-reliant Rural Development Policy for the Poor Peasantry of Sonar Bangladesh,* Ford Foundation, Dhaka, May 1973.

Dumont, Rene. *Problems and Prospects for Rural Development in Bangladesh,* Ford Foundation, Dhaka, November 1973.

Evens, T.M.S. 'The Predication of the Individual in Anthropological Interactionism', *American Anthropologist,* Vol. 79, 1977.

Faaland, J. and Parkinson, J.R. *Bangladesh — The Test Case of Development,* London, C. Hurst & Co., 1976.

Faaland, J., and Hossain, Mosharaff. 'Structural Transformation and Rural Development', in: *European Studies on Development,* edited by Jacques De Bandt, Peter Mandi and Dudley Seers, MacMillan, London, 1980.

Faaland, J. (ed.) *Aid and Influence,* MacMillan Press, 1981.

FAO/UNDP/Government of Bangladesh, Agricultural Mission. *Selected Policy Issues and Working Papers,* Dhaka, 1979.

Feldman, Shelley. 'Rural Infrastructural Development in Bangladesh and its Potential Consequences for Reproductive Behaviour', *Journal of Social Studies,* No. 7, 1980.

Feldman, Shelley and McCarthy, Florence E. 'Purdah and Changing Patterns of Social Control among Rural Women in Bangladesh', *Journal of Marriage and the Family,* Vol. 45, No. 4, November 1983.

Gait, E. *Census of India 1901,* Calcutta: Bengal Secretarial Press, Calcutta, 1902.

Gaudefroy-Demombynes, Maurice. *Muslim Institutions,* George Allen & Unwin Ltd, London, 1968.

Government of Bangladesh. *Statistical Pocket Book of Bangladesh 1981,* Bureau of Statistics, Dhaka, December 1982.

Government of Bangladesh, Planning Commission. *First Five Year Plan 1973–1978.*

Government of Bangladesh, Planning Commission. *Second Five Year Plan, 1980–85.*

Government of Bangladesh. *Bangladesh Population Census Report,* National Volume, Dhaka, 1978.

Government of Bangladesh. *World Fertility Survey: Bangladesh Fertility Survey 1975. First Report,* Dhaka: Ministry of Health and Population Control, Population Control and Family Planning Division, 1978.

Government of Bangladesh. *Land Occupancy Summary Report of 1977,* Bangladesh Bureau of Statistics, Dhaka, n.d.

Government of the Netherlands. *Bangladesh: Rural Development in Four Thanas in Kushtia District: Study on the Problems of the Rural Poor: Appraisal of an Experimental Programme,* Ministry of Foreign Affairs, International Assistance Department, February 1978.

Griffin, K., and Khan, A.R. 'Poverty in Third World: Ugly Facts and Fancy Models', *World Development,* Vol. 6, No. 3, 1978.

Haaland, Gunnar (ed.). *Problems in Savannah Development: The Sudan Case,* Occasional Paper No. 19, Department of Social Anthropology, University of Bergen, 1980.

Hannah, L.M. 'Hand Pump Irrigation in Bangladesh', *Bangladesh Development Studies,* Vol. 4, No. 4, October 1976.

Haq, Mahbub-ul. *The Strategy of Economic Planning: A Case Study of Pakistan,* Oxford University Press, 1966.

Hartmann, Betsy and James Boyce. *Needless Hunger: Voices from a Bangladesh Village,* Institute for Food and Development Policy, San Francisco, 1979.

Hartmann, Betsy and James Boyce. 'Who Works, Who Eats?', *Bulletin of Concerned Asian Scholars,* Vol. 13, No. 4, 1981.

Hossain, M., Rahman, S., and Aksah, M.M. *Agricultural Taxation in Bangladesh,* Bangladesh Institute of Development, 1978, mimeo.

Hossain, Mahabub. 'Farm Size, Tenancy and Land Productivity: An Analysis of Farm Level Data in Bangladesh Agriculture', *The Bangladesh Development Studies,* Vol. 5, No. 3, 1977.

Hossain, Mahabub. 'Nature of Tenancy Markets in Bangladesh', *Journal of Social Studies,* No. 3, 1979.

Hossain, Mahabub. *Foodgrain Production in Bangladesh, Performance Potential and Constraints,* BIDS, Dhaka, 1980, mimeo.

Hunter, W.W. *A Statistical Account of Bengal,* Trübner & Co., London, 1876.

Islam, A.K.M. Aminuel. *A Bangladesh Village: Conflict and Cohesion: An Anthropological Study of Politics,* Schenkman, Cambridge, Massachusetts, 1974.

Islam, A.K.M. Aminuel. *Victorious Victims, Political Transformation in a Traditional Society,* Schenkman, Cambridge, Massachusetts, 1978.

Islam, Rizwanul. 'What Has Been Happening to Rural Income Distribution in Bangladesh?', *Development and Change,* Vol. 10, No. 3, 1979.

Jacoby, Erich, H. 'Effects of the "Green Revolution" in South and South-east Asia', *Modern Asian Studies,* Vol. 6, No. 1, 1972.

Jahan, Rounaq. *Local Power Structure and the Mobilization of Vote: A Study of the Bangladesh Election 1979,* DERAP Working Paper A 155, Chr. Michelsen Institute, Bergen, August 1979.

Jahangir, B.K. *Differentiation, Polarization and Confrontation in Rural Bangladesh,* Centre for Social Studies, University of Dhaka, 1979.

Jahangir, B.K. *Rural Society, Power Structure and Class Practice,* Centre for Social Studies, University of Dhaka, 1982.

Jahangir, B.K. The State as a Relation of Production: Bangladesh, *Journal of Social Studies,* No. 18, 1982.

Jannuzi, F. Thomasson and Peach, James T. 'Note on Land Reform in Bangladesh: The Efficiency of Ceiling', *Journal of Peasant Studies,* Vol. 6, No. 3, April 1979.

Jannuzi, F. Thomasson and Peach, James T. 'Land Occupancy Survey, 1977', in: *The Agrarian Structure of Bangladesh, An Impediment to Development,* Boulder, Colorado, USA, Westview Press, 1980.

Jansen, Eirik G. 'Choice of Irrigation Technology in Bangladesh: Implications for Dependency Relationships between Rich and Poor Farmers', *Journal of Social Studies,* No. 5, 1979.

Jansen, Eirik G. *Possible Socio-Economic Implications of Norwegian Assistance to Bangladesh's Inland Waterways Transport Sector,* DERAP Working Paper A 197, Chr. Michelsen Institute, Bergen, February 1981.

Jansen, Eirik G. 'The Development of the Mechanized River Transport Sector in Bangladesh, Aid to the Poor?', in: *Poverty and Aid,* edited by J.R. Parkinson, Blackwell, Oxford, 1983.

Jansen, Eirik G., Jahangir, B.K., Maal, Bodil and Rahman, Nazibor. 'Dilemmas Involved in Defining and Delimiting Household Units in Rural Surveys in Bangladesh', *Journal of Social Studies,* No. 21, 1983, Dhaka.

Jenkins, A., Matin, N., Shaha, S. and Latif, M.A. *Unite and Survive: Developing Landless Organization in Bangladesh,* Oxfam, 1980.

Jenkins, A., Dulta, A.K., Hasan, M., and Khan, K.Z.T. *The Net: Power Structure in Ten Villages,* Bangladesh Rural Advancement Committee, Dhaka, 1980.

Jensen, Kurt Mørk. *A Study on the Economic Viability of Blacksmiths and Carpenters in Noakhali District,* BIDS-CDR Second Joint Noakhali Development Study, Centre for Development Research, Copenhagen and Bangladesh Institute of Development Studies, Dhaka, April, 1983.

Kamaluddin, S. 'Basket case to Bread Basket', *Far Eastern Economic Review,* 24 October, 1980.

Khan, N.I. (ed.). *Comilla, Bangladesh District Gazetteers,* Bangladesh Government Press, Dhaka, 1977.

Khan, Azizur Rahman, Islam, Riawanul and Huq, Mahfuzul. *Employment, Income and the Mobilization of Local Resources: A Study of Two Bangladesh Villages,* ILO, Geneva, 1980.

Khuda, Barkat-E. *The Use of Time and Underemployment in Rural Bangladesh,* University of Dhaka, 1982.

Maal, Bodil. *Statistical Material Collected from a Village in Bangladesh,* DERAP Working Paper A 191, Chr. Michelsen Institute, Bergen, December 1980.

Mahfuzullah. 'Sharecroppers' Rights', *Holiday,* Dhaka, 25 December 1982.

Mandal, Md. Abdus Sattar. *An Economic Analysis of Resource Use with Respect to Farm Size and Tenure in an Area of Bangladesh,* unpublished dissertation, Wye College, University of London, August 1979.

McCarthy, Florence E. *The Status and Condition of Rural Women in Bangladesh,* Planning and Evaluation Cell, Ministry of Agriculture and Forests, Dhaka, 1978.

McHenry, D.F. and Bird, Kai. 'Food Bungle in Bangladesh', *Foreign Affairs,* No. 27, 1977.

Miranda, Armindo. 'Nuptiality in Bangladesh', *Journal of Social Studies,* No. 9, 1980.

Mukherjee, Ramkrishna. *Six Villages of Bengal,* Popular Prakashan, Bombay, 1971.

Paine, Robert. *Second Thoughts about Barth's Models,* Royal Anthropological Institute Occasional Paper No. 32, London: Royal Anthropological Institute of Great Britain and Ireland, 1974.

Parkinson, J.R. 'Food Aid', in *Aid and Influence,* ed. by J. Faaland, MacMillan Press, 1981.

Parkinson, J.R. (ed.) *Poverty and Aid,* Blackwell, Oxford, 1983.

Patnaik, Utsa. 'Class Differentiation within the Peasantry: An Approach to the Analysis of Indian Agriculture', *Economic and Political Weekly,* 11 September, 1976.

Qadir, S.A. *Village Dhanishwar — Three Generations of Man-Land Adjustment in an East Pakistan Village,* Technical Publication No. 5, Pakistan Academy for Rural Development, Comilla, 1960.

Rahman, Anisur. *The Utilization of Labour in the Strategy for Development in the ECAFE Development Region,* paper prepared for ECAFE, United Nations, mimeo, n.d.

Rahman, Hussain Zillur. *Report from Raipur,* BIDS-CDR Joint Noakhali Development Study, Centre for Development Research, Copenhagen and Bangladesh Institute of Development Studies, Dhaka, 1980.

Rao, C.H.H. 'Urban vs. Rural or Rich vs. Poor', Review article in *Economic and Political Weekly,* 7 October, 1978.

Rao, V.M. 'Village Lease Markets for Agricultural Land: Some Approaches for Analysis', *Economic and Political Weekly,* Review of Agriculture, June 1974.

Rashid, Haroun Er. *Geography of Bangladesh,* University Press Limited, Dhaka, 1977.

Scott, Michael. *Aid to Bangladesh — For Better or Worse,* Oxfam of America, The Institute for Food and Development Policies, San Francisco, 1979.

Sen, Amartya. *Poverty and Famines: An Essay on Entitlement and Deprivation,* Clarendon Press, Oxford, 1981.

Siddiqui, Kamal. A Comment on Jannuzi and Peach, *Journal of Peasant Studies,* Vol. 6, No. 3, April 1979.

Siddiqui, Kamal. *The Political Economy of Rural Poverty in Bangladesh,* National Institute of Local Government, Dhaka, 1982.

Sobhan, Rehman. 'Politics of Food and Famine', *Economic and Political Weekly,* 1 December, 1979.

Sobhan, Rehman. *Food Politics and Famine in Bangladesh,* DERAP Working Paper No. 158, Chr. Michelsen Institute, Bergen, 1979.

Sobhan, Rehman. 'Bangladesh and the World Economic System: The Crisis of External Dependence', *Development and Change,* Vol. 12, No. 3, July 1981.

Sobhan, Rehman. *The Crisis of External Dependence, The Political Economy of Foreign Aid to Bangladesh,* University Press Limited, Dhaka, 1982.

Sobhan, Rehman. 'The Crisis of External Dependence: Some Policy Options for Bangladesh', *Journal of Social Studies,* No. 18, 1982.

Stepanek, Joseph R. *Bangladesh — Equitable Growth?* Pergamon Press, New York, 1979.

Tarrant, J.R. 'Food Policy Conflicts in Bangladesh', *World Development,* Vol. 10, No. 2, 1982.

Thomas, J.W. 'An Analysis of a Development Policy Decision', in: *Choice of Technology in Developing Countries* by Timmer, Thomas, Wells and Morawetz, *Harvard Studies in International Affairs,* No. 32, 1975.

Thompson, W.H. The Profits and Rent of Agricultural Land in a Corner of Bengal in 1989, *Bengal Economic Journal,* Vol. 2, No. 3, 1918.

Thorner, Alice. 'Semi-Feudalism or Capitalism? — Contemporary Debate on Classes and Modes of Production in India', *Economic and Political Weekly,* Vol. 17, No. 49, 50, 51, 1982.

United Nations. *Population of Bangladesh,* Country Monograph Series No. 8, New York, 1981.

Van Schendel, Willem. *Peasant Mobility — The Odds of Life in Rural Bangladesh,* Van Gorcum, Assen, The Netherlands, 1981.

Van Schendel, Willem. After the Limelight: Longer-Term Effects of Rural Development in a Bangladesh Village, *Bulletin of Concerned Asian Scholars,* Vol. 13, No. 4, 1981.

Vogel, Garson. *Overseas Development,* p. 4, UK Overseas Development Ministry, September 1978.

Webster, J.E. *Tippera, Eastern Bengal District Gazetteers,* Pioneer Press, Allahabad, 1910.

Westergaard, Kirsten. *The Relationship between the State and Rural Society in Bangladesh,* Institute of Political Studies, University of Copenhagen, 1979.

Westergaard, Kirsten. *Boringram: An Economic and Social Analysis of a Village in Bangladesh,* Rural Development Academy, Bogra, n.d.

White, Benjamin N.F. *Rural Household in Studies in Anthropological Perspective,* Revised version of a background paper prepared for the ADC-RTN Workshop in Household Studies, Singapore, August 3–7, 1976.

Who Gets What and Why: Resource Allocation in a Bangladesh Village, Bangladesh Rural Advancement Committee, Dhaka, 1979.

Wood, G.D. 'Class Differentiation and Power in Bandakgram: The Minfundist Case', in M.A. Huq (ed.), *Exploitation and the Rural Poor,* Bangladesh Academy for Rural Development, Comilla, 1976.

Wood, G.D. 'Rural Class Formation in Bangladesh, 1940–1980', *Bulletin of Concerned Asian Scholars,* Vol. 13, No. 4, 1981.

World Bank. *Bangladesh Land and Water Resources, Sector Study* (9 Volumes), World Bank, 1972.

Zahir, S., and Kamel, A. *Urban Rationing System in Bangladesh,* Bangladesh Institute of Development Studies, 1981, mimeo.

Zaidi, S.M. Hafeez. *The Village Culture in Transition: A Study of East Pakistan Rural Society,* Honolulu: East-West Center Press, 1970.

Index